Saving Strangers

Humanitarian Intervention in International Society

Nicholas J. Wheeler

OXFORD
UNIVERSITY PRESS

OXFORD

UNIVERSITY PRESS

Great Clarendon Street, Oxford OX2 6DP

Oxford University Press is a department of the University of Oxford.
It furthers the University's objective of excellence in research, scholarship,
and education by publishing worldwide in

Oxford New York

Auckland Bangkok Buenos Aires Cape Town Chennai
Dar es Salaam Delhi Hong Kong Istanbul Karachi Kolkata
Kuala Lumpur Madrid Melbourne Mexico City Mumbai Nairobi
São Paulo Shanghai Taipei Tokyo Toronto

Oxford is a registered trade mark of Oxford University Press
in the UK and in certain other countries

Published in the United States
by Oxford University Press Inc., New York

© Nicholas Wheeler 2000

The moral rights of the author have been asserted
Database right Oxford University Press (maker)

First published 2000
First published in paperback 2002

British Library Cataloguing in Publication Data
Data available

Library of Congress Cataloging in Publication Data
Wheeler, Nicholas J.
Saving strangers: humanitarian intervention in international society/
Nicholas J. Wheeler.
p. cm.
· Includes bibliographical references and index.
1. Humanitarian intervention. I. Title.
JZ6369.W49 2000   341.5'84—dc21   00–037484
ISBN 0–19–829621–5 (hbk)
ISBN 0–19–925310–2 (pbk)

3 5 7 9 10 8 6 4 2

Typeset in Stone Sans and Stone Serif by
Cambrian Typesetters, Frimley, Surrey
Printed in Great Britain
on acid-free paper by
Biddles Ltd.
Guildford and King's Lynn

SAVING STRANGERS

WITHDRÁWN

For John and Lola Wheeler

PREFACE AND ACKNOWLEDGEMENTS

Although this book has only been written in the last two years, my exploration of the ideas discussed in it can be traced back to the Western intervention in northern Iraq to protect the Kurds in the immediate aftermath of the Gulf War. Shortly before this action I had read a fascinating essay by one of my students taking the MA in International Law and Politics at the University of Hull that had introduced me to the concept of humanitarian intervention. Whether I would have ventured into this subject without the 'intervention' of Justin Morris is hard to say, but what attracted me to it was that it offered a vehicle for integrating my research interests in Strategic Studies—especially the ethics of force—and the 'English School' theory of international society. I had been engaged with the latter since reading Hedley Bull's *The Anarchical Society* as an undergraduate, but the writer who really started me thinking about humanitarian intervention was R. J. Vincent. After the 1991 Kurdish crisis, I re-read Vincent's two great contributions, *Nonintervention and International Order* and *Human Rights and International Relations*. These two books span twenty years of his thinking on the subject and reflect the tensions in Vincent's work between pluralist and solidarist conceptions of international society. It became clear to me that there was a book to be written that built on Vincent's contribution and examined how different theories of international society lead to different conceptions of the legitimacy of humanitarian intervention. This became the project that has culminated in *Saving Strangers*.

Justin Morris became a member of the Department at Hull, a close personal friend, and we wrote several pieces together exploring the legal, political, and philosophical issues raised by the interventions in Iraq, Somalia, and Rwanda. I owe Justin an enormous personal and intellectual debt, and whilst he has not read any page of the manuscript, his influence is to be found throughout. Four other friends at Hull also deserve a special mention. I was very fortunate to have Andrew Mason as a colleague; he brightened my days with his warm friendship and cheerful disposition, and I was constantly drawing on his enormous reservoir of philosophical knowledge. Andrew made many useful comments on earlier versions of the Introduction and Chapter One. Tim Huxley was also a great support to me and was an endless source of knowledge about the Vietnamese intervention in Cambodia. Martin Shaw's work on world society challenged my own English School thinking and we spent many enjoyable hours arguing over the merits of these theories. The final influence upon my thinking at Hull was Bhikhu (now Lord) Parekh who spent many hours with me discussing the ethics of humanitarian intervention.

I left Hull in 1993 and returned to the Department of International Politics at the University of Wales, Aberystwyth where I had been a tutor in 1985–86. Aberystwyth was once described to me by Lawrence Freedman as my 'natural home' and the years since 1993 have proved this to be true. The constructivist approach to language and the social world that permeates the following pages came to fruition in Aberystwyth. The Department is such a lively and stimulating place to work and so many colleagues and students have helped me to think about the questions raised in this book. However, I want to mention in particular the following: John Baylis, Susie Carruthers, Mick Cox, Jenny Edkins, Steve Hobden, Colin McInnes, Simon Murden, Richard Wyn Jones, Veronique Pin-Fat, and Lucy Taylor, who in their different ways challenged me to interrogate the assumptions underlying this book.

By the time I arrived in Aberystwyth I had decided to write a book developing the ideas in my 1992 article published in *Millennium* on 'Pluralist and Solidarist Conceptions of International Society'. This article defended a pluralist approach, but it was apparent that the practice of humanitarian intervention was outstripping the theory. In early 1993 the UN had embarked upon the most ambitious experiment to date, the reconstruction of a failed state in Somalia. I had watched with dismay through the summer of 1993 as the noble humanitarian purposes behind President Bush's *Operation Restore Hope* had turned into a US 'witch-hunt' for General Aidid. Adam Roberts, whose writings on humanitarian intervention have had an important impact on my thinking, had coined the phrase 'humanitarian war' in early 1993 and Somalia appeared to demonstrate that the idea of using force for humanitarian purposes was a contradiction in terms. Exploring whether force could be a servant of humanitarian values enlarged my original project and required an exploration of Just War theory.

The failure of the UN to prevent and stop the Rwandan Genocide of 1994 demonstrated the limits of the evolving norm of humanitarian intervention. The conventional wisdom emerging in the literature was that humanitarian intervention was securing a new legitimacy after the cold war, but as Rwanda showed, this claim exaggerated the impact of the end of the cold war on state behaviour. Here, I was struck by the parallel with the failure of the society of states to stop the atrocities in Cambodia at the end of the 1970s, and it was at this point that I decided to write a comparative analysis of cold war and post-cold war cases of humanitarian intervention.

By early 1995, I could begin to see the outlines of the book. I was very fortunate at this time to spend a period of my sabbatical leave with Robert Jackson at the University of British Columbia. I want to thank Robert, his wife Margaret, and their daughter Jennifer, for the kind hospitality they showed me during that period. Robert and I had met two years earlier and begun a conversation on the character of ethical statecraft that we have continued since. I am a great admirer of his work and he encouraged me to make my book a normative defence of solidarism. With it I hope to make a small dent into his pluralist skepticism about the possibilities of the solidarist project. The other person outside the Department who helped me to find my voice was Karin Fierke. Our rich and exhausting conversations about Wittgenstein, rules and the end of the cold war led me to appreciate the importance of language in constituting state practices in the society of states.

I began writing *Saving Strangers* in January 1998 and in doing so I was influenced by Oliver Ramsbotham and Tom Woodhouse's *Humanitarian Intervention in Contemporary Conflict*. This is the best book on the subject and I have been a constant borrower from it. The other two people whose writings on humanitarian intervention and international society have been a constant source of challenge and enlightenment over the last ten years are Chris Brown and James Mayall. Many other colleagues in our profession have enriched my thinking on the subject of this book, but I want to mention in particular the following: Barry Buzan, Richard Falk, Lawrence Freedman, Fred Halliday, Emily Haslam, Chris Hill, Andrew Hurrell, Richard Little, Nick Rengger, Paul Rogers, Caroline Thomas, Brian White, and Peter Wilson. I was very fortunate during the copy-editing stage of the manuscript to attend a workshop at Cambridge University organized by James Mayall and Gene Lyons on the future of international human rights, and over dinner I struck up a fascinating conversation with Hurst Hannum and especially Jack Donnelly, as to the claims I was advancing in this book. The ensuing discussion led me to make some minor but nonetheless important modifications to the argument that is defended in the following pages.

In researching the cold war cases of humanitarian intervention in this book, I owe special thanks to the following. The Indian High Commission in London; the Vietnamese Embassy; the Tanzanian Embassy; and Mr Lamin of the Organisation of African Unity who was kind enough to supply me with papers relating to the OAU's involvement in the Tanzanian-Ugandan conflict. I gained a deeper understanding of the political context at the UN during the Cambodian and Ugandan cases as a consequence of my interview with Britain's then Ambassador on the Security Council, Ivor (now Lord) Richard. I am also grateful to Ted Rowlands MP who, as a junior minister in the Foreign Office in the period 1975–79, shared his reflections on the Tanzanian intervention in Uganda; to Michael Leifer for our email conversation about Vietnam's motives and justifications for its intervention in Cambodia, and to Rob Dixon for his comments on an earlier version of Chapter 4. I owe a special debt of thanks to my then PhD student, Babu Rahman, who as one of the three research assistants who collected the case study materials used in this book, worked assiduously in the National Library of Wales at Aberystwyth which is an UN Documentation Centre. Here I must say a huge thank you to Mrs Ann Cornwell-Long who is responsible for the UN collection at Aberystwyth, and who was always ready to help me in finding UN documentation.

Turning to my research on the post-cold war cases, I have the following to thank. First, I am grateful to Sir David Hannay who spent two hours talking with me about his time as British Ambassador on the Security Council during the Iraqi, Somali, and Rwandan crises. Secondly, I would like to express my gratitude to Malcolm Harper for sharing his experiences of working in Somalia in 1993-94 for the United Nations Association. Next, I would like to acknowledge James Gow, and especially Alex Bellamy, for sharing their deep knowledge of the wars in the former Yugoslavia. Alex, a doctoral student in the Department, worked as a research assistant on this part of the book. He also provided very detailed and searching comments on an earlier version of Chapter 8. I also want to express my thanks to Linda Melvern who has become a close friend in the course of writing this book and who generously shared information and ideas with me from her forthcoming book, *A People Betrayed: The Role of the West in Rwanda's Genocide*. Michael Barnett and David Malone also provided exceptionally helpful comments on earlier versions of Chapter 7. The final research assistant on the book was my PhD student, Daniela Kroslak, who worked indefatigably to gather materials on the Iraqi, Somali, and Rwandan cases, and who also made many valuable comments on an earlier draft of Chapter 7 based on her own research on the Rwandan Genocide.

My gratitude goes to those people who read the manuscript. Maja Zehfuss made many useful comments on the Introduction and Chapter One. Colin Wight's knowledge of social theory and IR never ceases to amaze me and his advice on my use of rules, norms, and Quentin Skinner's work were invaluable. Andrew Linklater's contribution to my thinking on the possibilities for a solidarist theory of international society cannot be overestimated. I am thrilled that he is now a colleague in the Department and in addition to being a constant source of intellectual stimulation and encouragement, he also provided many valuable comments on the chapters in Part One and Part Two. Four people read the entire manuscript, Ken Booth, Steve Smith, Ian Clark and Tim Dunne.

Ken and Eurwen Booth have been close and trusted friends since my first temporary appointment in Aberystwyth over fifteen years ago. Ken is an intellectual giant in our field and a source of inspiration to me in every aspect of academic life. It is largely due to him that I was so keen to return to the Department in 1993. We disagree over humanitarian intervention—taking very different sides over NATO's action in Kosovo in March 1999—as we did over British and American nuclear weapons in the 1980s. We also have our differences on the potentialities for the society of states to act as a guardian angel rather than a global gangster, but these disagreements conceal what we share: a commitment to an emancipatory politics with human rights at its centre. I also have to thank Ken for coming up with the title *Saving Strangers*.

I owe so much to Steve Smith who in the seven years that I have been in the Department has become a very good friend. Apart from being a scholar with a renowned international reputation and an excellent Head of Department who steered the Department to new heights of success in the second half of the 1990s, he also has a tremendous feel for how a book should hang together. And it is this latter skill that he generously shared with me after reading the entire manuscript in one sitting.

I was delighted when Ian Clark decided to leave Cambridge for the West Wales coastline. Ian and I had written a co-authored book in the late 1980s on British nuclear strategy and having him in the Department is a real treat. Ian is an internationally recognised scholar, and a model teacher and first-rate administrator. He supported me totally throughout this project, reading all the chapters that I passed him within a matter of days and returning them with detailed comments and suggestions that improved the manuscript enormously.

Finally, I come to the biggest intellectual debt of all. Tim Dunne and I enjoy a very close and productive writing partnership. We are both committed to the same normative agenda of radicalizing the English School and our work on ethics and foreign policy is an attempt to advance the solidarist project of exploring how states might act as guardians of human rights. *Saving Strangers* is my attempt to defend the solidarist voice in the conversation over the legitimacy of humanitarian intervention, but the argument would never have taken this form without our collaborative work. It has been my good fortune that our intellectual paths crossed in Aberystwyth. There were times when I wondered whether I would ever finish such a marathon project, and whilst Tim probably hopes that he never has to hear the words 'human int' again, he pushed me to finish my first single-authored book more than anyone else.

In terms of the commissioning and production of the manuscript, I was very fortunate to work with Dominic Byatt at OUP who was always cheerfully encouraging about the project. Amanda Watkins was very helpful in steering the manuscript through to completion and I was blessed in having Hilary Walford as my copy-editor. She accepted with better humor than I deserved the numerous changes that I made to the manuscript at copy-editing stage.

I also want to thank the support staff inside the Department. Two first-rate administrators, Mari Duller and Caroline Haste, help keep the ship of 'Interpol' (as the Department is affectionately known on the corridor) on an even keel, and I want to thank both for their professionalism and friendship. I also want to thank our secretaries Elaine Lowe and Donia Richards, and especially Ardwyna Davies and Vicki Jones. I also want to thank Nicola Richards for typing up the transcripts of my interviews.

I have dedicated this book to my Mother and Father for all the love and support they have shown me over the years. They gave me the opportunities that made possible an academic career. For that they will always have my deepest thanks.

Nick Wheeler

Aberystwyth
May 2000

CONTENTS

ABBREVIATIONS

ABM	anti-ballistic missile
AFSCME	American Federation of State, County, and Municipal Employees
APC	armoured personnel carrier
ASEAN	Association of South East Asian Nations
CDR	Coalition pour la Défense de la République
CIA	Central Intelligence Agency
CNN	Cable News Network
CPS	Centre for Policy Studies
CSCE	Conference on Security and Cooperation in Europe
DK	Government of Democratic Kampuchea
DPKO	Department of Peacekeeping Operations
EC	European Community
ECOWAS	Economic Community of West African States
EU	European Union
FCO	Foreign and Commonwealth Office
FRY	Federal Republic of Yugoslavia
GDR	German Democratic Republic
GAOR	General Assembly Official Records
HDZ	Hrvatska Demokratska Zajednica (Croatian Democratic Union)
KFOR	Kosovo Force
ICJ	International Court of Justice
ICRC	International Committee of the Red Cross/Red Crescent
IFOR	Implementation Force
IISS	International Institute of Strategic Studies
ILA	International Law Association
IMF	International Monetary Fund
INGO	international non-governmental organization
JNA	Jugoslavenski Narodna Armija (Yugoslav Peoples Army)
LDK	Democratic League of Kosovo
MNRD	Mouvement National pour la Révolution et le Développement
MOU	Memorandum of Understanding
MSF	Médecins sans Frontières
NAC	North Atlantic Council

NATO	North Atlantic Treaty Organization
NGO	non-governmental organization
NSC	National Security Council
OAU	Organization of African Unity
OFDA	Office of Foreign Disaster Assistance
OSCE	Organization on Security and Cooperation in Europe
PDD	Presidential Decision Directive
PKK	Partiya Karkeren Kurdistan (Kurdistan Workers' Party)
PLA	People's Liberation Army
PRK	People's Republic of Kampuchea
PUK	Patriotic Union of Kurdistan
QRF	Quick Reaction Force
RAF	Royal Air Force
RPF	Rwandan Patriotic Front
RTLMC	Radio Télévision Libre Mille Collines
SCOR	Security Council Resolution
SDI	Strategic Defense Initiative
SDS	Srpska Demokratska Zajednica (Serbian Democratic Party)
SFOR	Stabilization Force
SFRY	Socialist Federal Republic of Yugoslavia
SHZ	safe humanitarian zone
SNA	Somali National Alliance
SNF	Somali National Front
SSDF	Somali Salvation Democratic Front
TNC	Transitional National Council
UCK	Ushtria Clirimtare e Kosoves (Kosovo Liberation Army)
UN	United Nations
UNAMIR	United Nations Assistance Mission for Rwanda
UNHCR	United Nations High Commissioner for Refugees
UNICEF	United Nations Children's Fund
UNITAF	Unified Task Force
UNOSOM	United Nations Operation in Somalia
UNPROFOR	United Nations Protection Force
UNSCR	United Nations Security Council Resolution
USC	United Somali Congress
VJ	Vojska Jugoslavije (Yugoslav Army)
WEU	Western European Union

INTRODUCTION

The dilemma of what to do about strangers who are subjected to appalling cruelty by their governments has remained with us throughout the post-1945 world. While the question remains the same, the normative context has changed markedly. As a result of the international legal obligations written into the United Nations system, clear limits were set on how governments could treat their citizens.[1] For the first time in the history of modern international society, the domestic conduct of governments was now exposed to scrutiny by other governments, human rights non-governmental organizations (NGOs), and international organizations. But the new human rights regime was severely limited by the weaknesses of its enforcement mechanisms. The UN Charter restricts the right to use force on the part of individual states to purposes of self-defence, and it was widely accepted during the cold war that the use of force to save victims of gross human rights abuses was a violation of the Charter. The Security Council is empowered under the Chapter VII provisions of the Charter to authorize the use of force to maintain 'international peace and security', but there is considerable controversy about how far this permits the Council to authorize intervention to stop humanitarian emergencies taking place inside state borders.

This gap between normative commitments and instruments allows governments to abuse human rights with virtual impunity. Intervention by force might be the *only* means of enforcing the global humanitarian norms that have evolved in the wake of the Holocaust, but this fundamentally challenges the established principles of non-intervention and non-use of force. This dilemma is one that leaves state leaders nowhere to hide.[2] 'Doing something' to rescue non-citizens facing the extreme is likely to provoke the charge of interference in the internal affairs of another state, while 'doing nothing' can lead to accusations of moral indifference.

The extent to which humanitarian intervention has become a legitimate practice in international society is the subject of the book. In order to

---

[1] The international legal obligations that protected individuals against the power of the state can be found principally in the UN Charter, the 1948 Universal Declaration of Human Rights, the 1948 Genocide Convention, and the two International Covenants on human rights drawn up in 1966. Cumulatively, these established important limits on the exercise of sovereign prerogatives. See J. Donnelly, 'The Social Construction of Human Rights', in T. Dunne and N. J. Wheeler (eds.), *Human Rights in Global Politics* (Cambridge: Cambridge University Press, 1999).

[2] This phrase was used by Ken Booth in a different context. The source is, however, very relevant to this discussion. See K. Booth, 'Human Wrongs in International Relations', *International Affairs*, 71/1 (1995), 103–36.

investigate this question, I examine the legitimacy of intervention in seven cold-war and post-cold-war cases where the target state was either massively abusing human rights or had collapsed into lawlessness and civil strife. Crucially, the volume investigates *how far states have recognized humanitarian intervention as a legitimate exception to the rules of sovereignty, non-intervention, and non-use of force.*[3] While there are studies of each case of intervention—in East Pakistan, Cambodia, Uganda, Iraq, Somalia, Rwanda, and Kosovo—there is no single work that examines them in a comparative framework and from a theoretical perspective concerned with investigating whether a new norm of humanitarian intervention is emerging. Each chapter tells a history of an intervention, weaving together a study of the motives of the actors, their public legitimating reasons, the international response, and the success of the action in humanitarian terms. Together, they explore the interplay between motives, justifications, and outcomes in the seven cases under consideration.

The discipline that dominates existing studies of humanitarian intervention is international law, and I have drawn heavily from this body of work. With some notable exceptions, there has been little interchange between the disciplines of international relations and international law, and this is a pity, since both have much to learn from each other.[4] The tendency among realist-inclined international-relations scholars is to assume that, since states are judge and jury in their own courts, international law is not proper law because it lacks the authority to create obligations that are binding. I fundamentally reject this proposition and believe, like Rosalyn Higgins, that law 'is the interlocking of authority with power'.[5] What is important, then, *is to distinguish between power that is based on relations of domination and force, and power that is legitimate because it is predicated on shared norms.*[6]

---

[3] Although humanitarian intervention can be defined to encompass non-military forms of intervention such as the activities of humanitarian non-governmental organizations (NGOs) such as Médecins sans Frontières (MSF) and Oxfam, this book focuses on the legitimacy of using force to end appalling abuses of human rights. I agree with Oliver Ramsbotham and Tom Woodhouse that the traditional state-centric approach to humanitarian intervention is too limited because it provides no framework for accommodating the non-military humanitarian activities of states and humanitarian NGOs, but my point of departure is that force is sometimes the right means to avert or stop a greater evil. O. Ramsbotham and T. Woodhouse, *Humanitarian Intervention in Contemporary Conflict* (Cambridge: Polity Press, 1996).

[4] The most ambitious attempt by international-relations scholars to date to integrate the concerns of both disciplines is F. Kratochwil, *Rules, Norms, and Decisions: On the Conditions of Practical and Legal Reasoning in International Relations and Domestic Affairs* (Cambridge: Cambridge University Press, 1989). See also A. Hurrell, 'International Society and Regimes', in V. Rittberger (ed.), *Regime Theory and International Relations* (Oxford: Oxford University Press, 1999), 49–73. For texts that seek to bridge the two disciplines from an international-law perspective, see T. Franck, *The Power of Legitimacy among Nations* (Oxford: Oxford University Press, 1990), and M. Byers, *Custom, Power and the Power of Rules: International Relations and Customary International Law* (Cambridge: Cambridge University Press, 1999).

[5] R. Higgins, *Problems and Process: International Law and How We Use It* (Oxford: Oxford University Press, 1994), 4

[6] This theme is developed by Jürgen Habermas, who argues that the key question is whether power is manifestly exercised through the threat or use of violence or whether it is legitimated. In

Law can be the servant of particular interests rather than an expression of the general will. In these circumstances, a space opens up between legality and legitimacy. It is quite possible in the domestic realm to have legal rules that are not viewed with moral approval by the majority of citizens. Think of the case of the racial laws upholding apartheid in South Africa or how we would view the citizenship laws passed by the Nazis in the 1930s that stripped the Jews of their rights. These examples raise the question as to what legitimacy should be attached to a legal order that institutionalizes gross human rights abuses? For example, were the victims of apartheid morally entitled (or even obligated) to disobey the laws of the South African state? And how far was armed resistance by the African National Congress legitimate?

In this context, situations can arise where an alternative moral practice develops that secures approval but that breaks the existing law. If this persists over time, there are two possible pathways that have been identified by Tom J. Farer: first, an explicit exception might be carved out of the existing law that permits the action under specified conditions provided that the actor invoking the new rule can demonstrate that his or her action satisfies these. The second approach is to deny exceptions that are formally enshrined in the law but to recognize a practice of mitigation based on successive cases where judges and jurors have imposed lesser sentences on the basis of a plea that the action should be treated leniently. A good example of this is euthanasia, which is outlawed in most European states and the USA (though not the Netherlands). On some occasions, individuals who have assisted with 'mercy killing' are able to persuade the court that the circumstances were such as to justify a verdict of not guilty.[7]

Applying these analogies to the question of humanitarian intervention is both difficult and necessary: it is difficult because the international legal process lacks an authoritative decision-maker that can adjudicate on the applicability of legal rules in the manner performed by judges in domestic society. The International Court of Justice (ICJ) in The Hague is the closest approximation to this and its judgments are a key element in the formation of customary international law. However, it is individual states that decide which cases will be subject to compulsory jurisdiction by the ICJ. The reason why it is necessary to investigate the legality of humanitarian intervention is twofold: first, to ascertain whether it is subject to an implicit code of mitigation or a set of legal exceptions grounded in a rule of customary international

this context, Habermas suggested in an interview after the 1991 Gulf War that the UN's action marked a significant step in developing the rule of law in interstate relations and that: 'It would therefore be a reasonable policy to strengthen the authority of the UN sufficiently for the resolutions of the world community to be enforced, if necessary by military means.' See J. Habermas (interviewed by M. Haller), *The Past as Future*, trans. M. Pensky (Cambridge: Polity Press, 1996), 10.

[7] T. J. Farer, 'A Paradigm of Legitimate Intervention', in L. F. Damrosch, *Enforcing Restraint: Collective Intervention in Internal Conflicts* (New York: Council on Foreign Relations Book, 1993), 327.

law, and, second, because it throws into sharp relief the conflict between actions that might be moral but not legal.

Legitimacy and International Society

Before proceeding further, it is necessary to establish the usage of the concept of legitimacy in the book. There is an extensive treatment of this concept in political and legal theory in relation to domestic orders, but there are few works that explicitly interrogate the idea of legitimacy at the international level.[8] The reason for this neglect is the general acceptance of the assumption that the international realm is governed by considerations of power and not legitimacy. This implies that power and legitimacy are in an antithetical relationship, but, as Inis Claude argued, writing in the 1960s, the two concepts are complementary, since the 'obverse of the legitimacy of power is the *power of legitimacy*; rulers seek legitimization not only to satisfy their consciences but also to buttress their positions'.[9] Claude argued that legitimacy was important to power-holders because it made them more secure. In this book, I will be advancing a different although not incompatible argument: legitimacy is constitutive of international action. Put boldly, my contention is that state actions *will be constrained if they cannot be justified in terms of a plausible legitimating reason*. The 'power of legitimacy' to constrain state actions is a more powerful statement of Claude's original thesis, and it acts as the framing question around which the empirical case studies are structured.[10]

The notion of 'constraint' employed in this book is derived from constructivist understandings of how actors are embedded within a normative context structured by rules.[11] The latter are guidance devices that tell us how to act in particular circumstances and that proscribe certain forms of conduct as unacceptable. In claiming that norms and rules play a constraining role, I am not arguing that they physically prevent actions from being

---

[8] A brief but thought-provoking treatment of this issue is provided by Martin Wight's essay 'International Legitimacy' in H. Bull (ed.), *Systems of States* (Leicester: Leicester University Press and the LSE, 1977). Other works that focus on this question from the broad theoretical perspective adopted here are R. J. Vincent, *Human Rights and International Relations* (Cambridge: Cambridge University Press, 1986), and R. H. Jackson, *Quasi-States: Sovereignty, International Relations and the Third World* (Cambridge: Cambridge University Press, 1990).

[9] I. Claude, 'Collective Legitimation as a Political Function of the United Nations', *International Organization*, 20 (1966), 368.

[10] The American international lawyer Thomas Franck developed this theme in his 1990 work titled *The Power of Legitimacy*, which explored how legal rules exerted a 'compliance pull' on states. I discuss Franck's thesis below.

[11] I will be examining in more detail the constructivist understanding of norms and rules as they relate to the workings of international society in Part One. The key text on constructivism is A. Wendt, *Social Theory of International Politics* (Cambridge: Cambridge University Press, 1999).

carried out. It is a norm that I do not insult guests whom I invite to dinner, but there is nothing that is intrinsic to the norm that physically stops me from doing this. Norms are not material barriers and their constraining power derives from the social disapproval that breaking them entails. In the case of dinner parties, it is the adverse consequences that this would have on my friendships that constrain me. Norms that acquire the status of law take the costs of violation onto another level carrying with it the threat of legal sanctions.

There is a further germane point here, which is that violations of a norm or law do not necessarily mean that it has ceased to exist. It all depends upon how widespread the non-compliance is, since, if violators are subject to exclusion by their peers, then this will confirm the efficacy of the norm despite acts of non-compliance with it.[12] Alternatively, a norm violator might set in motion what Martha Finnemore and Kathryn Sikkink call a 'norm cascade'. What is meant here is that, if a large enough group of supporters are prepared to adopt the new norm as the standard of appropriate behaviour, it will replace the previously accepted practice. Finnemore and Sikkink argue that, when new norms are raised, there always follows a process of contestation as the supporters of the old norm seek to resist the advocates of the new norm. This struggle is rarely resolved quickly and the result is either the defeat of the new norm or its acceptance as a legitimate practice.[13] To return to my example of dinner parties, if I insult my guests, this could lead to a 'norm cascade' where this habit catches on, as the guests begin to inflict the new rules upon different circles of friends.

The same arguments apply at the international level because norms and rules 'establish intersubjective meanings that allow the actors to direct their actions towards each other, communicate with each other, appraise the quality of their actions, criticize claims and justify choices'.[14] In the absence of

[12] Friedrich Kratochwil and John Ruggie argue that compliance with norms is not a variable that can be monitored by studying overt behaviour because all human actions stand in need of interpretation. Applying this methodology to the international realm leads Kratochwil and Ruggie to argue that it is 'precisely because state behaviour within regimes is interpreted by other states . . . [that] the rationales and justifications for behaviour which are proffered, together with pleas for understanding or admissions of guilt, as well as the responsiveness to such reasoning on the part of other states . . . are absolutely critical components of any explanation involving the efficacy of norms' (F. Kratochwil and J. G. Ruggie, 'International Organization: A State of the Art or an Art of the State', in F. Kratochwil and E. D. Mansfield (eds.), *International Organization: A Reader* (London: Harper Collins, 1994), 11).

[13] M. Finnemore and K. Sikkink, 'International Norm Dynamics and Political Change', *International Organization*, 2/4 (1998), 895–905.

[14] Kratochwil, 'Neorealism and the Embarrassment of Changes', *Review of International Studies*, 19/1 (1993), 76. Kratochwil highlights the crucial importance of language in constituting shared meanings, and here he brings speech-act theory into international relations. He gives the example of saying 'I do' in a wedding ceremony, which does not describe an action but is one without which the practice of marriage would be impossible. Threats, promises, and contracts are all speech-acts that constitute actions, since 'language *does not mirror* action by sticking a descriptive label on the activity: it is action' (F. Kratochwil, 'Neorealism', 75–6).

this shared language, it is as hard to imagine international relations taking place as it is to believe that two people could play chess if they were given a board and wooden carvings but knew nothing of the rules of the game. John Searle, a philosopher who has written widely on the construction of reality, uses the chess analogy to illustrate the fact that the rules did not evolve in order to prevent collisions; rather, it is the rules that constitute the identities of the pieces (pawns, rooks, knights, and so on) and establish what moves they are permitted to make.[15]

The rules that this book is interested in are those that constitute international society and the focus is on how far the society of states recognizes the legitimacy of using force against states who grossly violate human rights. Here, my key starting point is the assumption—shared by English School theorists and constructivists[16]—that states form a society of states constituted by rules of sovereignty, non-intervention, and non-use of force. I develop the international- society approach below, but for the moment I want to focus on the general claim that *rules and norms both constrain and enable actors.* This is necessary to prepare the ground for what is to follow, since a key focus of the case-study chapters is to investigate how far humanitarian intervention belongs to the legitimate range of reasons that states can invoke in justifying the use of force. The starting point for this study is the actors' justifications, because they identify the reasons that states believe they can legitimately invoke to justify their actions.[17]

The key point about notions of international legitimacy is that they are not within the control of individual agents. Here, I disagree with writers like E. H. Carr who argue that states are always able to create a legitimacy convenient to themselves. Carr contended that theories of international morality or legitimacy are always 'the product of dominant nations or groups of nations'.[18] Realists argue that powerful states consciously espouse those moral principles that serve their interests, but Carr's critique is an even more damning one. The charge is not one of moral hypocrisy, since Carr acknowledges that actors might sincerely believe in the principles they profess; the problem

---

[15] J. R. Searle, *The Construction of Social Reality* (London: Penguin, 1995). For an important development of this argument that applies it to changing normative practices, see K. M. Fierke, *Changing Games, Changing Strategies: Critical Investigations in Security* (Manchester: Manchester University Press, 1998).

[16] The English School is usually taken to refer to the works of Charles Manning, E. H. Carr, Herbert Butterfield, Martin Wight, Adam Watson, Hedley Bull, and R. J. Vincent. For a detailed history, see T. Dunne, *Inventing International Society: A History of the English School* (London: Macmillan, 1998). The book aligns itself with the view that the English School and constructivism occupy the same terrain. The lineage can clearly be seen in Wendt, *Social Theory of International Politics*, esp. ch. 6, which builds directly on Wight's and Bull's work. For an early argument of this kind, see T. Dunne, 'The Social Construction of International Society', *European Journal of International Relations*, 1/3 (1995), 367–89.

[17] M. Finnemore, 'Constructing Norms of Humanitarian Intervention', in Peter Katzenstein (ed.), *The Culture of National Security* (Columbia: Columbia University Press, 1996), 159.

[18] E. H. Carr, *The Twenty Years Crisis 1919–1939* (London: Macmillan, 1939), 111.

is the deeper one that these 'supposedly absolute and universal principles . . . [are] not principles at all, but the unconscious reflexions of national policy based on a particular interpretation of national interest at a particular time'.[19] This view relegates the prevailing norms and rules of any international order to reflections of the underlying distribution of power. There is clearly a relationship between power and norms, but it is not as one-dimensional as Carr would have us believe. Once established, norms will serve to constrain even the most powerful states in the international system.

Those who reject the above premiss could profit from reading Quentin Skinner's contribution to the way in which we understand language. As he argues, the range of legitimating reasons that any actor can invoke is limited by the prevailing morality in which she finds herself. Crucially, the agent 'cannot hope to stretch the application of the existing principles indefinitely; correspondingly, [the agent] can only hope to legitimate a restricted range of actions'.[20] If Skinner's argument that 'any course of action is inhibited from occurring *if it cannot be legitimated*,'[21] can be sustained at the international level, then this book will be making a significant inroad into the claim that states can always create a legitimacy convenient to themselves. In the cases of humanitarian intervention considered in the book, I aim to incorporate the Skinner thesis into a broad-based constructivist approach.

This gives rise to the following questions: were states constrained during the cold war by the rules of international society from raising humanitarian claims to justify their use of force? The empirical cases in Part Two discuss India's, Vietnam's and Tanzania's justifications for their use of force against Pakistan, Cambodia, and Uganda in the 1970s: how did they defend their actions and to what extent did the society of states name these actions as rule-breaking ones that justified sanctioning behaviour? Based on these cases, is there any evidence that humanitarian claims were accepted as legitimate in cold-war international society? By focusing on how rules influence the reasoning process of the actors, is it possible to account for why India's, Vietnam's, and Tanzania's non-compliance with the rules of sovereignty, non-intervention, and non-use of force were treated so differently? Is it the case, that what counts as a violation of the rule 'is not simply an "objective description" of a fact but an inter-subjective appraisal' that can be understood only by analysing the justifications proffered for action and the responsiveness of other states to such arguments.[22]

To investigate the question of whether India's and Vietnam's use of force secured collective legitimation, I focus on the justifications and public-reasoning

---

[19] Ibid.
[20] Q. Skinner, 'Analysis of Political Thought and Action', in J. Tully (ed.), *Meaning and Context: Quentin Skinner and his Critics* (Cambridge: Polity Press, 1988), 117.
[21] Ibid., emphasis added.
[22] Kratochwil and Ruggie, 'International Organization', 11.

process in the UN Security Council and General Assembly in 1971 and 1979. In the case of Tanzania, the issue was not brought before either the Security Council or the General Assembly, but it was hotly debated at the 1979 Organization of African Unity (OAU) Summit. I examine these deliberations to assess how far Tanzania's justifications were validated by African states. Given that I am interested in how far other states were persuaded by the justifications offered up by India, Vietnam, and Tanzania, the study relies on an interpretative method that examines the process of argumentation that takes place in the various international institutions (the Security Council, the General Assembly, and the OAU). By listening in on the conversations that took place, the aim is to evaluate the constructivist claim that actors are inhibited from making arguments that cannot be legitimated.

If certain actions are ruled out because they cannot be legitimated, then it follows that a change in legitimating principles will enable new actions that were previously inhibited. I argue that humanitarian claims were not accepted as a legitimate basis for the use of force in the 1970s but that a new norm of UN-authorized humanitarian intervention developed in the 1990s. What remains contested at the beginning of the new century is the legitimacy of states or regional organizations employing force without express Security Council authorization. I refer to this as unilateral humanitarian intervention[23] to distinguish it from UN-authorized intervention, and it was NATO's intervention in Kosovo in March 1999 and the subsequent debates in the Security Council that dramatized the growing disagreements among states over the legitimacy of using force in the absence of explicit Security Council authorization.

The argument in Part Three traces the changing normative context that made possible new practices of humanitarian intervention in the 1990s. In describing this context, I employ the same interpretative method to examine the justifications and public-reasoning process in the UN Security Council. This body was paralysed by cold-war politics in the 1970s, but in the 1990s the Security Council embarked upon a period of activism that saw it extend the scope of its powers into matters previously considered part of the 'domestic jurisdiction' of states. By studying the justifications offered by Security Council members for their voting behaviour in different cases of intervention, I examine the contest within the Security Council over its interventionary competence.

Even if a new norm of humanitarian intervention is emerging, how should we respond to the criticism that states can agree to humanitarian norms in

[23] This is a useful term to describe the interventions of individual states, but it is less useful in describing interventions where a group of states are involved as in Western intervention in northern Iraq or NATO action in Kosovo. Nevertheless, I have decided to adopt it to cover all cases where intervention is not explicitly authorized by the UN Security Council. I use the label humanitarian intervention to refer to generic cases of intervention that include both unilateral and UN authorized ones.

principle, but violate them in practice? Putting this point in philosophical terms, Martin Hollis and Steve Smith have usefully referred to this discrepancy as one where the legitimating function of language ('the language of manœuvre') contrasts with the motivations for the action ('inward reasons for action which agents can keep to themselves').[24] Skinner's reply to this problem is to argue that whether the actor is sincere or not is beside the point since what matters is that, once an agent has accepted the need to legitimate his behaviour, he is committed to showing that his actions

were in fact motivated by some accepted set of social and political principles. And this in turn implies that, *even if the agent is not in fact motivated by any of the principles* he professes, *he will nevertheless be obliged to behave in such a way* that his actions remain compatible with the claim that these principles genuinely motivated him.[25]

The difficulty with this argument, and one that sophisticated realists make, is that in international politics states can always find a justification for their actions because the rules are sufficiently indeterminate. They can be stretched to provide enough legitimacy for practically any action—for example, the appeal to self-defence that routinely accompanies acts of aggressive unilateralism.

There can be no conclusive response to the sceptic who argues that public legitimating reasons are always *post hoc* rationalizations. Practitioners might claim at the time, or later in memoirs and interviews, that they would not have acted without these legitimating reasons, but how can we know that this is the case? As I argue in Chapters 6, 7, and 8, the existence of specific Security Council resolutions enabled the use of force by Western states in Iraq, Somalia, and Rwanda, but to prove Skinner's thesis it would have to be shown that Western states would have been inhibited from intervening in the absence of these resolutions. Given the impossibility of this task, the book nevertheless provides good reasons to support the proposition that decision-makers are inhibited by legitimation concerns.

In exploring the constraining power of norms, the book also investigates how changing domestic and international norms enable state actions that were previously unthinkable. This should not be read as indicating that new norms guarantee changed actions, since, just as their constraining power does not physically prevent actions, 'new or changed norms enable new or different behaviours; they do not ensure such behaviours'.[26] Changing norms provide actors with new public legitimating reasons to justify actions, but they do not determine that an action will take place. This is very pertinent to the subject of humanitarian intervention, for, as I argue in relation to the case

---

[24] M. Hollis and S. Smith, *Explaining and Understanding International Relations* (Oxford: Oxford University Press, 1990), 176.

[25] Skinner, 'Analysis of Political Thought and Action', 116; emphasis added.

[26] Finnemore, 'Constructing Norms', 158.

of Rwanda, the problem was not that the sovereignty norm blocked effective Security Council action, but the fact that in the vital early weeks of April 1994—when hundreds of thousands could have been saved—no government was prepared to risk its soldiers to rescue victims of the genocide.

If an intervention does take place, then the publicly articulated reasons might be sufficient to explain the action, since there may not be a gap between motives and justifications (a proposition investigated in Parts Two and Three). However, cases might arise where justification is a necessary but not a sufficient explanation of an action. In such cases, it is important to explore the additional motivating factors that led governments to use force. This requires an investigation on a case-by-case basis of the role played by what Hollis and Smith call the 'off-the-board'[27] reasons. In explaining specific decisions on intervention in humanitarian crises in the 1970s and 1990s, I investigate how important these reasons were as against the public legitimating ones. Yet, in arguing that we should study both justifications and motives, it is central to my argument that justification is a critical enabling condition of action and not simply a rationalization of decisions taken for other reasons.

How legitimation concerns constrain and enable state actions in relation to the use of force for humanitarian purposes is central to this study, but it is not sufficient to restrict our understanding of legitimacy to that of the practice of the actors themselves. This is the way that I have talked about legitimacy so far, defining it in terms of the standards of acceptable conduct set by the prevailing morality of society, be it domestic society or international society. Actions that are collectively interpreted as falling outside these boundaries are named as illegitimate, leading to social disapproval and perhaps sanctioning. The problem with this conception of legitimacy is that it tells us nothing about the normative content of the norms and rules, or why they should be adhered to. Legitimacy is bestowed upon those who keep to the rules of the game and actions that violate these are judged as deviant and dangerous.[28]

This legalist interpretation is problematic for the reason that a commitment to its cherished rules led international society to condemn the resort to force by India and especially Vietnam, even though in each case the effect was to rescue the victims of mass murder. In examining state practice in the 1970s, this book seeks to explore how it was that the victims of mass murder were excluded from the discourse of the society of states. If you had asked the people suffering under the brutal tyrannies in East Pakistan, Cambodia, or

---

[27] Hollis and Smith, *Explaining and Understanding*, 185.

[28] A good example of this conception of international legitimacy is Franck, *The Power of Legitimacy*, where he argues that the legitimacy of a rule is measured by its 'compliance pull'; the more legitimate the rule the greater the compliance. The problem here is that it shows us *how* leaders are constrained, but not *why*.

Uganda how they viewed the legitimacy of India's, Vietnam's and Tanzania's interventions, their answer would have been very different from the meaning given to these actions by international society.

Order and Justice in International Society

As the above examples illustrate, *humanitarian intervention exposes the conflict between order and justice at its starkest*. To elucidate these tensions, and hopefully overcome them, I turn to the conception of international society supplied by the English School. Within the school, theorists generally divide into 'pluralists' or 'solidarists', and the importance of these categories is that each provides a very different understanding of the legitimacy of humanitarian intervention.[29] Pluralist international-society theory defines humanitarian intervention as a violation of the cardinal rules of sovereignty, non-intervention, and non-use of force. Pluralists focus on how the rules of international society provide for an international order among states sharing different conceptions of justice. States and not individuals are the principal bearers of rights and duties in international law, and pluralists are sceptical that states can develop agreement beyond a minimum ethic of coexistence. Indeed, as I explore further in Part One, they argue that attempts to pursue individual justice through unilateral humanitarian intervention place in jeopardy the structure of inter-state order.

This view of the moral possibilities of international society is challenged by the more radical—or solidarist—voice that looks to strengthen the legitimacy of international society by deepening its commitment to justice. Rather than see order and justice locked in a perennial tension, solidarism looks to the possibility of overcoming this conflict by developing practices that recognize the mutual interdependence between the two claims. Bull defined solidarism as 'the solidarity, or potential solidarity, of the states comprising international society, with respect to the enforcement of the law'. This conception of international society recognizes that individuals have rights and duties in international law, but it also acknowledges that individuals can have these rights enforced only by states. Consequently, the defining character of a solidarist

---

[29] The idea that there are pluralist and solidarist conceptions of international society was first developed by Hedley Bull in 'The Grotian Conception of International Society', in H. Butterfield and M. Wight (eds.), *Diplomatic Investigations* (London: Allen & Unwin, 1966), 51–74. This approach to thinking about the moral possibilities of international society was not developed by Bull, but is finding favour today. In addition to N. J. Wheeler, 'Pluralist or Solidarist Conceptions of Humanitarian Intervention: Bull and Vincent on Humanitarian Intervention', *Millennium: Journal of International Studies*, 21/2 (1992), see A. Hurrell, 'Society and Anarchy in the 1990s', in B. A. Roberson (ed.), *The Structure of International Society* (London: Pinter, 1998); Dunne, *Inventing, International Society*, and Andrew Linklater, *The Transformation of Political Community* (Cambridge: Polity Press, 1998).

society of states is one in which states accept not only a moral responsibility to protect the security of their own citizens, but also the wider one of 'guardianship of human rights everywhere'.[30] Writing in 1966, Hedley Bull argued that it was not possible to find much support for the view that international society should police human rights violations, or that it bestowed a legal right of humanitarian intervention upon individual states. This was one of the reasons that led him to the conclusion that the solidarist conception of international society was 'premature'.[31] *Saving Strangers* builds upon Bull's contribution by showing how pluralism and solidarism generate competing approaches to the legitimacy of humanitarian intervention, and by charting the stamp of these conceptions on state practice during and after the cold war. Crucially, it asks how far the society of states has developed a new collective capacity for enforcing minimum standards of humanity.

The existing English School writings on the legitimacy of humanitarian intervention are rather fragmentary. While writers such as Adam Roberts, Robert Jackson, and James Mayall have made important contributions to our thinking in several key articles written through the 1990s, there has been no systematic attempt to develop a theory of humanitarian intervention. Furthermore, these pluralists share a deep scepticism about the moral value of the doctrine of humanitarian intervention and question its support in state practice. What is curious is that solidarists have done so little work on the question of the theory and practice of humanitarian intervention in the period since Bull wrote his essay. R. J. Vincent's writings in the mid-1980s stand out as the only significant contribution to this debate, and I explore these in greater detail in Part One. However, he did not develop a solidarist theory of humanitarian intervention, nor did he challenge the criticisms of the pluralists or the realists. In this book, I set out to do the following: develop a comprehensive framework for deciding what is to count as a legitimate humanitarian intervention; examine how pluralist and solidarist conceptions of international society shaped the diplomatic dialogue over humanitarian intervention; provide a rebuttal of realist and pluralist critiques of humanitarian intervention; and integrate legal and political approaches.

Part One shows in more detail how the various arguments of lawyers, social constructivists, philosophers, and Just War theorists all contribute to our understanding of the practice of humanitarian intervention in international society. I consider the normative justifications marshalled in support of the rules that constitute a pluralist international society, and open up the question as to why the rules should be valued if they enable states to commit gross abuses of human rights. This is a prelude to the enunciation of the following solidarist claim: *states that massively violate human rights should forfeit their right to be treated as legitimate sovereigns, thereby morally entitling*

---

[30] Bull, 'The Grotian Conception', 63.   [31] Ibid. 73.

other states to use force to stop the oppression. I then show how this solidarist position is strongly opposed by pluralists and realists, before turning to the construction of a theory of humanitarian intervention that seeks to address these objections. Here, I set up a framework for assessing the humanitarian qualifications of particular interventions, and argue that humanitarian intervention is a moral duty in cases of what I call 'supreme humanitarian emergencies'.

Before turning to an overview of the cold-war empirical cases analysed in the volume, it is necessary to explain why these cases have been chosen. The normal response of states to humanitarian outrages during the cold war was non-intervention: examples include the slaughter of millions of Tutsis in Burundi in the early 1960s; the murder of hundreds of thousands of Ibos during the war over Biafra's attempted secession from Nigeria; and Indonesia's mass murder of East Timorese after its conquest and annexation of that country in 1975. However, there are three cases of unilateral intervention during the cold war that are the subject of considerable controversy in terms of their credentials as humanitarian interventions: India's 1971 intervention in East Pakistan, which led to the ending of gross human rights abuses and the creation of the state of Bangladesh; Vietnam's intervention in Cambodia in December 1978, which precipitated the overthrow of the murderous Pol Pot regime; and Tanzania's intervention in Uganda a few months later, which ended Idi Amin's reign of terror. The secondary literature, predominantly in the field of international law, has focused extensively on these cases but is divided on two key issues: first, did India, Vietnam, and Tanzania act for humanitarian reasons, and, secondly, were their actions legitimated by other states as exceptions to the rules of sovereignty, non-intervention, and non-use of force?

Organization of the Case-Study Material

These issues are taken up in the first case study through an examination of the justifications, motives, and outcomes surrounding India's use of force against Pakistan in December 1971. After a short discussion of the background context, I examine India's justifications for its use of force. Is there any evidence to suggest that its public legitimating reasons were different from its motives? Were the justifications in conformity with the rules of international society? From the outset India pointed to the humanitarian benefits of its actions, but to what extent did it defend its actions on humanitarian grounds? Chapter 2 assesses the extent to which international society accepted India's violation of Article 2 (4) of the UN Charter (which prohibits the unilateral use of force except for purposes of self-defence) on humanitarian grounds, as some lawyers suggest.

Chapter 3 investigates why it was that Vietnam was so heavily sanctioned for its use of force against the murderous regime of Pol Pot. In contrast to India, Vietnam did not make any appeal to humanitarian reasons; indeed, it even went so far as publicly to repudiate this as a legitimate basis for its use of force. Given that Vietnam had a strong case for justifying its actions on humanitarian grounds, it is surprising that it did not make more of this justi-fication, and I consider the reasons for this. Part of the explanation for the condemnation can be found in the cold-war context: there was no support for Vietnam because it was perceived to be acting as an agent of Soviet imperial-ism, and the action was condemned by the Western bloc and the Association of South East Asian Nations (ASEAN), which took the view that Vietnam's justification of self-defence masked expansionist ambitions. I reject this inter-pretation: according to the criteria to be developed in Part One, Vietnam's use of force qualifies as a humanitarian intervention and should have been approved by the society of states.

Vietnam was suffering the opprobrium of the society of states at the same time that Tanzania's use of force against Uganda was being treated with leniency. Chapter 4 examines why Tanzania's overthrow of Idi Amin was greeted with 'almost tacit approval'.[32] Realists would argue that the selective treatment of Vietnam's and Tanzania's actions shows how responses to the use of force are always governed by calculations of interests. Fernando Teson takes a different view, arguing that the Tanzanian case was treated differently because it was viewed by the society of states as 'a precedent supporting the legality of humanitarian intervention in appropriate cases'.[33] To investigate this claim, the chapter considers how far Tanzania resorted to humanitarian justifications in defending its actions, and how far these were approved by the wider society of states? The new Ugandan Government argued that the OAU should welcome Tanzania's action on humanitarian grounds. This claim chal-lenged the dominant pluralist conception that humanitarian intervention is not legitimate; but, as I go on to argue, this solidarist conception failed to secure normative legitimacy among African states.

The importance of studying the justifications and public reasoning process of the actors in the cold-war cases is that it provides the basis for a compar-ative analysis of post-cold-war cases of intervention. Part Three of the book shows that in the 1990s, there was a growing tendency to invoke humanitar-ian justifications by Western governments to legitimate their use of force. Chapter 5 opens by briefly describing the changing international context that made possible the UN mandated use of force against Iraq following its inva-sion of Kuwait in 1990. It then focuses on the post-war situation in Iraq, which led to the passing of UN Security Council Resolution 688 on 5 April

[32] C. Thomas, *New States, Sovereignty and Intervention* (Aldershot: Gower, 1985), 122–3.
[33] Fernando Teson, *Humanitarian Intervention: An Inquiry into Law and Morality* (Dobbs Ferry, NY: Transnational Publishers, 1988), 167.

1991. The key legal issue in relation to India's, Vietnam's, and Tanzania's use of force focused on whether their interventions breached Article 2 (4), but debate shifted in the 1990s to the question of whether the Security Council can legitimately intervene inside state borders, given the prohibition against intervention by UN organs under Article 2 (7).[34] The only exception to this is Security Council enforcement action under Chapter VII of the Charter, but this requires a finding that there is a 'threat to the peace, breach of the peace, or act of aggression [that threatens] international peace and security'.[35]

The process of argumentation within the Security Council during the adoption of Resolution 688 shows that some states resisted broadening the interpretation of threats to 'international peace and security' for the reason that it exceeded the Security Council's legitimate competence to act under the Charter. What, then, are we to make of the claim of Western governments that Resolution 688 provided legal cover for their military deployment inside northern Iraq to create 'safe havens' for the victims of Iraqi oppression? I examine the domestic and international enabling conditions of Western action, and identify other 'off-the-board' reasons that played a role in the decision to intervene. The final part of the chapter considers whether the actions of Western governments were in conformity with their humanitarian claims.

Chapter 6 analyses how the USA came to intervene militarily in Somalia in 1990–1 given that it was an area of little or no strategic significance. Was the Bush Administration influenced by domestic pressures? Or, did the President act for personal humanitarian reasons? Security Council authorization enabled US action, but would the Bush Administration have acted without a Security Council mandate? In contrast with Resolution 688, where two states abstained and three voted against, all fifteen states on the Security Council endorsed Resolution 794, which authorized US military action in Somalia. This has led many commentators to argue that this indicates acceptance of a new norm of collective humanitarian intervention in international society; I argue that this interpretation needs to be qualified in several important respects. The narrative then considers the expansion of the Somali operation from a short-term mission of famine relief into a long-term political project aimed at nothing less than the demilitarization of Somali society. Apart from addressing the obvious question why the mission ended in disaster, it is also important to look at the impact this had on the UN and on American public opinion. Moreover, what conclusions can be drawn about the viability of forms of intervention that try and address the underlying causes of human suffering?

Any claim that the interventions in northern Iraq and Somalia demonstrate a new practice of legitimate humanitarian intervention runs up against

---

[34] Ramsbotham and Woodhouse, *Humanitarian Intervention*, 79.
[35] Charter of the United Nations, Article 39.

the international response to the Rwandan genocide of 1994. There was US military intervention to deliver humanitarian aid in the aftermath of the genocide, but the brutal fact is that over one million people died during a period of two months, and international society failed to come to the rescue. Chapter 7 considers whether the genocide could have been prevented. Why was there no attempt to stop the bloodbath in the crucial period between April and the end of May? After weeks of inaction at the UN, France finally decided to act and requested Security Council authorization for a limited military intervention to protect displaced persons inside Rwanda. This action was viewed with suspicion by other members of the Security Council, who worried that French humanitarian justifications masked its real reasons for acting, and I examine how far the French action satisfies the requirements of a legitimate humanitarian intervention.

Prior to the adoption of Resolution 929, which authorized its intervention in Rwanda, France had declared that it would intervene in Rwanda only if it had explicit Security Council authority. The implication is that it would have been constrained from acting in the absence of this collective legitimation. NATO's use of force against the Federal Republic of Yugoslavia in March 1999 pushed against the boundaries of legitimate intervention because it occurred without explicit Security Council authorization. Central to how far this case sets a legal precedent is the groundbreaking debate in the Security Council on 24 and 26 March, where the majority of members either approved or acquiesced in NATO's action. I open Chapter 8 by reflecting on the decision to use air power to defend the Kosovars, showing how this judgment relied on a particular reading of the lessons of international intervention in Croatia and Bosnia. NATO leaders defended the action as a 'humanitarian war'. Prior to, and during, the bombing, a fierce debate raged about whether the humanitarian war was necessary, just, proportionate, and effective. What lessons will world leaders draw from Kosovo? Will it be that we need to develop 'new rules' outlining the conditions under which intervention is legitimate—as Tony Blair has suggested[36]—or should we draw the conclusion that violent means rarely bring about good ends?[37]

The concluding chapter of the book takes up these themes by reflecting on how far humanitarian intervention secured a new legitimacy in the 1990s. Here I argue that, whilst a new norm of Security Council-authorized humanitarian intervention has developed at the beginning of the new century, the practice of unilateral humanitarian intervention continues to be treated with

---

[36] Tony Blair, 'Doctrine of the International Community', Speech given in Chicago, USA, 22 Apr. 1999.

[37] K. Booth, 'The Kosovo Tragedy: Epilogue to Another "Low and Dishonest Decade"?', unpublished lecture given at the South African Political Science Association Biennial Congress, held at the Military Academy, Saldanha, 29 June 1999.

great suspicion by international society. The chapter challenges this caution on the part of the society of states, arguing that a practice of unilateral humanitarian intervention can support a new solidarity in the society of states based on the reconciliation of the imperatives of order and justice.

PART ONE

Theories of Humanitarian Intervention

1

Humanitarian Intervention and International Society

It is the contention of this chapter that international society, like other organizations in the social world, is constituted by rule-governed actions. The first part of this chapter builds upon the discussion in the Introduction by exploring further how the rules of the society of states constrain and enable state actions. I argue for an understanding of international society that avoids the twin fallacies of making rule-following the result of conscious rational calculations or the product of deep social structures existing independently of the practices of human agents. The next part of the chapter turns to the question of how pluralist and solidarist international-society theory interprets the legitimacy of the practice of humanitarian intervention. Here, I set out the objections of pluralists and realists to legitimating this practice in international politics. The final part of the chapter offers a rebuttal of these objections by developing a solidarist theory of humanitarian intervention.

Procedural accounts of international legitimacy are predicated on the assumption that the test of legitimacy is state practice. This is certainly an important criterion for judging acts of intervention, but it should not be the definitive one. What is needed is a *substantive* conception that can be used to evaluate the humanitarian qualifications of specific cases of intervention, and critically to reflect upon the normative responses of the society of states. This chapter supplies such a conception by establishing minimum or threshold conditions that should define a legitimate humanitarian intervention. Actions that satisfy these should be legitimated by the society of states, but there are additional tests above the threshold that correspondingly increase the legitimacy of the action in humanitarian terms.

The Nature of International Society

Charles Manning was the first to liken international society to a game with its own self-contained rules.[1] In answer to the fundamental question as to

---

[1] C. Manning, *The Nature of International Society*, 2nd edn. (London: Macmillan, 1975).

why states obey the law when it cannot be enforced, he argues that 'the on-going diplomatic process is indeed like a game, and like any other game, it has to have rules, and compliance with those rules'.[2] Manning's contribution is to show how practices such as sovereignty and international law belong to a game that diplomats and state leaders reproduce through their actions. If we want to understand how international society becomes possible, then it is necessary to recognize that the practices that constitute it have no real-world existence independent of the 'communal imagining'[3] that conjure them into existence. Martin Wight argued that the defining mark of the society of states is the reciprocal recognition of sovereignty, but sovereignty is not a physical object that we can touch, feel, or measure. Rather, to take one of Manning's favourite analogies, it is like the existence of Father Christmas: Santa Claus is 'real' but he exists only because we all participate in the shared understand-ings that make his existence possible; similarly, sovereignty exists by virtue of the intersubjective meanings that conjure it into existence.[4]

This begs the question as to who does the conjuring? One answer is that states are the agents who, through their interactions, constitute the practices of the society of states. Thus, we talk about Britain, Russia, or China taking this or that action. But how can this be, since we all know that states do not exist in the way that flesh and blood individuals do? The way round this problem is to think of states not as agents, but as structures that constrain and enable those individuals who hold positions of responsibility in the state.[5] Thus, foreign ministers—like university lecturers—are enabled and constrained by the rules that constitute their respective positions of author-ity. How they play their role within international society or the university is not predetermined; rather, it is up to each individual to manoeuvre within the rules as he or she sees fit. The result in both walks of life is that some indi-viduals live up to their responsibilities better than others, but all individuals who accept either of these positions of authority are subject to a set of constraints. As I discussed in the Introduction, these constraints are not phys-ical but normative ones, and the fact that they are socially constructed does not make them any less real.

The purpose of the above is to make clear that, when I personify states in this book, it is a shorthand to describe those individuals who, as Robert Jackson puts it, 'act on behalf of states: statesmen—or, in other words pres-idents, chancellors, prime ministers, foreign ministers, ambassadors'.[6] It is

---

[2] Manning, *The Nature of International Society*, 112.

[3] Ibid. 19.

[4] The best exploration of how sovereignty becomes constructed is provided by Alexander Wendt in his 1992 article 'Anarchy is what States Make of it: The Social Construction of Power Politics', *International Organization*, 46/2 (1992).

[5] For this insight I am grateful to Colin Wight.

[6] R. H. Jackson, 'The Political Theory of International Society', in K. Booth and S. Smith (eds.), *International Relations Theory Today* (Cambridge: Polity Press, 1995), 111.

individuals who sign treaties like the UN Charter, but this action does not bind them as individuals, it binds the states that they represent.[7] And, in signing treaties or sending diplomats to act as Ambassadors to other countries, state leaders reproduce the shared meanings that constitute the society of states.

The contention that the practices of the society of states are rule-governed raises the question as to whether state leaders are conscious that they are following rules. This is how realists would conceive of international society in that they would argue that governments pursue their interests while paying lip service to the rules. State leaders recognize that they have to justify their actions in terms of the rules, but this owes nothing to a normative commitment to the rules and everything to being seen to play the game so as to avoid moral censure and sanctions.[8] And, in response to the argument advanced in this book that the rule structure is sufficiently determinate to constrain actions that cannot be plausibly defended in terms of the rules, realists reply that good players of the game, like a skilled advocate defending a hard case in a court of law, can always find arguments to justify their positions.

This realist view that states use language 'strategically'[9] to advance their interests is open to the objection that it fails to understand how 'nothing is simultaneously freer and more constrained than the action of the good player'.[10] This is the thesis of Pierre Bourdieu, who criticizes those who make rule following the product of rational calculation, while also denying accounts of the social world that take agents out of the picture by relying on structural causes that exist independently of the practices of the actors. Bourdieu's contribution is to develop the idea of 'strategizing', which he defines as that 'feel for the game' that comes from a practical sense of what is required to play the game well. Two players might learn the rules of football but one of them is a poor player who has no real sense of where the ball is; the other knows instinctively what is required by the game and moves around the pitch in a way that suggests that 'the ball were in command of him'. Bourdieu's key point is that this shows that 'he is in command of the ball'. The best footballers achieve success by doing more than skilfully applying the rules; they have a 'feel for the game' that is not reducible to knowledge of these. Yet at the same time they are successful only because they work within

---

[7] The two best expositions of this argument are in Carr, *The Twenty Years Crisis*, and Manning, *The Nature of International Society*.

[8] I owe this point to Andrew Mason.

[9] I am borrowing this idea of strategic language use from Jürgen Habermas, who defines it as 'action orientated to success' where the defining characteristic is that agents pursue ends instrumentally based on means–ends calculations of efficiency. 'Strategic action', then, is at the opposite end of the spectrum to Habermas's idea of 'communicative action', which he defines as 'action orientated to understanding' (J. Habermas, *Theory of Communicative*, i. *Reason and the Rationalization of Society*, trans. T. McCarthy (London: Heinemann, 1984), 285).

[10] P. Bourdieu, *In Other Words: Essays towards a Reflexive Sociology*, trans. M. Adamson (Stanford: Stanford, Calif. University Press, 1987), 63.

the constraints imposed by the rule structure of the game. As Bourdieu puts it, mastery of the game brings with it a real sense that 'you can't do just anything and get away with it'.[11] Players, then, will act in ways that reproduce the game without this necessarily being a product of conscious calculation. Bourdieu argues that the production and reproduction of the game are 'outside conscious control and discourse (in the way that, for instance, techniques of the body do)'.[12]

Three important implications follow from Bourdieu's understanding of strategizing in understanding the nature of international society. The first is that the realist model of states consciously calculating their moves is too limited because it ignores how states are socialized into a set of predispositions that are not questioned. States follow their interests, but the way they define these is shaped by the rules prevailing in the society of states.[13] Thus, in response to the realist argument that states obey international law only when it is in their interest to do so, Hedley Bull responds that what is more surprising is that states 'so often judge it in their interests to conform to it'.[14] Adopting Bourdieu's argument, states define their interests in ways that take into account the constraints that '*impose themselves* on those people . . . who, because they have a feel for the game . . . are prepared to perceive them and carry them out'.[15]

This leads into the second and related point, which is that successful players recognize the constraints that membership of international society imposes. The major fault-line that divides realism from the English School is, in Hedley Bull's words, that, even if a state decides to break the rules, it recognizes 'that it owes other states an explanation of its conduct, in terms of rules that they accept'.[16] This is very different from the realist account, where the rules are instruments that states manipulate in their self-interest, and it reflects the core assumption of the English School that states 'form a society in the sense that they conceive themselves to be *bound* by a common set of

[11] Bourdieu, *In Other Words: Essays towards a Reflexive Sociology*, 64.

[12] Ibid. 61. John Searle makes the same argument as Bourdieu and gives the example of a baseball player who learns the rules and then begins playing the game seriously. As he or she develops as a player, his or her actions become more fluent and responsive to the demands of the game. Searle argues that it is misleading to think that he or she is applying the rules more skillfully, since what has happened is that the player has acquired a set of predispositions and skills that are determined by the rules of the game, but which do not rely on actors consciously following rules. See Searle, *The Construction of Social Reality*, 141–2.

[13] This is the significance of the constructivist claim that identities and interests are not exogenous to interaction; rather, as Wendt so powerfully argues, identities are constituted through interaction and changing identities generate different conceptions of interests.

[14] H. Bull, *The Anarchical Society: A Study of Order in World Politics* (London: Macmillan, 1977), 140.

[15] Bourdieu, *In Other Words*, 63. This argument bears an important family resemblance to constructivist claims that identities constitute interests, and that membership of the society of states brings with it an obligation to accept the binding character of international law that leads states to define their interests in ways that reinforce this legal obligation.

[16] Bull, *The Anarchical Society*, 45.

rules in their relations with one another'.[17] And, even if it is conceded that states participate in this ritual of legitimation when breaking the rules only to avoid moral censure and sanctions, this realist criticism ignores how far this need to justify in terms of the rules constrains state action. Confirming the relevance of Skinner's argument to the international level, Bull argues that 'rules are not infinitely malleable and do circumscribe the range of choice of states which seek to give pretexts in terms of them'.[18]

The third issue raised by understanding international society as a rule-governed activity is what happens when the rules are disputed? Experienced footballers might not be conscious of the rules constituting the game for most of a match, but, if there is a dispute over a penalty, then both teams will invoke the rules to try and win the referee over. Without the existence of the rules to provide common reference points, it would be impossible to argue over the merits of the referee's decision. The referee is the arbiter of competing claims on the football field and it is relatively easy to make decisions because the rule structure is highly determinate. The difficulty arises when choices have to be made between conflicting rules, the application of which is contested. This is the problem that faces the law-making process in both domestic and international society. One view of the law is that the task of judges is to find the appropriate rule and apply it, but, as Rosalyn Higgins argues, this overlooks the fact that determining the relevant rule is part of the decision-making function of judges. Such a determination, according to Higgins, requires making choices between alternative legal claims and it cannot be divorced from wider political and social considerations.

If we turn to the international realm, then the legal process is even more intimately bound up with the political process because of 'the lack of authoritative decisions concerning the applicability and scope of legal norms'.[19] Nevertheless, states can argue over whether an action belongs to a particular legal rule only because they share enough of a common language to structure the public reasoning process. In the Cuban Missile Crisis, for example, the USA and the Soviet Union disagreed over whether the Soviet deployment of missiles could be justified under the rule of self-defence, but it was only because they shared this common language that they could argue over the merits of competing claims.

---

[17] Ibid. 13; emphasis added.

[18] Bull's point about the constraining power of the rules is captured well in Louis Henkin's comment that the 'fact that nations feel obliged to justify their actions under international law, that justifications must have plausibility, that plausible justifications are often unavailable or limited, inevitably affects how nations will act' (L. Henkin, *How Nations Behave: Law and Foreign Policy* (New York: Columbia University Press, 1979), 45). Further evidence for this proposition is that a senior Foreign Office official told me privately that the British Government would never make a move unless it could present a plausible legal defence of its action that would be meaningful to others.

[19] Kratochwil, *Rules, Norms, and Decisions*, 254.

It does not follow from the above that the process of public argumentation always shapes decisions. This would be claiming too much, since, as Kratochwil points out, the lack of an authoritative arbiter to interpret the application of legal rules ensures that decisions are often settled by 'bargaining and coercive moves rather than by persuasion and by appeals to common standards, shared values, and accepted solutions'.[20] How far this is the pattern of interstate interactions is an empirical question, but, unless states choose to promote their interests through naked threats, it is incumbent upon those who want to legitimate their actions to domestic and international constituencies to make appeals to shared rules and norms.[21] And actors who invoke these to defend their actions can find themselves entrapped by their own justifications in ways that serve to constrain their subsequent actions.[22]

Having shown the importance of rules and norms in understanding the nature of international society, *the question is how far humanitarian intervention is a legitimate move in international society.* This question has both a descriptive and normative component: the descriptive one requires a study of state practice and this is the subject of the empirical investigations in the remainder of the volume; the normative dimension relates to the question of whether humanitarian intervention should be permitted in a society of states constituted by rules of sovereignty, non-intervention and non-use of force. This is the question to which I now turn.

---

[20] Kratochwil, *Rules, Norms, and Decisions,* 254.

[21] As Martti Koskenniemi argues, actors 'pressured by argument . . . occasionally submit themselves to critiques and counter-arguments that invoke the same norms' (M. Koskenniemi, 'The Place of Law in Collective Security', in A. J. Paolini *et al.* (eds.), *Between Sovereignty and Global Governance: The United Nations, the State and Civil Society* (London: Macmillan, 1998), 45).

[22] A good example of this is the argument over the interpretation of the ABM Treaty during the Reagan Administration. The administration was committed to deploying a space-based defence system (the Strategic Defense Initiative (SDI)), but this was incompatible with the existing terms of the 1972 Anti-Ballistic Missile (ABM) Treaty. Consequently, the Reagan Administration proposed a new 'broad' interpretation of the provisions of the treaty, but this was opposed and defeated by a coalition of forces in the USA that supported the existing treaty interpretation. What is interesting about this example is that the common reference point for the argument in the USA was that treaties are binding (the principle of *pacta sunt servanda*). The Reagan Administration could have argued that it was no longer going to be bound by the treaty, but it realized that such a move would lack legitimation both domestically and internationally. Having argued that treaties were binding, and having lost the public argument for broadening the treaty, the administration was forced to constrain its space-based testing to the parameters set by a narrow interpretation of the treaty. In making this argument, Hasenclever, Mayer, and Rittberger cite Harald Muller's earlier study of the impact of the ABM Treaty on the Reagan Administration's SDI programme, which stressed the importance of regime rules and norms in constraining US policy. See A. Hasenclever, P. Mayer and V. Rittberger, *Theories of International Regimes* (Cambridge: Cambridge University Press, 1997), 183, and H. Müller, 'The Internationalization of Principles, Norms and Rules by Governments: The Case of Security Regimes' in V. Rittberger (ed.), *Regime Theory and International Relations* (Oxford: Oxford University Press, 1999), 361–91.

Pluralist and Realist Objections to Humanitarian Intervention

The issue of humanitarian intervention arises in cases where a government has turned the machinery of the state against its own people, or where the state has collapsed into lawlessness. Pluralist international-society theory defends the rules of the society of states on the grounds that they uphold plural conceptions of the 'good'.[23] However, the point of departure for solidarist international-society theory is the glaring contradiction between the moral justification of pluralist rules and the actual human rights practices of states. It takes only a quick glance at Amnesty International's annual report to appreciate how many states fail to protect the basic rights of their citizens. Following Henry Shue, R. J. Vincent defined basic rights as security from arbitrary violence and minimum subsistence rights.[24] International society is constituted by a rule-governed framework that enables sovereigns, in Michael Walzer's words, to protect 'the values of individual life and communal liberty'[25] within their borders. Following from this, if a state abuses the human rights of its citizens, should its sovereignty be respected? As Chris Brown puts it, if 'diversity entails that states have the right to mistreat their populations, then it is difficult to see why such diversity is to be valued'.[26] What moral value attaches to the rules of sovereignty and non-intervention if they provide a licence for governments to violate global humanitarian standards? And what are outsiders legally and morally permitted—or even required—to do in the face of such violations of international law?

---

[23] Pluralist international-society theorists are rarely explicit about the normative value to be attached to the society of states, but there is in Bull's work an occasional glimpse of the claim that the moral value of the society of states is be judged in terms of its contribution to individual well-being. He writes, 'if any value attaches to order in world politics, it is order among all mankind which we must treat as being of primary value, not order within the society of states' (Bull, *The Anarchical Society*, 22). The implication of this is that the rules of the society of states are to be valued only if they provide for the security of individuals who stand at the centre of Bull's ethical code. What is implicit in Bull has been made explicit by Robert H. Jackson, who explores the morality of international society in terms of the 'egg-box' conception of international society developed by R. J. Vincent and Hidemi Suganami. 'Sovereign states are the eggs . . . the box is international society' and the purpose of the box in Vincent's words 'is to separate and cushion, not to act'. This leads Jackson to reflect that 'regulating states by international law to avert or reduce the incidence or extent of damaging collisions between them only makes sense if those entities are valuable in themselves . . . There is no point in egg-boxes if eggs are not only breakable but also valuable . . . international society presupposes the intrinsic value of all states and accommodates their inward diversity . . . But it requires and postulates their outward uniformity as indicated by their equal legal status'. See R. H. Jackson, 'Martin Wight, International Theory and the Good Life', *Millennium: Journal of International Studies*, 19/2 (1990), and Vincent, *Human Rights and International Relations*, 123.

[24] Vincent, *Human Rights and International Relations*, 14. Henry Shue conceptualized 'basic rights' as those that are necessary before any other rights can be satisfied. See Henry Shue, *Basic Rights: Subsistence, Affluence and US Foreign Policy* (Princeton: Princeton University Press, 1980), 18–22.

[25] M. Walzer, *Just and Unjust Wars: A Moral Argument with Historical Illustrations* (London: Allen Lane, 1978), 108.

[26] C. Brown, *International Relations Theory: New Normative Approaches* (Hemel Hempstead: Harvester Wheatsheaf, 1992), 125.

Gross human rights violations are now a matter of legitimate international concern, but my interest in this volume is in the legitimacy of using force to prevent or stop such violations. English School solidarists like R. J. Vincent have recognized that 'states should satisfy certain basic requirements of decency before they qualify for the protection which the principle of non-intervention provides'.[27] Moreover, Vincent suggests that, if states systematically and massively violated human rights, '*then* there might fall to the international community a duty of humanitarian intervention'.[28] Michael Walzer argues that 'morality, at least, is not a bar to unilateral action, so long as there is no immediate alternative available'. Humanitarian intervention for Walzer 'is justified when it is a response (with reasonable expectations of success) to acts "that shock the moral conscience of mankind" '.[29] The argument is not that the rules of sovereignty and non-intervention should be jettisoned, since these remain the constitutive rules of international society. Instead, Walzer's solidarist argument is that states should be denied protection of these in those extraordinary cases where governments are committing acts of mass murder, since they are guilty of 'crimes against humanity'.[30] At this point, states are morally entitled to use force to stop these atrocities, and, for some solidarists like Vincent, the obligation is even stronger and the society of states has a duty to act.

As I argued in the Introduction, humanitarian intervention exposes the conflict between order and justice at its starkest, and it is the archetypal case where it might be expected that international society would carve out an explicit legal exception to its rules. After all, what is the point of upholding these if governments are free to slaughter their citizens with impunity? In his discussion of how the conflict between order and justice might be mitigated, Bull argues that two key considerations have to be borne in mind: the consequences for international order of any attempt to promote individual justice; and the degree of injustice embodied in the existing order.[31] Bull is not prepared to assert a general priority of order over justice, suggesting that the 'question of order *versus* justice will always be considered by the parties

---

[27] R. J. Vincent and P. Watson, 'Beyond Non-Intervention', in I. Forbes and M. J. Hoffmann (eds.), *Political Theory, International Relations and the Ethics of Intervention* (London: Macmillan, 1993), 126.

[28] Vincent, *Human Rights and International Relations*, 127.

[29] Walzer, *Just and Unjust Wars*, 107. Writing over ten years after Walzer, Fernando Teson argued that 'a government that engages in substantial violations of human rights betrays the very purpose for which it exists and so forfeits not only its domestic legitimacy, but its international legitimacy as well. Consequently, I shall argue, foreign armies are morally entitled to help victims of oppression in overthrowing dictators, provided that the intervention is proportionate to the evil which it is designed to suppress' (Teson, *Humanitarian Intervention*, 15).

[30] Walzer, *Just and Unjust Wars*, 106. Michael J. Smith argues that because 'the rights of states rest on the rights of individuals . . . a state that is oppressive and violates the autonomy and integrity of its subjects forfeits its moral claim to full sovereignty' (M. J. Smith, 'Humanitarian Intervention: An Overview of the Ethical Issues', *Ethics and International Affairs*, 3 (1989), 74).

[31] Bull, *The Anarchical Society*, 97–8.

concerned in relation to the merits of a particular case'.[32] However, when it comes to the question of humanitarian intervention, Bull emphasizes the dangers that such a practice poses to international order, given that states have conflicting claims of justice. He argues that the society of states had not experimented with a right of humanitarian intervention because of an 'unwillingness to jeopardize the rules of sovereignty and non-intervention by conceding such a right to individual states'.[33] The pluralist concern is that, in the absence of an international consensus on the rules governing a practice of unilateral humanitarian intervention, states will act on their own moral principles, thereby weakening an international order built on the rules of sovereignty, non-intervention, and non-use of force.[34] Bull's critique of humanitarian intervention is a moral one because he views the provision of international order as a necessary condition for the protection and promotion of individual well-being.[35] This defence of the non-intervention rule is based on what philosophers call rule consequentialism. The well-being of all individuals is better served by a legal rule that prohibits humanitarian intervention than by allowing it in the absence of agreement over what principles should govern such a right.[36] To permit humanitarian intervention in such circumstances is to accept that 'it is always going to be based on the cultural predilections of those with the power to carry it out'.[37]

The pluralist objection to legitimating a practice of unilateral humanitarian intervention is a powerful one, but there are four further objections that I want to consider that are raised by realists.[38] The first is that humanitarian claims always cloak the pursuit of national self-interest and that legalizing a right of humanitarian intervention would lead to states abusing it. This concern led Thomas Franck and Nigel Rodley to argue in 1973 that humanitarian intervention should not be permitted as a further exception to the rule prohibiting the use of force in Article 2 (4) of the UN Charter. They argue that the exception contained in the rule of self-defence was already vulnerable to abuse without adding another escape clause that might further weaken the restraint found in Article 2 (4). Because humanitarian concerns will be manipulated by intervening states, a doctrine of humanitarian intervention

[32] Ibid. 97.

[33] H. Bull (ed.), *Intervention in World Politics* (Oxford: Oxford University Press, 1984), 193.

[34] It is important to note here that, while Vincent argued for a 'duty of humanitarian intervention' on the part of the collectivity of states, he shared Bull's pluralist caution about issuing a right of humanitarian intervention to states, since this would 'issue a license for all kinds of interference, claiming with more or less plausibility to be humanitarian, but driving huge wedges into international order' (Vincent, *Human Rights and International Relations*, 114).

[35] See n. 23.

[36] A. Mason and N. J. Wheeler, 'Realist Objections to Humanitarian Intervention', in B. Holden (ed.), *The Ethical Dimensions of Global Change* (London: Macmillan, 1996), 101–2.

[37] Brown, *International Relations Theory*, 113.

[38] In making this distinction between realist and pluralist objections, I recognize that pluralists could share some or all of these realist objections. However, they have not figured prominently in their writings on the legitimacy of humanitarian intervention.

becomes a weapon that the strong will use against the weak. Having surveyed pre-1945 and post-1945 cases of possible humanitarian intervention, Franck and Rodley conclude that in 'very few, if any, instances has the right been asserted under circumstances that appear more humanitarian than self-interested and power seeking'.[39] The problem of abuse confirms the realist view that language is rhetorical, a public disguise that masks the real reasons why states act.

The next realist criticism is the descriptive one that, unless vital interests are at stake, states will not intervene if this risks soldiers' lives or incurs significant economic costs. The contention here is that states will not intervene for primarily humanitarian reasons because they are always motivated by considerations of national self-interest. Realists would agree with Bhikhu Parekh's definition of humanitarian intervention as action 'wholly or primarily guided by the sentiment of humanity, compassion or fellow-feeling'[40] while simultaneously maintaining that this normative statement does not speak to how states actually behave in world politics. Realists who advance this view might concede that humanitarian considerations can play a part in motivating a government to intervene, but states will not use force unless they judge vital interests to be at stake. Thus, the best we can hope for is a happy coincidence where the promotion of national security also defends human rights.[41] The strength of this position is that it recognizes the reality of state interests and power; its weakness is that it makes humanitarianism dependent upon shifting geopolitical and strategic considerations. Realists would argue that there is no alternative to this and buttress this argument against humanitarian intervention by pointing to the problem of selectivity.

Do states always apply principles of humanitarian intervention selectively? Realism answers yes and contends that the selective way humanitarian intervention has been applied in the past is a guide to how a legal right would be applied in the future. Indeed, Franck and Rodley argue that legitimating humanitarian intervention would increase the risks that states would apply the rules selectively. They argue that 'one is not encouraged by the blatant

---

[39] T. Franck and N. Rodley, 'After Bangladesh: The Law of Humanitarian Intervention by Military Force', *American Journal of International Law*, 67 (1973), 290. One of the most notorious examples of this is Hitler's manipulation of humanitarian rationales to justify his intervention in Czechoslovakia in 1938. In a letter to Prime Minister Neville Chamberlain, Hitler wrote that 'ethnic Germans and "various nationalities" . . . have been maltreated in the unworthiest manner, tortured, economically destroyed and, above all, prevented from realizing for themselves also the right of nations to self-determination'. Hitler claimed that in protecting ethnic Germans, he was acting in conformity with the minority rights provisions of the League of Nations. These justifications were treated as bogus by most states, but Hitler could only make them because there existed a regime for the protection of minority rights. See Franck and Rodley, 'After Bangladesh', 284.

[40] B. Parekh, 'Rethinking Humanitarian Intervention', in Bhikhu Parekh (ed.), *The Dilemmas of Humanitarian Intervention*, special issue of the *International Political Science Review*, 18/1 (1997), 54.

[41] Solidarists like Michael Walzer have recognized the force of this realist criticism, he himself argues that 'states don't send their soldiers into other states, it seems, only in order to save lives' (Walzer, *Just and Unjust Wars*, 101).

failure of the international community or of states with the undeniable power to effect rescue to save Jews . . . to intervene with force on behalf of the Armenians . . . to rescue the Hutu of Burundi . . . to aid the Biafrans in their struggle for independence'.[42] The problem of selectivity arises when an agreed moral principle is at stake in more than one situation, but national interest dictates a divergence of response.

The fourth objection is the normative one that states have no business risk-ing their soldiers' lives or those of their non-military personnel to save strangers. This criticism of humanitarian intervention is in tension with the descriptive claim noted above that states do not engage in intervention motiv-ated by primarily humanitarian considerations. If the argument that states will never intervene for primarily humanitarian reasons was true, then this question of soldiers' lives would never arise. However, it does arise, as the cases of Somalia and Kosovo clearly testify, and what is being advanced here is a normative objection to humanitarian intervention predicated on the claim that it is our identity as citizens that constitutes the outer limits of our moral duties. State leaders and publics do not have duties to stop 'barbarities beyond borders',[43] and, if a government has broken down into lawlessness, or is behaving in an appalling way towards its citizens, this is the moral respons-ibility of that state's citizens and political leaders. Outsiders are not under any duty to intervene, even if they believe that they have the capacity to prevent or mitigate such evils. The reason is that 'citizens are the exclusive responsi-bility of their state, and their state is entirely their own business. Citizens should be morally concerned only with the activities of their own state, and the latter is responsible to and for its citizens alone'.[44] This extreme statist position that the only justification for risking soldiers' lives is in defence of the national interest is well summed up by Samuel P. Huntington, who asserted in relation to US intervention in Somalia that 'it is morally unjustifi-able and politically indefensible that members of the [US] armed forces should be killed to prevent Somalis from killing one another'.[45]

Pushed to its logical extreme, the implication of the statist paradigm is that governments should not risk the life of even one soldier to save hundreds of thousands or even millions of non-nationals. Very few realists would follow Huntington and adhere to such a strict rule, but how many of our 'boys and girls' are we prepared to risk? How many of us would agree with David Hendrickson that 'the prospect of moderate casualties'[46] should not deter humanitarian interventions? How is moderate to be defined? It would surely

[42] Franck and Rodley, 'After Bangladesh', 288.
[43] The phrase is Ken Booth's.
[44] Parekh, 'Rethinking Humanitarian Intervention', 56.
[45] Quoted in Smith, 'Humanitarian Intervention', 63.
[46] David C. Hendrickson, 'In Defense of Realism: A Commentary on Just and Unjust Wars', *Ethics and International Affairs*, 11 (1997), 46.

be more than the eighteen US Rangers lost in a firefight in Somalia in October 1993, which, as I argue in Chapter 6, played a key role in leading President Clinton to withdraw US forces from that conflict. Hendrickson undermines his position by arguing that even moderate losses would be politically unsustainable in democratic polities. The problem here is that televisual and print media nurture humanitarian sentiments on the part of democratic publics that create pressures for intervention, but this has to be balanced against the risk 'that domestic public opinion will revolt against any costly or protracted involvement'.[47] In Chapters 5, 6, 7, and 8 I examine how successfully Western governments balanced these conflicting considerations, and how far the risk of casualties deterred them from using force in defence of humanitarian values.

Even if it is argued that states have a right to risk their soldiers in defending humanitarian values, there is the objection that such interventions are likely to end in disaster. This objection is not unique to realists and some liberals share this concern with crusading interventionism. The worry here is that noble humanitarian intentions are no guarantee against failure and humiliating exit, and that there is a dangerous arrogance in the idea that the secure liberal societies of the West have the answers, let alone the will, to solve the problems of states such as Somalia and Rwanda.[48] A good example of this view is Simon Jenkins, who, when giving evidence before the House of Commons Foreign Affairs Committee on 25 November 1997, stated:

What is the basis on which you decide that a particular outrage against human rights in a particular country which has not, necessarily, threatened cross-borders is something in which you should involve yourself? What is the military objective that you take . . . How do you know that you have won this particular conflict? Most important of all, it becomes quite difficult, at a certain stage, to justify asking your own troops . . . to commit their lives to the defence of—what?[49]

Despite being much more sympathetic to the project of liberal interventionism, Michael Ignatieff expressed similar sentiments when he questioned the 'traces of imperial arrogance' that led the USA to believe that it could go into Somalia, stop the clan warfare, and then exit within a few months having handed the problem over to the UN.[50] Ignatieff remains committed to

---

[47] Hendrickson, 'In Defense of Realism: A Commentary on Just and Unjust Wars', 45.

[48] Martin Woollacott cites that doyen of American realism, George F. Kennan, who wrote in his diary after the US intervention in Somalia that he regarded 'this move as a dreadful error'. According to Woollacott, Kennan's concern is that 'intervention in Somalia and other places was predicated on a vastly exaggerated idea of what a nation, even a very powerful one, could do for other societies, especially damaged and anarchic ones' (M. Woollacott, 'Busybodies can Do More Harm than Good', *Guardian*, 19 July 1997).

[49] 'Foreign Policy and Human Rights', Foreign Affairs Committee, Minutes of Evidence, 25 Nov. 1997, 4.

[50] M. Ignatieff, *The Warrior's Honor: Ethnic War and the Modern Conscience* (London: Chatto & Windus, 1998), 94.

the project of international rescue, but, writing before Kosovo, he expressed his concern that the failure of liberal interventionism in the 1990s (how far this is a fair description of the outcomes of the interventions in Iraq, Somalia, and Rwanda is addressed later in the book) had led the West to pull up the moral drawbridge on suffering humanity. How far Kosovo has changed this and how far the 'seductions of moral disgust'[51] continue to grip the mindsets of policy-makers and publics are issues that are taken up in the concluding chapter of the volume.

It is clear from the above list of objections that solidarist international-society theory has quite a challenge on its hands in defending humanitarian intervention as a legitimate practice. Replying to these criticisms by developing a solidarist theory of humanitarian intervention is the task of the final part of this chapter.

A Solidarist Theory of Legitimate Humanitarian Intervention

My argument is that interventions have to satisfy certain tests to count as humanitarian. This is a minimum requirement, and, once this threshold has been crossed, there are additional criteria that if met correspondingly increase the legitimacy of a particular action.[52] It is necessary to make two points at this stage: first, others might agree with the criteria specified here but disagree over which ones should be built into the threshold. For example, the argument that the primacy of humanitarian motives is not a threshold criterion is likely to arouse controversy. Secondly, identifying criteria for legitimate humanitarian intervention does not resolve the problem of deciding whether a particular case has satisfied these tests. What it does do, however, is establish the common reference within which argumentation can take place.

There are four requirements that an intervention must meet to qualify as

---

[51] Ignatieff makes a fascinating parallel here with Joseph Conrad's *The Heart of Darkness* and comments that this was 'a fable about late nineteenth-century imperialism paralyzed by futility and consumed by nihilistic rage'. It is here that he introduces the idea of the 'seductivness of moral disgust' considering that, 'having failed to civilize the savages, Kurtz [Conrad's fictional colonial overlord who goes to Africa in search of ivory but who justifies this to himself and to others in terms of a higher civilizing mission] turns against them all the force of his own moral self-disillusion' Ignatieff (*The Warrior's Honor*, 92).

[52] The best existing attempts to develop a framework for conceptualizing the legitimacy of humanitarian intervention are: Ramsbotham and Woodhouse, *Humanitarian Intervention*, and Teson, *Humanitarian Intervention*. Ramsbotham and Woodhouse identify five key questions: '(i) was there a *humanitarian cause*? (ii) was there a declared humanitarian end in view? (iii) was there an appropriate *humanitarian approach*—in other words, was the action carried out impartially, and were the interests of the intervenors at any rate not incompatible with the humanitarian purpose? (iv) were *humanitarian means* employed? (v) was there a *humanitarian outcome*?' (*Humanitarian Intervention*, 73). Their framework builds on Teson's pioneering work by not privileging motives over outcomes, and by emphasizing the importance of the character of the means employed. The solidarist framework in *Saving Strangers* develops these formative ideas and applies them to seven empirical case studies.

humanitarian and these are derived from the Just War tradition. First, there must be a just cause, or what I prefer to call a supreme humanitarian emergency, because it captures the exceptional nature of the cases under consideration; secondly, the use of force must be a last resort; thirdly, it must meet the requirement of proportionality; and, finally, there must be a high probability that the use of force will achieve a positive humanitarian outcome.

Turning to the first criterion, there is no objective definition of what is to count as a supreme humanitarian emergency, but some claims will be more persuasive than others. It is no good trying to define an emergency in terms of the numbers killed or displaced, because this is too arbitrary. A supreme humanitarian emergency exists when the only hope of saving lives depends on outsiders coming to the rescue. It is incumbent upon those who wish to legitimate an armed intervention as humanitarian (this would hopefully include the intervening state but it is not a stipulation since humanitarian justifications are not part of the threshold requirements) to make the case to other governments and domestic and international public opinion that the violations of human rights within the target state had reached such a magnitude that, to paraphrase Walzer, they shock the conscience of humanity. Thus, it is important to distinguish between what we might call the ordinary routine abuse of human rights that tragically occurs on a daily basis and those extraordinary acts of killing and brutality that belong to the category of 'crimes against humanity'. Genocide is only the most obvious case but state-sponsored mass murder and mass population expulsions by force also come into this category. I also include state breakdown, such as the Somali case, which led to famine and a collapse of law and order.

Humanitarian intervention is clearly justified in these situations, but, if we wait until the emergency is upon us, it will come too late to save those who have been killed or forcibly displaced. This raises the vexed problem of how early rescue should be. What about a case where only a few hundred have been killed but intelligence points to this being a precursor to a major campaign of killing and ethnic cleansing? This appears to have been the story in Kosovo and the justification for humanitarian intervention was a preventative one. This brings us to an important point: in all the cases covered in this volume, with the possible exception of the Kosovo one (see Chapter 8), military intervention came too late to protect civilians from their killers. Even though it is easier to justify a military intervention at home and abroad after blood has been spilt on a significant scale, governments should not wait for thousands to die before they act. Here I agree with Michael Bazyler that the 'intervening nation or nations need not wait for the killings to start if there is clear evidence of an impending massacre'.[53] The problem, of course, as

---

[53] M. Bazyler, 'Reexamining the Doctrine of Humanitarian Intervention in the Light of the Atrocities in Kampuchea and Ethiopia', *Stanford Journal of International Law*, 23 (1987), 600.

Kosovo illustrates so well, is that this assessment is likely to be disputed by other governments and domestic publics, and this begs the question as to who decides what counts as 'clear evidence' in such cases.

The other problem that confronts us is how to reconcile the moral imperative for speedy action with the Just War requirement that force always be a last resort. This is sometimes called the principle of necessity and Nigel Rodley defines it as a condition where 'nothing short of the application of armed force would be sufficient to stop the human rights violations in question'.[54] He argues that, unless the case can be made that delay would result in 'irreparable harm', this requires that states exhaust all peaceful remedies. In the case of humanitarian intervention this dilemma is posed starkly because, during the time that policy-makers are trying to achieve a halt to the abuses through non-violent means, massacres and expulsions might be continuing on the ground. It is too demanding to require politicians to exhaust all peaceful remedies; rather, what is required is that they are confident that they have explored all avenues that are likely to prove successful in stopping the violence. If there is doubt on this score, then state leaders are morally obliged to continue to pursue their humanitarian ends through non-violent means since, while the use of force can promote good consequences, it always produces harmful ones as well.[55]

The above calculation is made all the more difficult by the fact that any decision to opt for the use of force must satisfy the proportionality requirement. And, if there are strong doubts here, then the right action is to eschew the use of force on the grounds that it could lead to a worst situation. The principle of proportionately, according to Rodley, requires 'that the gravity and extent of the violations be on a level commensurate with the reasonably calculable loss of life, destruction of property [and] expenditure of resources'.[56] The requirement that the level of force employed not exceed the harm that it is designed to prevent or stop raises the fundamental question as to whether violent means can ever serve humanitarian purposes or whether the oxymoron of 'humanitarian war' hides a tragic contradiction.[57] Reflecting

---

[54] N. S. Rodley, 'Collective Intervention to Protect Human Rights', in N. S. Rodley (ed.), *To Loosen the Bands of Wickedness* (London: Brassey's, 1992), 37.

[55] M. Fixdal and D. Smith, 'Humanitarian Intervention and Just War', *Mershon International Studies Review*, 42/2 (1998), 302.

[56] Rodley, 'Collective Intervention', 37.

[57] This is the argument of Ken Booth and Richard Falk, who are strong advocates of cosmopolitan values in world politics but suspicious of the doctrine of humanitarian intervention. Booth argues that non-humanitarian means rarely serve humanitarian ends and that in all the cases in the 1990s where 'humanitarian war' was tried it was found wanting on pragmatic grounds. Falk is more inclined to believe that the use of force 'can be an emancipatory instrument, at least in certain extreme situations', but this requires governments 'to commit significant numbers of lives and resources over a prolonged period, with the prospect of possibly heavy losses, and even then with no assurance of success'. Given that no government has been prepared to make this commitment of resources and lives, Falk concludes dismally that 'military action in an interventionary mode virtually always produces destructive and counterproductive results'. See Booth, 'The Kosovo

on the Kosovo case, Adam Roberts argues that, in 'the long history of legal debates about humanitarian intervention, there has been a consistent failure to address directly the question of the methods used in such interventions'.[58]

A key moral question that arises when employing violent means to secure humanitarian ends is the question of what counts as a legitimate military target. The laws of war require that civilians never be deliberately targeted, but the stipulation that they be protected as far as possible from the exigencies of war begs the question as to what risks intervenors should take in order to avoid civilian losses. Military necessity can be used to justify the killing of innocents on the grounds that this happens to be an inadvertent consequence of attacks against legitimate military targets. This is the doctrine of 'double effect', developed by Catholic theologians in the Middle Ages, which allows soldiers to harm civilians provided that this is not the intention of the act.[59] The problem, as Walzer argues, is that this provides a 'blanket justification' for civilian deaths that are 'unintended but foreseeable'.[60] According to Mona Fixdal and Dan Smith, Just War theory would proscribe that a humanitarian intervention is 'just if it produces a surplus of good over harm—taking all affected parties into consideration'.[61] However, this form of consequentialist moral reasoning is open to the objection that, given the terrible imponderables associated with such calculations, 'even a good cause', in Guenter Levy's words, 'is not worth any price'.[62]

The moral risk that opens up for leaders who decide to play the consequentialist or utilitarian game is that they can never know in advance that their decision to play god with the lives of others will lead to the just ends they hope for. In a situation where civilians are being killed by their government and where there is evidence that the target government is planning to escalate the scale of the killing, it can never be known in advance that more lives will be saved by intervention than will be lost by it, or that the means employed will not take on such a character that the moral credentials of the intervenors begin to look little different from those they are fighting against.

Tragedy: Epilogue to Another "Low and Dishonest Decade"?' and R. Falk, 'Hard Choices and Tragic Dilemmas', Nation, 20 Dec. 1993, 758.

[58] A. Roberts, 'NATO's Humanitarian War over Kosovo', Survival, 41/3 (1999), 110. This point is also made by Ramsbotham and Woodhouse, who argue that a key criterion is 'the means employed compatible with a humanitarian mission' (Ramsbotham and Woodhouse, Humanitarian Intervention, 75).

[59] As Walzer puts it, 'double effect is a way of reconciling the absolute prohibition against attacking non-combatants with the legitimate conduct of military activity . . . The good and evil effects that come together, the killing of [enemy] soldiers and nearby civilians, are to be defended only insofar as they are the product of a single intention, directed at the first and not the second' (Walzer, Just and Unjust Wars, 153).

[60] Ibid. Walzer argues that the doctrine of the double effect is too permissive and invites the following reply: 'what difference does it make whether civilian deaths are a direct or an indirect effect of my actions? It can hardly matter to the dead civilians, and if I know in advance that I am likely to kill so many innocent people and go ahead anyway, how can I be blameless?'

[61] Fixdal and Smith, 'Humanitarian Intervention', 304.   [62] Quoted in ibid.

These are the risks that face contemporary humanitarian warriors, since, as Richard Falk argues, 'an initially humanitarian orientation is no assurance that the undertaking will retain that character under pressure'.[63] Decision-makers can argue that their actions were required by necessity and that there were no alternatives to stop the atrocities, but, even if intervention produces a surplus of good over harm, it will never be known whether non-violent alternatives might have achieved the same result at less cost.

In saying that the humanitarian consequences of using violent means can be known only with the benefit of hindsight, we come to the final threshold or minimum criterion for a legitimate humanitarian intervention, which is that decision-makers must believe the use of force will produce a humanitarian outcome. Clearly any judgement here will be crucially influenced by how far the operation is deemed to have satisfied the proportionality requirement. Accepting that the violent character of the means does not always contradict the morality of the ends, I agree with the Argentinian international lawyer Fernando Teson that a positive humanitarian outcome is characterized by 'whether the intervention has rescued the victims of oppression, and whether human rights have subsequently been restored'.[64] Teson's notion of human rights being 'restored' is a problematic one because it implies that the citizens of the target state enjoyed human rights protection before the killings started, which is a question that would have to be investigated in specific cases. Consequently, I prefer to substitute the word *protection* for restored. The requirement is that a political order be established by the intervening state(s) that is hospitable to the protection of human rights. One test of this is that the withdrawal of the intervening force does not lead to a resumption of the killing and brutality. The twin requirements of *rescue* and *protection* reflect the division of humanitarian outcomes into short- and long-term ones: the former referring to the success of intervention in ending the supreme humanitarian emergency, and the latter being defined in terms of how far intervention addresses the underlying political causes that produced the human rights abuses.

Now that I have defined the threshold conditions for an intervention to qualify as humanitarian, it will be immediately apparent that I have not included the primacy of humanitarian motives as a defining test. At first sight this seems counter-intuitive, since how can an action be labelled humanitarian if it is not inspired by humanitarian ideals or purposes? The primacy of humanitarian motives in determining the humanitarian credentials of an intervention is the conventional wisdom among realists and those international lawyers who write on humanitarian intervention.[65] For example, as I

---

[63] Falk, 'Hard Choices', 760.   [64] Teson, *Humanitarian Intervention*, 106.

[65] Ramsbotham and Woodhouse cite the following definition by Wil Verwey in 1992 as representative of this emphasis on the primacy of motives. Verwey defined humanitarian intervention as: 'The threat or use of force by a state or states abroad, *for the sole purpose of preventing or putting a halt*

discuss in Chapters 3 and 4, most lawyers writing on the Vietnamese and Tanzanian interventions in Cambodia and Uganda disqualify them as humanitarian for this reason. The problem with this approach is that it takes the intervening state as the referent object for analysis rather than the victims who are rescued as a consequence of the use of force. Solidarism is committed to upholding minimum standards of common humanity, which means placing the victims of human rights abuses at the centre of its theoretical project, since it is commtted to exploring how the society of states might become more hospitable to the promotion of justice in world politics. Thus, changing the referent from state motivations to victims of state power leads to a different emphasis on the importance of motives in judging the humanitarian credentials of intervenors.

The one international lawyer who has challenged the motives-first approach is Teson, who argues that making motives the defining test of a humanitarian intervention is predicated on a flawed methodology. He can be located in the solidarist wing of the English School, because he argues that governments that massively violate human rights forfeit their right to protection of the rules of sovereignty and non-intervention, and as a result, other states are morally entitled to intervene. Having set out the moral justification for any such action, Teson argues that:

The intervenor must also employ *means* that are consistent with the humanitarian purpose. But unless other motivations have resulted in further oppression by the intervenors . . . they do not necessarily count against the morality of the intervention . . . The true test is whether the intervention has put an end to human rights deprivations. That is sufficient to meet the requirement of disinterestedness, even if there are other, non-humanitarian reasons behind the intervention.[66]

The primacy of humanitarian motives is not a threshold condition. But if it can be shown that the motives behind the intervention, or the reasons behind the selection of the means, are inconsistent with a positive humanitarian outcome, then it is disqualified as humanitarian. It follows that, even if an intervention is motivated by non-humanitarian reasons, it can still count as humanitarian provided that the motives, and the means employed, do not undermine a positive humanitarian outcome. In advancing this claim,

---

to a serious violation of fundamental human rights, in particular the right to life of persons, regardless of their nationality, such protection taking place neither upon authorization by relevant organs of the United Nations nor with permission by the legitimate government of the target state' (cited in Ramsbotham and Woodhouse, *Humanitarian Intervention*, 43; emphasis added).

[66] Teson, *Humanitarian Intervention*, 106–7. Teson's critique of motives as the determining factor in judging the legitimacy of humanitarian intervention is shared by Bruce Jones, who argues that a 'robust theory of intervention should consider *both* motivation and outcomes in assessing the humanitarian character of actions'. Jones produces a matrix that maps humanitarian motives and outcomes in different cases of intervention in the Rwandan conflict in the 1990s, but the weakness of his approach is that he does not make the Tesonian point that motives are relevant only if they undermine humanitarian outcomes. See B. Jones, 'Intervention without Borders: Humanitarian Intervention in Rwanda, 1900–94', *Millennium: Journal of International Studies*, 24/2 (1995), 225–48.

I am not arguing that the society of states should praise those governments that are fortunate in achieving this happy coincidence of non-humanitarian motives, means, and outcomes. But I am arguing that, because they save lives, such interventions should be legitimated by states and not condemned or sanctioned. The society of states should reserve its praise and material support *only* for those governments that accord humanitarian reasons a significant factor in their decisions to intervene, and that satisfy some or all of the additional criteria discussed below.

The next criterion above the threshold that I want to consider is the question of whether an intervention is justified in humanitarian terms. The realist worry that states will abuse humanitarian rationales for ulterior reasons raises its ugly head at this point, but the reply to this is threefold. The first is that abuse is an objection to humanitarian intervention only if the non-humanitarian motives behind an intervention undermine its stated humanitarian purposes.

Secondly, the criticism of hidden motives simply ignores the possibility that justification might correspond with motivation, and that state leaders might recognize a moral responsibility to defend human rights. As I argued in the Introduction, a key premiss of solidarism is that governments are responsible not only for protecting human rights at home but also for defending them abroad. This responsibility includes putting their military personnel and citizens at risk to save the victims of gross and systematic violations of human rights. This view is predicated on the assumption that sovereign boundaries are moral constructions that are not immutable. Once it is accepted that there is nothing natural or given about sovereignty as the outer limit of our moral responsibilities, it becomes possible to argue for a change in our moral horizons such that it becomes legitimate for state leaders to risk the lives of their soldiers and citizens to stop gross abuses of human rights. Realists argue that governments are not morally entitled to ask their soldiers to die for humanitarian causes, but this is a weak argument, because, when soldiers join the military, they accept an obligation to serve wherever they are sent by the government.[67]

The third response to the argument that humanitarian claims will be abused is that it underestimates how far actors become 'entangled in their justifications'.[68] Governments that justify intervention in humanitarian terms establish a normative benchmark against which we can judge their subsequent actions. Moroever, since states cannot hope to justify any action

---

[67] I recognize that governments might legally send their soldiers to die in particular wars without these actions having legitimacy in the eyes of those soldiers or domestic public opinion. The obvious example here is US military participation in the Vietnam War in the late 1960s. However, my point is that governments should not be inhibited from undertaking humanitarian intervention because soldiers have not explicitly volunteered for such actions.

[68] K. M. Fierke, 'Dialogues of Manœuvre and Entanglement: NATO, Russia and the CEEC's', *Millennium: Journal of International Studies*, 28/1 (1999), 30.

as humanitarian, it follows, as Skinner argues, that actors who accept the 'need to legitimate' will be limited to actions that can plausibly be defended in terms of the legitimating reasons that are claimed to have motivated the action.[69] And, having claimed the moral high ground, governments that fail to deliver on their promises will have to defend themselves against the suspicion that they had hidden motives that undermined the stated humanitarian purposes of the mission. A discrepancy between justifications and outcomes does not prove the case, however, since there might be situations where intervention is justified and motivated in humanitarian terms but which ends in disaster. Here, it is important to ask how far the means employed were responsible for this outcome, and what reasons explain the selection of these as against other means of intervention.[70] Nevertheless, it is possible to imagine cases where there is no contradiction between humanitarian motives and means on the one hand, and outcomes on the other, but where intervention ends in disaster. It would be wrong to make success the defining test of legitimacy in such cases, since this would lead to the conclusion that we can judge the legitimacy of an intervention motivated by humanitarian reasons only with the benefit of hindsight. As long as decision-makers who justify their actions in humanitarian terms have done everything in their power to ensure that there is no contradiction between their humanitarian motives and the character and conduct of the intervention, then even an intervention that fails disastrously can be defined as humanitarian.[71]

In addition to the question of motives and justifications, the other two criteria excluded from the threshold that are likely to generate most controversy are the issue of whether humanitarian intervention should always be lawful and the question of selectivity.

The legality of humanitarian intervention without Security Council authorization has become a subject of considerable normative debate since NATO's action in Kosovo. As I discuss in Chapter 8 and in the Conclusion, the UN Secretary General was sufficiently seized by the seriousness of this question to make it a key part of his opening speech to the 1999 session of the UN

---

[69] Skinner, 'Analysis of Political Thought and Action', 112. Skinner gives the example of the merchant class who tried to justify their accumulation of profit in the Europe of the sixteenth and seventeenth centuries by appealing to religious justifications. What is important, he argues, is that, having invoked this legitimating reason, the 'merchant cannot hope to describe *any* action he may choose to perform as being "religious" in character, but only those which can be claimed with some show of plausibility to meet such agreed criteria as there may be for the application of the term. It follows that if he is anxious to have his conduct appraised as that of a genuinely religious man, he will find himself restricted to the performance of only a certain range of actions'. (Q. Skinner, 'Language and Social Change', in Tully (ed.), *Meaning and Context*, 131–2). See also Fierke, 'Dialogues', 30–1.

[70] When I use the word *means* in the book, I am using the term broadly, as in *The New Oxford Dictionary of English*, to refer to 'an action or system by which a result is brought about'. This encompasses not only the type of intervention—air power or ground forces for example—but also how the intervention is conducted.

[71] I am grateful to Jack Donnelly for alerting me to the significance of this point.

General Assembly. The starting point for reflecting on the legality of humanitarian intervention is that the majority of international lawyers argue that
this practice is unlawful. Pointing to the legal drafting of the UN Charter,
these jurists, often labelled 'restrictionists', argue that the ban in Article 2 (4)
on the use of force against the 'territorial integrity and political independence' of states prohibits humanitarian intervention. These jurists recognize
that the Security Council has the legal authority under the Chapter VII provisions of the Charter to authorize military enforcement action, but they point
out that the Security Council has jurisdiction to act under Article 39 of
Chapter VII only if it determines that there is a threat to 'international peace
and security'. It cannot authorize military intervention on humanitarian
grounds alone.

There are both legal and moral responses to the restrictionist argument
that humanitarian intervention without Security Council authorization is
illegal. The moral argument is that humanitarian intervention is one of those
hard cases where ethical concerns should trump legality, and that, while we
should always try and obtain Security Council authorization, this legal
requirement can be overridden in cases of supreme humanitarian emergency.
This view that humanitarian intervention is morally permitted but should
not be legalized is expressed by Franck and Rodley when they argue that
humanitarian intervention 'belongs in the realm not of law but of moral
choice, which nations, like individuals, must sometimes make'.[72] Their position is that this moral imperative cannot be legally recognized because of the
dangers that such a legal right would be abused.

The difficulty with this resolution of the problem is that it serves to high-
light the normative limitations of a system of international law that encour-
ages law-abiding states to break the law when this is demanded by the
requirements of common humanity. I agree with Wil Verwey that accepting
this conflict between legality and morality fatally weakens international law
because it 'would imply the recognition—no more, no less—that international law is incapable of ensuring respect for socially indispensable standards
of morality'.[73]

Consequently, the second response to the restrictionists is to argue that
international law should recognize a right of unilateral humanitarian intervention. This argument was pressed by a minority of international lawyers
during the cold war and it gained additional adherents in the 1990s. This
'counter-restrictionist' position is predicated on the claim that there is
support for a legal right of humanitarian intervention in both the UN Charter
and customary international law. The contention is that the promotion of

[72] Franck and Rodley, 'After Bangladesh', 304.
[73] W. Verwey, 'Humanitarian Intervention in the 1990s and Beyond: An International Law
Perspective', in J. N. Pieterse (ed.), *World Orders in the Making: Humanitarian Intervention and Beyond*
(London: Macmillan, 1998), 200.

human rights should rank alongside peace and security in the hierarchy of UN Charter principles. Here, counter-restrictionists point to the language in the preamble to the UN Charter and Articles 1 (3), 55, and 56, which impose a legal obligation on member states to cooperate in promoting human rights. According to Teson, the 'promotion of human rights is as important a purpose in the Charter as is the control of international conflict'.[74] Consequently, counter-restrictionists argue that the Security Council has a legal right to authorize humanitarian intervention irrespective of whether it has found a threat to 'international peace and security' under Article 39. Some jurists go even further and assert that, if the Security Council fails to take remedial action in cases of massive human rights abuses, then individual states should act as armed vigilantes and take the enforcement of the human rights provisions of the Charter into their own hands. Michael Reisman and Myers McDougal claim that, were this not the case, 'would be suicidally destructive of the explicit purposes for which the United Nations was established'.[75]

Witnessing the images on their television sets of the atrocities committed against the minority Ibos by Nigerian troops during the civil war over the secession of Biafra from Nigeria, Reisman and McDougal produced their now famous 1969 memorandum, 'Humanitarian Intervention to Protect the Ibos'. This claimed that there was a legal right of unilateral humanitarian intervention, and they concluded their memorandum with the proposal that the UN institutionalize a system of humanitarian intervention, and suggested that the International Law Association (ILA) be asked to draft a protocol. This invitation was taken up by the ILA in the early 1970s, and, in a series of reports, it attempted to draft a set of criteria for judging the legality of unilateral humanitarian intervention.[76] Richard Lillich argues that these studies generated a broad consensus on the following:

1. There must be an imminent or ongoing gross human rights violation.
2. All non-intervention remedies available must be exhausted before a humanitarian intervention can be commenced (see also criteria 9).
3. A potential intervenor before the commencement of any such intervention must submit to the Security Council, if time permits, its views as to the specific limited purpose the proposed intervention would achieve.
4. The intervenor's primary goal must be to remedy a gross human rights violation and not to achieve some other goal pertaining to the intervenor's own self-interest.
5. The intent of the intervenor must be to have as limited an effect of [sic] the

---

[74] Teson, *Humanitarian Intervention*, 131.

[75] A. C. Arend and R. J. Beck, *International Law and the Use of Force: Beyond the UN Charter Paradigm* (London: Routledge, 1993), 133.

[76] This story is told in R. B. Lillich, 'The Development of Criteria for Humanitarian Intervention', unpublished paper, 6.

authority structure of the concerned State as possible, while at the same time achieving its specific limited purpose.

6. The intent of the intervenor must be to intervene for as short a time as possible, with the intervenor disengaging as soon as the specific limited purpose is accomplished.

7. The intent of the intervenor must be to use the least amount of coercive measures necessary to achieve its specific limited purpose.

8. Where at all possible, the intervenor must try and obtain an invitation to intervene from the recognized government and thereafter to cooperate with the recognized government.

9. The intervenor, before its intended intervention, must request a meeting of the Security Council in order to inform it that the humanitarian intervention will take place only if the Security Council does not act first (see also criteria 2 & 3).

10. An intervention by the United Nations is preferred to one by a regional organization, and an intervention by a regional organization is preferred to one by a group of States or an individual state.

11. Before intervening, the intervenor must deliver a clear ultimatum or 'peremptory demand' to the concerned State insisting that positive actions be taken to terminate or ameliorate the gross human rights violations.

12. Any intervenor who does not follow the above criteria shall be deemed to have breached the peace, thus invoking Chapter VII of the Charter of the United Nations.[77]

There are two important points to note about the above criteria: first, humanitarian outcomes do not even feature in the ILA list of requirements. Instead, the stipulation is the standard one in the international-law literature that the 'primary goal must be to remedy a gross human rights violation'. Where the ILA criteria do have something to offer is in their discussion of the role that the Security Council should play in the legitimation process. States contemplating humanitarian intervention are required to report to the Security Council that the action will take place only if the Council does not act first. There is no guarantee that Council authorization will be forthcoming at this point, and it is possible that a resolution might be passed condemning the proposed action. On the other hand, the great value of this criterion is that it legitimates states raising humanitarian claims before the Security Council. This opens up the possibility that the Security Council will recognize an obligation to include the protection of human rights under its Chapter VII responsibilities. It is equally possible that the Security Council might be divided on the question of the legitimacy of using force, which complicates the picture still further, raising the following questions: how many Council members have to be opposed to an action before we can say that it lacks collective legitimation, and does it matter if some or all of these

[77] Third Interim Report of the Subcommittee on the International Protection of Human Rights by General International Law, ILA Report of the Fifty-Sixth Conference 217 (New Delhi, 1974). Quoted in Lillich, 'The Development', 7–8.

are veto-bearing members of the Council? I take up these questions in the empirical chapters.

The dispute between restrictionists and counter-restrictionists over the legality of humanitarian intervention comes down to the question of whether this practice is legally exempt from the prohibition on the use of force in Article 2 (4). Restrictionists like Rosalyn Higgins contend 'that the Charter *could* have allowed for sanctions for gross human-rights violations, but deliberately did not do so'.[78] Set against this, Reisman and McDougal counter that:

> Since a humanitarian intervention seeks neither a territorial change nor a challenge to the political independence of the state involved and is not only not inconsistent with the purposes of the United Nations but is rather in conformity with the most fundamental peremptory norms of the Charter, it is a distortion to argue that it is precluded by Article 2 (4).[79]

Anthony Arend and Robert Beck identify four criteria that an intervention must meet if it is to be exempted from the ban on force in Article 2 (4): it must not involve a prolonged military presence by the intervening state(s) in the target state; a loss of territory by the target state; a regime change there; any actions inconsistent with the purposes of the UN Charter.[80]

Given that the legal basis of unilateral humanitarian intervention is hotly disputed, what is the basis for deciding between the conflicting claims? The standard answer supplied by lawyers is to have recourse to customary international law. Article 38 of the statute of the ICJ refers to this 'as evidence of a general practice accepted as law'.[81] Customary law is different from treaty law because it is not created by written agreements between states that set down the rules to regulate their interactions in a specific area. Instead, as Arend and Beck put it, 'if over a period of time, states begin to act in a certain way and come to regard that behaviour as being required by law, a norm of customary international law has developed'.[82] It is not enough that states actually engage in the practice that is claimed to have the status of customary law; they must do so because they believe that this practice is 'accepted as law'. This subjective element is referred to by lawyers as *opinio juris* and is essential in identifying which rules are legally binding upon states.

Restrictionists argue that state practice in the post-Charter period does not support a legal right of unilateral humanitarian intervention. Here, they point to the following: General Assembly standards on non-intervention, such as the 1965 Declaration on the Inadmissability of Intervention, which denied legal recognition to intervention 'for any reason whatever'; the 1970 Declaration on Principles of International Law Concerning Friendly Relations and Co-opera-

---

[78] Higgins, *Problems and Process*, 255.
[79] Quoted in A. C. Arend and R. J. Beck, *International Law and the Use of Force*, 134.
[80] Ibid.
[81] Charter of the United Nations, Article 38.
[82] Arend and Beck, *International Law and the Use of Force*, 6.

tion, which confirmed that 'no State or group of states has the right to intervene, directly or indirectly, for any reason whatever, in the internal or external affairs of any other State'; and the 1987 Declaration on the Enhancement of the Effectiveness of the Principle of Refraining from the Threat or Use of Force in International Relations, which stated that 'no consideration of whatever nature may be invoked to warrant resorting to the threat or use of force in violation of the Charter'. The ICJ in the *Nicaragua* judgment considered the question of whether there were legal exceptions to the non-intervention rule, and its judgment was that this 'would involve a fundamental modification of the customary law principle of non-intervention', for which there was no support in state practice.[83] Indeed, the court cited with approval the following statement by the International Law Commission: 'The law of the Charter concerning the prohibition of the use of force in itself constitutes a conspicuous example of a rule in international law having the character of *jus cogens*.'[84] The concept of *jus cogens* is widely accepted in international law and denotes a peremptory norm of general international law that is described in the 1969 Vienna Convention of the Law of Treaties as 'a norm accepted and recognized by the international community of States as a whole as a norm from which no derogation is permitted and which can be modified only by a subsequent norm of general international law having the same character'.[85]

Counter-restrictionists deny that the prohibition on the use of force is *jus cogens*, claiming that there is custom from the pre-Charter and post-Charter period supporting a rule of unilateral humanitarian intervention. The latter proposition is investigated in Chapters 2, 3, and 4 in relation to India's, Vietnam's and Tanzania's use of force, but what of their argument that there existed such a right prior to 1945? This book is not the place to document the history of the doctrine of humanitarian intervention, but lawyers date the origins of the doctrine to the seventeenth-century Dutch International lawyer Hugo Grotius, who considered that the rights of the sovereign could be limited by principles of humanity. In a famous passage that shows why Grotius is the father of solidarist international society theory, he considered that, 'if a tyrant . . . practices atrocities towards his subjects, which no just man can approve, the right of human social connexion is not cut off in such a case . . . It would not follow that others may not take up arms for them.'[86] The doctrine was the subject of debate among international lawyers during the eighteenth century, but it was not pressed into service by states until the early part of the nineteenth century.

---

[83] Quoted in M. Weller, 'Access to Victims: Reconceiving the Right To "Intervene" ', in W. P. Heere, *International Law and The Hague's 750th Anniversary* (Leidon: A. W. Sijthoff, 1972), 334.

[84] Quoted in Byers, *Custom, Power and the Power of Rules*, 184.

[85] Quoted in ibid. 183.

[86] Grotius, *De Jure Belli est Pacis*, quoted in F. Kofi Abiew, *The Evolution of the Doctrine and Practice of Humanitarian Intervention* (The Hague: Kluwer Law International, 1999), 35.

The 1827 intervention by Britain, France, and Russia to protect Greek Christians from the oppressive rule of Turkey set the pattern for subsequent interventions in the Ottoman Empire. In language that was little different from that used by NATO at the end of the twentieth century to justify its use of force against the Milosevic regime, the intervening states claimed that their action was required 'no less by sentiments of humanity, than by interests for the tranquillity of Europe'.[87] The next case where the doctrine was invoked to justify intervention was the French intervention in 1860–1 to rescue the Christian population in Syria.[88] Turkish rule had led to the suppression of the traditional religious rights of the Maronite Christians and to the massacre of thousands. France was authorized by the other great powers meeting at the Conference of Paris in 1860 to end the massacres and restore order. The Sultan 'consented' to the intervention of the 6,000 French troops, but only because it was clear that non-compliance with the wishes of the European great powers would lead to strategic coercion being exercised by the Concert powers against Turkey.[89]

Restrictionists challenge the proposition that these cases demonstrate that the doctrine of humanitarian intervention was recognized in pre-Charter customary international law. Franck and Rodley make three important rebuttals: first, they point out that the interventions of the nineteenth-century Concert powers in the internal affairs of the Ottoman Empire have to be seen in the context of 'relations between unequal states . . . in which "civilized" states exercise *de facto* tutorial rights over "uncivilized" ones'. As such, these cases are not particularly helpful in thinking about relations between states where sovereign equality is the key legitimating principle of the society of states. Secondly, they argue that intervention was legitimated only when it was collectively authorized by the Concert of Europe; individual state action was not permissible, as in the case of Russia's assertion of a unilateral right to protect Christians living in the Ottoman Empire that led to Britain and France going to war against Russia to enforce the rules of the Concert system. Finally, Franck and Rodley question how far the interventions in Turkey's internal affairs were motivated by primarily humanitarian considerations. They recognize that humanitarian impulses played some role in the decisions to intervene, and that these reasons had legitimacy in the eyes of domestic public opinion in Western Europe and Russia, but 'these motives were certainly neither wholly pure, nor were they consistently pursued in the absence of other power considerations'.[90] This objection to state practice supports the realist view that states will never act for purely humanitarian reasons, but, as

---

[87] Quoted in Abiew, *The Evolution*, 49.

[88] This case is discussed in B. M. Benjamin, 'Note: Unilateral Humanitarian Intervention: Legalizing the Use of Force to Prevent Human Rights Atrocities', *Fordham International Law Journal*, 16 (1992–3), 128.

[89] Abiew, *The Evolution*, 50.   [90] Franck and Rodley, 'After Bangladesh', 281.

I have argued earlier, the key question is not the purity of motives but the relationship between motives and humanitarian outcomes.

The importance of this discussion is that, if a doctrine of unilateral human-itarian intervention is part of customary international law, then we should expect to see states employing this justification and having it validated in cases where the doctrine could be plausibly invoked. Evidence of such state practice and *opinio juris* provides an important indication that the society of states has established rules to regulate this practice. Moreover, the existence of any past cases of intervention justified in humanitarian terms would provide an important reply to the pluralist objection that legitimating the practice of unilateral humanitarian intervention will open the floodgates to intervention driving huge wedges into international order.

The thesis to be developed in subsequent chapters is that there is no custom supporting the practice of unilateral humanitarian intervention in the cases of Bangladesh, Cambodia, and Uganda, but that new humanitarian claims were advanced in the 1990s. This raises the question as to whether post-cold-war practices of humanitarian intervention have created a new custom. To lay the groundwork for answering this question in Part Three, it is necessary to examine how a new rule of customary international law is created.

The formation of new custom requires both state practice and *opinio juris*, but it would be wrong to think that non-compliance with a rule means that it has lost its normative character as legally binding. Rosalyn Higgins gives the example of the international prohibition on torture, which is widely recognized as a customary rule in international law, but this recognition does not stop the majority of states from committing such abuses. The effi-cacy of norms, as Ruggie and Kratochwil remind us, is not measured solely by rates of compliance; rather, what is critical are the justifications given for actions and the responsiveness of other states to these. Thus, as Higgins argues, the reason why torture continues to be a legally binding rule of customary international law despite widespread non-compliance is 'because *opinio juris* as to its normative status continues to exist . . . No state, not even a state that tortures, believes that the international law prohibition is unde-sirable and that it is not bound by the prohibition.'[91] This leads her to argue that a new custom cannot emerge without the vast majority of states engag-ing in a contrary practice and crucially, 'withdrawing their *opinio juris*'.[92] In

---

[91] Higgins, *Problems and Process*, 22.

[92] Higgins argues that this reasoning was invoked by the ICJ in determining the law on the use of force in *Nicaragua* v. *United States*. The Court stated: 'if a state acts in a way prima facie incom-patible with a recognized rule, but defends its conduct by appealing to exceptions or justifications contained within the rule itself, then whether or not the State's conduct is in fact justifiable on that basis, the significance of that attribute is to confirm rather than to weaken the rule' (quoted in ibid. 20). In relation to the same case, Michael Byers points out that, faced with a history of state prac-tice that contradicted the rule of non-intervention, the Court expressed the opinion that 'the signi-

its judgment that non-intervention was a customary rule of international law in the case of *Nicaragua* v. *the US*, the ICJ expressed its view that 'reliance by a State on a novel right or an unprecedented exception to the principle might, if shared in principle by other States, tend towards a modification of customary international law'.[93] This emphasizes the fact that new custom requires states to raise novel claims that by definition cannot be contained in the existing law and this means that such claims are always open to the rejoinder that they are deviant and unlawful. On the other hand, the advocacy of new norms by a state or group of states might lead, as I argued in the Introduction, to a 'norm cascade', where a significant number of states embrace the norm, leading to the development of a new rule of customary international law.

The final criterion above the threshold for judging the humanitarian character of an intervention is the vexed issue of selectivity. The criticism that humanitarian intervention is selective because states intervene only for self-interested reasons resonates across the political spectrum. In reflecting on this criticism, it is important to distinguish between actions that are selective because states privilege selfish interests over the defence of human rights, and those that are selective because of prudential concerns. Robert H. Jackson makes an important distinction between 'instrumental' prudence, which is 'where leaders are expediently thinking only of themselves or their regimes', and 'normative or other-regarding prudence—where the other is anyone whose rights, interests and welfare depend upon the decisions and actions of state leaders'.[94] Addressing the charge of selectivity requires treating like cases alike, but, with the best will in the world, it is just not possible to take the same action in every case where human rights are threatened, because prudence as a moral virtue dictates different responses in different cases. As Vincent put it, 'considerations of prudence do not determine the moral agenda, but they do condition its treatment'.[95] Franck and Rodley lose sight of this crucial point in their criticisms of the society of states for not preventing the destruction of European Jewry or saving the Armenians. In the latter case, as Hendrickson points out, 'it is difficult to see what outside powers might have done',[96] a conclusion echoed by William Rubinstein in his persuasive study of how the allied powers could not have done more to save Jews during the Second World War.[97] The extreme cases of human suffering,

---

ficance for the Court of cases of State conduct *prima facie* inconsistent with the principle of non-intervention lies in the nature of the ground *offered as justification*' (quoted in Byers, *Custom, Power and the Power of Rules*, 133, emphasis added).

[93] Quoted in ibid. 133.

[94] R. H. Jackson, 'The Situational Ethics of Statecraft', unpublished paper in possession of the author, 12.

[95] Vincent, *Human Rights* and *International Relations*, 124.

[96] Hendrickson, 'In Defense of Realism, 43.

[97] William Rubinstein, *The Myth of Rescue: Why the Democracies could not have Saved More Jews from the Nazis* (London: Routledge, 1997).

Hendrickson argues, 'are those where there usually—perhaps invariably—exist imperative considerations on the other side that make the duty of humanitarian intervention either impossible or fraught with enormous risk'.[98] I will have more to say about this problem later in the book since it is probably the most commonly cited objection to legitimating humanitarian intervention, but for the moment I want to note that just because governments are selective in their interventions does not necessarily mean that we should treat their humanitarian justifications as bogus in every case where they are employed. This is an empirical question that needs examining on a case-by-case basis.

The criticism that intervention is selective depending upon considerations of interests raises the question whether humanitarian intervention is a moral duty. Solidarism establishes that humanitarian intervention is *morally permitted but is it also morally required*? A simple example of this is the decision of a bystander not to rescue a drowning child. Assuming that the bystander can swim, we would argue that the individual failed in his or her duty to rescue the child. And in some European states such as France and Germany, it is written into the law that individuals should act as rescuers in such circumstances. Yet moral choices rarely present themselves to us in this simplified way. Consider the case of the rescuers in Nazi-occupied Europe who risked their lives to save Jews from the concentration camps. We should certainly praise their actions as heroic, but would we want to argue that those who did not take similar risks were failing in their moral duty? Many refused to shelter Jews not because they were selfish or cowardly (and it was easy to be cowardly in the context of Nazi Germany) but because they feared for the safety of their own loved ones.

The story of the rescuers is one of conflicting moral imperatives, and it is the same with the claim that humanitarian intervention is a moral duty. Solidarism agrees with realism that state leaders have a responsibility to protect the security and well-being of their citizens, but it parts company with it on the question of whether this obligation exhausts obligations to non-citizens. The debate within solidarist international-society theory is over the character of these obligations. Solidarism argues that states committed to these principles—'good international citizens'—are not required to sacrifice vital interests in defence of human rights, but they are required to forsake narrow commerical and political advantage when these conflict with human rights.[99] The hard question is whether solidarism requires state leaders to *risk* and *lose* soldiers' lives to save non-citizens. The solidarist battle cry that state

---

[98] Hendrickson, 'In Defense of Realism', 44.

[99] The idea of states as 'good international citizens' was first employed by the former Australian Minister for Foreign Affairs and Trade, Gareth Evans, to describe his pursuit of a foreign policy that reconciled 'enlightened self-interest' and 'idealistic pragmatism'. The concept was developed by Andrew Linklater in 'What is a Good International Citizen?', in P. Keal (ed.), *Ethics and Foreign Policy* (Camberra: Allen & Unwin, 1992).

leaders are 'burdened' with the defence of human rights begs the question as
to how this should be balanced against their responsibility to protect the lives
of citizens.[100]

The solidarist argument advanced in this book is that, in exceptional cases
of supreme humanitarian emergency, state leaders should accept the risk of
casaulties to end human rights abuses. To develop this argument, I want to
apply Walzer's notion of 'supreme emergency' in *Just and Unjust Wars* to the
moral choices facing state leaders in decisions on humanitarian intervention.
Walzer's book is a powerful defence of the principle of non-combatant immunity in the Just War tradition, but, having built up the argument as to why war
cannot escape moral discourse, he argues in chapter 16 that exceptional
circumstances can arise where the survival of the state requires leaders to
violate the prohibition against killing civilians. A supreme emergency exists
when the danger is so immiment, the character of the threat so horrifying,
and when there is no other option available to assure the survival of a particular moral community than violating the rule against targeting civilians. He
gives the example of Britain in 1940, where British leaders employed strategic
bombing against German cities as their only defence against the evil of
Nazism.[101] Walzer does not praise leaders who violate the war convention of
non-combatant immunity, claiming that 'we say yes *and* no, right and
wrong'. He captures the 'agonizing' character of this by claiming that those
who make these decisions 'only prove their honor by accepting responsibility
for those decisions and by living out the agony'.[102]

If we apply this framework to a solidarist theory of humanitarian intervention, the survival of our state is not on the line (and in that sense it is not
a supreme emergency in the way it was for Britain in 1940), but it is a supreme
emergency for those human beings facing genocide, mass murder, and ethnic
cleansing. Supreme humanitarian emergencies are extraordinary situations
where civilians in another state are in immiment danger of losing their life or
facing appalling hardship, and where indigenous forces cannot be relied upon
to end these violations of human rights. As Walzer argues in relation to
supreme emergencies, state leaders find themselves confronted with these

---

[100] The problem of balancing these conflicting moral imperatives is revealed in Jackson's attempt
to construct a theory of moral responsibility in foreign-policy decision-making. He recognizes the
inevitablity of normative conflicts between what he calls 'national', 'international', and 'humanitarian' conceptions of moral responsibility in foreign policy, contending that good statecraft lies in
balancing all three of these. Jackson clearly moves beyond a realist ethic when he argues that state
leaders have a responsibility to defend human rights because they are 'human beings themselves
[and] are in a better position than anyone else to help or hinder their fellow humans in other countries'. However, this commitment to solidarism does not extend to accepting casualties in defence
of human rights because decisions on humanitarian intervention always 'have to pay final respects
to national responsibility'. The implication is that state leaders have humanitarian responsibilities
but these are trumped by a *primary* responsibility to protect the security of their citizens. This does
not rule out humanitarian intervention in all cases, but it does restrict it to cases where there is little
or no risk of casualties. Jackson, 'The Political Theory of International Society', 123.
[101] Walzer, *Just and Unjust Wars*, 251–68.   [102] Ibid. 326.

situations only on rare occasions. But, when they do, they are confronted with the ultimate choice between realist and solidarist conceptions of moral responsibility in statecraft. The latter demands that state leaders override their *primary* responsibility not to place citizens in danger and make the agonizing decision that saving the lives of civilians beyond their own borders requires risking the lives of those who serve in the armed forces. Having decided that humanitarian intervention is *morally required*, state leaders must still satisfy themselves that using force meets the requirements of necessity and proportionality, and that there is every expectation that the use of force will be successful.

Even if it is agreed that state leaders who have the power to make a difference are required in emergency situations to risk and lose soldiers' lives to save non-citizens, this still leaves unresolved the appalling moral question as to what is the threshold of unacceptable losses. The bar is considerably higher for solidarism than realism, but how high? I argue in Chapter 8 that NATO should have been prepared to launch a ground intervention to rescue Kosovars rather than rely on an air campaign that posed low risks to NATO aircrew. But how many NATO soldiers would it have been right to risk and lose to save the lives of Kosovar strangers? It cannot be a 1.1 exchange, because the consequentalist ethics that justify humanitarian intervention demand that any loss of life, as a consequence of intervention, be outweighed by the number of lives saved as a result of it. As I argued earlier, these judgements are difficult enough to make with the benefit of hindsight; for politicians who bear the awesome responsibility of taking them at the time, they impose agonizing moral choices.

Certainly, those state leaders who have to make the godlike consequentialist calculation as to whether X number of soldiers' lives should be risked to save a greater number of civilians facing imminent death beyond their borders deserve both our sympathy and our empathy. I will examine in later chapters how Western state leaders resolved this conflict between their responsibilities to citizens and strangers in the cases of Iraq, Somalia, Rwanda, Bosnia, and Kosovo.

Conclusion

Having explored how the rules of international society enable and constrain state actions, I examined solidarist claims for a doctrine of humanitarian intervention. Here, I drew on the work of R. J. Vincent, Michael Walzer, and Fernando Teson (locating the writings of the latter two within the camp of solidarism). The analysis then turned to a discussion of pluralist and realist objections to legitimating a practice of unilateral humanitarian intervention in the society of states. The task of the final part of the chapter was to reply to these objections by setting out a solidarist theory of humanitarian intervention. The latter identified four minimum criteria (supreme humanitarian emergency, necessity or last resort, proportionality, and a positive humanitarian outcome) that interventions have to satisfy to qualify as humanitarian. This framework challenges the conventional wisdom in the existing literatures in international relations and international law that the primacy of humanitarian motives is the defining characteristic of a humanitarian intervention. Instead, I argued that non-humanitarian motives disqualified an intervention as humanitarian only if it could be shown that these, or the means employed, undermined a positive humanitarian outcome. Interventions that satisfy the criteria of humanitarian motives, humanitarian justifications, legality, and selectivity have progressively better humanitarian qualifications than those that meet only the minimum or threshold requirements.

It might be objected at this point that an intervention should satisfy all eight requirement listed above to qualify as humanitarian. There are three replies here: first, there are no cases of intervention since 1945 that meet all these criteria and it is very implausible to think that future cases will satisfy such a demanding range of requirements. Secondly, the argument is not that we should praise interventions that meet only the threshold requirements; rather, as I argued above, we should make all efforts in our individual and collective capacities to persuade and cajole state leaders into living up to a solidarist ethic of responsibility. Confronted with supreme humanitarian emergencies, governments should be prepared to risk and lose soldiers' lives for primarily humanitarian reasons, justify their actions in humanitarian terms, work to secure Security Council authorization, and treat like cases alike.

Finally, this solidarist theory of humanitarian intervention rejects the pluralist proposition that state practice is the defining test of a legitimate humanitarian intervention. To anticipate the argument developed in Part Two, by placing the defence of human rights at the centre of a solidarist theory of humanitarian intervention, we arrive at the conclusion that the society of states should have legitimated India's, Vietnam's and Tanzania's interventions as humanitarian, because they met the minimum requirements of a legitimate action. This interpretation of the legitimacy of these actions stands in sharp contrast to state practice, and this illustrates the moral bankruptcy of cold-war international society. Solidarism gives a very different meaning to humanitarian intervention than pluralism, and it supplies us with a normative standard by which to judge the success of international society in acting as a guardian of human rights in the cold war and post-cold-war cases covered in the chapters to follow.

PART TWO

Humanitarian Intervention during the Cold War

2

India as Rescuer? Order versus Justice in the Bangladesh War of 1971

The Pakistani Government's brutal repression of the Bengali people living in East Pakistan resulted in the deaths of over a million Bengalis. The atrocities took place between March and December 1971, when Indian intervention brought the massacres to an end and led to the creation of the new state of Bangladesh. This level of human rights abuses clearly meets the criteria of a supreme humanitarian emergency, and it might be expected that the society of states would have recognized India's use of force as an exception to its rules. As we will see, India relied primarily on the justification of self-defence, but it also invoked humanitarian claims to justify its use of force. This appeal to justice fell on deaf ears in the great debating chambers of the society of states, where the Indian action was widely viewed as a breach of the rules that jeopardized the pillars of interstate order.

After a short discussion of the background context that led to the intervention, I examine how persuasive India's justifications were for its use of force, and how far these belied the real motives behind the action. Here, two key arguments are advanced: first, India's public legitimating reasons were themselves a key determinant of the action; and, secondly, non-humanitarian motives were present in the decision to act, but these did not undermine a positive humanitarian outcome. Having argued that India's intervention meets the minimum requirements of a legitimate humanitarian intervention, the second part of the chapter traces the radically different meaning given to the legitimacy of India's action by governments on the Security Council and in the General Assembly.

The Background to Intervention

The causes of the Indo-Pakistan War of 1971 can be traced back to the violent partition in 1947 of post-colonial India into the new states of India and Pakistan. The latter was geographically split by more than 1500 kilometres into West Pakistan and East Pakistan. In addition to geography, there were important cultural, linguistic, and economic disparities between the two parts of Pakistan. In West Pakistan, there were fifty-five million people speaking the official language of Urdu compared to 2 per cent in East Pakistan, where over 95 per cent of the seventy-five million people spoke Bengali. Of these, between ten and twelve million were Hindus, who naturally looked to India for cultural and commercial interactions.[1] By contrast, West Pakistan developed trading links with its Arab neighbours and identified with this grouping within the Islamic bloc.

The relationship between East and West developed into an increasingly polarized one as the Bengalis began to feel that they were being treated as a colonial outpost by the West Pakistan Government. Conditions in the East began to deteriorate as the Western part became increasingly prosperous and industrialized. At the time of partition the per capita income of the West had exceeded the East by 10 per cent and by 1969 this had risen to 60 per cent.[2] Economic domination facilitated political control, with West Pakistan controlling the military and bureaucracy. This economic and political discrimination spawned a movement—the Awami League—for greater regional autonomy in Pakistan's Eastern wing. Pakistan had been ruled since partition by long periods of military dictatorship, but in 1969 General Yahya Khan took over as President from Marshal Ayub Khan and agreed to hold elections to choose a civilian government.

In the elections the Awami League campaigned on a platform of maximum autonomy but not separation. It secured 288 of the 300 seats in the East Pakistani Assembly and also gained 167 of the 169 seats allocated to East Pakistan in the National Assembly. This made it the biggest single party in Pakistan. The Pakistan People's Party, the second largest in the National Assembly, argued that, since each was the biggest single party in each of the wings, there should be parity rights for both parties in drafting the new constitution. However, the Awami League refused on the grounds that it controlled the majority of seats in the Assembly. General Yahya Khan postponed the convening of the National Assembly and the Awami League responded by a campaign of non-violent non-cooperation in the East.[3] This was met by a declaration of martial law and the deployment of government troops onto the streets of East Pakistan. At the same time, the Pakistani Government sought to reopen negotiations, the condition being that the context for talks was maintenance of the territorial integrity of East Pakistan.[4] The Government feared that the Awami League was developing secessionist tendencies and it was determined to stamp these out.

---

[1] The differences are discussed in L. Kuper, *The Prevention of Genocide* (New Haven: Yale University Press, 1985), 45.   [2] This figure is given in ibid. 46.
[3] R. Sisson and L. E. Rose, *War and Secession: Pakistan, India, and the Creation of Bangladesh* (Berkeley and Los Angeles: University of California Press, 1990), 92.   [4] Ibid. 99.

The last attempt at resolving the conflict took place between 16 and 24 March 1971 and involved face-to-face meetings between the leader of the Awami League, Sheikh Mujibur Rahman, President Yahya Khan, and the leader of the West Pakistan People's Party, Zulfikar Ali Bhutto. Initially, these talks appeared to be going well and there was progress on many of the issues that divided the parties. However, the use of the word 'confederation' by Awami League negotiators to describe their position on the role of East Pakistan in the constitution was perceived by the military as evidence of the League's secessionist ambitions.[5] President Yahya Khan had asked his generals shortly after the negotiations had begun to prepare contingency plans for the restoration of law and order in the Eastern wing, but no decision had been made on implementing this decision. As the talks foundered over the issue of the constitutional relationship between the two wings of Pakistan, Yahya Khan and his generals decided that what was needed in East Pakistan was a proper show of force to end the rebellion of the Awami League and its supporters.

On 25 March 1971 West Pakistani garrisons 'struck with devastating force'[6] against the political leaders of the Awami League and its supporters. This was a brutal act of repression that involved the widespread killing of civilians. The East Pakistan Staff Study of the International Commission of Jurists wrote in its 1972 report that the killing 'was done on a scale which was difficult to comprehend',[7] and Leo Kuper adds that the brutality included the 'additional horror of torture and extermination camps'.[8] As the Bengalis began to organize a campaign of armed resistance, the army responded with the 'annihilation'[9] of Bengali villages.

India's immediate reaction was to express its concern at developments in East Pakistan.[10] This hardened two days later when both Houses of the Indian Parliament adopted a resolution describing the repression in East Pakistan as 'amounting to genocide'.[11] The Indian Parliament blamed the current crisis on the failure of the Pakistani Government 'to transfer, power to the legally-elected representatives of the people of East Bengal', stating that: 'The House wishes to assure them that their struggles and sacrifices will receive the wholehearted sympathy and support of the people of India.'[12] Although the Indian Government allowed Awami League escapees to set up a provisional government-in-exile on Indian soil, it did not recognize the new government of Bangladesh when it proclaimed its independence on 10 April. However,

---

[5] Ibid. 132–3. [6] Kuper, *The Prevention of Genocide*, 47.
[7] East Pakistan Staff Study by the Secretariat of the International Commission of Jurists, in *Review of the International Commission of Jurists*, 8 (1972), 26.
[8] Kuper, *The Prevention of Genocide*, 47. [9] Ibid. 47.
[10] Robert Jackson notes that Foreign Minister Sworn Singh 'expressed his government's concern' on 26 March. See Robert Jackson, *South Asian Crisis: India-Pakistan–Bangladesh* (London: Chatto & Windus for the IISS, 1975), 36.
[11] Quoted in ibid. [12] Quoted in ibid.

Indian Prime Minister, Indira Gandhi, secretly trained and equipped Bengali guerrilla forces operating from bases within Indian territory.[13]

In the face of mass killing in East Pakistan, the overwhelming reaction of the society of states was to affirm Pakistan's right to sovereignty and the rule of non-intervention.[14] There were expressions of concern at the humanitarian situation inside East Pakistan, but the dominant view was expressed by UN Secretary General U Thant in his letters to President Yahya Khan on 5 and 22 April. The Secretary General accepted the Pakistan Government's position that the conflict inside East Pakistan fell within the domestic jurisdiction of Pakistan under Article 2 (7) of the UN Charter. This was certainly the position taken by the USA, which, whilst calling for international assistance to relieve the suffering of the people of East Pakistan, stopped short of condemning Pakistan for its use of force against its own people. Indeed, President Nixon continued to supply Pakistan with arms, leading Indian Foreign Minister, Sawan Singh, to issue a protest against the USA. In a speech to the lower House of the Indian Parliament on 12 July, he stated that US actions amounted to 'condonation of genocide in Bangladesh' and support for the military regime of West Pakistan against the people of East Bengal.[15] The Soviet Union in a letter to President Yahya Khan on 2 April called for an end to the bloodshed and repression, but President Podgorny was careful to affirm his commitment to the territorial integrity of Pakistan.[16]

Although there was a strong consensus in international society that the conflict inside East Pakistan was covered by Article 2 (7), it was also becoming apparent that the growing number of Bengalis fleeing for safety to India risked internationalizing the crisis. The slaughter and mass rape produced a situation where eventually some 9–10 million people escaped across the border to West Bengal. The refugees had to be fed and sheltered and given protection from epidemics (for example, cholera broke out in Calcutta, whose population had swelled to twelve million with the addition of the refugees). The influx of these numbers into Indian society created enormous social and economic tensions in West Bengal's border areas as well as imposing an 'unbearable' economic strain that was costing the exchequer millions every day.[17] According to Adams and Whitehead, this produced a public outcry in

---

[13] J. Adams and P. Whitehead, *The Dynasty: The Nehru-Gandhi Story* (London: Penguin Books for the BBC, 1997), 234.

[14] Britain and France took this view in statements in late March and late April respectively. China lined up behind its ally Pakistan in emphasizing the importance of keeping Pakistan unified. Similarly, the non-Arab Muslim powers were among the first to give public support to Pakistan, and, at the end of June, a conference of twenty-two Muslim states in Jiddah expressed the common view that Pakistan's territorial integrity should be maintained. For a fuller discussion, see Jackson, *South Asian Crisis*, 38–43.

[15] 'India Accuses US of Condoning Genocide', *The Times*, 12 July 1971.

[16] Jackson, *South Asian Crisis*, 40.

[17] 'Pakistan Means War, India Says', *The Times*, 19 Nov. 1971.

India for the army to intervene in the territory of what the Indian Government now named as 'East Bengal'.[18] In an effort to get wider international support for India's situation, Prime Minister Gandhi visited Western capitals, which ensured publicity of the continuing atrocities in East Pakistan. The Indian leader emphasized to Western leaders and publics that 'the refugee situation was intolerable, the problem was not of India's making, but if necessary India would take action'.[19]

The cold-war line-up, with the USA and China aligned with Pakistan and the Soviet Union supporting India, prevented effective pressure being brought to bear on the growing conflict. According to U Thant's memoirs, the major powers did not even discuss the matter.[20] Given what the Secretary General called in his memoirs the 'extraordinary apathy'[21] of the Security Council, he had to restrict himself to organizing an international aid programme. However, in July he took the step of distributing a confidential memorandum to the Council (made public in August) that warned member states that the internal conflict in East Pakistan could all too easily escalate into war on the subcontinent, and that it was the responsibility of the Council to prevent this occurring.[22] In making this argument, the Secretary General reversed his earlier position that the UN was debarred from intervening because of Article 2 (7) of the UN Charter. By arguing that Pakistan's internal repression constituted a threat to 'international peace and security', the possibility was opened up for the Security Council to act under Chapter VII of the Charter, which enables the Council to override the ban on UN intervention in Article 2 (7). This position received some support from France and Italy, but the Council did not convene to discuss the crisis until war had actually broken out on 3 December 1971.

Hostilities between India and Pakistan escalated throughout November as Bangladeshi guerrillas continued to raid Pakistani positions. Indeed, by the third week of November, Pakistan alleged that India had actually invaded, as border skirmishes led to Indian forces advancing several kilometres inside Pakistani territory.[23] At the same time, Pakistani forces were shelling Indian towns on the border. According to the then Indian Chief of Army Staff, Sam Manekshaw, a full-scale attack was planned for 4 December. They did not have to wait until then. On 3 December Pakistan launched an attack on eight Indian airfields, precipitating an immediate Indian intervention. As the subcontinent exploded into war, the Security Council met in emergency session at 5.00 p.m. the following day.

---

[18] Adams and Whitehead, *The Dynasty*, p. 236.   [19] Quoted in ibid.
[20] U Thant, *View from the UN* (London: David & Charles, 1978), 424.
[21] Ibid. 422.   [22] Ibid. 423.
[23] 'Pakistan Says India Launched Big Attack', *Financial Times*, 23 Nov. 1971.

India's Justifications for its Use of Force

In addition to the five permanent members, ten members are elected by the General Assembly every two years to serve on the Security Council. In 1971 neither India nor Pakistan was a member, but, under Article 31 of the UN Charter, any state is entitled to 'participate, without vote, in the discussion of any question brought before the Security Council whenever the latter considers that the interests of that member are specially affected'.[24] The Security Council agreed that India and Pakistan should participate in its deliberations, and the Indian Ambassador opened proceedings by defending his government's use of force as a response to Pakistan's aggressive actions. Ambassador Sen denied that his government had breached the prohibition on the use of force in Article 2 (4) since Pakistan had struck first. The implication was that India's military response was consistent with the rule of self-defence in Article 51 of the Charter.[25] A study of India's justifications, however, provides scant support for this case, with the evidence pointing to the conclusion that India considered Article 51 a weak public justification for its use of force. To develop this argument, it is necessary to go deeper into the law relating to self-defence.

According to Article 51 of the UN Charter, the right of individual and collective self-defence exists in the event of 'an armed attack . . . against a Member of the United Nations, until the Security Council has taken measures necessary to maintain international peace and security'.[26] In addition to the Charter requirement that an 'armed attack' must have taken place, customary international law places further restrictions on the right to self-defence. This goes back to the *Caroline* case of 1837, which has its origins in the protest sent by US Secretary of State, Daniel Webster, to the British Government following its armed expedition into US territory to capture the vessel *Caroline*, which was allegedly preparing to transport guerrilla forces to assist the Canadian rebels who were challenging British colonial rule in Canada.[27] The British Government argued that its action was justified on grounds of self-defence, but Webster claimed that the British Government would have to satisfy the following conditions if the plea of self-defence was to be accepted: 'It will be for [the British] Government to show a necessity of self-defence, instant, overwhelming, leaving no choice of means, and no moment for deliberation.'[28]

---

[24] Charter of the United Nations, Article 31.

[25] This is the standard interpretation of India's defence in the existing literature. See e.g. East Pakistan Staff Study, *Review of the International Commission of Jurists*, 53–62, and M. Akehurst, 'Humanitarian Intervention', in H. Bull (ed.), *Intervention in World Politics* (Oxford: Oxford University Press, 1984), 96.   [26] Charter of the United Nations, Article 51.

[27] For a fuller discussion of the *Caroline* case, see J. S. Davidson, *Grenada: A Study in Politics and the Limits of International Law* (Aldershot: Gower, 1987), 103–4, and R. Y. Jennings, 'The *Caroline* and *McLeod* Cases', *American Journal of International Law*, 32 (1938), 82.

[28] Quoted in Davidson, *Grenada*, 101.

The British Government accepted Webster's formulation of the self-defence rule, and its legal counsel, Lord Ashburton, sought to argue that British action in the *Caroline* case was in conformity with this rule.[29] A further requirement that has become part of customary international law since the *Caroline* case is that any use of force in self-defence must be proportionate to the initial attack. In their study of the legality of India's intervention in East Pakistan, the International Commission of Jurists' East Pakistan Staff Study concluded that, whilst Pakistan's attacks against Indian territory justified a military response under Article 51, the scale of India's response was not proportionate to the initial attack. The report stated that, 'we find it difficult to accept that the scale of India's armed action was motivated solely by military considerations based on the need to protect her national frontiers and territory'.[30]

The fact that there was no explicit reference to Article 51 or the rule of self-defence in Ambassador Sen's defence before the Security Council suggests that the Indian Government recognized that it was on dubious grounds in invoking this rule. Instead, Ambassador Sen put forward a new claim to justify India's use of force based on the premiss that Pakistan had committed a new crime of 'refugee aggression'.[31] He argued that the meaning of 'aggression' should also encompass the aggression that resulted from ten million people coming to India as refugees. 'Now, was that not a kind of aggression?', he asked. 'If aggression against another foreign country means that it strains its social structure, that it ruins its finances, that it has to give up its territory for sheltering the refugees . . . what is the difference between that kind of aggression and the other type, the more classical type, when someone declares war, or something of that sort.'[32] Repeating a theme that had been prominent in Indian Government statements since the Pakistani Government's use of force against the East Bengali people, the Ambassador said that it was not India that was breaking up Pakistan, but 'Pakistan that is breaking up Pakistan itself and, in the process, creating aggression against us'.[33]

India was seeking to persuade the Security Council that its use of force was a legitimate response to Pakistan's 'refugee aggression' and its 'military aggression'. A measure of the threat that the Indian Government perceived in the flow of millions of refugees across its borders can be seen in the fact, that hours before Pakistani jets had attacked Indian airbases, Mrs Ghandi had told Congress Party workers in New Delhi that she would 'do what is best in our national interest'. Moreover, she issued a warning to Western states that

[29] Ibid. 103.

[30] East Pakistan Staff Study, *Review of the International Commission of Jurists*, 57.

[31] Security Council Resolution (SCOR), 1606th Meeting, 4 Dec. 1971, 17. If India's Chief of Army Staff in 1971, Sam Manekshaw, is to be believed, India planned to strike the first blow. As a result, it can be speculated that the Indian Government had already decided to legitimize its actions in terms of Pakistan's 'refugee aggression'. This bolsters the argument that India was not expecting to justify its intervention in terms of the rule of self-defence.

[32] SCOR, 1606th Meeting, 4 Dec. 1971, 15.   [33] Ibid.

naming India as an 'aggressor' would not deter her from protecting India's 'territorial integrity and sovereignty'.[34] Mrs Gandhi and her ministers' fear was that the presence of millions of refugees in West Bengal and Tripura threatened to create a revolutionary situation threatening the intercommunal harmony of the Indian state.

How seriously, then, should we take India's justification of 'refugee aggression' in explaining its decision to resort to force? By breaking up Pakistan, India certainly weakened the power of its arch-enemy. In addition, Mrs Gandhi's party was doing badly in the polls as a consequence of the refugee crisis, and solving this would boost the electoral fortunes of the Congress Party. Consequently, it might be argued that there was a gap between justification and motivation, but, even if this were the case, it does not follow from this that justification is merely an *ex post facto* rationalization of actions taken for different reasons. Rather, this case supports Skinner's proposition that the public legitimating reasons supplied by an actor are themselves a key factor in the decision to act. To argue the opposite case it would be necessary to show that, in the absence of the legitimating reason of 'refugee aggression', the hidden motives behind India's use of force could have been invoked to justify this action. But it is simply not credible to argue that an Indian Government could have gone to war and justified it on the basis of weakening an enemy and improving its electoral fortunes. This would have shown contempt for UN Charter principles and in so doing placed in jeopardy the shared meanings and understandings that constitute the society of states. Nevertheless, in arguing that India's public legitimating reason was a necessary condition of action, I am not arguing that this determined the action. The best explanation of India's decision to intervene is one that combines the enabling condition of its occurrence (the refugee crisis) with the 'off-the-board' reasons that led Mrs Gandhi and her ministers to decide for war rather than peace.

India's primary justification for its use of force was Pakistan's 'refugee aggression', but it did invoke humanitarian claims. Since India's position throughout the crisis was that any settlement depended upon respect for the democratic and human rights of the Bengali people, it is not surprising that its humanitarian justifications were bound up with its advocacy of self-determination for the people of East Bengal. Those Awami League leaders who had escaped Pakistan's repression had declared independence for the state of Bangladesh in April 1971, but neither India nor the rest of the world recognized the new government-in-exile. India's position dramatically changed as fighting raged on the subcontinent, its decision to recognize Bangladesh on 6 December being foreshadowed two days earlier when the Indian Ambassador claimed in the Security Council that the rule of self-determination might be

---

[34] 'Mrs Ghandi Says Being Named an Aggressor would not Deter India', *The Times*, 3 Dec. 1971.

applied to the people of East Pakistan. He stated that the appalling human suffering of the Bengali people justified declaring 'East Pakistan a non-self-governing territory'.[35] In making this argument, India was asking for an exception on humanitarian grounds to the rule that international society had applied in previous cases where claims of self-determination had arisen—namely, that the right of self-determination cannot be applied to the territories of member states.[36]

In seeking to justify India's intervention on humanitarian grounds, Ambassador Sen argued that the 'military repression' in East Pakistan was on a sufficient scale to 'shock the conscience of mankind'.[37] He directed this appeal at his fellow members of the Security Council: 'What . . . has happened to our conventions on genocide, human rights, self-determination, and so on?' Two days later, he returned to this theme pointing out that members were focusing on the pluralist principles of sovereignty and territorial integrity to the exclusion of the human rights norms enshrined in the UN Charter. 'Why', he asked, were members 'shy about speaking of human rights . . . What has happened to the justice part [of the UN Charter]?'[38]

As Franck and Rodley point out, the 'answer was that justice was being enforced, at that moment, by Indian troops'.[39] In their study of the legal basis of the Indian action, the International Commission of Jurists, East Pakistan Staff Study concluded that India's armed intervention would have been justified 'if she had acted under the doctrine of humanitarian intervention'.[40] The failure of the Security Council to stop the massive violations of human rights taking place inside East Pakistan, and the appalling situation facing those trapped in the refugee camps on the Indian border, gave India a legal right to act unilaterally. As I discussed in the previous chapter, the ILA report in 1970 setting out criteria for a legitimate humanitarian intervention stipulated that before intervening a state must request a meeting of the Security Council.

[35] SCOR, 1606th Meeting, 4 Dec. 1971, 18. At a meeting of the Security Council held on 12 Dec., 1971, Indian Foreign Minister Sworn Singh argued that 'international law recognizes that where a mother State has irrevocably lost the allegiance of such a large section of its people as represented by Bangla Desh and cannot bring them under its sway, conditions are suitable for that section to come into being as a separate state' (SCOR, 1611th Meeting, 12 Dec. 1971, 13). In its balanced analysis of India's legal justifications, the East Pakistan Staff Study of the International Commission of Jurists rejected India's argument, claiming that, if the General Assembly's Declaration of Principles of International Law is accepted as the rules for claiming a right of self-determination, 'it is difficult to see how it can be contended that in March 1971 the people of East Pakistan, or the leaders of the Awami League on their behalf, were entitled in international law to proclaim the independence of Bangladesh under the principle of the self-determination of people' (East Pakistan Staff Study, *Review of the International Commission of Jurists*, 53–62).

[36] For a discussion of this, see Kuper, *The Prevention of Genocide*, 76–82.

[37] SCOR, 1606th Meeting, 4 Dec., 1971, 15. This language is virtually identical to that used by Walzer in *Just and Unjust Wars*, where it will be recalled he argues that 'humanitarian intervention is justified when it is a response . . . to acts "that shock the moral conscience of mankind"'.

[38] SCOR, 1606th Meeting, 4 Dec. 1971, 32, and SCOR, 1608th Meeting, 6 Dec. 1971, 27.

[39] Franck and Rodley, 'After Bangladesh', 276–7.

[40] East Pakistan Staff Study, *Review of the International Commission of Jurists*, 62.

Although India failed to request such a meeting, the East Pakistan Staff Study did not consider that this disqualified the action as a legitimate one. In addition, the ILA Report claimed that the intervening states, 'primary goal must be to remedy a gross human rights violation'. The East Pakistan Staff Study does not address whether humanitarian motives were primary, preferring to justify India's action on the grounds that it met the test of proportionality because the level of 'force used was no greater than was necessary in order to bring to an end . . . violations of human rights'.[41]

In arguing that India should have justified its use of force in terms of the principle of humanitarian intervention, the East Pakistan Staff Study emphasized that this was not the 'ground of justification'.[42] However, this ignores India's attempt to persuade members of the Security Council that its intervention was justifiable in terms of UN Charter principles relating to the protection of human rights. That said, at no point did India explicitly justify its use of force in terms of the legal doctrine of humanitarian intervention. The closest it came to invoking this legal defence was in giving the meaning of a 'rescue' to its military intervention. The Indian Ambassador stated: 'We are glad that we have on this particular occasion absolutely nothing but the purest of motives and the purest of intentions; to *rescue* the people of East Bengal from what they are suffering. If that is a crime, the Security Council can judge for itself.'[43]

The Ambassador's claim that India had acted for primarily humanitarian reasons sits uneasily with the earlier justification of 'refugee aggression'. And, if India was motivated solely by humanitarian reasons, then why did it not act earlier to rescue the Bengali people? India could have used force to stop the killings within weeks of the massacres and invoked the legal doctrine of humanitarian intervention to justify this. Mrs Gandhi's Government intervened nine months after the atrocities began—not for humanitarian reasons—but because it perceived in the exodus of ten million refugees a vital threat to the security of the Indian state and the survival of the Congress Party.

As I discuss below, the humanitarian claims raised by India did not succeed in changing the norms of the society of states. Yet, given the legitimating power of the rules of sovereignty, non-intervention, and non-use of force, India's appeal that the Security Council treat its use of force as an exception

[41] East Pakistan Staff Study, *Review of the International Commission of Jurists*, 56.

[42] Ibid. 62.

[43] SCOR, 1606th Meeting, 4 Dec. 1971, 18; emphasis added. Most commentators follow Michael Akehurst in arguing that, having raised this claim, India retracted it in the final published version of the Official Records of the Security Council (every government is allowed to edit the record of its representatives). He suggests that India underwent a change of mind on the legitimacy of humanitarian intervention as a consequence of the negative reception that this claim received in the Security Council. But, *contra* Akehurst, the claim raised by India remains in the final version of the Official Records. See Akehurst, 'Humanitarian Intervention', 96.

to these because it was defending the 'justice part' of the UN Charter challenged existing norms. This is the significance of Franck and Rodley's comment in 1973 that the 'Bangladesh case is an instance, by far the most important in our times, of the unilateral use of military force justified *inter alia*, on human rights grounds'.[44] By raising humanitarian claims to justify its use of force, India created an opportunity for the Security Council to reverse the normal priority accorded order over justice in the society of states.

The International Reaction

India's contention that it was responding to Pakistan's 'refugee' and 'military' aggression was rejected by the Pakistani Government, which alleged that India's defensive justifications hid its real motive of breaking up Pakistan. Reiterating the position that his government had taken since the beginning of the crisis, the Pakistani Ambassador argued that the internal situation inside East Pakistan was part of Pakistan's 'domestic jurisdiction', and there could be no valid grounds for any outside intervention. Repeating the standard pluralist justification for the rules of sovereignty and non-intervention, he stated: 'One principle is basic to the maintenance of a peaceful world order, and it is that no political, economic, strategic, social or ideological considerations may be invoked by one state to justify its interference in the internal affairs of another state.'[45] This position was strongly supported by China, which condemned India for what it interpreted as an act of aggression. The Chinese Ambassador rejected the reasons put forward by India and called upon the Council to name India as an aggressor and demand that it unconditionally withdraw its forces from East Pakistan.

In contrast to China's insistence that the question of East Pakistan was solely the internal affair of Pakistan, the USA acknowledged that the cause of the human suffering of the Bengali people lay in the failure of both India and Pakistan to arrive at a political accommodation. Nevertheless, the USA followed China in rejecting India's justifications for resorting to force, which it saw as a clear violation of the UN Charter. The US priority was a ceasefire and it proposed a draft resolution that called upon India and Pakistan to withdraw their forces from foreign territories.[46] Speaking on television three days after the Indian invasion, the American Ambassador to the UN, George Bush, stated that India was guilty of 'clear-cut aggression'.[47] The following day a senior White House Official in an off-the-record briefing condemned India's

---

[44] Franck and Rodley, 'After Bangladesh', 303.
[45] SCOR, 1606th Meeting, 4 Dec. 1971, 10.
[46] Ibid. 19.   [47] Jackson, *South Asian Crisis*, 125.

action as 'an unjustified move that could lead to international anarchy'.[48] The meaning given to India's intervention by Nixon Administration officials legitimated the following punitive sanctions: licences for military sales were revoked, all current economic aid was suspended, and it was announced that there would be no provision for aid in the next year's budget.[49]

The only states to condone India's action in the Security Council were the Soviet Union and its Warsaw Pact ally Poland. India and the Soviet Union had signed a Treaty of Peace, Friendship, and Cooperation on 9 August 1971 and this made it very difficult for Moscow not to support India at the UN. As we have seen, India justified its intervention in terms of 'refugee aggression', East Bengal's claim to self-determination, and an implicit plea of humanitarian intervention. All three reasons figured in the Soviet Union's defence. Ambassador Malik appealed to the Council to imagine what it must be like to be overrun by ten million refugees, and he linked this issue to the demand raised by India as to whether the representatives of the government-in-exile of Bangladesh should be invited to speak to the Security Council. Ambassador Sen had stated that discussing the problem of East Pakistan without the voice of the victims of the conflict was akin to 'playing Hamlet without the Prince of Denmark'.[50] Similarly, the Soviet Ambassador contended that the seventy-five million people in Pakistan's Eastern wing, and the ten million who had fled across India's borders, had undergone 'unbelievable suffering' and should not be deprived of an 'opportunity to speak'.[51] Without explicitly defending India's use of force as a humanitarian intervention, the Soviet Union argued that India's recourse to force had to be located in the context of the massive human suffering caused by Pakistan's repressive policies, which frustrated the will of the population of East Pakistan as expressed in the elections of 1970. In advancing the claim of the East Bengali people to justice and the right of self-determination, the Soviet Union challenged the view championed by Pakistan, China, and the USA that inviting the representatives of the provisional government of Bangladesh to speak would issue a licence for secession in the society of states.

As the deliberations of the Council unfolded through the early hours of 5 December, India, the Soviet Union, and Poland opposed the position of the rest of the Security Council, which supported an immediate ceasefire. In response to the charge that India's use of force had breached the rules of the

---

[48] There were alternative interpretations of the Bangladeshi war available to US policy-makers but these were excluded from the policy-making process. A few hours before the White House briefing on 7 Dec., the Nixon Administration was attacked by Senator Edward Kennedy and Senator Edmund Muskie for its support of Pakistan, when the latter was responsible for the 'repression of the independence movement . . . [and] for the outbreak of the conflict'. For a discussion of these competing views, see 'White House Hits Hard at India over Launching a Full-Scale War', *The Times*, 8 Dec. 1971.

[49] Jackson, *South Asian Crisis*, 125.   [50] SCOR, 1606th Meeting, 4 Dec. 1971, 5.

[51] Ibid. 4.

society of states, India defended its army's presence in East Pakistan on humanitarian grounds. In a powerful passage, Ambassador Sen pleaded to the Council:

Shall we release the Pakistan soldiers by a so-called cease-fire so that they can go on a rampage and kill the civilians in Dacca, in Chittagong, and in other places? Is this the kind of cease-fire we desire.

I wish to give a very serious warning to the Council that we shall not be a party to any solution that will mean continuation of oppression of East Pakistan people . . . So long as we have any light of civilized behavior left in us, we shall protect them.[52]

Reflecting several years later on the deliberations in the Security Council, U Thant considered that, whilst many states felt that India had a legitimate grievance against Pakistan, this did not justify what they perceived as India's deliberate exploitation of the crisis in order to dismember Pakistan.[53] The 1970 ILA report on the criteria for legitimate humanitarian intervention identified the exhaustion of all non-forcible remedies as a key requirement, and the Security Council's position was that India had failed to fulfil this. Most states on the Security Council considered that negotiations with President Yayha Khan to resolve the crisis should have been given more time. As a result, any attempt by India to defend its action as a rescue mission was always going to run up against the objection that it had acted prematurely. The problem with this criticism of India's use of force is that every extra day spent trying to arrive at a settlement allowed Pakistani forces to abuse human rights with impunity.

After several hours of argument, the Security Council voted on a number of draft resolutions proposed by the USA, China, the Soviet Union, and the non-aligned members of the Council. With the exception of the Soviet resolution, which demanded a political settlement as part of any ceasefire (this resolution secured only two votes and was lost, as all resolutions must secure at least nine votes), all the other resolutions called for an immediate ceasefire and were vetoed by the Soviet Union. The Security Council met again the following day to try and resolve the diplomatic deadlock among the major powers. It did so against the background of the Indian Government's decision to recognize the state of Bangladesh. The antagonists repeated their positions of the previous day, with Pakistan insisting that the Security Council condemn India for its dismemberment of Pakistan.[54] The major powers lined up behind their clients in the region: the USA reiterated its call for an immediate ceasefire; China repeated its condemnation of India; and the Soviet Union argued for a ceasefire as part of a political settlement.

The most imaginative attempt to bridge these conflicting positions came from the Soviet Union, which pressed the claim that there could be no order

---

[52] Ibid. 16–17.   [53] Thant, *View from the UN*, 428.
[54] SCOR, 1607th Meeting, 5 Dec. 1971, 4.

on the subcontinent without respect for justice. In response to Pakistan's and China's argument that the internal situation inside East Pakistan was covered by the non-intervention principle, the Soviet Union argued that the domestic jurisdiction clause in the UN Charter did not apply because the consequence of the human suffering was an 'unprecedented' situation that 'had serious international consequences'.[55] Ending the violence between India and Pakistan—and within East Pakistan itself—required addressing both the interstate and intrastate aspects of the situation.

This argument that there is an interdependence between order and justice failed to win over the Security Council and it remained paralysed as war raged on the subcontinent. After a third meeting had failed to make progress, the non-aligned group managed to persuade the major powers to refer the issue to the General Assembly under the Uniting for Peace Resolution of 1950.[56] The discussion in the General Assembly reveals little or no support for a practice of humanitarian intervention in the society of states. Whilst India was condemned as an aggressor by only two states—China and Albania—none of the other forty-seven states speaking justified its use of force in terms of the doctrine of humanitarian intervention. The Soviet Union and the other members of the Warsaw Pact, in rejecting the demand for a ceasefire, did emphasize the atrocities committed by Pakistan. However, at no point did the Soviet Union or its allies argue that India's use of force should be recognized as an exception to the rules. Fernando Teson argues that an examination of the debate in the General Assembly shows that a number of states did not view the case as only an interstate problem. It is a huge jump to claim, however, that this is evidence for the proposition that the society of states 'implicitly acknowledged that the normative force of [Article 2 (4)] is attenuated where acts of genocide are concerned'.[57] With the exception of the Eastern bloc, those states that stressed the intrastate dimensions of the crisis were emphatic, *contra* Teson, that there could be no justification for actions that violated Article 2 (4) of the Charter. Sweden, for example, highlighted the inhuman conditions inside East Pakistan, but reaffirmed the UN Charter's prohibition against the use of force except in self-defence.[58]

India suffered a major defeat in the General Assembly as the majority of states backed a resolution calling for an immediate ceasefire, passed by 104

---

[55] SCOR, 1607th Meeting, 1, 7, 12.

[56] This provides that, 'if the Security Council, because of lack of unanimity of the permanent members fails to exercise its primary responsibility for the maintenance of international peace and security in any case where there appears to be a threat to the peace, breach of the peace, or act of aggression, the General Assembly shall consider the matter immediately with a view to making appropriate recommendations to Members for collective measures, including in the case of a breach of the peace or act of aggression the use of armed force when necessary, to maintain or restore international peace and security' quoted in Kuper, *The Prevention of Genocide*, 56.

[57] Teson, *Humanitarian Intervention*, 188.

[58] N. Ronzitti, *Rescuing Nationals Abroad through Military Coercion and Intervention on Grounds of Humanity* (Dordrecht: Martinus Nijhoff, 1985), 97.

votes to eleven with ten abstentions. Although there was reference in the Preamble to the necessity of securing an early political settlement, the Assembly legitimated a position that left the Pakistani army free to continue its repression inside East Pakistan. Leo Kuper argues that this resolution demonstrates a 'rejection of humanitarian intervention and [an] overriding commitment to norms protective of state sovereignty and territorial integrity and noninterference in the internal affairs of member states'.[59] The importance of the speech acts in the Assembly is that they reproduced the intersubjective understandings that constitute a pluralist society of states. The claims of justice were raised in debate, but Resolution 2793 secured such overwhelming support because it was accepted as a given that, even in cases of mass murder, there could be no exceptions to the constitutive rules of a pluralist international society.

India might have lost the moral argument in the General Assembly but it was winning on the battlefield. Its response to the vote was to state that it, did not feel bound by it, since 'the good thing about a General Assembly resolution is that it is recommendatory, not mandatory. It is one thing to vote, but another to grapple with a complex situation.'[60] The crisis on the subcontinent was once again thrown back to the Security Council, which met for one last time to try and resolve the crisis from 12 to 21 December. There was a growing sense of urgency and frustration in the Council given India's rejection of the General Assembly Resolution and its continuing military advance into East Pakistan.

The USA had requested that the Security Council meet and its Ambassador opened his address by repeating a White House statement that condemned India for its 'defiance of world opinion'[61] in not complying with Resolution 2793. The USA acknowledged once again that Pakistan's use of force in East Pakistan had produced 'tragic' consequences that had placed India in a very difficult situation. Ambassador Bush was emphatic, however, that this did not 'justify the actions of India in intervening militarily and placing in jeopardy the territorial integrity and political independence of its neighbor Pakistan'.[62] It was fidelity to this rule that had produced the overwhelming majority in support of Resolution 2793. And in a last-ditch attempt to avert disaster for his country, the Pakistani Foreign Minister, Bhutto (who had flown in specially for this meeting of the Security Council), appealed to the Council to avoid setting a precedent that could fatally erode the bases of order in the society of states. He argued that Pakistan's diplomatic success in the General Assembly was not due to 'power politics' because, in that game, India held the stronger cards. Rather, he claimed that Pakistan's arguments won legitimacy because they were

[59] Kuper, *The Prevention of Genocide*, 84.

[60] Indian Government spokesperson speaking after the vote in the General Assembly (quoted in Thant, *View from the UN*, 431).

[61] SCOR, 1611th Meeting, 12 Dec. 1971, 2.   [62] Ibid.

based, not on the interests of Pakistan conceived selfishly and subjectively, but on a world principle—universally accepted, universally recognized—that a sovereign State, brought into being by its own blood and toil and sweat, cannot be dismembered by a predatory neighbor wanting to tear it apart limb by limb. Today it is Pakistan; tomorrow it will be other parts of the world . . . Today it is in the subcontinent, tomorrow it will be in other parts of Asia, Africa and Latin America; it can be anywhere. So it is a basic issue which is involved in the present situation.[63]

The argument that there could be no exceptions to this rule—even in situations where a state was murdering its own people—prevailed within the Council. This position was reflected in a US draft resolution calling for a ceasefire and immediate withdrawal of all forces, but it was killed by a Soviet veto despite securing eleven votes in favour and two abstentions (Poland and the Soviet Union voting against). By this stage it was becoming obvious that there was no possibility of reaching an agreement within the Council. Attention now began to focus on the political issues raised by the decision of the civilian regional government in East Pakistan to resign. When the Security Council met on 15 December, Britain and France tabled a resolution that recognized that power had to be handed over to the elected representatives in East Pakistan.[64] The fall of Dacca to Indian forces was imminent, and, on 16 December, India's Foreign Minister Sworn Singh announced to the Council that India had ordered a ceasefire following the surrender of Pakistani forces in East Pakistan. This was followed by President Yahya Khan ordering a ceasefire, and the last meeting of the Security Council took place on 21 December, when it was finally possible to pass a compromise resolution. Security Council Resolution 307 called for a durable ceasefire, withdrawal of armed forces to their own borders, and action to bring the voluntary return of refugees home. However, the facts on the ground were that Indian arms had defeated the Pakistani army and created the new state of Bangladesh. Against this background, it is easy to agree with Kuper that the resolution 'was quite meaningless, even as a face-saving device'.[65]

Given the position expressed by a majority in the Security Council and General Assembly on the legitimacy of India's use of force, it is surprising that Teson argues that Resolution 307 supports a doctrine of humanitarian intervention in the society of states. What is crucial for him is the fact that the resolution did not condemn India.[66] But this reads too much into a resolution that was passed primarily because it represented a compromise between the positions taken by the USA and Soviet Union during the crisis. Equally problematic is Gary Klintworth's contention that the recognition of Bangladesh by the vast majority of states in the following months, including the USA after the final withdrawal of Indian forces in March 1972, indicates

---

[63] SCOR, 1611th Meeting, 16.
[65] Kuper, *Prevention of Genocide*, 84.

[64] Thant, *View from the UN*, 433–4.
[66] Teson, *Humanitarian Intervention*, 188.

'the acquiescence of states in the Indian invasion and dismemberment of Pakistan'.[67] He claims that India's use of force was treated leniently because it was seen to be acting for humanitarian reasons.[68] He supplies no evidence to support this claim and as an interpretation of state practice during the Bangladeshi case it is simply out of line with the positions taken by governments in the Security Council and General Assembly.

The problem with both Teson's and Klintworth's arguments is a methodological one: they succumb to the positivist fallacy of assessing the legitimacy of a normative practice by studying overt behaviour. The fact that India was not condemned in the General Assembly, and that, with the exception of the USA, governments did not impose sanctions should not be interpreted as evidence of the legitimacy of humanitarian intervention in the society of states. It is only by analysing the responsiveness of other states to India's justifications that we can understand the legitimacy of the practice of humanitarian intervention in the society of states. It is true that India could have been treated more harshly, but it does not follow from this that the intervention was excused on humanitarian grounds. The weakness of this claim is that, in the absence of governments publicly justifying their actions in these terms, it is open to the rejoinder that other reasons might equally well explain the international response to India's intervention other than the desire to mitigate it. And, even if it is conceded that a form of legal mitigation was operating in this case, it is a mistake to confuse mitigation with moral approval. This interpretation of the international reaction to events in East Pakistan shows that India's humanitarian claims were emphatically rejected as a legitimate basis for the use of force.

Conclusion

Pluralist international-society theory defines humanitarian intervention as a breach of the rules of sovereignty, non-intervention, and non-use of force, and this interpretation dominated state practice during the Bangladeshi case. The significance of this case is that it was the first time in post-1945 international society that humanitarian claims were raised to justify the use of force. By invoking global humanitarian norms in its defence, India appealed for its use of force to be treated as an exceptional case. Franck and Rodley argue that India's case for human rights 'succeeded',[69] but they can only be referring to India's success on the battlefield. In the debating forums of the Security Council and the General Assembly, India's cries for justice fell on deaf ears.

---

[67] G. Klintworth, *Vietnam's Intervention in International Law* (Canberra: Australian National University Press, 1984), 49.

[68] Ibid. 50.　　　　　　　　　　　　　　[69] Franck and Rodley, 'After Bangladesh', 303.

Nearly all the Ambassadors participating in the conversation in the Security Council acknowledged the human tragedy inside East Pakistan, but they balanced this against the moral consequences of legitimating an action that weakened the prohibition on the use of force, and risked opening the door to secessionist claims in the society of states.

If the dominant discourse in the Security Council and General Assembly was a pluralist one, then what of the realist argument that states employ this language to mask their real interests? Applying this theory to the contending positions taken by the players in this case, the US and Chinese advocacy of pluralist rules can be explained in terms of their geopolitical interest in supporting Pakistan against a Soviet-backed India. Conversely, power political reasons led the Soviet Union to support India's forcible break-up of Pakistan. One important test of the sincerity of actors' arguments is consistency in relation to like cases. Here, the Soviet Union is open to the charge that it changed its traditionally robust doctrinal position on the inviolability of territorial borders and non-use of force because this suited its interests. It sang a very different tune because this frustrated the search for a ceasefire in the Security Council, enabling the Indian army to emerge victorious from the war. Such a victory bolstered its alliance with India, opened up the prospect of exerting some control over the new state of Bangladesh, and, most important of all, gave Moscow important advantage in the geopolitical competition against China and the USA.

Two important responses can be made to the realist argument that this case supports the strategic view of language. First, even if the Soviet Union acted strategically, it recognized that legitimating its claims depended upon advancing arguments that could plausibly be argued to belong to the rules of the society of states. As Nicholas Smith puts it, in 'order for the manipulation of meanings to be possible, there must first be meanings to manipulate'.[70] The dominant view in the Security Council was that justice had to be subordinated to that of order, but the Soviet Union argued that this position was contradictory because there could be no order on the subcontinent without satisfying the demands for justice. The key argument fiercely contested on the one hand by India and the Soviet Union, and on the other by Pakistan and China, revolved around whether the interstate dimensions of the crisis could be separated from Pakistan's internal repression. U Thant had argued as early as July that there was a critical linkage between domestic events in Pakistan's Eastern wing and wider international security. At that time the Soviet Union had disagreed with U Thant. Its new-found conversion to the view that there was an interrelationship between order and justice leaves it open to the accusation that this was motivated by selfish reasons. Whatever its ulterior motives, the Soviet Union challenged the existing intersubjective consensus

---

[70] Quoted in Fierke, 'Dialogues', 31.

in the Security Council and General Assembly that order could be satisfied only at the expense of justice.[71] And, in justifying its opposition to a ceasefire on the grounds that this would actually serve to undermine order, the Soviet Ambassador appreciated that his government's case would be strengthened if it could justify its position in terms of the shared meanings (the priority of order over justice) that set the limits for legitimate argumentation in the Security Council.

Whether actors play strategically or not, there is the question of how conflicting claims get resolved. In a situation where language is being used strategically, the only possibility for reaching an agreement is if actors change their understanding of their interests through argumentation. In cases where actors are sincere in their claims it relies on reaching a new intersubjective consensus through the process of what Habermas calls the 'unforced force of the better argument'.[72] This case provides no support for either of these propositions. In his memoirs, U Thant laments the failure of the Security Council to be anything other than a debating forum. It is true that the conflicting arguments raised in the Council failed to persuade any of the participants to change their positions, but it does not follow from this that actors were insincere in their arguments. What it illustrates is how the exist-ence of common reference points—in this case the assumption that the primary value was maintaining international order—is no guarantee that agreement will be reached between the parties. The Soviet argument that order was best supported by opposing a ceasefire was always going to be opposed by its adversaries in the cold war, but it failed to win any support among the non-aligned because it was viewed as subversive of the pluralist rules that maintained international order.

The second problem with viewing language strategically is that it overlooks the power of discourse in constraining the choices of agents. The contribu-tion of Bourdieu's theoretical and empirical investigations is to introduce the idea of 'the socialized agent', rather than the subject, and to show how strat-egy is the product 'of the practical sense (and not the projects or calculations of any conscious mind)'.[73] This idea captures well the workings of the society of states because governments become socialized into certain norms and rules

---

[71] Leo Kuper concludes that, while the position taken by the Soviet Union 'is hardly to be explained as reflecting an overriding concern for human rights', it argued strongly against a posi-tion that would have left the Pakistani Government in a position to continue its repression of the Bengali people. See Kuper, *Prevention of Genocide*, 83–4.

[72] This idea is based on what Habermas calls 'discourse ethics', which are characterized by actors entering into dialogue where there is an openness to change one's position through the process of argumentation. It is no good viewing the dialogue as an opportunity to score points or to harangue opponents. Habermas argues that it is impossible to eliminate all differences of power and privilege between actors and that these will distort the process of communication, but he argues that the 'communication community (unlimited, that is, in social space and historical time) is an idea that we can approximate in real contexts of argumentation' J. Habermas, *Justification and Application Remarks on Discourse Ethics*, trans. Ciaron Cronin (Cambridge: Polity Press, 1993), 163.

[73] Bourdieu, *In Other Words*, 62.

that constitute the givens of discourse. We have seen how the Soviet Union supported by its Eastern-bloc allies raised new claims that served its interests, but at no point did the Soviet Government seek to justify India's action in terms of the doctrine of humanitarian intervention. No member of the Security Council or General Assembly questioned the pluralist rules of sovereignty, non-intervention, and non-use of force; these constituted the space within which legitimate argumentation could take place.

The only exception was India, which raised humanitarian claims to justify its use of force. This was not its primary rationale, and, after the attempt to present its action as a 'rescue' mission had failed to secure any legitimation from other members of the Security Council, India never mentioned it again. India's humanitarian argument failed to succeed, but what is important is that it felt able to raise this claim in the first place. Without the human rights norms in the 'justice part' of the UN Charter and Genocide Convention, India would have lacked the normative language to name Pakistan's repression as a 'shock to the conscience of mankind'. However, this attempt to stretch the human rights norms of the Charter to legitimate the use of force failed to win any adherents in the Security Council.

The international response to India's intervention demonstrates that there was no support for a doctrine of unilateral humanitarian intervention in state practice. As I argued in the previous chapter, the normative practices of the actors should not be the defining test of a legitimate humanitarian intervention. Applying the solidarist theory of humanitarian intervention developed in the previous chapter to India's action leads to the conclusion that its use of force meets the threshold requirements, and consequently it should have been welcomed by the society of states.

Pakistan's slaughter of over one million Bengalis constituted a supreme humanitarian emergency that justified humanitarian intervention. India should have issued a clear statement that it would invade unless Pakistan ceased its human rights abuses, but the Indian action still meets the Just War requirement of necessity or last resort, because outside military action was the only means available to end the atrocities. The 1972 report of the East Pakistan Staff Study of the International Commission of Jurists concluded that India's use of force also met the requirement of proportionality. Ending Pakistan's repression required nothing less than the defeat of its army in war, and, however awesome a moral calculation, the requirement of proportionality is met because the costs in life to the Indian armed forces and to civilians killed on both sides during the fighting were outweighed by the number of lives saved as a result of the intervention. It will never be known how many more Bengalis would have been killed had India not acted, but there is no evidence to suggest that Pakistan's campaign of repression was over by the time it intervened. It is true that India's intervention came too late to save hundreds of thousands of Bengalis, but it deserves credit for stopping the massacres and creating a political context within which the human rights of Bengalis could be protected.

Although India's intervention was not motivated by primarily humanitarian reasons, it counts as a humanitarian one, because (in addition to meeting the requirements of necessity and proportionality) the security reasons that led it to intervene and the means employed did not undermine the humanitarian benefits of the intervention. As Michael Walzer puts it, the Indian action is a good example of humanitarian intervention 'because it was a *rescue*' and 'its various motives converged on a single course of action that was also the course of action called for by the Bengalis'.[74]

Whatever the humanitarian benefits of India's action, it was the fear of setting a precedent that could shake the foundations of international order that became the recurring theme in the debates within the Security Council and General Assembly. State practice in the Bangladeshi case supports the majority view of international lawyers who argue that the prohibition in Article 2 (4) makes humanitarian intervention unlawful, and that any use of force for purposes other than self-defence has to be authorized by the Security Council. The opposing counter-restrictionist viewpoint that humanitarian intervention is not a breach of Article 2 (4) can be heard in India's argument that its use of force was in conformity with the humanitarian purposes of the UN Charter.

The legal claim that India's intervention can be justified under Article 2 (4) is open to the reply that it fails to meet two of the key tests that counter-restrictionists propose for the legitimate use of force under Article 2 (4). Humanitarian intervention must not involve a regime change in the target state nor a loss of its territory. India's action fails on both counts, but, as I argue in the next chapter in relation to Vietnam's overthrow of Pol Pot, this legal stipulation ignores the political reality that ending crimes against humanity on the scale of the Bangladeshi and Cambodian cases requires such drastic actions. The counter-restrictionist test that India's intervention easily satisfies is that it quickly withdrew its forces and did not try to make Bangladesh a satellite state.

Counter-restrictionists also require that states contemplating humanitarian intervention should request a meeting of the Security Council to inform it that intervention will only take place if the Council does not act first. India requested that the Security Council meet to discuss the growing security threat on its border, but no action had been forthcoming. The Security Council became actively involved in the crisis only when war broke out, but the time for collective UN intervention would have been in the weeks after March, when the scale of the killing became apparent. However, at this time there was consensus in the Security Council that the massacres taking place

---

[74] Walzer, *Just and Unjust Wars*, 105, emphasis in original.

inside East Pakistan did not pose a threat to international security and were a matter of Pakistan's internal affairs. India's intervention in East Pakistan revealed the myopic character of this thinking, but it would have strengthened the moral credentials of its action had it informed the Security Council that it was planning to use force to stop Pakistan's human rights abuses because this posed a major threat to its security and was an outrage against common humanity.

I argued in the previous chapter that the absence of Security Council authorization does not disqualify an action as humanitarian provided it meets the threshold tests. But what of the pluralist argument voiced in the Security Council and General Assembly during the Bangladesh case that unilateral action of this kind sets a dangerous precedent? The solidarist reply is twofold: first, if the argument was that India's intervention in stopping the massacres in East Pakistan set a precedent for the use of force that other states might follow, I would argue that this was a good precedent if it led states to end future human rights violations that shocked the conscience of humanity. The ethical blindness of the pluralist criticism of India's action is that it focused on the moral consequences of a breach of the rules without considering how far these had protected Pakistan from UN action as it violated human rights with impunity after March 1971.

The second argument against the pluralist objection of precedent-setting is that it exaggerates how far a new precedent had been set. India did not justify its use of force in terms of the self-defence rule in Article 51 of the Charter, but its argument of 'refugee aggression' came close to invoking this defence, which is the legitimate right of all states. India had tried to interest the Security Council in the growing security threat on its borders, and, when this had failed to elicit an effective international response, it had unilaterally acted to protect its vital interests. As the Soviet Ambassador put it in the Security Council debate on 4 December, 'not one of the 15 members of the Security Council . . . would want his Government and his people suddenly to find on its own territory within such a short space of time such a huge number of refugees, forced to flee from their own country to the territory of a neighbouring state'.[75] For other members of international society legitimately to invoke the Bangladeshi case as a precedent, they would have to make the case that they faced an equally severe threat to their security as a consequence of the influx of large numbers of refugees. The fact that India was heavily censured for its use of force also weakens any claim that it set a precedent that others might invoke to justify the use of force.

A full-blown solidarist defence of its use of force on the grounds of both security and humanity would not have saved India from moral censure and US economic sanctions, given the cold-war context and the grip of a pluralist

---

[75] SCOR, 1606th Meeting, 4 Dec. 1971, 4.

mindset on state leaders and diplomats. However, it would have forced the society of states publicly to debate the legitimacy and legality of the doctrine of unilateral humanitarian intervention. This conversation was beginning to take place among international lawyers, and the Bangladeshi case served as a catalyst for further work in this area, but it was not present in the diplomatic dialogue that surrounded India's intervention. In raising human rights claims to justify its use of force, India challenged the dominant rules of international society, but this solidarist argument failed to change the shared meanings that constituted the practices of a pluralist international society. In establishing the boundaries of permissible action, the pluralist discourse excluded a human rights justification for the use of force, because this was viewed as being fundamentally opposed to the maintenance of international order.

The solidarist counter to this pluralist privileging of order over justice is to argue that human rights can be defended without this undermining order, and that satisfying the demand for justice is necessary to the provision of order. Both these propositions find support in an open letter written by Mrs Ghandi to President Nixon immediately after the war. She wrote: 'The fact of the matter is that the rulers of West Pakistan got away with the impression that they could do what they liked because no one, not even the United States, would choose to take a public position that while Pakistan's integrity was certainly sacrosanct, human rights, liberty were no less so and that there was a necessary interconnection between the inviolability of states and the contentment of their people.'[76] It is easy to read into this letter the claim that Pakistan had forfeited its right to protection of the rules of sovereignty and non-intervention because of its failure to live up to minimum standards of humanity within its borders. This solidarist argument failed to find any favour in the international response to India's intervention in East Pakistan. The task of the next two chapters is to investigate how far the society of states became more open to solidarist themes during the course of the 1970s.

[76] Text of Prime Minster Gandhi's Letter to President Nixon, quoted in *New York Times*, 17 Dec. 1971.

3

Vietnam's Intervention in Cambodia: The Triumph of Realism over Common Humanity?

Vietnam's overthrow of the Pol Pot regime in early 1979 is another case where the society of states should have legitimated an intervention on humanitarian grounds. The new Vietnamese installed government claimed that the Khmer Rouge were responsible for three million deaths out of a population of six to seven million. However, most independent observers accept Amnesty International's estimate that between one and two million died, mostly through malnutrition and disease as they worked in forced labour camps. Amnesty put the number of political killings at 200,000 in 1975–7 and a further 100,000 in 1978.[1] Despite the Khmer Rouge's attempt to seal Cambodia off from the outside world, reports of the 'killing fields' began to filter out through 1978. In response to this, there was pressure from a number of states for the Government of Democratic Kampuchea (DK) to be invest-igated by the UN's Human Rights Committee. Before this body could report, Vietnam took the law into its own hands and forcibly removed Pol Pot. Eight months earlier US President Jimmy Carter had named the DK as the 'worst violator of human rights in the world',[2] but Washington joined the chorus of condemnation that greeted Vietnam's use of force. Instead of breathing a huge sigh of relief at the ending of such a murderous regime, Vietnam was heavily sanctioned by international society (with the exception of the Soviet Union and its communist allies) for breaking the rules of sovereignty, non-intervention, and non-use of force.

This chapter traces the background context that led Vietnam to resort to force. What role, if any, did humanitarian considerations play in the decision to intervene? Next, I examine Vietnam's public justifications for its action. Faced with the charge of aggression, Vietnam replied that it had used force only in self-defence and that this was restricted to the border areas where it had been

---

[1] Quoted in G. Evans and K. Rowley, *Red Brotherhood at War: Vietnam, Cambodia and Laos since 1975*, 2nd edn. (London: Verso, 1990), 99. See also 'Amnesty International, *Political Imprisonment and Torture* (London: Amnesty International, 1986), 16–17.

[2] Quoted in Ronzitti, *Rescuing Nationals Abroad*, 190.

attacked by the Khmer Rouge. Although some analysts have sought to justify Vietnam's overthrow of the Pol Pot regime as an act of self-defence, Vietnam did not try to make this case. Instead, it maintained that Pol Pot had been removed from power by an internal uprising of the Cambodian people. This claim was easily exposed as a fabrication, given the presence of over 100,000 Vietnamese soldiers inside Cambodia, and it was totally rejected by thirteen members of the UN Security Council. Vietnam could have tried to justify its use of force on humanitarian grounds, but, even when confronted with a barrage of criticisms in the Security Council, it did not employ this line of reasoning.

The fact that Vietnam did not appeal to a legal right of unilateral humanitarian intervention did not prevent international society from legitimating its action on these grounds. Many states in the Security Council and General Assembly recognized the terrible suffering of the Khmer people under Pol Pot, but they also affirmed the principle that human rights violations could not justify the unilateral use of force. This pluralist argument echoed the position taken by the majority of the Security Council and General Assembly in response to India's action, but the sanctioning was different in the two cases. Although the US initially imposed a range of economic sanctions against India, within a matter of months it had joined the rest of the world in recognizing the new state of Bangladesh. Compare this with the decision of the General Assembly to deny recognition to the new government in Phnom Penh and to accredit Cambodia's UN seat to an anti-Vietnamese guerrilla movement dominated by the ousted Pol Pot. In examining the reasons behind this hostile international response to Vietnam's action, I consider how far the discourse of pluralism in the Security Council and General Assembly masked the play of power politics. The final part of the chapter critiques state practice, especially the policies of Western states, by arguing that Vietnam's use of force meets the minimum requirements of a legitimate humanitarian intervention and that it should have been welcomed rather than condemned.

The Background to Intervention

The Vietnamese and Khmer peoples have a long history of enmity and conflict stretching back centuries, and in this respect the war between Cambodia and Vietnam in 1978–9 can be seen as another chapter in this long story. Immediately after the Khmer Rouge came to power in 1975 there were reports of border clashes with Vietnam. Pol Pot visited Hanoi in mid-1975 to resolve these disputes and this led to the setting-up of local cross-border committees that would meet to settle any problems.[3] This was followed by a high-level meeting in June 1976 to work out a treaty on the disputed land and

---

[3] Evans and Rowley, *Red Brotherhood*, 82.

maritime borders. But this broke down when the Cambodians walked out.[4] As Evans and Rowley argue, the Khmer Rouge's approach to the border issue differed radically from Vietnam's. The latter adopted the norm of post-colonial international society that borders inherited at the time of independence can be changed only through mutual consent. This is the legal principle of *uti posseditis*, which denotes territoriality and not ethno-nationality as the defining criteria of statehood.[5] In keeping with its revolutionary fanaticism to turn the clock back to 'year zero' at home, the Khmer Rouge believed that the Mekong Delta and the area around Saigon were 'lost territories'[6] that the Vietnamese had taken by force against the old Khmer Empire. Consequently, they expected to be compensated for these losses.[7] If Vietnam had accepted this argument, it would have allowed the Pol Pot Government to make similar claims against Thailand, Laos, and Burma. Moreover, it would have set a dangerous precedent, since all post-colonial states can make claims of this sort, and it is fear of the consequences of such territorial revisionism that underpins the rules of sovereignty, non-intervention, and non-use of force.

Despite the fact that Vietnam and the DK held radically different views on how to settle their border disputes, the second half of 1976 witnessed few serious border incidents, and those that occurred were dealt with by the border committees. Yet by early 1977 the situation had deteriorated, with the Khmer Rouge destroying Vietnemese villages along the disputed border and massacring civilians. During 1975–7, Pol Pot had fought off domestic challenges to his leadership and his emergence as the undisputed leader of the Khmer Rouge led him to apply his method of 'resolving contradictions' to Cambodia's foreign relations.[8] According to Nayan Chanda, the Khmer Rouge manipulated the traditional fears of the Khmer people by claiming that Vietnam had a plan to conquer Kampuchea and that this could be met only by the annihilation of the Vietnamese.[9] This is supported by Gary Klintworth, who claims that 'Vietnamese civilians seemed to have been the main victims' of the Khmer Rouge's attacks.[10] The Khmer Rouge used the

---

[4] Elizabeth Becker argues that Vietnam made it very difficult for the Cambodians to do anything else by presenting the Khmer Rouge with 'a difficult series of foreign confrontations'. See E. Becker, *When the War was Over: The Voices of Cambodia's Revolution and its People* (New York: Simon & Schuster, 1986), 207. Evans and Rowley challenge Becker's argument, considering that it was the 'trigger-happy approach of the Khmer Rouge' that was responsible for the breakdown of negotiations. See Evans and Rowley, *Red Brotherhood*, 81.

[5] An excellent exegesis of this position is provided in Jackson, *Quasi-States*, 40–7.

[6] Evans and Rowley, *Red Brotherhood*, 84.

[7] Ibid. Evans and Rowley quote Stephen Heder, who argues that: 'The Cambodians approached the question as the sole aggrieved party, and expected a certain recompense for their historical losses and their willingness to cease contesting them. They offered not negotiations in the regular sense, but unilateral resolutions of outstanding problems' (S. R. Heder, 'The Kampuchean–Vietnamese Conflict', in D. W. P. Elliot (ed.), *The Third Indochina Conflict* (Boulder, Colo.: Westview, 1981), 25).

[8] Evans and Rowley, *Red Brotherhood*, 104.

[9] N. Chanda, *Brother Enemy: The War after the War* (New York: Collier, 1986).

[10] Klintworth, *Vietnam's Intervention in International Law*, 20.

same barbarous methods in their killing of the Vietnamese that they employed against opponents at home. Khieu Samphan, a leading member of the Khmer Rouge, told Prince Sihanouk in 1978 that it was a deliberate policy to foster hatred of the Vietnamese, since this would encourage the Cambodian people to forget about their own hardships and work even harder: 'the Khmer people', Samphan said, 'would undergo every sacrifice as soon as the flag of Vietnamophobia is waved in front of them'.[11] Prince Sihanouk later claimed that the Pol Pot regime had needlessly provoked Vietnam in its quest for national unity at home. The Khmer Rouge was motivated by 'supernationalism and their visceral nostalgia for "Kampuchea Krom" [the Khmer name for the "lost territories" of the Mekong Delta and the area around Saigon]'.[12]

An alternative reading of the Khmer Rouge's use of force against Vietnam is supplied by Stephen Heder. He maintains that it was part of a negotiating strategy designed to induce greater flexibility on the part of Hanoi by showing that Cambodia could hurt Vietnam militarily.[13] Even if this was the intention, the attempt to use force to back up its claim to a 'greater Cambodia' was perceived by Vietnam as a declaration of hostilities. Nevertheless, the Vietnamese decided to respond defensively in the hope that restraint might produce a negotiated settlement. The DK rejected Vietnam's continuing diplomatic overtures, and when on 24 September 1977 Khmer Rouge forces killed hundreds of civilians in an attack on Tay Ninh province, Vietnam decided to respond militarily.[14]

In October armoured columns moved up to twenty-five kilometres into Cambodia and then pulled back. This show of resolve did not deter further Cambodian attacks and in December the Vietnamese launched an attack with 50,000 troops and then withdrew. Fearful that China's backing for the Khmer Rouge might produce a war on two fronts, Vietnam continued to try the path of dialogue. Foreign Minister Nguyen Co Thach proposed on 5 February 1978 an end to all hostilities, withdrawal of all forces to five kilometres from the border, international inspection of the frontier, and a treaty based on respect for territorial integrity within existing borders.[15] Pol Pot went on Phnom Penh radio to reject this proposal and repeat his government's 'demand [for] the revision of border documents and changes in the demarcation of land and sea borders' and 'resettlement of the "Kampuchea Krom" issue'.[16]

The Khmer Rouge's rejection of its latest proposal for negotiations convinced Vietnam that its long-term security required the removal of Pol Pot.[17] The Politburo met in February and decided actively to assist opposition

---

[11] Ibid.   [12] Quoted in ibid. 19.

[13] Heder, 'The Kampuchean–Vietnamese Conflict', 28.

[14] Evans and Rowley, Red Brotherhood, 106.   [15] Ibid.

[16] Quoted in ibid. 107.

[17] Vietnamese proposals for negotiations were restated in April and June 1978, and in March the Vietnamese had called for the Security Council to appoint a mission to mediate the border dispute.

forces inside Cambodia to overthrow the Khmer Rouge, with military force if necessary.[18] Direct military intervention was considered, but, since this risked war with China and would be perceived as aggressive by ASEAN, it was decided to pursue the alternative strategy of building up resistance inside Cambodia.[19]

This shift in policy was made public when Hanoi Radio began to condemn Pol Pot's domestic atrocities and issue calls for the Cambodian people to overthrow him.[20] This was the first time that Vietnam had spoken out against the human suffering inside Cambodia and it only occurred in the context of a deliberate campaign to turn the Khmer people against their leaders.[21] There were 160,000 Cambodian refugees in South Vietnam, and Hanoi sought to organize them into a guerrilla movement that could infiltrate Cambodia and support opposition groups in overthrowing the Khmer Rouge. By August there were reports of uprisings in the eastern part of Cambodia and it seemed that Vietnam might secure its objective of overthrowing Pol Pot without having to invade. A key aspect of this strategy was linking up the Vietnamese-based insurgent movement with the resistance movement in the east. Before this could happen Pol Pot struck decisively against the rebels and Evans and Rowley argue that this was a bitter blow for Vietnam since it 'ended the possibility of Pol Pot's overthrow by an internal upheaval'.[22]

Vietnam had wanted to avoid the costs and risks of direct military intervention by relying on an internal uprising. However, it had decided by late 1978 to throw the might of the Vietnamese army against the Khmer Rouge, given the security imperative of removing Pol Pot. Elizabeth Becker suggests that the motive was to realize Hanoi's longstanding ambition of controlling the Mekong Valley.[23] Other states were quick to impute such expansionist motives to Vietnam, but, if the intention was to create a 'greater Vietnam', why did it try so hard to achieve an agreement with the DK in 1977–8? A better explanation is that policy-makers sought to address their security concerns through cooperation, and it was only when this was unreciprocated that they opted for unilateral measures. Michael Leifer stresses the security motivations, arguing that intervention 'was a matter of strategic imperative

According to Klintworth, the UN Secretary General, Kurt Waldheim, 'reportedly told the Vietnamese Chargé d'Affaires at the United Nations, Phan Duong, that it would be difficult to reach a consensus in the Security Council, by which Vietnam understood that China would be opposed and could use its veto power in the Security Council'. Sino-Vietnamese relations had deteriorated to the point of armed clashes on the border by early 1978. Two principal factors explain this: first, China was suspicious about growing links between the Soviet Union and Vietnam, and, secondly, it did not like the impact of Vietnam's economic policies on the overseas Chinese in Vietnam. See Klintworth, *Vietnam's Intervention in International Law*, 22.

[18] Evans and Rowley, *Red Brotherhood*, 107–8.

[19] N. Chanda, 'A Dry Season Infiltration', *Far Eastern Economic Review*, 3 Nov. 1978.

[20] Evans and Rowley, *Red Brotherhood*, 108, and 'Hanoi Wages War by Radio', *Observer*, 16 Apr. 1978.   [21] Ibid.   [22] Evans and Rowley, *Red Brotherhood*, 108.

[23] Becker, *When the War was Over*, 336. Quoted in Evans and Rowley, *Red Brotherhood*, 107. Evans and Rowley point out that Becker does not supply any evidence to back up her claim.

rooted in geopolitical doctrine [which] contemplated Indochina as a natural entity in strategic terms which had to be maintained'. He compares this to a version of the Brezhnev Doctrine, where Vietnam has 'a licence to intervene' in the states of Cambodia and Laos if outside powers use them to threaten its security.[24] The outside power that most worried Vietnam was China, which through 1978 developed an increasingly close relationship with the DK. A major constraint on attacking Cambodia was the fear of China's reaction, but the Vietnamese Politburo had concluded by November 1978 that the growing threat from China could be contained only if Vietnam struck decisively in the South first. The immediate danger was the nineteen Khmer Rouge divisions massing on the border, and intervention was aimed at neutralizing this threat so that Vietnam would be able to deal with any future Chinese threat from the North. Klintworth captures well the security interests that motivated the decision to use force:

Vietnam faced a dilemma. Its northern border with China was becoming insecure while attempts at negotiating a peaceful solution with Cambodia in the south had failed . . . Vietnam's situation in 1977 and 1978 was precarious . . . The Khmer Rouge attacks and the growing pressure from China on the Sino-Vietnamese border were seen in Hanoi as a Chinese pincer strategy aimed at threatening Vietnam on two fronts . . . In Vietnam's view, its invasion and occupation of Kampuchea was unavoidable.[25]

In deciding to remove the security threat posed by the Khmer Rouge and its backers in Beijing, Vietnam sought a measure of insurance in the form of a treaty of friendship with the Soviet Union that was signed in November. The other concern that worried Vietnam was the reaction of ASEAN states if it used force to remove Pol Pot. The Vietnamese Premier, Pham Van Dong, made a tour of ASEAN capitals in late 1978 offering treaties of friendship and assurances that Vietnam did not pose a threat to the region.[26]

There is some evidence that Vietnam's initial war aim was not to drive for Phnom Penh but to control Cambodia east of the Mekong. Limited action of this kind would surely not have received the regional and international condemnation that met Vietnam's installation of a puppet government in the Cambodian capital. Nayan Chanda cites interviews conducted by Heder in 1981 with members of the new Cambodian Government to support the claim that the seizure of Phnom Penh was an act of 'strategic opportunism'.[27] Chea Soth, a Politburo member of the Kampuchean People's Revolutionary Party, claimed that: 'We were just thinking in terms of taking over half the country,

---

[24] M. Leifer, 'Vietnam's Intervention in Kampuchea; The Rights of State v. the Rights of People', in I. Forbes and M. Hoffman (eds.), *Political Theory, International Relations, and the Ethics of Intervention* (London: St Martin's Press for Macmillan, 1993), 146. In private correspondence with the author, Michael Leifer confirmed that it was made clear to him in interviews in Hanoi in 1984 that 'the invasion was required as a matter of strategic necessity' (letter to the author, 9 Oct. 1998).

[25] Klintworth, *Vietnam's Intervention in International Law*, 22–7.

[26] Evans and Rowley, *Red Brotherhood*, 109.   [27] Chanda, *Brother Enemy*, 345.

the half on one side of the Mekong, and leaving the rest to Pol Pot.'[28] On Christmas Day 1978, Vietnam launched twelve divisions (around 100,000 soldiers) against Pol Pot's forces. After a few days of heavy fighting, the forces of the Khmer Rouge collapsed, tempting 'Hanoi to go for broke'.[29] A member of the Central Committee told Heder, 'when we attacked and pursued them and saw how easy it was, we just kept going'.[30]

On 3 January, Hanoi Radio admitted that fighting was under way in Cambodia, the action being credited to the recently formed Cambodian Front for National Salvation (National Salvation Front).[31] This was to be Vietnam's key defence in the ensuing debates in the Security Council. The National Salvation Front had been inaugurated to the world by the Vietnamese at the beginning of December with Hanoi Radio claiming on 5 December that the Front had been established two days previously in a 'liberated zone' in eastern Cambodia and was committed to the overthrow of the Khmer Rouge.[32] Pol Pot's attack against the resistance forces in the east had put an end to Vietnam's hope that the Khmer Rouge could be removed through an internal uprising, and the declaration of the National Salvation Front was an attempt to lay the ground for the claim that Vietnam had played no part in the toppling of the Pol Pot regime.

Although Pol Pot was still broadcasting news of mythical victories on 5 January, two days later he fled the city, as Vietnamese forces entered unopposed. The new government declared itself as the People's Republic of Kampuchea (PRK) and was led by Heng Samrin (who had been Deputy Commander of the eastern resistance forces) and was made up of other members of the National Salvation Front (including that great survivor of Cambodian politics, Hun Sen, who became Foreign Minister). Having lost on the battlefield, Pol Pot tried to gain international support for Cambodia's position. Foreign Minister Ieng Sary demanded that the UN Security Council convene an emergency meeting to condemn Vietnam. This was opposed by the Soviet Union and Czechoslovakia, which supported the argument of Vietnam and the new Cambodian Government that the Security Council could not respond to a request from a government that had ceased to exist, since this represented interference in the new government's internal affairs. This was a procedural issue (and hence the veto could not be used) and the Soviet Union was outvoted by the other members of the Council. Nine days after the original request, the Security Council met on 11 January.

---

[28] Quoted in ibid. 345–6.   [29] Evans and Rowley, *Red Brotherhood*, 110.

[30] Quoted in Chanda, *Brother Enemy*, 346.

[31] 'Vietnam Invades Cambodia', *Daily Telegraph*, 3 Jan. 1979.

[32] 'Hanoi Steps up Support for Khmer Insurgents', *Financial Times*, 5 Dec. 1978.

Vietnam's Justifications for its Use of Force

The Vietnamese Ambassador, Mr Ha Van Lau, repeated his government's earlier claim that Pol Pot had been overthrown by the National Salvation Front. He admitted that Vietnam's forces had engaged Khmer Rouge forces but defended this on grounds of self-defence. He argued that there were 'two wars' taking place, 'one, the border war started by the Pol Pot–Ieng Sary clique against Viet Nam . . . the other, the revolutionary war of the Kampuchean people'.[33] It was the latter that had made possible the fall of the Pol Pot government; Vietnam's use of force had been restricted to the exercise of the 'sacred right of self-defence of peoples in the face of aggression'.[34] Despite the presence of over 100,000 Vietnamese soldiers in Cambodia, Ha Van Lau tried to persuade the Council that the overthrow of the DK had been achieved by the guerrilla forces of the National Salvation Front and an uprising of the Cambodian people.

Given that the two-wars argument was easily exposed as a sham, why did Vietnam invoke it? One explanation is that Vietnam knew that it had broken the rules of the game but recognized that it owed its peers a justification in terms of the accepted rules. It may be recalled that this is Bull's defining mark for the existence of a society of states, and the significance of this is the claim that the rules cannot be endlessly stretched to provide a pretext for any action. Actors hope that their justifications will be persuasive and that this will reduce any risk of sanctioning. But, if justifications lack plausibility, actors will be robbed of legitimacy as they find themselves confronted with a discrepancy between their rhetoric and their actions. As I show below, the ridicule that greeted Vietnam's two-wars argument illustrates the costs of treating the rules as 'infinitely malleable'.[35]

By taking the fateful decision to drive its tanks to Phnom Penh, Vietnam confronted the unexpected problem of how to justify the removal of a neighbouring government. Realists might argue that Vietnam's decision to place the toppling of Pol Pot prior to concerns about international legitimacy demonstrates the weakness of the claim that actions are constrained if they cannot be legitimated. I argued in the previous chapter that India's use of force became possible only because it could be legitimated, but this case appears to demonstrate the opposite. The problem of legitimation was a constraining factor in the decision to rule out military intervention in early 1979, but this was overridden as Vietnam confronted a deteriorating security environment. Certainly, there is evidence that Vietnam believed that the world would quickly forget its invasion of Cambodia. Singapore's then Foreign Minister, Kishore Mahbubani, revealed in an article in *Foreign Affairs*

[33] SCOR, 2108th Meeting, 11 Jan. 1979, 12.   [34] Ibid. 13.
[35] Bull, *The Anarchical Society*, 45

in the early 1980s that Vietnam's Ambassador at the UN had informed him in January 1979 that in 'two weeks, the world will have forgotten the Kampuchea problem'.[36] This assumption proved to be a major miscalculation, with Vietnam paying a heavy political and economic price for its decision to act: it was named as an international pariah; its puppet government in Phnom Penh was denied a seat at the UN; and its action had the effect of uniting China, ASEAN, and the West in a common front against it. Vietnam's justification was easily exposed as bogus and, as I show below, Western states exploited this to the full in legitimating their imposition of political and economic sanctions against Hanoi.

According to Klintworth, Vietnam could have mitigated the extent of international condemnation had it argued a better case. He contends that the intervention should have been defended on grounds of both self-defence and humanitarian intervention. He goes much further than Vietnam was prepared to and argues that the overthrow of Pol Pot 'was a reasonable act of self-defence'.[37] The series of attacks launched against Vietnam by the Khmer Rouge in 1977–8 constituted, according to Klintworth, an 'armed attack' that legitimated a response under Article 51 of the UN Charter. According to Vietnamese Government figures, 30,000 soldiers were killed in 1977–8; twenty-five townships and ninety-six villages destroyed; 250,000 people rendered homeless and large areas of farmland abandoned.[38] The claim of self-defence is implicitly supported by Evans and Rowley, who point out that 'no government can tolerate such destruction for long without striking back'.[39] As discussed in the previous chapter, customary international law requires that an act of self-defence must meet the requirements of both necessity and proportionality. Thus, the fact that Vietnam repeatedly tried to reach a peaceful solution with the DK, only resorting to military action after the failure of negotiations, is pointed to as evidence that the action met the legal requirement of necessity.[40]

As with Pakistan's attack against India in December 1971, the DK's use of force against Vietnam certainly justified a military response under Article 51. However, was overthrowing the government of another state a proportionate response to the initial attack? If Vietnam had stuck to what seems to have been the original invasion plan of creating a security buffer east of the

---

[36] I am grateful to Michael Leifer for bringing this to my attention. See K. Mahbubani, 'The Kampuchean Problem: A Southeast Asian Perspective', *Foreign Affairs*, 62/2 (1983–4), 408.

[37] Klintworth, *Vietnam's Intervention in International Law*, 28.

[38] Ibid. See also Evans and Rowley, *Red Brotherhood*, 107.   [39] Ibid.

[40] The *Caroline* case establishes that the danger must be 'instant, overwhelming, leaving no choice of means and no moment for deliberation'. As Klintworth notes, Vietnam had been deliberating the option of armed intervention for months, and its generals had prepared contingency plans for an invasion. Although this does not strictly meet the requirements of self-defence set out in the *Caroline* case, he contends that it 'is too much to expect a state facing the threat of a major attack, or a series of border incursions, to be prepared to respond immediately' (Klintworth, *Vietnam's Intervention in International Law*, 25).

Mekong, then it could have defended this action as one of self-defence. It can only be speculated how persuasive this justification would have been in the Security Council, but it is likely that a limited counter-attack of this kind would have elicited a very different response to an action that toppled a neighbouring government. Consequently, the two-wars justification looks like a hasty attempt to deny responsibility for the forcible overthrow of Pol Pot in a context in which the Vietnamese Government believed it had exhausted the boundaries of legitimate self-defence.

This interpretation is not shared by Klintworth, who argues that Vietnam's forcible change of government meets the requirement of proportionality. He cites Oscar Schachter's argument that a state might be forced in self-defence to counter-attack against 'the source of the attack, on a scale that would deter future attacks'.[41] According to Klintworth, Vietnam's forcible ejection of the existing government was proportionate, because the continuing threat to Vietnam was the 'Pol Pot regime based in Phnom Penh [and] Military and political logic demanded its overthrow and replacement by a government less committed to war with Vietnam'.[42] The claim of proportionately depends upon showing that this response was essential to Vietnam's continued existence and Klintworth claims that Vietnam drew a comparison between its use of force and the Allied invasions and occupations of Germany and Japan in 1945.[43] This analogy between Allied actions in the Second World War and Vietnam's use of force is open to the rebuttal that Vietnam's survival did not depend upon the removal of Pol Pot. Nevertheless, since the two-wars argument was ridiculed in the Security Council, Vietnam clearly missed an opportunity in not invoking this argument to justify its use of force.

[41] Schachter argues that Article 51 leaves unimpaired the right of self-defence that existed prior to the UN Charter. He follows Ian Brownlie, who argues that it is not 'unreasonable to allow a state to retaliate beyond the immediate area of attack when that state has sufficient reason to expect a continuation of attacks from the same source'. Nevertheless, following the precedent set by the *Caroline* case, Schachter argues that the imminence of attack must be so clear that defensive action is a prerequisite for self-preservation. He is explicit that his position on Article 51 does not legitimate pre-emptive strikes or anticipatory attacks in response to 'perceived attacks' and criticizes Israel's reliance on this argument to justify its strike against Iraq's Osirak nuclear reactor in 1981. Schachter's view is discussed in Klintworth, *Vietnam's Intervention*, 16, 27. For Schachter's original argument, see Oscar Schachter, *A United Nations Legal Order* (Cambridge: Cambridge University Press, 1995).

[42] Klintworth, *Vietnam's Intervention in International Law*, 27.

[43] Klintworth argues that the Allied interventions were justified 'as necessary . . . to eradicate fascism, to restructure the political and legal processes in those countries and thereby to make it safe for neighbors of Germany and Japan as well as for the world'. Unfortunately, the only evidence that he cites to support his claim that Vietnam advanced the precedent of the Allied actions is the statement of a member of the PRK. However, there is no evidence in any of the official statements by the Vietnamese Government before the Security Council or General Assembly to buttress Klintworth's assertion. See Klintworth, *Vietnam's Intervention in International Law*, 27. Klintworth's view that Vietnam's action met the requirement of proportionately is also supported by Evans and Rowley, who argue that Vietnam had 'reasonable grounds' for judging that the Pol Pot government 'constituted a grave threat to it . . . [which] justified . . . eliminating the threat by invading and occupying Cambodia—just as the Allies were justified in invading and occupying Germany and Japan in 1945, (Evans and Rowley, *Red Brotherhood*, 190).

Stretching Article 51 to justify the overthrow of a neighbouring govern- ment is unlikely to prove convincing in a society of states dominated by a pluralist interpretation of the UN Charter. However, what if this self-defence argument is buttressed by the claim that the use of force is also justified on humanitarian grounds? Given the failure of the UN to stop the grotesque violations of human rights taking place inside Cambodia, did Vietnam have a legal right unilaterally to use force to end the violations? This was the argu- ment made by the International Commission of Jurists, East Pakistan Staff Study in relation to India's intervention in East Pakistan, and it might be extended to Vietnam. India raised humanitarian claims in 1971 but it did not explicitly invoke the doctrine of humanitarian intervention. By contrast, Leifer argues that Vietnam justified intervention in terms of the 'need to remove a genocidal regime'.[44] It will be recalled that for Leifer the primary motive behind Vietnam's intervention was strategic, and he is, therefore, identifying a gap between justification and motivation—the significance of this being his claim that the language of manœuvre was an 'appeal to the humanitarian norms of the international community'.[45] In the face of the worst human rights violations since the Nazis, Vietnam espoused a specious humanitarian justification for its use of force because it hoped that this would attenuate any criticism that it had violated Article 2 (4) of the UN Charter.

This analysis of Vietnam's justification would make its manipulation of humanitarianism a clear-cut case of abuse. But the problem with Leifer's argu- ment is that, in contrast to India, Vietnam at no point advanced humanitar- ian claims to justify its use of force.[46] Indeed, if anything, the evidence points in the opposite direction, with Vietnam repudiating human rights as a legit- imate basis for the resort to force. For example, the Vietnamese Foreign Minister, Nguyen Co Thach, stated that Vietnam was primarily concerned with its security and that human rights were the concern of the Cambodian people.[47] The closest Vietnam came to appealing to 'humanitarian norms' was in its description of the 'inhuman policies' of the 'monstrous regime of Pol Pot–Ieng Sary' that had led to the 'revolutionary war of the Kampuchean

---

[44] Leifer, 'Vietnam's Intervention in Kampuchea', 145.   [45] Ibid. 148.

[46] Leifer advances no evidence to support his claim that Vietnam invoked a humanitarian justi- fication, but he does point to the Treaty of Friendship signed between Vietnam and the PRK on 18 February 1979. This treaty legitimated the Vietnamese troop presence in Cambodia, and in his state- ment the Vietnamese Premier welcomed the Kampuchean people's victory over the Khmer Rouge, which has 'eliminated for good the genocide and slavery imposed by this clique' (quoted in Leifer, 'Vietnam's Intervention in Kampuchea', 146–7). However, it is hard to read this statement as supporting Leifer's argument that Vietnam justified its use of force on humanitarian grounds. In correspondence with the author, Leifer has modified his claim somewhat. He writes: 'I would revise my statement to suggest that although the Vietnamese adhered to the national salvation front thesis plus their rights under treaty, there was an ambiguity in their apologetics exemplified in the strong emphasis on the fact that they had been confronted with a genocidal regime and a recurrent denial of the legitimacy of "the Pol Pot clique of genocidal criminals" ' (letter to the author, 9 Oct. 1998).

[47] Quoted in Klintworth, *Vietnam's Intervention in International Law*, 70.

people'.[48] Human rights violations in Cambodia elicited Vietnam's condemnation only when it became politically convenient[49] and the Vietnamese Ambassador was trying to exploit the widespread revulsion against Pol Pot to lend credibility to the two-wars justification.[50] He emphasized the terrible suffering of the Khmer people in an effort to persuade the Council that the fall of Pol Pot had been caused by a 'mass uprising'[51] and stressed the improved human rights situation and security benefits for the region that had arisen from the change of government in Phnom Penh. Ha Van Lau stated:

Within Kampuchea, all the inhuman policies of the Pol Pot–Ieng Sary regime will be abolished and replaced by a democratic regime . . . A new era is now dawning in Indo-China and in South-East Asia . . . a serious threat to the peace and stability of the area, has been abolished. The victorious United Front for the National Salvation of Kampuchea has formed its new government and has advocated building a truly independent and free Kampuchea . . . That is a new factor which should benefit peace and stability in South-East Asia.[52]

Three possible explanations might be adduced for Vietnam's refusal to justify its action under the doctrine of humanitarian intervention. First, Vietnam might simply have accepted the legitimacy of the rules of sovereignty, non-intervention, and non-use of force. Certainly, the two-wars justification suggests a strong desire to legitimate its action in terms of the accepted rules. Secondly, Vietnam might have reasoned that a plea of humanitarian intervention would lack credibility, given that it had been silent on the question of human rights violations during the first four years of the Pol Pot regime. Finally, it is possible that the Politburo in Hanoi feared setting a precedent for humanitarian intervention that might be used by other states to attack Vietnam or its friends in the future. Consequently, any construction of Vietnam's intervention as a humanitarian one depended upon wider international society giving this meaning to it.

The International Reaction

The hostile response that greeted Vietnam's intervention emanated from three groups of actors: the USA and its allies, who interpreted Vietnam's action as a move in the game of cold-war power politics; ASEAN, which feared that Vietnam's use of force against Cambodia heralded the beginning of a Vietnamese drive for regional hegemony; and the neutral and non-aligned

---

[48] SCOR, 2108th Meeting, 11 Jan. 1979, 12–13.
[49] Leifer, 'Vietnam's Intervention in Kampuchea', 146.
[50] I owe this point to Michael Leifer.
[51] SCOR, 2108th Meeting, 11 January 1979, 12.   [52] Ibid. 13–14.

states, which worried that Vietnam's action eroded the rule of law in international relations. The first arena for moral censure of Vietnam was the Security Council. As in the Bangladeshi case, this was paralysed by cold-war politics, and the issue was eventually placed before the General Assembly at the prompting of ASEAN. Here, debate focused on two issues: first, should Cambodia's UN seat be accredited to the new government in Phnom Penh or be given to the deposed Pol Pot government, which was fighting to regain power? Secondly, what was to be done about the presence of Vietnamese troops in Cambodia, which was perceived by some ASEAN states as a vital threat to their security?

The two-wars justification was totally rejected by the representative of the DK invited to speak before the Security Council. Prince Sihanouk claimed that Vietnam's action was a clear-cut case of aggression and annexation that represented a fundamental threat to regional security. He argued that the National Salvation Front was a 'pitiful smoke-screen designed to hide from the outside world the criminal and repugnant anti-Kampuchean undertaking of the Socialist Republic of Viet Nam'.[53] This position was strongly supported by the Chinese representative, Chen Chu, who argued that the two-wars defence was 'foolish lies', since 'how can a puppet organization that was brought into being only a few weeks ago possess a dozen or so divisions of regular troops and launch attacks on all parts of Kampuchea . . . This is a great mockery of and an insult to the United Nations and its Member States.'[54] China sponsored a resolution condemning Vietnam's 'aggression' and calling for the withdrawal of Vietnamese forces from Cambodia.

China's interest in opposing and reversing Vietnam's intervention reflected its fear that the Soviet Union would profit from this action. By the end of the 1970s China perceived the Soviet Union as intent on 'global hegemonism' and this explains its willingness to develop closer strategic links with the USA, which was equally concerned about the growth of Soviet power in South-East Asia. China's security fears about the consequences of Soviet Vietnamese collusion can be seen in the following statement by Chen Chu:

Viet Nam relies on Soviet support for realizing its ambitions of seeking hegemony in South-East Asia. The Soviet Union, on the other hand, regards Viet Nam as its 'strategic base' . . . in an attempt to control the sea lane from the west Pacific to the Indian Ocean and link up its strategic deployments in the two oceans so as to prepare for the seizure of oil resources and important strategic positions in west Asia and the Middle East.[55]

There is no mention in China's testimony of the human rights violations of the Pol Pot regime; instead, it emphasized the geopolitical imperative of containing the security threat posed by Vietnam and the Soviet Union to the region. There is no reason to suspect a gap between justifications and moti-

---

[53] SCOR, 2108th Meeting, 11 January 1979, 8.   [54] Ibid. 10.
[55] Ibid. 11.

vations here, since China's subsequent actions were in conformity with its virulent rhetoric against the Soviet Union and Vietnam. Only a few weeks after Vietnam's use of force against Cambodia, China punished Vietnam by launching an offensive against it.

If the voice of realism shaped China's deliberations, then the USA introduced pluralist considerations into the conversation. The US Ambassador, Andrew Young, argued that international society should have brought the full weight of its moral pressure to bear on a regime that violated its most basic humanitarian principles, stressing the view that the way a government treats its own citizens is a legitimate matter for international censure. However, he was equally adamant that a commitment to defend human rights could not justify breaching the rules of non-intervention, territorial integrity, and non-use of force.[56] The USA recognized that Vietnam had legitimate security anxieties relating to Cambodian attacks against its citizens in the border areas, but Young argued that 'border disputes do not grant one nation the right to impose a government on another by military force'.[57] In rejecting Vietnam's plea of the two-wars argument, the US Ambassador stated that the National Salvation Front ruled Cambodia only 'thanks to Vietnamese bayonets'.[58] The US position was that Vietnam should immediately withdraw its forces and respect the territorial integrity of the Cambodian state.

In expressing its moral revulsion at the atrocities committed by the Khmer Rouge, the USA overlooked the basic fact that its prescription for security in the region risked bringing the Khmer Rouge back to power. The Carter Administration had sought to elevate human rights in the hierarchy of foreign-policy principles, but, when it came to a choice between upholding the rule of law or permitting an exception in the name of rescuing the Cambodian people, an absolutist interpretation of the rules won out. Young asserted that international society could not permit Vietnam's violation of the rules 'to pass in silence', since this 'will only encourage Governments in other parts of the world to conclude that there are no norms, no standards, no restraints'.[59]

The Carter Administration's denunciation of a unilateral action that had the effect of removing a barbaric regime would be more understandable if there had existed a credible alternative of collective UN action against the Khmer Rouge. A few months before the Vietnamese intervention, Senator McGovern, speaking before the Subcommittee on East Asian and Pacific Affairs of the US Senate Committee on Foreign Relations, had called for the use of force to end human rights violations in Cambodia. Speaking later on the floor of the House, McGovern asked whether 'any thought is being given either by our Government or at the United Nations or anywhere in the international community of sending in a force to knock this Government out of power, just on humanitarian grounds'.[60]

---

[56] Ibid. 7.   [57] Ibid. 8.   [58] Ibid.
[59] Ibid.   [60] Quoted in Ronzitti, *Rescuing Nationals Abroad*, 98.

McGovern envisaged any such action taking place under the authority of Chapter VII of the UN Charter, which would have enabled China to veto any proposed action against its ally. In addition to its strategic interests in protecting Pol Pot, any attempt by Western states to press Chapter VII into service to justify humanitarian intervention would have been opposed by China and the non-aligned states on the Security Council, who were jealously protective of sovereign rights. To legitimate military enforcement action, the Security Council is required under Article 39 of the Chapter VII provisions of the Charter to make a finding of a threat to 'international peace and security'. But stretching this rule to cover the removal of tyrants like Pol Pot would have raised fears that this was weakening the non-intervention principle in Article 2 (7) of the Charter. Given these political and doctrinal constraints, it is not surprising that the Carter Administration took the view that McGovern's proposal was not a 'live option'.[61]

The normative rubicon that McGovern was not prepared to cross, however, was endorsing a unilateral use of force that ended human rights abuses. Consequently, he joined the administration in condemning Vietnam for taking the law into its own hands. The Carter Administration moved immediately to block Vietnam's participation in international economic institutions such as the International Monetary Fund (IMF) and World Bank and to prevent its puppet government in Phnom Penh from being welcomed into the club of states. Realists would argue that this response is explained by two factors: first, the US psyche remained traumatized by the Vietnam War, in which over 50,000 Americans had been killed; secondly, the collapse of superpower *détente* led the USA to view itself as locked into a global confrontation with a Soviet Union promoting its interest through the support of proxies. Vietnam provided the Soviet Navy with an important base at Can Ranh Bay and its use of force against Cambodia was interpreted in zero-sum terms as an advance of Soviet power in South-East Asia. The USA set about making common cause with China and ASEAN in reversing this Soviet gain, even if this meant supporting Pol Pot and his killers in the Khmer Rouge. These political and strategic reasons reinforced the US defence of pluralist norms, but the question is how far would the Carter Administration have argued this case if its interests had been defined differently? If the same legal principle had been at stake in relation to a US friend, would the Carter Administration have been such a staunch defender of the rules?

Britain and France shared Washington's strategic concerns and they were also conscious of supporting the position taken by ASEAN at a time when the EC was keen to develop closer economic and political links with this grouping. The EC, accompanied by Japan, immediately withdrew all economic aid to Vietnam. These reasons were not part of Britain and

---

[61] Quoted in Ronzitti, *Rescuing Nationals Abroad*, 98.

France's public justifications; instead, they argued that Vietnam's action was an intolerable breach of the rules. Whatever the record of Pol Pot's human rights abuses, this could not justify Vietnam's use of force. The British Ambassador, Ivor (now Lord) Richard, followed the USA, China, and ASEAN in calling for an immediate withdrawal of Vietnamese forces from Cambodia, arguing that, 'whatever is said about human rights in Kampuchea, it cannot excuse Viet Nam, whose own human rights record is deplorable, for violating the territorial integrity of Democratic Kampuchea'.[62] By pointing out that Vietnam was not a paragon of virtue at home, Ambassador Richard pre-empted any attempt by Vietnam's friends on the Council to play up the humanitarian aspects of its action. The same view was taken by France, which also had bitter memories of its intervention in the jungles of Indochina. What is noteworthy about the French Ambassador's statement in the Security Council is his explicit repudiation of any defence of Vietnam's action on humanitarian grounds. Ambassador Leprette stated:

The notion that because a régime is detestable foreign intervention is justified and forcible overthrow is *legitimate* is extremely dangerous. That could ultimately jeopardize the very maintenance of international law and order and make the continued existence of various régimes dependent on the judgement of their neighbours.[63]

Britain and France had clear security and economic reasons for playing the pluralist card against Vietnam. Again, this prompts the realist question as to whether these states would have taken such a strong line if their interests had pointed in a different direction? Constructivists would counter this focus on interests by claiming that what matters is how interests get defined, and that requires an analysis of how identities become constructed. Membership of the society of states carries with it obligations that lead governments to define their interests in terms of a general commitment to uphold the rules. Thus, it is often not a case of choosing between state interests and the rules of international society, since the latter constitutes the definition of the former. I am not arguing that specific cases do not arise when states decide to pursue short-term advantages at the expense of the rules, but this happens less frequently than realists would have us believe. Because actors worry about finding plausible justifications to legitimate their actions, they define their interests in terms of playing within the rules. This leaves room for argumentation over whether particular actions belong to the rules, but, as Vietnam discovered, there is a price to be paid for thinking that legitimating reasons can be stretched endlessly to cover any action.

Evidence for this socialization thesis might be seen in the uncompromising position taken by the smaller constitutional governments who spoke in

---

[62] SCOR, 2110th Meeting, 13 Jan. 1979, 6.
[63] SCOR, 2109th Meeting, 12 Jan. 1979, 4; emphasis added.

the Security Council debates over Vietnam's intervention in Cambodia. Norway, Portugal, Australia, and New Zealand are all strong defenders of human rights internationally, but they all rejected humanitarian justifications for Vietnam's action. The Norwegian Ambassador, for example, stressed that his government had expressed 'strong objections' to Pol Pot's violations, but the domestic abuses of the Khmer Rouge 'cannot—we repeat, cannot—justify the actions of Viet Nam over the last days and weeks'.[64] A similar position was taken by Portugal, which argued that Vietnam's action was a 'clear violation of the principle of non-intervention' that could not be justified despite the 'appalling record' of human rights violations inside Cambodia. The Portuguese Ambassador stated: 'there are no nor can there be any socio-political consider-ations that would justify the invasion of the territory of a sovereign State by the forces of another State.'[65] And Ambassador Francis speaking for New Zealand recognized that the DK had not followed 'the principles of the Charter either in its internal affairs or in its dealings with other states . . . But the misdeeds of one State do not, in our view, justify the invasion of its territory by another.'[66] Solidarism argues that governments should forfeit protection of the rules of sovereignty, non-intervention, and non-use of force if they massively violate human rights, and the Australian Ambassador addressed himself directly to this question. Pointing out that Australia had refused to enter into diplomatic relations with the Pol Pot regime because of its violations of human rights, he stated that Australia gave its 'full support to Democratic Kampuchea's right to independence, sovereignty and territorial integrity. Like other Governments, we cannot accept that the internal policies of any Government, no matter how *reprehensible*, can justify a military attack upon it by another Government.'[67] States that abuse human rights are exposed to international moral censure, but what is apparent from the position taken by these constitutional governments is that this was the limit of solidarism in international society at the end of the 1970s.

This doctrinal rejection of humanitarian intervention was reinforced by Singapore, which was the only member of ASEAN to address itself directly to this question in the Security Council.[68] Ambassador Koh asserted that, even if governments act as tyrants at home, there could be no exceptions to the rules of the society of states:

---

[64] SCOR, 2109th Meeting, 12 Jan. 1979, 2.

[65] SCOR, 2110th Meeting, 13 Jan. 1979, 3.

[66] Ibid. 6.

[67] SCOR, 2111th Meeting, 15 Jan. 1979, 3; emphasis added.

[68] Malaysia, Thailand, the Philippines, and Indonesia had requested an opportunity as non-members of the Council to participate in the debate and ASEAN sang from the same pluralist hymn sheet. Malaysia emphasized the inviolability of the principles in Article 2 of the UN Charter and argued that 'armed intervention by any country . . . irrespective of its military or political justifica-tion, cannot be condoned' (SCOR, 2110th Meeting, 12 Jan. 1979, 4). Similarly, the Philippines stated that it was 'against interference by any State in the domestic affairs of any other State, for that was the quintessence of the Charter and the basis of international law' (SCOR, 2111th Meeting, 15 Jan. 1979, 9).

It has been said by others that the Government of Democratic Kampuchea, led by Pol Pot, has treated its people in a barbarous fashion. Whether that accusation is true or false is not the issue before the Council. We hold the view that the Government of Democratic Kampuchea is accountable to the people of Democratic Kampuchea. No other country has a right to topple the Government of Democratic Kampuchea, however badly that Government may have treated its people. To hold to the contrary principle is to concede the right of a foreign Government to intervene and overthrow the Government of another country.[69]

In addition to this principled stand, Singapore stated that it was worried about Vietnam's action because it threatened Singapore's security as well as wider regional security. At a special meeting of Foreign Ministers held at Bangkok on 12 and 13 January, ASEAN had issued a statement deploring the Vietnamese intervention and calling for the withdrawal of its forces from Kampuchea. ASEAN felt betrayed by what it saw as Vietnam's contravention of the assurances that Pham Van Dong had given to the region during his tour of ASEAN capitals prior to the invasion. In condemning Vietnam's action, ASEAN did not mask its strategic reasons behind legal ones;[70] rather, governments invoked both sets of arguments in the Security Council.

Finally, we come to the position taken by the non-aligned on the Security Council. These states had no immediate security interests at stake and nor did they have a reputation for acting as guardians of human rights at home or abroad. Consequently, it is not surprising that their contribution was to stress that there could be no exceptions to the rules. The voice of solidarism was a silent one in the arguments made by Bolivia, Gabon, Kuwait, Zambia, Nigeria, and Bangladesh. Although these governments avoided directly condemning Vietnam, they did not provide any support for that beleaguered government. Instead, they stressed the sacrosanct nature of the non-intervention rule. For example, Bangladesh stated that its position was governed by its commitment to 'the cardinal principle that States shall refrain, in their international relations, from the threat or use of force against the territorial integrity or political independence of any State'.[71] The pluralist view espoused by Bangladesh illustrates how newly independent states quickly develop a feel for playing the game of international society, because Bangladesh's existence as a sovereign state had been made possible only because of a breach of the rules.[72] The only non-aligned state to raise the issue of human rights was Bolivia, which stated that

---

[69] SCOR, 2110th Meeting, 13 Jan. 1979, 5.

[70] This is the argument of Evans and Rowley, who claim that 'Vietnam's military intervention in Cambodia was condemned by ASEAN . . . for basically strategic reasons, but the grounds given officially were legal ones' (Evans and Rowley, *Red Brotherhood*, 187).

[71] SCOR, 2109th Meeting, 15 Jan., 1979, 6.

[72] Justin Morris comments that 'It is particularly interesting to note that Bangladesh adopted such a position [pluralism] when one considers the means by which it achieved independence' (J. Morris, 'The Concept of Humanitarian Intervention in International Relations' MA dissertation (Hull, 1991), 25).

its willingness to hear Prince Sihanouk's testimony in no way implied 'support for or solidarity with the acts of the regime of Pol Pot'; instead, Bolivia's position was based on 'full respect for the principle of non-intervention'.[73]

It will be recalled that China had introduced a draft resolution that explicitly condemned Vietnam as the aggressor. It decided not to press this to a vote because Kuwait introduced an alternative resolution sponsored by the non-aligned group on the Council. This resolution did not explicitly condemn Vietnam, but it called upon all foreign forces to withdraw from Cambodia, the primary demand expressed by all those opposing Vietnam's use of force. The vote was thirteen in favour with two against (Czechoslovakia and the Soviet Union), but, since the Soviet Union wielded the veto, the resolution was not adopted.

The Soviet Union and Czechoslovakia were the only members of the Council to support Vietnam's position (they were supported by the GDR, Hungary, Poland, and Cuba, who had asked to make representations to the Council) and they did so by endorsing the two-wars argument. The Soviet Ambassador, Oleg Troyanovsky, turned upside down the claim that Vietnam had violated the non-intervention principle by arguing that the Security Council was intervening in the internal affairs of the PRK. According to Leifer, the Soviet Union 'stressed humanitarian arguments',[74] but this claim has to be located in the context of Moscow's advocacy of the two-wars argument. At no point did the Soviet Union seek to justify Vietnam's use of force under the doctrine of unilateral humanitarian grounds. Instead, it persisted with Vietnam's claim that the National Salvation Front as the 'genuine expression of the Kampuchean people' was responsible for the overthrow of Pol Pot. In an effort to legitimate the new government, Ambassador Troyanovsky highlighted the 'monstrous crimes' committed by the Pol Pot regime. However, this tactic of confronting the Security Council with the humanitarian implications of taking a pro-Pol Pot line left Ambassador Troyanovsky exposed to the charge made by the British Ambassador that his government was manipulating human rights for political purposes. The British Ambassador pointed out that, when Britain had submitted a draft resolution on Pol Pot's human rights violations to the Commission on Human Rights, the Soviet Union and Cuba had failed to support it. Indeed, he noted that the former 'Soviet Deputy Foreign Minister, Mr. Zorin, then said that the matter was being raised "purely for political ends". But there it is. I welcome their recent conversion.'[75] Ambassador Richard's exposure of the contradictions in the Soviet Union's

---

[73] SCOR, 2109th Meeting, 13 Jan. 1979, 7.

[74] Leifer, 'Vietnam's Intervention in Kampuchea', 150.

[75] SCOR, 2110th Meeting, 12 Jan. 1979, 6. According to an article in the *International Herald Tribune*, Ambassador Richard's comments 'moved the council to laughter . . . the Chinese rocked in their seats with laughter. Prince Sihanouk beamed with pleasure [whilst] Oleg Troyanovsky wore "as deep a frown as we have seen", one delegate said'. ('US Joins Denunciation of Invasion of Cambodia', *International Herald Tribune*, 15 Jan. 1979).

stance on human rights shows how actors become entangled in their justifi-cations, leaving them open to charges of double standards if there is a discrep-ancy between the arguments they employ in different forums.

The Soviet Union found itself in an uncomfortable position in the Security Council. The only vote in favour of the Soviet position was a Czech one, a government that the Soviet Union had installed into power by force in 1968.[76] Moreover, it was forced to veto a resolution sponsored by the non-aligned members of the Council calling for the withdrawal of 'all foreign forces', whilst at the same time denying that Vietnamese forces had invaded Kampuchea. As *The Economist* put it, 'by first claiming that there were no invaders, and then blocking a call for their withdrawal, Mr Troyanovsky has destroyed some of his government's remaining credibility in the eyes of the non-aligned states'.[77]

The Chinese delighted in seeing their Soviet and Vietnamese adversaries embarrassed in the eyes of the world, but they wanted more than rhetorical declarations. Two days after the vote in the Council, 100,000 Chinese People's Liberation Army (PLA) troops poured across the Vietnamese border. The war lasted about a month and China suffered 20,000 casualties as it confronted tough Vietnamese resistance.[78] The Security Council convened from 23 to 27 February to try and resolve the war, but, with the exception of the Soviet bloc and Cuba, the Council linked China's use of force to Vietnam's continuing occupation of Kampuchea.[79] This issue continued to preoccupy the majority of the states on the Council, who reaffirmed their pluralist critique of Vietnam's action.[80] No resolution was put to the vote during the Security Council meetings in late February and the Council convened again on 16 March to vote on a draft resolution sponsored by ASEAN. This called for a ceasefire between all parties in the region, withdrawal of foreign forces to their own borders, and the settlement of disputes by peaceful means. For the second time in a month, the Soviet Union felt compelled to veto a resolution backed by a majority in the Security Council.

The controversy over Vietnam's use of force shifted to the General Assembly in late 1979, when the question of who should represent the legit-

---

[76] 'Echo-slovakia', *The Economist*, 20 Jan. 1979, 16.   [77] Ibid.

[78] Evans and Rowley, *Red Brotherhood*, 115–16.

[79] The Chinese defended their use of force as an act of self-defence, but this plea was not accepted by the USA, ASEAN, or the non-aligned members of the Council, who considered it an unaccept-able violation of UN Charter principles. For example, the USA argued that the principle of the non-use of force applied 'to the present attack by China on Viet Nam just as they apply to the earlier invasion of Cambodia by Viet Nam' (SCOR, 2114th Meeting, 23 Feb. 1979, 4).

[80] Given the argument advanced in the previous chapter that India raised humanitarian justifi-cations to justify its use of force, it is revealing to note that India speaking as an invited represen-tative stated that the principles of sovereignty and non-intervention were of 'universal applicability' and that there could be 'no exceptions'. India had tried to justify its intervention in East Pakistan by stretching Article 51 and raising humanitarian claims; the latter clearly depended upon persuad-ing the Council to treat its use of force as a legitimate 'exception' to the rules of sovereignty, non-intervention, and non-use of force.

imate government of Cambodia at the UN was debated by the General Assembly at its 34th session. The Assembly's Credentials Committee had recommended by six votes to three acceptance of the Pol Pot's government claim to recognition. The report of the Committee was considered by the Assembly during two plenary meetings on 21 September 1979. Vietnam, the Soviet bloc, and eleven friends of the Soviet Union in the eighty-eight-member Non-Aligned Movement had recognized the PRK and these states backed its right to the Cambodian seat at the UN. This position was defeated by a vote of 71 to 35, with 34 abstentions.

What is noteworthy about the debate in the General Assembly on the credentials question is that no state tried to justify Vietnam's use of force under the doctrine of humanitarian intervention. It is true that Vietnam and its supporters in the Soviet bloc tried hard to exploit the revulsion felt in the General Assembly at the terrible atrocities committed by the Pol Pot regime, but this attempt at persuading states to look more favourably upon Vietnam's breach of the rules failed. This implicit plea for mitigation on the part of Vietnam and the Soviet bloc was rejected by Ambassador Koh of Singapore, who addressed himself directly to this justification for the use of force. He asserted that, 'if we were to recognize a doctrine of humanitarian intervention, I submit that the world would be an even more dangerous place than it is now for us small countries'. His position was that, however terrible the human rights violations of a state, there could be no exception to the rules, because this would be open to abuse by larger states who 'on the pretext of saving a people from its inhumane Government' would intervene and impose a government backed by that power.[81] The importance of this argument is that the Singapore Ambassador was giving a moral justification for pluralist rules that depended upon the realist argument of abuse rather than the pluralist objection voiced by European states in the Security Council, which focused on the dangers of legitimating humanitarian intervention in a world where states had different conceptions of justice. Both of these arguments were invoked to varying degrees by governments in the General Assembly who argued that their opposition to Vietnam's action did not in any way imply support for the past actions of the Pol Pot regime.

Supporters of the PRK's right to be recognized as the legitimate government argued that it had come to power as a result of an uprising by the Cambodian people, and that Vietnam's presence was the result of a formal Treaty of Friendship signed with the PRK. Set against this, the majority of states argued that the PRK should be denied recognition because it lacked popular legitimacy and had come to power only as a result of Vietnamese arms. For example, China stated that the claim of the PRK was unacceptable because it was a puppet regime of Vietnam that had been repudiated by the

---

[81] General Assembly Official Records (GAOR), 34th Session, A/34/PV.3, 21 September 1979.

Khmer people. Singapore reinforced this by arguing that Assembly recognition of a government installed by 'over 10 divisions' of the Vietnamese army would violate the UN's non-intervention principle.[82] China and ASEAN's common front against Vietnam is understandable, given their anxiety that Vietnam's Soviet-backed action changed the balance of power in the region. The anti-Vietnamese grouping continued to have the backing of the USA and most EC states (France abstained on the issue of the 'two Kampucheas', arguing that neither party had the right to represent Cambodians at the UN[83]), the former motivated by cold-war imperatives and the latter mindful of its growing economic interests in South-East Asia. This stance on recognition was also taken by many other states that did not have immediate interests in seeing Vietnam punished.

There was a third possibility open to the General Assembly, which was to keep the Cambodian seat vacant pending a settlement of the conflict. This proposal, raised by India, had received some endorsement at a Summit of the Non-Aligned states meeting in Havana the previous month. On the floor of the Assembly, it was defeated by eighty votes to forty-three in a move that upheld a UN legal office opinion that to leave the seat vacant would be unconstitutional.[84]

ASEAN continued to apply the pressure on Vietnam by initiating in November a three-day debate in the General Assembly on the situation in Cambodia. Leading the debate on a draft resolution sponsored by thirty states, Malaysia (speaking for ASEAN) argued that armed intervention in the internal affairs of the DK was the cause of the deteriorating security situation in South-East Asia. ASEAN was particularly worried that conflict might spill over into Thailand, as the Vietnamese were stepping up attacks against Khmer Rouge forces operating on the Thai–Cambodian border.[85] This regional security concern was reinforced by a general interest in upholding the rules of the society of states. Speaking in the General Assembly, the Malaysian Ambassador, Tan Sri Zaiton, acknowledged that the Khmer Rouge was guilty of causing the deaths of hundreds of thousands, but he was equally adamant that barbaric behaviour at home could not justify Vietnam's military intervention. The rule of non-intervention, he argued, protected the weak against the strong, the alternative being 'the law of the jungle where might is right'.[86]

The draft resolution advanced by ASEAN called once again for the withdrawal

---

[82] Ambassador Koh's speech is cited in 'Of Snakes and Ladders', *Far Eastern Economic Review*, 5 Oct. 1979, 14.   [83] Ibid.

[84] Thailand argued that to keep the seat vacant would be to condone armed aggression and Zaire said that it would deny the sovereign rights of a member state. Similarly, Senegal and Yugoslavia argued that it would create a dangerous precedent. Austria, France, Spain, Surinam, and Sweden all abstained on the issue of the 'two Kampucheas', arguing that neither party had the credentials to act as the legitimate representative of the Kampuchean people. See 'The Diplomats Dig in', *Far Eastern Economic Review*, 5 Oct. 1979.

[85] Evans and Rowley, *Red Brotherhood*, 196–7.   [86] 'The Diplomats Dig in'.

of all foreign forces from Cambodia and the right of self-determination for its people. It also acknowledged the urgent need for humanitarian assistance to prevent starvation in the country, which was emerging as the latest threat to the Khmer people (this is discussed in detail below). The UN held an emergency Pledging Conference to raise funds to stop the developing famine in Cambodia a few days before the General Assembly debate. And this consideration was stressed in the contributions of Bangladesh, Bhutan, Nepal, New Zealand, Australia, and Singapore.

Opposing this draft resolution was a counter one drawn up by Vietnam and its supporters in the Soviet bloc and Third World that stated that the ASEAN-sponsored resolution was an act of interference in the internal affairs of the PRK Government. This argument failed to convince the Assembly, which voted ninty-one to twenty-one (with twenty-nine abstentions) in support of the ASEAN resolution. In a parallel response to India's negative reaction to the General Assembly's condemnation of its intervention in East Pakistan, Vietnam's reported reply to Resolution 34/22 was the realist one that 'the decision is made on the battlefield and not on a piece of paper'.[87] An alternative response would have been to argue that Resolution 34/22 was contradictory in that it called upon all parties to respect human rights whilst demanding the withdrawal of the Vietnamese army, which was all that stood between the Cambodian people and a return of Pol Pot.[88] Moreover, by continuing to give international legitimacy to Pol Pot's armed struggle against the Heng Samrin regime, the General Assembly fuelled the civil war that was contributing to the massive humanitarian crisis inside Cambodia at the end of 1979.

As Western publics were exposed to media images of starving Cambodians, Vietnam was accused by Western governments of playing politics with the lives of Cambodians. This charge would have carried greater moral authority had Western governments acted as guardians of human rights in Cambodia in the period 1975–9. Instead, as I argue below, it was the Vietnamese government that rescued the Khmer people from the brutal prison of Pol Pot's tyranny.

The Humanitarian Credentials of Vietnam's Action

The Khmer people have traditionally viewed their larger Vietnamese neighbour with suspicion and fear. But there can be little question that the vast majority welcomed the Vietnamese as rescuers. Based on interviews with

---

[87] Quoted in N. Chanda, 'Hanoi Ponders its Strategy', *Far Eastern Economic Review*, 7 Dec. 1979, 21.

[88] This argument is made in Morris, 'The Concept of Humanitarian Intervention', 27.

survivors of the Pol Pot regime, William Shawcross concluded that 'the Vietnamese intervention had been a true liberation'[89] and an Oxfam report written by Eva Mysliwiec reached the same judgement.[90] Further evidence for this claim is provided by Prince Sihanouk, who said that the Cambodian people welcomed the Vietnamese as 'saviours'.[91] A seasoned observer of the region, Nayan Chanda, reflected that:

In hundreds of Cambodian villages, the Vietnamese invasion was greeted with joy and disbelief. The Khmer Rouge cadres and militia were gone. People were free again to live as families, to go to bed without fearing the next day . . . it was as if salvation had come . . . One refrain that I heard constantly from the survivors was 'If the Vietnamese hadn't come, we'd all be dead'.[92]

Therefore the evidence points strongly to the conclusion that Vietnam's intervention was initially welcomed as an act of liberation by the Khmer people.[93] This positive response to Vietnam's action on the part of the victims of the Khmer Rouge stands in sharp contrast to the hostile international reaction. There can be no doubt that Cambodia's 'killing fields' constituted a supreme humanitarian emergency and that outside military intervention was the only means of bringing an end to the barbarities of the Pol Pot regime. Eventually local forces might have asserted themselves and overthrown the government, but in the interim how many more Cambodians would have been killed and brutalized? Vietnam's use of force meets the requirement of proportionality because it was commensurate with the gravity of the human rights violations that it ended. The final threshold requirement for an intervention to qualify as humanitarian is that any non-humanitarian motives for acting and the means employed must not undermine a positive humanitarian outcome. The result of Vietnam's decision to remove Pol Pot was the

---

[89] Quoted in Klintworth, *Vietnam's Intervention in International Law*, 65.

[90] E. Mysliwiec, *Punishing the Poor: The International Isolation of Kampuchea* (Oxford: Oxfam, 1988), quoted cited in Klintworth, *Vietnam's Intervention in International Law*, 66.

[91] *Cambodian Information Office Newsletter*, May 1997, 19, quoted in Klintworth, *Vietnam's Intervention in International Law*, 65.

[92] Chanda, *Brother Enemy*, 370.

[93] As the presence of thousands of Vietnamese troops became a permanent fixture on the Cambodian landscape, the Khmer people's traditional fear of Vietnamese colonization began to express itself. Between 200,000 and 300,000 Vietnamese settled in Cambodia after the intervention, raising the spectre that the Khmer people would loose their identity. The Vietnamese did not help their case by plundering Phnom Penh for anything of material value, but the claim of 'Vietnamization' has to be seen in the context of the state of the country in 1979. It was, Chanda writes, 'a land without money, markets, postal system, or schools; it was a land littered with mass graves and charnel houses'. These problems were compounded by the fact that the new government was the subject of international opprobrium and sanctions. Rebuilding the state required the assistance of thousands of Vietnamese officials, engineers, teachers, and doctors, since the elimination of this professional class was a key goal of the Khmer Rouge. Vietnam set about rebuilding the infrastructure and providing training for the Khmers in how to run a modern economy and society. The latter vigorously threw themselves into the task of reconstruction, but this would not have been possible without Vietnamese assistance. The results were impressive: children returned to school, basic health care was provided, and currency replaced the system of barter. See Chanda, *Brother Enemy*, 371.

rescue of the Khmer people from a government that was committing mass murder against its citizens, and this humanitarian outcome is evident in the fact that it was welcomed by the Cambodians as a liberation.

Accepting that Vietnam's action meets the threshold requirements for a humanitarian intervention, how far does it satisfy the lawyers' tests for permissible use of force under Article 2 (4)? It will be recalled from the previous chapter that the key requirements here are that there is no loss of territory by the target state, no regime change, and the immediate withdrawal of the intervening forces. The Indian intervention in East Pakistan failed to satisfy the first two of these, but it met the third. Vietnam, on the other hand, meets the first criterion but falls down on the other two. Rather than undermining the humanitarian credentials of its action, this illustrates, as in the Bangladeshi case, the limitations of this legal framework in assessing the legitimacy of cases of humanitarian intervention. The proposition that to be lawful humanitarian intervention should not involve a regime change begs the question as to how Pol Pot's abuses could have been ended without his removal from power? As Tom Farer points out, 'usually there is a connection between the severity of violations and the irremediable character of the delinquent regime'.[94] A regime change in Phnom Penh, then, was a prerequisite for ending the grotesque human rights violations perpetuated by the Khmer Rouge.

Vietnam is criticized for not withdrawing its forces until the late 1980s, and the comparison is drawn with India, which as we saw promptly disengaged its forces from Bangladesh (India's decision to withdraw being a key factor in the US decision to recognize the new government and lift its sanctions against India).[95] Set against this, Gary Klintworth considers that Vietnam's long-term military presence in Cambodia 'is explicable on the grounds that it [had] to contend with a Khmer Rouge force that . . . [was] . . . supplied materially by other powers'.[96] Had Vietnam responded to the General Assembly vote by immediately pulling its forces out, there would have been nothing to stop the Khmer Rouge from returning to power. Given that disengagement by Vietnam would probably have returned the Khmer people to the tyranny of Pol Pot, its long-term military presence was probably the only means of preventing a return to the slaughter.[97] Vietnam, of

---

[94] T. Farer, 'An Inquiry into the Legitimacy of Humanitarian Intervention', in L. F. Damrosch and D. J. Scheffer (eds.), *Law and Force in the New International Order* (Oxford: Westview Press, 1991), 198.

[95] For example, Bazyler argues that the 'Vietnamese invasion was not limited. After the overthrow of the Khmer Rouge, the Vietnamese did not leave the country' (Bazyler, 'Reexamining the Doctrine of Humanitarian Intervention', 609).

[96] Klintworth, *Vietnam's Intervention in International Law*, 76.

[97] In a balanced appraisal, Farer considers that by 'remaining in Cambodia to support the government it had imposed, Vietnam appeared indictable for an ongoing violation of the country's political independence and territorial integrity . . . But despite its own tarnished record [on human rights], the post-invasion regime seemed a long step up from Pol Pot. And given the geopolitical setting—intense superpower competition and Chinese–Soviet enmity, the exhausted condition of

course, did not prolong its occupation because of these concerns, but its key strategic interest in eliminating the military and political threat from the Khmer Rouge coincided with the goal of protecting the Khmer people against a return of Pol Pot.[98]

Vietnam's intervention fails the counter-restrictionist tests of a permissible humanitarian intervention under Article 2 (4), but had it fulfilled these requirements, there would have been at best a temporary cessation of atrocities before the normal business of killing was resumed by the Khmer Rouge upon returning to power. In arguing that Vietnam saved the Cambodian people from the barbarism of Pol Pot, it is important to recognize that the new Vietnamese-backed government was itself guilty of human rights abuses. A 1985 report by the USA-based Lawyers' Committee for Human Rights listed abuses such as arbitrary arrest, detention, and torture as a 'daily reality'.[99] This reinforced the finding of a 1984 *Amnesty International Report* that stated that 'Vietnamese security and military personnel grossly and consistently violated the human rights of Kampucheans subject to their authority'.[100] Although the humanitarian qualifications of Vietnam's intervention are clearly weakened by these rights violations, any assessment has to be balanced against the appalling human rights situation that prevailed under the Pol Pot regime. Whatever the moral failings of the PRK, its abuses do not even begin to outweigh the fact that its installation by Vietnamese arms saved seven million people from the mass murderer Pol Pot and his henchmen.

Vietnam also stands accused of violating human rights by using hunger as a political weapon. Paradoxically, the famine that spread across Cambodia in late 1979 was an unintended consequence of the liberation from Pol Pot. Freed at last from their imprisonment by the Khmer Rouge on the land, thousands of Cambodians left in search of their homes and loved ones. This, coupled with the fighting between the Vietnamese and Khmer Rouge, especially in Battambang province (a rich rice-producing area), meant that the main rice planting was largely missed. The situation was aggravated by the fact that Vietnam had little rice to spare owing to poor harvests.[101] Vietnam is charged with slowing down the international relief effort by insisting that the PRK control the distribution of aid, a move resisted by UNICEF, the Red Cross, and Oxfam.[102] The reason why Vietnam was so anxious about controlling distribution was its fear that food aid distributed by international bodies

Cambodian society, and the continued coherence and zeal of Pol Pot's cadres—the Vietnamese Army may then have been the only plausible means for preventing a Khmer Rouge restoration' (Farer, 'An Enquiry', 193–4).

[98] Klintworth, *Vietnam's Intervention in International Law*, 73.

[99] Lawyers' Committee for Human Rights, Kampuchea, *After the Worst* (1985), 5–6, quoted in Bazyler, 'Reexamining the Doctrine of Humanitarian Intervention', 610.

[100] Quoted in Bazyler, 'Reexamining the Doctrine of Humanitarian Intervention', 610.

[101] 'Freedom to Starve', *The Economist*, 25 Aug. 1979.

[102] 'The Cambodian Government at Last Seems Willing to Accept Supervised Aid for its Starving People. Now, Speed', *The Economist*, 6 Oct. 1979, 16.

would find its way into the hands of the Khmer Rouge, thereby sustaining its war effort.[103] Under international pressure, Vietnam agreed to allow the relief agencies to distribute aid, but there continued to be frustration in the West with what was perceived as its obstructionist tactics.

The issue came to the fore at the UN Pledging Conference that met a few days before the General Assembly session on Kampuchea. In a context where Western publics were being exposed to media images of starving Cambodians, some Western governments argued for a form of humanitarian intervention. The French Foreign Minister, Jean-François Poncet, stated that the 'need . . . to save lives' might require 'exceptional' actions such as the air-dropping of food and medication into Cambodia.[104] The airdrop plan was supported by Canadian Foreign Minister Flora McDonald, who even went so far as to draw a parallel with the diplomatic timidity shown over the famine in Cambodia and the international response to the Holocaust. 'People will demand', she said, 'that extraordinary measures be taken'.[105] The French–Canadian airdrop plan was backed by the USA, but it received a lukewarm reception from UNICEF and the Red Cross, which worried about delivering humanitarian aid without the consent of the Cambodian Government.[106]

This concern was borne out by the PRK's Ambassador in Moscow, Keo Prasat, who stated that 'we will do everything to defend our airspace and land and water routes from any violations of our territory'.[107] The reference to land routes is significant, because the USA had also proposed the opening of an overland route for aid supplies through Thailand. However, this had been rejected by the government in Phnom Penh. An article in *The Economist* high-lighted the security reasons behind this decision:

Although this is the most direct way, the roads lead through areas held either by right-wing Khmer Serei guerrillas or the remnants of Pol Pot's Khmers Rouges; and from there directly into the path of the Vietnamese army, which is moving heavy units all along the border [Cambodian–Thai]. Although Vietnam has allowed the relief operation to go ahead, its compassion is unlikely to extend to taking the pressure off its enemies to keep Cambodian civilians from starving.[108]

Although Vietnam was heavily criticized by the West for blocking relief

---

[103] The Foreign Ministry in Phnom Penh expressed its fears that international aid is 'the pretext . . . to supply war material to the Pol Pot–Ieng Sary bandits and other reactionary forces, enemies of the Kampuchean people' (quoted in 'Leading towards a new realism', *Far Eastern Economic Review*, 7 Dec. 1979, 23).

[104] 'Take a Figure and Double it', *Far Eastern Economic Review*, 16 Nov. 1979, 27.   [105] Ibid.

[106] Alain Modoux of the ICRC told the *Far Eastern Economic Review* in an interview that aircraft operating over Kampuchea without the consent of the Phnom Penh government risked being 'shot out of the skies', adding that the ICRC 'has had that experience, in Biafra' (ibid.).

[107] Vietnam's Ambassador to the UN, Ha Van Lau, reinforced this warning by claiming that any relief aircraft flying without permission over Cambodia 'would be brought down' (ibid).

[108] 'Slowly Comes the Rice', *The Economist*, 3 Nov. 1979, 48. Also see 'Take a Figure and Double it', and 'The Cambodian Government at Last Seems Willing to Accept Supervised Aid for its Starving People. Now, Speed'.

efforts, a different message was given by the head of UNICEF after a visit to Cambodia in December. After returning from his fact-finding tour, Henry Labouisse said that he was satisfied that the PRK was cooperating with international relief efforts, and he blamed the Khmer Rouge for the destruction of Cambodia's infrastructure, which was complicating relief efforts.

Moreover, the Western charge that Vietnam used hunger as a political weapon overlooked the fact that it was only because of foreign support—including the USA and Britain—that the Khmer Rouge posed a significant threat to the government in Phnom Penh. Had Vietnam's intervention been legitimated by the society of states, the PRK could have received international aid for the rebuilding of Cambodia rather than facing economic sanctions, and in such a climate it would have had no anxieties about opening its doors to humanitarian relief efforts to save the Cambodian people.

Vietnam was accused of playing politics with the lives of the Cambodian people, but those who levelled this charge voted in the UN General Assembly to condemn Vietnam for toppling a regime guilty of some of the worst crimes against humanity since the Holocaust. What is more, the Assembly supported Pol Pot's guerrillas fighting in the hills of Cambodia as the only legitimate government, a move that risked bringing the Khmer Rouge back to power. It also made Vietnam very suspicious of international relief efforts to alleviate the famine that gripped Cambodia in late 1979. Is this the triumph of realism over common humanity or the moral consequences of defending the rule of law in a pluralist society of states?

Conclusion

Realists argue that states do not intervene for primarily humanitarian reasons, and this assessment is borne out by this study of Vietnam's intervention in Cambodia. If the primacy of a humanitarian motive is the defining characteristic of a legitimate humanitarian intervention, then this case fails to meet the test. There is no evidence that Pol Pot's human rights violations played any part in the decision to invade Cambodia: Vietnam criticized these only when it became politically convenient to do so, and, had a diplomatic settlement been secured with the DK on its borders, it would have coexisted with its murderous neighbour. It is fortuitous for the Cambodian people that such an interstate agreement proved elusive, since Vietnam's subsequent use of force rescued the Khmer people from what one commentator has described as 'auto-genocide'.[109]

---

[109] Based on a detailed investigation by the UN Subcommission on Prevention of Discrimination and Protection of Minorities into human rights in Cambodia, the Chairman of the Committee, Mr Bouhdiba, described the human rights situation under the Khmer Rouge as the worst 'since nazism . . . [it] constituted nothing less than autogenocide' (quoted in Klintworth, *Vietnam's Intervention in International Law*, 62).

Advocates of the motives-first approach, like Bazyler, argue that rescue 'was merely a *by-product* of Vietnam's goals of achieving political dominance over Kampuchea'.[110] This leads him to argue that Vietnam's action cannot be justified under the legal doctrine of humanitarian intervention. Bazyler interprets Vietnam's use of force as designed to further its historic drive for regional hegemony in Indochina, but the weight of evidence points to a different conclusion: it was the belief that vital security interests were at risk that led Vietnam to invade Cambodia. As with India's intervention in East Pakistan, Vietnam was prepared to risk its soldiers' lives and expend scarce resources only because it perceived a fundamental threat to its security from China in the North and the DK in the South. As Klintworth puts it, 'saving human beings from being killed was an inevitable consequence of intervention by Vietnam . . . [but] it was always a secondary consideration to the overriding priority imposed by concern for vital security interests'[111]—the implication being that victims of human rights abuses will be rescued only if this coincides with the vital security interests of a state.[112]

The Vietnamese intervention in Cambodia, like the Indian action in East Pakistan, poses a hard case for a solidarist theory of humanitarian intervention: how can we meaningfully describe these actions as humanitarian when this reason played no part in the decision to intervene? The problem with motives as the defining criterion of a humanitarian intervention is that it simply ignores the question of humanitarian outcomes. The referent for analysis is the state and its motivations rather than the victims of human rights abuses. By reversing the traditional privileging of motives over outcomes, the test of legitimacy becomes how far intervention rescues those in danger and creates the political conditions to safeguard human rights in the future. The critical qualification here is that neither the non-humanitarian motives that explain the decision to intervene nor the means of the intervention must undermine the humanitarian benefits of the action. The humanitarian credentials of the Vietnamese action are tarnished by the subsequent human rights abuses under the PRK. But this does not alter the fact that Vietnam's security interests in removing the Khmer Rouge, and preventing its return to power, required actions that ended the appalling abuses of the Pol Pot regime and provided a new measure of security for the Khmer people.[113] Consequently, it can be agreed with Klintworth that Vietnam's use of force

---

110 Bazyler, 'Reexamining the Doctrine of Humanitarian Intervention', 610; emphasis added, 608.

111 Klintworth, *Vietnam's Intervention in International Law*, 60.

112 This is the conclusion of Morris. See his 'The Concept of Humanitarian Intervention', 46.

113 Given that this case supports Teson's view that we should look 'primarily at whether the intervention has rescued the victims of oppression, and whether human rights have subsequently been restored', it is curious that he does not include this case in his extensive study of post-1945 state practice. Arend and Beck tentatively suggest that he does not include this case because Vietnam's 'regional hegemonistic motives for invading Kampuchea seem clear', but this completely misreads Teson's position that it is a flawed methodology to rely on motives in judging the legitimacy of humanitarian interventions. Arend and Beck, *International Law and the Use of force*, 123.

meets 'the criteria for an excusable humanitarian intervention', because 'the net result of Vietnam's intervention was to interrupt the killing that was underway inside Cambodia'.[114]

A difficulty with the argument that international society should have legitimated Vietnam's action on humanitarian grounds is that, in contrast to India, it did not try to justify its actions in these terms. There is no evidence that the Politburo in Hanoi ever considered defending its action in humanitarian terms; Vietnam felt compelled to breach the rules of the game in this particular instance but it did not want to issue a general challenge to them. Even if the Vietnamese Government privately debated the merits of raising humanitarian claims in the hope of mitigating international condemnation, it had to weigh this against the danger that this might set a precedent that could come back to haunt it. Vietnam's own record on human rights was not a good one—British Ambassador Ivor Richard described it as 'deplorable'— and it might have been aware that it could become a target for future humanitarian interventions. Moreover, having stayed silent for four years about the terrible rights violations taking place inside Cambodia, members of the Security Council and General Assembly could have pointed to the hypocrisy that led Vietnam to disguise power political motives behind the cloak of humanitarian claims.

If the legitimacy of humanitarian intervention should be judged in terms of whether it produces a positive humanitarian outcome, then how is this claim to be legitimated in a society of states that is deeply suspicious that states can be trusted with such a doctrine? It is not that governments were unaware of this legal justification for the use of force, as can be seen from Ambassador Koh's statement in the General Assembly. What is striking about his speech is the conviction that the doctrine would always be abused by the strong as a weapon against the weak. It was simply unthinkable to him that states might act for humanitarian reasons or that their non-humanitarian motives might lead to a course of action that rescues victims from genocide and mass murder. In addition to the objection of abuse, Western governments invoked the pluralist concern that, given conflicting claims of human rights, humanitarian intervention threatens interstate order. France put this position most explicitly when it argued that legitimating humanitarian intervention would 'make the continued existence of various regimes dependent on the judgement of their neighbours'. Most states did not feel it necessary to advance such moral justifications for the rules, simply affirming it as an article of faith that, even when a government is committing mass murder against its citizens, there can be no exceptions to these.

The solidarist response to the above pluralist and realist objections is to argue that it exaggerates how far legitimating humanitarian intervention

---

[114] Klintworth, *Vietnam's Intervention in International Law*, 76.

would undermine the restraints against the use of force. Governments that want to invoke humanitarian justifications with any plausibility would have to make the case that their use of force is justified because it is the only means of ending human rights abuses that shock the conscience of humanity. This is the argument that Vietnam should have employed in defending its overthrow of Pol Pot. Given the cold-war context and the fact that Vietnam had only recently defeated the USA in war, the solidarist defence that its use of force was justified because it had ended mass killing and did not pose a threat to regional security would probably have made little difference to the international reaction. However, this argument was much more convincing than the two-wars justification and it might have forced states to address explicitly the legitimacy of the doctrine of humanitarian intervention. Moreover, instead of being pilloried in the Security Council and General Assembly, Vietnam would have been able to claim the moral high ground by exposing the fact that Western governments were condemning an action that had ended the 'killing fields' inside Cambodia.

Had Vietnam defended its action under the doctrine of humanitarian intervention, it is possible that some states might have been persuaded to change their views on the legitimacy of this practice. Certainly, it is only by governments raising such claims that there is any prospect of developing a new norm of unilateral humanitarian intervention in international society. However, one major obstacle to this dialogical approach is that governments might invoke pluralist objections to humanitarian intervention in order to protect interests that remain hidden from public debate. The concern expressed about precedent setting in the debates in the Security Council and General Assembly might be viewed as an example of the language of manœuvre—that is, actors manipulating justifications in order to further 'off-the-board' interests.

The above argument fails to explain the actions of China and ASEAN, however, since these states were explicit about both the legal and the strategic reasons that led them to oppose Vietnam's action. Britain, France, and the USA were less explicit about the political, economic, and security interests behind their criticism of Vietnam's use of force, but it is too narrow a perspective to view these states as espousing pluralist arguments only because they served their interests. This instrumental view of language is open to the objection that it underestimates the power of discourse in predisposing actors to accept certain practices as both natural and unchangeable. It is not that states consciously calculated the costs and benefits of various strategies, rather as Bourdieu would argue it is actors' feel for the rule structure of the game that leads them to play within its constraints and enablements. What is fascinating about the Cambodian case is that humanitarian intervention as an alternative moral practice is visible in the speech acts of the players, but pluralist rules constitute the givens of the discourse in such a way that legitimating

Vietnam's action as humanitarian is rendered unthinkable. The agency of state leaders and diplomats is crucial in reproducing the rules that constitute a pluralist society of states, but, once pluralist practices become habitual and taken for granted by states, it is very difficult to change them.

Normative change depends upon states raising new claims that challenge existing rules, and the group of states that could most dramatically have changed the normative context of Vietnam's intervention was the Western bloc. It was this group that was responsible for the imposition of such draconian political and economic sanctions against Vietnam and the new PRK government. In response to the argument that Western security interests required condemnation of Vietnam and support for the guerrilla army of Pol Pot, critics argue that Western governments are guilty of grossly exaggerating the threat to security interests posed by Vietnam's action. According to John Girling, apart from Thailand, it 'posed almost no direct security threat to others'.[115] Had Western governments been able to break out of the straitjacket imposed by a cold-war mindset and the pluralist habits of the society of states, they would have seen that they were in the fortunate position of being able to welcome Vietnam's use of force in ending the Pol Pot regime without risking vital security interests. The loss of political and economic influence within ASEAN as a consequence of taking a pro-Vietnam line was a small price to pay for bringing an end to the worst human rights violations since the Holocaust. Moreover, by treating Vietnam as a Soviet proxy, the West and ASEAN created a self-fulfilling prophecy by pushing it further into the arms of the Soviet Union. Indeed, had the West and ASEAN legitimated Vietnam's action on humanitarian grounds, this would have created a security climate where Vietnam felt able to withdrawal its forces from the PRK, making possible a normalization of its relations with Thailand and ASEAN. Thus, even on security grounds, Western policy was driven by myopic considerations of self-interest.

How should we morally judge a society of states that condemns the practice of humanitarian intervention on the twin grounds that such a right will be abused and set a dangerous precedent? The Canadian Foreign Minister, Flora McDonald, accused the society of states of diplomatic timidity in responding to the Cambodian famine. The real timidity came earlier: first, in the collective failure to do more to end the atrocities of the Pol Pot government during the period 1975–9; and, secondly, in the poverty of the diplomatic imagination that prevented the Security Council and General Assembly from critically reflecting on the moral implications of privileging pluralist rules over the defence of human rights. Governments were well aware of the human consequences for the Khmer people of their adherence to pluralist

[115] J. Girling, 'Lessons of Cambodia', in J. Girling (ed.), *Human Rights in the Asia-Pacific Region* (Canberra: Australian National University, 1991), 28.

rules. Despite this, it was the moral consequences for interstate order of weakening these that dominated the discourse. Vietnam was no saint, but its intervention should have been treated as an exception to the rules and legitimated because it ended the barbarism inside Cambodia. The moral bankruptcy of pluralist international society in the face of mass killing is well captured by John Girling: 'The lesson of Cambodia is . . . whose security? That of Pol Pot? Or of China and the United States against the security—that is, the lives—of Cambodians? To claim that the sanctity of frontiers (as breached by the Vietnamese) should have priority over the safety of thousands of Cambodians represents an appalling "reversal of values".'

The pluralist objection that legitimating Vietnam's action on humanitarian grounds risked setting a dangerous precedent would carry greater conviction if there was consistency across cases. However, the fact is that, at the same time as Vietnam was being condemned and sanctioned for a breach of the rules, Tanzania's violation of the same principle went virtually unchallenged? If pluralist predispositions were so deeply ingrained in the habits and attitudes of international society, then what explains the different responses to these two cases? This is the subject of the next chapter.

4

Good or Bad Precedent? Tanzania's Intervention in Uganda

Tanzania's use of force against Uganda in early 1979 removed a barbaric regime that had become an embarrassment to other African governments. After seizing power in 1971, Idi Amin imposed an eight-year dictatorship upon Uganda, which, according to Amnesty International, killed up to 300,000 people.[1] Ugandan citizens lived in daily fear of their security and there was a complete breakdown of the rule of law as government forces killed and tortured civilians with impunity. The horrors perpetuated by the Ugandan regime ashamed even those African heads of state who were themselves guilty of abuses of human rights. However, African governments failed to condemn Amin's grotesque behaviour towards his own citizens, hiding behind Article III of the OAU, which prohibits intervention in the internal affairs of member states. The only exception to this general silence was the Tanzanian President, Julius Nyerere, who did condemn Amin's abuses and challenge the legitimacy of his rule.

Relations between Tanzania and Uganda had deteriorated through the 1970s, and in October 1978 Uganda invaded Tanzania; this gave Nyerere his opportunity and he launched a counter-attack that led to Tanzanian forces overthrowing the government of Idi Amin in April 1979. This chapter traces the background context that led to the Tanzanian intervention and examines how Tanzania tried to legitimate its breach of the OAU's non-intervention rule. Here, I consider how far Tanzania raised humanitarian claims and how far these justifications equalled its motivations for acting.

In breaking the OAU's rules of sovereignty and non-intervention, Tanzania's use of force posed the conflict between order and justice at its starkest for African states fiercely protective of their sovereignty. The second part of the chapter focuses on the international, and especially the African, reaction to Tanzania's use of force. In the Bangladeshi and Cambodian cases, the Security Council was the forum where conflicting claims were debated,

---

[1] F. Hassan, 'Realpolitik in International Law: After Tanzanian–Ugandan Conflict "Humanitarian Intervention" Reexamined', *Willamette Law Review*, 17 (1981), 893.

but the Tanzanian–Ugandan conflict was never discussed by the Security Council. As the victim of an armed attack, the Government of Democratic Kampuchea had requested that the Security Council debate Vietnam's intervention, and Uganda tried to repeat this tactic when confronted by Tanzania's intervention. However, there was no support among African states at the UN for the Security Council to hear the Ugandan case. And, since the great powers showed no interest in coming to Uganda's defence, the issue never came before the Security Council. Moreover, and in stark contrast to the response to Vietnam's intervention, there was no imposition of sanctions against Tanzania by any member of international society. A key question posed by this case is whether the tacit acceptance of Tanzania's use of force is a precedent supporting humanitarian intervention as a rule of customary international law. Can the different responses to Vietnam's and Tanzania's actions be explained in terms of legal principles or do they reflect the play of power politics?

The legitimacy of Tanzania's use of force against Uganda was debated at the 1979 OAU Summit in Monrovia, and Nyerere's action was criticized by the outgoing OAU Chairman and Nigeria. However, what is surprising about the summit is that so few African states challenged the action. The significance of the debate at Monrovia is that it represented a clash between pluralist and solidarist conceptions of international society, with the argument being raised in debate that tyrants like Amin should be deprived of the protection afforded by the OAU Charter. I consider how far this solidarist claim succeeded in changing the dominant norm within the OAU that there is no relationship between a government's treatment of its citizens at home and its right to sovereign prerogatives.

The Background to Tanzania's Intervention

The origins of the Tanzanian–Ugandan War of 1979 can be traced back to President Julius Nyerere's condemnation of Idi Amin's seizure of power in a military *coup* in 1971. Nyerere was generally opposed to *coups* in Africa and he disliked this one in particular because it deposed his friend and fellow socialist revolutionary Milton Obote. The latter had been democratically elected and Nyerere viewed him as the legitimate leader of Uganda. The Tanzanian leader provided asylum for Obote and his supporters, who included 1,000 soldiers. Within a week of the *coup* Nyerere was describing Amin as a 'murderer'.[2] Eighteen months later, he allowed Obote's exile forces to launch an invasion of Uganda. The attack failed, because Libya rushed

---

[2] *African Contemporary Record*, 11 (1978–9), B393.

forces to support Amin and Nyerere decided not to intervene in support. Instead, under the auspices of the OAU, Tanzania signed the Mogadishu Agreement on 5 October 1972, which committed both Tanzania and Uganda to refrain from military operations against each other.[3] Whilst Nyerere respected the agreement, he continued to condemn Amin for his brutality. Launching a bitter attack against him to coincide with the opening of the 1975 OAU Summit in Kampala (Nyerere refused to attend as a protest against Amin), the Tanzanian President claimed that the horrors committed by the Ugandan Government shamed all Africans. Nyerere was appalled that he was the only African leader prepared to condemn Amin's human rights abuses, believing that the principles of the OAU should safeguard justice as well as order.[4] His reasoning is well reflected in the following statement by one of his ministers in 1975:

> when massacres, oppression and torture are used against Africans in the independent states of Africa there is no protest anywhere in Africa . . . It is made to appear that Africans lose their right to protest against State-organized brutality on the day that their country becomes independent through their efforts. For on all such matters the OAU acts like a trade union of the current Heads of State and Government, with solidarity reflected in silence if not in open support for each other.[5]

In addition to his moral repugnance at Amin's atrocities, Nyerere's opposition reflected his desire to weaken an unpredictable and threatening neighbour. His fear of future Ugandan intentions was confirmed in October 1978, when Ugandan forces invaded Tanzanian territory and occupied the Kagera Salient. Uganda's bogus pretext was that this territory rightfully belonged to it as part of the old colonial division between the German and British spheres of influence in Africa.[6] What appears to have happened is that a section of the Ugandan army had mutinied, and, during the rout of these forces by troops loyal to Amin, some had escaped across the border into Tanzania.[7] To distract attention from the growing erosion of his power base at home, and to direct the energies of the Ugandan army outwards, Amin allowed two of his battalions to pursue the mutineers across the Tanzanian border. And, finding little resistance, they occupied the 1,000 square kilometres of the Kagera Salient. It is reported that Ugandan forces killed indiscriminately, driving 40,000 into the bush and leaving 10,000 unaccounted for. According to one Tanzanian official, Ugandan forces 'stole everything movable and destroyed everything immovable'.[8]

---

[3] Ibid.   [4] Thomas, *New States, Sovereignty and Intervention*, 92.

[5] Quoted in C. E. Welch, 'The OAU and Human Rights: Towards a New Definition', *Journal of Modern African Studies*, 19/3 (1981), 405.

[6] Thomas, *New States, Sovereignty and Intervention*, 92. Amin's claim to the Kagera Salient relied on the same repudiation of the rules of post-colonial international society that underpinned the Pol Pot Government's claim on the 'lost territories' of Kampuchea Krom.

[7] The background to the mutiny is discussed in Thomas, *New States, Sovereignty and Intervention*, 93.   [8] *African Contemporary Record*, 11 (1978–9), B393.

Nyerere was incensed at Amin's actions and determined to throw out the invaders. However, it took several weeks to mobilize Tanzanian forces and move them into the Kagera, since artillery and other equipment had to be transported from the southern border.[9] Tanzania is one of the world's poorest countries and mobilizing an army required taking buses and other vehicles into military service, which massively disrupted the economy and society. To pay for this effort, Tanzanian Finance Minister Edwin Mtei imposed higher taxes on a wide range of goods. The result of Uganda's invasion was that the Tanzanian economy went onto a war footing that it could ill afford.[10]

At the same time as Tanzania was mobilizing to repel Ugandan forces, Nigeria and Libya sent envoys to mediate in the dispute. Nyerere told the Libyan delegation that their efforts would be better directed at condemning Amin's aggression.[11] And, in response to Nigerian efforts at mediation, Nyerere stormed: 'How', he asked, 'do you mediate between somebody who breaks into your house and the victim of the assault?'[12] Recognizing in Tanzanian military preparations that he might have bitten off more than he could chew, the Ugandan leader offered in early November to withdraw from the occupied territory, provided that Tanzania agreed to cease supporting anti-Amin forces. The offer was rejected by Nyerere, who was determined to throw out and punish Amin. By early December Tanzanian forces had driven Ugandan forces back to the border, and this, coupled with widespread condemnation of Uganda's aggression, convinced Amin that he should withdraw from Tanzania.[13]

Yet it was becoming clear that Nyerere wanted more than a withdrawal of Ugandan forces from Tanzanian territory. In his meeting with the Nigerian mediator, Army Chief of Staff Lt. Gen. Theophilus Danjuma, the Tanzanian leader stated that pushing Amin out was 'no longer the problem. The problem is, what next? Is Africa asking Tanzania to pay for those massacres and wanton destruction of property?'[14] It seems that Nyerere had decided to embark on a two-pronged approach: first, to punish Amin's soldiers for their brutality against his people and destruction of Tanzanian property, and, secondly, to remove any future military threat to Tanzania by toppling Amin from power. However, it was never part of Nyerere's original intention that this would be done by Tanzanians; rather he hoped that, by wiping out Amin's southern units, the way would be paved for exile forces and the Ugandan people to overthrow him.[15] To legitimate the economic burden that

[9] *African Contemporary Record*, 11 (1978–9), B393.
[10] Thomas, *New States, Sovereignty and Intervention*, 96.
[11] *African Contemporary Record*, 11 (1978–9), B.394.   [12] Ibid.
[13] Thomas, *New States, Sovereignty and Intervention*, 94. The USA, Britain, Denmark, Finland, Iceland, Norway, Angola, Botswana, Mozambique and Zambia, Ethiopia, Algeria, Madagascar, and Kenya all condemned the Ugandan aggression.
[14] 'Tanzania Bars Mediation in Conflict with Uganda', *International Herald Tribune*, 18–19 Nov. 1978.
[15] Thomas, *New States, Sovereignty and Intervention*, 98. Also see 'Tanzania May Enter Uganda', *Observer*, 19 Nov. 1978.

such an ambitious strategy imposed on the Tanzanian people, the official press, Dar es Salaam radio, and Nyerere himself stressed the appalling nature of the Amin regime and the need for Tanzania to act to put an end to its excesses. The Tanzanian Government newspaper, the *Daily News*, stated in an editorial on 7 November that Uganda's seizure of the Kagera Salient 'must be the last of Amin's mad actions',[16] and the weekly *Sunday News* suggested that, if Africa would not act against Amin, then Tanzania must act alone: 'Tanzanians owe it to themselves, the OAU and the rest of peace-loving mankind to end once and for all Amin's eccentricities which have culminated in mass murders, and untold human suffering both within Uganda and in Tanzania.'[17]

Caroline Thomas argues that, given Nyerere's decision to remove Amin from power, the visit in December by the Chairman of the OAU, President Jaafar Mohammed al Numeiry of Sudan, to mediate the Ugandan–Tanzanian conflict was 'fruitless'.[18] This is an accurate interpretation, given Numeiry's position that the best way to get Ugandan forces out of Tanzania was for Nyerere to reach agreement with Amin. This could not be achieved if the OAU was to accept Tanzania's demand that Amin be named the 'aggressor'.[19] It is not the practice of the OAU to condemn member states, and, even in a situation where Uganda had flagrantly violated the OAU's non-intervention rule, Chairman Numeiry recommended a ceasefire, an end to territorial claims, withdrawal of forces to recognized borders, and adherence to the rules of the OAU Charter. Nyerere did not want mediation from the OAU; he wanted it to condemn Uganda's actions and for other African states to provide Tanzania with practical support in the fight against Amin. In particular, he would have liked Kenya to cut off oil supplies to Uganda. The Kenyan Government refused, because this would break the agreement on landlocked states in Africa.

The OAU Chairman's refusal to support Tanzania's claims reinforced Nyerere's view that the rules of the OAU Charter should be changed so that they did not protect rulers like Amin. It was not only Amin's external excesses that preoccupied Nyerere. Speaking three days before Numeiry's visit on the seventeenth anniversary of Tanzania's independence, he stated that there was

A strange tendency in Africa . . . a tendency which, if we do not consider it carefully, will badly damage respect for our continent . . . Amin is a killer. Since he took over the leadership of Uganda—and I am not sure whether I should call it leadership or oppression—he has killed many more people than Smith has done. He has killed many more people than Vorster has done in SA [South Africa]. But there is a strange habit in Africa: an African leader, so long as he is an African, can kill Africans just as he pleases, and you cannot say anything. If Amin was White, we would have passed many resolutions

---

[16] 'Tanzania Hints Decision to End Amin Presidency', *International Herald Tribune*, 7 Nov. 1978.
[17] Quoted in Thomas, *New States, Sovereignty and Intervention*, 95–6.   [18] Ibid. 99.
[19] *African Contemporary Record*, 11 (1978–9), B394.

against him. But he is Black, and Blackness is a licence to kill Africans. And therefore there is complete silence; no one speaks about what he does.[20]

In another speech on the following day, he explicitly called for a change to the rules that would deny protection of the OAU Charter to those who massively abuse human rights at home. Nyerere claimed that it 'did not matter what a Head of State did; he could kill as many people as he liked in his country and he would still be protected by the Charter. Where it was concerned, there is no African fascist—yet there are several.'[21] However, it was one thing to argue for a change of rule within the OAU to protect the victims of human rights abuses; it was quite another to justify unilateral intervention against Uganda in the name of human rights, since this threatened the very principles of sovereignty and non-intervention upon which the OAU was built.

Paralleling Vietnam's deliberations, Nyerere and his advisers hoped to rely on an internal uprising to remove Amin, because they did not want Tanzania to be seen as violating the bedrock rules of the society of states. Nyerere was prepared to assist an uprising by covertly building up the strength of exile forces committed to the overthrow of Amin, and to coordinate their intervention with a Tanzanian attack against Amin's southern battalions. Contrary to Amin's claims, both Nyerere and Obote had honoured the Mogadishu Agreement of 1972. However, at the end of October Nyerere had discussed with Obote his plan to overthrow Amin by bringing together exiled Ugandan political groups.[22] As a result of this secret meeting, an invitation was sent to all Ugandan political leaders in exile to come to Dar es Salaam to discuss the plan. The Front for the National Salvation of Uganda led by Yoweri Museveni was not pro-Obote but it was prepared to join the common fight against Amin in the hope of bringing democratic change to Uganda. The other key political grouping in the coalition was the Ugandan Nationalist Organization based in Nairobi. It also opposed Obote, but, like Museveni's group, it was prepared to submerge these differences to get rid of Amin. Following their defeat in 1972, Obote's supporters had turned their hands to farming and charcoal selling. Now they were handed arms and given training by the Tanzanian army. Colonel David Oyite and Colonel Tito Okello, veterans of the 1972 campaign, assumed military control of the Obote forces and later of the whole armed insurgency.[23] On 13 January 1979 Obote broke an eight-year silence calling on Ugandans to launch an armed struggle against the Amin regime.

[20] *African Contemporary Record*, 11 (1978–9), B394.   [21] Ibid.
[22] Ibid.   [23] Thomas, *New States, Sovereignty and Intervention*, 100.

Tanzania's Justifications for its Use of Force

By mid-January Tanzania had amassed some 30,000–40,000 soldiers on the Tanzanian–Ugandan border, and the *Daily News* reported on 27 January that Tanzanian forces had crossed into Uganda after Amin's forces had shelled Tanzanian positions.[24] At the same time as Tanzanian forces were attacking Ugandan forces in the border areas, opposition groups inside Uganda began a campaign of sabotage.[25] The *Observer* reported on 28 January that exile forces had crossed into Uganda from Tanzania to support the growing insurrection against Amin. Three border areas of Mutukula, Kabuyu, and Minziri were reportedly in the control of the exiles, but Tanzania denied that its army was occupying these areas.[26]

Despite Tanzanian denials, it seems that Nyerere's plan was for a two-pronged attack by Tanzanian and exile forces against the towns of Masaka and Mbarara, the headquarters of the two battalions that had inflicted such destruction against the Tanzanian people. By mid-February Western diplomatic sources confirmed that Tanzanian forces had advanced about sixty kilometres inside Uganda and were not encountering serious resistance. And, in the last week of February, Radio Uganda announced the fall of Masaka and Mbarara. Both of these towns were strategically vital, since they are on the road that carries supplies, crucially oil, from Kenya.[27]

As Tanzanian and exile forces achieved military successes, with elements of the Ugandan army joining forces with the invaders, an increasingly desperate Amin appealed to the OAU to stop the conflict. The OAU had set up an *ad hoc* Mediation Committee of nine African states and this met with ministers of the OAU Council in Nairobi on 23 February. The Tanzanian delegation led by Foreign Minister Ben Mkapa repeated Nyerere's demand that the OAU condemn Uganda's 'aggression' against the Kegara, expressing his disapproval that the Mediation Committee's report did not use the word 'invasion'.[28] Tanzania's position was that a resolution of the conflict depended upon the OAU condemning Amin's actions; Uganda renouncing any claim to the Kagera salient; a promise from Amin never again to invade Tanzania; and the payment of compensation for the damage resulting from the invasion. This was supported by its front-line partners Angola, Mozambique, Botswana, and Zambia. The strongest condemnation of Amin came from the official newspaper, *The Times of Zambia*, which stated that 'Amin's Uganda is the aggressor nation. It is in breach of the OAU Charter. Amin's regime should be roundly condemned by the OAU.'[29] Given that Nyerere knew that the OAU

---

[24] See ibid. 101, and 'Tanzania Troops Raiding Uganda, Says Nyerere', *Guardian*, 27 Jan. 1979.
[25] Thomas, *New States, Sovereignty and Intervention*, 101.
[26] 'Nyerere Steps up his Bid to Topple Amin', *Observer*, 28 Jan. 1979.
[27] Hassan, 'Realpolitik in International Law', 873.
[28] African Contemporary Record 11 (1978–9), A59.   [29] Ibid. A60.

would not publicly condemn a brother African state, his sincerity in seeking a peaceful solution has been questioned.[30] But Nyerere's rejection of the OAU's efforts reflected his conviction that it should be prepared to condemn states that flagrantly violated the Charter.

Given this principled stand, it was very difficult for Nyerere to justify Tanzania's use of force against Uganda on humanitarian grounds. He would have been open to the charge that he was defending his action in terms that violated the very rule he accused Uganda of breaking. Nyerere had championed a change of the OAU Charter so that it did not shelter tyrants like Amin, but he was not prepared to argue that massive human rights abuses legitimated armed intervention by outside states. In a speech on 28 February, Nyerere revealed his strong commitment to the OAU's principle of the inviolability of territorial frontiers:

Despite my dislike for Amin—and I really do not like him—the Government of Tanzania has no right to enter Uganda in order to topple Amin . . . No other government or anyone else in the world has the right to overthrow Amin's regime. That is the matter of *principle* . . . But Amin's regime is a brutal one, and the people of Uganda have that right.[31]

Nyerere never intended Tanzanian forces to advance deeply into Uganda, certainly not beyond the towns of Masaka and Mbarara. This strategy was based on three key factors: first, it was believed that the growing unrest within Uganda coupled with the intervention of the exile forces would be enough to overthrow Amin. Next, it was believed that Amin would not receive support from his normal backers in Libya and the Soviet Union. However, were Tanzanian forces to drive deeply into Uganda, this might change, with Arab states and the Soviet Union coming to the economic and even military aid of Amin's regime. Finally, Tanzania could not take on the main task of overthrowing Amin without violating the OAU Charter, which was something Nyerere was determined to avoid. In this context, his speech stressing the illegitimacy of using force to change even a murderous regime like Amin's is clear evidence that Nyerere rejected the doctrine of unilateral humanitarian intervention.

To legitimate Tanzania's use of force against Uganda, Nyerere resorted to the two-wars argument that Vietnam had invoked and been pilloried for in the Security Council. In a nationwide address on 27 March, the Tanzanian leader stated: 'First there are Ugandans fighting to remove the Fascist dictator. Then there are Tanzanians fighting to maintain national security.'[32] Nyerere did not follow the Vietnamese in explicitly employing the language of self-defence, but

---

[30] Hassan, 'Realpolitik in International Law', 873 n. 79.
[31] *African Contemporary Record*, 11 (1978–9), B430; emphasis added.
[32] 'Libya Delivers Ultimatum over Uganda to Tanzania', *International Herald Tribune*, 27 Mar. 1979.

he was clearly intent on presenting Tanzania's action as a legitimate defensive one. Whatever its legal niceties, the two-wars justification was equally unsustainable in this case because 'action taken against Amin's army amounted to action taken against Amin and his regime'.[33] By forcing Amin to keep Ugandan artillery and armour tied up in the southern border areas, it was difficult for his forces to deal with attacks from exile forces sweeping in from the east, and with uprisings of the Ugandan people in the north and in Amin's own fiefdom in the west Nile.[34] Moreover, Nyerere's initial hopes that Tanzanian forces could be confined to the border areas were dashed as they were forced to take on a greater share of the fighting inside Uganda, making an increasing mockery of the two-wars theory.

Two key factors contributed to this change in Tanzanian strategy: the first was the decision by Libya to intervene in the conflict by sending supplies and troops. By early March it was becoming clear that 1,000–2,000 Libyan soldiers were fighting with Amin as well as several hundred Palestinians, 500 of whom were guarding the radio station at Kampala.[35] The second problem for the intervening forces was the Ugandan army's Soviet supplied 122mm artillery, which had a range of up to forty kilometres and which was holding up the exile forces heading for Kampala, Entebbe, and Jinja.[36] One immediate consequence of this was the defeat of exile forces at a battle at Torono on 2 March. The exiles supported by Tanzanian artillery had achieved initial success but had later been defeated by loyalist forces retaking the town. Farooq Hassan argues that the real significance of this defeat was that it 'shattered the argument that the intervention was by Ugandan exiles alone without the physical combat help of Tanzanian forces'. According to Hassan, a spokesperson for the Ugandan Nationalist Organization admitted that the original plan had been for Tanzanian troops to march from the south towards Kampala, while the exiles moved in from the east, the purpose being to 'permit the exiles to march alone victoriously into the capital giving the illusion of their independent success'.[37] But, after the defeat at Torono, the exiles were forced to rejoin the Tanzanian force advancing from the south. As the campaign developed through March, Tanzanian and exile forces moved steadily towards Kampala. An important turning point came during the third week of March, when Tanzanian forces encountered Libyan forces for the first time during the conflict and inflicted a defeat on what had become Amin's last line of defence.

In response to this defeat, Libyan President Mu'ammar al-Quaddafi escalated the conflict by threatening to declare war on Tanzania unless it withdrew

---

[33] Thomas, *New States, Sovereignty and Intervention*, 102.

[34] 'Nyerere Steps up his Bid to Topple Amin'.

[35] Hassan, 'Realpolitik in International Law', 875, and Thomas, *New States, Sovereignty and Intervention*, 103

[36] *African Contemporary Record*, 11 (1978–9), B396.

[37] Hassan, 'Realpolitik in International Law', 874.

its forces from Uganda within twenty-four hours. This ultimatum was rejected and, as the war turned increasingly into a Tanzanian–Libyan one, Tanzania's two-wars justification became increasingly untenable.[38] Foreign journalists reporting on the war were in no doubt that 'the bulk of the fighting army, the suppliers of guns and ammunition and the drivers of the tanks were Tanzanian, as were the top military planners'.[39] Nyerere never intended Tanzanian forces to participate in the final overthrow of Amin, but it was clear that, without the direct involvement of Tanzanian forces, Amin might be able to hold onto power given the support of the Libyans. The Ugandan leader had around 2,000 Libyan troops defending Kampala and Nyerere took the difficult decision on 4 April to employ Tanzanian forces in a final push against Amin. As the *African Contemporary Record* puts it, 'having started the job, Nyerere decided it had to be completed, even if this meant going back on his earlier decision not to allow the Tanzanian forces to participate in liberating the capital'.[40] The invading force of Tanzanians and exiles left an escape route for pro-Amin troops and Nyerere told Quadaffi that he would allow the Libyans to escape.[41] Quadaffi took up this invitation and, after a few days more fighting, Kampala fell on 10 April to the victorious Tanzanian and exile forces. A week later Tanzanian forces began an offensive to take the rest of Uganda.

The perception among African states and wider international society was that Tanzania had forcibly replaced Amin's regime, and the question that confronted the Tanzanian President was how to justify Tanzania's actions, given his commitment to OAU Charter principles? He seems to have recognized that the two-wars argument was a weak defence, given that the Tanzanian army was sitting in Kampala. To head off the criticism that Tanzania had acted illegally, he now claimed that the action was a legitimate response to Ugandan aggression and that Tanzanian forces had fought alongside exiles and Ugandans seeking to liberate their country. In a speech in Dar es Salaam on 12 April, he stated that 'there are people who are accusing me of breaking international law . . . What law did we contravene? Should one let a thief get away with his crime.'[42] Two days later, he declared himself ready to go to the UN to defend his intervention, claiming that 'it is a good precedent . . . If Africa, as such, is unable to take up its responsibilities, it is incumbent upon each State to do so . . . it is a lesson to Amin and people of his kind.'[43]

Although the Tanzanian President was prepared to argue his case at the

38 Hassan, 'Realpolitik in International Law', 874.
39 'A Victory for Tanzania, a Worry for Africa', *New York Times*, 16 Apr. 1979.
40 *African Contemporary Record*, 11 (1978–9), B396.
41 Thomas, *New States, Sovereignty and Intervention*, 107.
42 'Invaders Establish Control in Kampala and Call on All Ugandans to Hunt Amin', *New York Times*, 13 Apr. 1979.
43 Quoted in Ronzitti, *Rescuing Nationals Abroad*, 103.

UN, he would have had a hard time persuading the Security Council that the removal of a neighbouring government constituted a legitimate act of self-defence. Tanzania's eviction of Ugandan forces from the Kegara Salient clearly meets the criteria of self-defence, because it was necessary to use force to repel the invaders and the amount employed was proportionate to the initial attack. However, taking the war into Uganda was a very different matter and to justify this on grounds of self-defence would require making the same argument that Klintworth advances to justify Vietnam's removal of Pol Pot—namely, that the removal of Amin was essential for Tanzania's continued existence. As I discuss below, Tanzania came close to making this defence at the OAU Summit at Monrovia, and a key motive in removing Amin was to prevent a second attack against Tanzania. Consequently, the legal question is how far the threat posed by Amin justified Tanzania using force on such a scale that the threat to Tanzania was eliminated. As I pointed out in the previous chapter, it is not enough to point to the possibility of future attack; rather, as Schachter argues, the imminence of attack must be so clear that defensive action is a prerequisite for survival. On this criterion, it is hard to justify Tanzania's action as an act of self-defence.

The second justification employed by Nyerere was retaliation against Uganda for its unlawful action in invading the Kegara Salient. Nyerere and his ministers were incensed by Amin's killing and destruction, with Tanzanian officials talking of a 'blood debt which must be settled'.[44] The UN Charter provides no legal provision for reprisals and this is not surprising given that the purpose of the Charter is to restrict the recourse to force by individual states to purposes of self-defence. The status of reprisals in customary international law is controversial, but three conditions were established by the Permanent Court of International Justice in an arbitration ruling in 1928. The first condition is that an illegal act has been committed; secondly, all peaceful means of redress must have been exhausted; and, finally, the action must be proportionate to the wrong inflicted.[45] Tanzania's action clearly did not meet the third criteria, since overthrowing Amin was not commensurate with the Ugandan leader's initial transgression.[46]

Assisting exile forces was the final argument employed by the Tanzanian Government to justify its actions. As we have seen, the two-wars theory lacked credibility in the eyes of foreign observers, who reported that up to 20,000 Tanzanian troops were involved in the intervention as against 3,000–5,000 Ugandan exiles. Moreover, it is estimated that the war cost

[44] 'Tanzania May Enter Uganda', *Observer*, 19 Nov. 1978.

[45] See Thomas, *New States, Sovereignty and Intervention*, 119.

[46] Ibid. Thomas also suggests that Nyerere's rejection of OAU mediation failed to meet the second criterion of seeking peaceful means of redress. This view is also supported by Hassan, who concludes that 'Tanzanian authorities cannot legitimize their behaviour by claiming an extrajudicial right to punish those violating their boundaries' ((Hassan, 'Realpolitik in International Law', 907).

Tanzania at least one million dollars a day, which was a massive strain on the economy and indicates the significance of Tanzania's role in bringing about the demise of the Amin regime.[47] This leads Hassan to argue that 'it is absurd to suggest the Tanzanian military was not the decisive element in the confrontation . . . Tanzania's claim for legitimacy represents an exaggerated fiction'.[48]

Nyerere seems to have reasoned that his best line of defence was to admit Tanzania's pivotal role in the overthrow of Amin and hope that the rest of the world condoned this. Although Vietnam could point to border attacks and massacre of civilians by the Pol Pot regime, Tanzania had been invaded and several hundred kilometres of its territory had been temporarily annexed. Nevertheless, legitimating the toppling of a government on self-defence grounds where there was no immediate threat fundamentally challenged the rules of international society. Indeed, Vietnam's intervention, which arguably is more justifiable on these grounds than Tanzania's, was interpreted as a clear-cut violation of the principles of non-intervention and non-use of force. What, then, explains the different international response to Tanzania's intervention?

The International Reaction: Tanzania's Insulation from Superpower Geopolitics

The first factor that differentiates the Tanzanian and Vietnamese interventions is that the Tanzanian–Ugandan conflict was never debated by either the UN Security Council or the General Assembly. On 13 February 1979 Amin had written to the UN Secretary General, Kurt Waldheim, requesting a meeting of the Security Council to deal with the 'serious and explosive situation now prevailing on the border'.[49] Kuwait was the President of the Security Council for February and the Kuwaiti Ambassador replied that neither he nor the Secretary General considered the request a properly worded one. As Thomas points out, such a reply indicates that Uganda was not seen by the Security Council as the injured party at this time.[50] Six weeks later, when it was clear to foreign diplomats that Tanzanian forces were heavily involved in the defeat of Amin's forces, the Ugandan President pressed once again for a

---

[47] On 13 July it was disclosed in Dar el Salamm that a month earlier Tanzania had appealed to the governments of the USA, West Germany, Canada, Sweden, Netherlands, Norway, Denmark, Japan, and the Britain for $375,000,000 in aid to avert economic collapse as a result of the Tanzanian–Ugandan war. The British Foreign and Commonwealth Office estimated that the war had cost Tanzania more than $250,000,000, threatening the very economic survival of the country. See *Keesing's Contemporary Archives* Bristol, 21 Sept. 1979, 29838.

[48] Hassan, 'Realpolitik in International Law', 905.

[49] Thomas, *New States, Sovereignty and Intervention*, 115.   [50] Ibid.

meeting of the Security Council. A few days later he withdrew his request after the fifty-member African group at the UN sent him a message advising him against involving the Security Council in the conflict.[51] Given that African states condemned Vietnam's breach of the non-intervention rule, it might seem surprising that they opposed Amin's attempt to secure a meeting of the Security Council. But this outcome reflected both the skill of Tanzanian diplomacy at the UN and the fact that most Africans were glad to see the back of Amin.[52]

The Security Council was the arena in which great power rivalries were played out in relation to Vietnam's use of force against Cambodia (as it had been eight years earlier when India had intervened in East Pakistan), but Tanzania's action was not drawn into the geopolitical conflict between the great powers. Although the USA and the Soviet Union competed for influence in relation to the strategically important conflict between Somalia and Ethiopia, they did not have important security interests at stake in the Tanzanian–Ugandan conflict. There was competition between China and the Soviet Union for influence, with China acting as a patron for Tanzania while the Soviet Union backed Amin. However, two factors moderated Sino-Soviet rivalry: the absence of US involvement and the Soviet Union's growing embarrassment at Amin's actions.

The Soviet Union was Uganda's main supplier of arms through the 1970s, with Soviet military and civilian advisers training the Ugandan army and air force.[53] After Amin's invasion of the Kegara Salient, the Soviet Union stopped supplying arms and it made no effort to support the Libyans in their counter-intervention against Tanzania. Moreover, having supported Amin without any criticism of his regime's human rights abuses for the previous seven years, the Soviet Union tried to open a new chapter in its relations with Tanzania and Uganda after the fall of Kampala. It endorsed Tanzania's defensive claim by describing the Tanzanian action as 'a countermeasure'[54] and denounced Amin for 'causing thousands of people to disappear'.[55] This reference to human rights abuses could have led the Soviet Union to endorse Tanzania's intervention on humanitarian grounds, but the Soviet Government's use of the word 'countermeasure' indicates that it preferred the convenient fiction that Tanzania's action was one of self-defence.

Western states reacted cautiously to Tanzania's forcible removal of Amin, neither praising nor offering any direct comment on the legitimacy of its use of force. The USA resumed normal diplomatic relations with the new

[51] 'A Victory for Tanzania, a Worry for Africa', *New York Times*, 16 Apr. 1979.

[52] Lord Richard, who was Britain's Ambassador on the Security Council at the time, puts a lot of weight on the role played by Salim Ahmed Salim, who was Tanzania's Ambassador to the UN and a significant influence on the policies of the African group at the UN. Interview with Lord Richard, House of Lords, Mar. 1999.

[53] *African Contemporary Record*, 11 (1978–9), B439.

[54] Quoted in Klintworth, *Vietnam's Intervention in International Law*, 51.   [55] Ibid.

Ugandan Government, suspending the trade sanctions that the Carter Administration had imposed on Uganda because of its human rights abuses. These steps were not coupled with any moral or material support for Tanzania's intervention. Britain recognized the new Ugandan Government on 16 April, with Foreign Secretary David Owen expressing his approval that the Ugandan dictator had been removed from power. Britain did make one million pounds available to the new regime, but, like the USA, it refrained from offering any direct comment on Tanzania's role in bringing about Amin's demise.

Western states were on difficult ground in recognizing the new government in Kampala, given their non-recognition of the PRK government in Phnom Penh. The USA and Britain refused to recognize the Heng Samrin government because it had been installed by Vietnamese arms, but they recognized a government in Kampala that had been installed by Tanzanian ones.[56] In the eyes of Western governments, the key difference between the two cases was that Vietnam was an expansionist state acting as a proxy for Soviet imperialism, whereas Tanzania had been provoked and was not a predatory state. The weakness of this argument is twofold: it overlooks the provocation of Vietnam by the Pol Pot regime, and, more importantly, it suggests that, had Vietnam been perceived as having benign motives, its use of force would have been treated differently. If this is the case, then why did Western states not make this argument instead of invoking the pluralist one that Vietnam's action undermined international order? The question that Western governments failed to answer was why Tanzania's toppling of Amin did not equally challenge the rule structure of international society.

China was also faced with a major difficulty in its reaction to Tanzania's use of force, since its strategic interests conflicted with its doctrinal principles. Tanzania was a valued ally, but if China blessed its client's action in overthrowing Amin, then this would weaken its case against Vietnam. Publicly, China preferred a negotiated settlement of the Tanzanian–Ugandan conflict along the lines proposed by the OAU's Mediation Committee, but it can be agreed with Thomas that 'it must have basked in the reflected glory of its client's achievement . . . Sino-Soviet rivalry by proxy had worked this time to the advantage of China.'[57] China recognized the new Ugandan Government on 2 May, and it is hard to avoid the realist judgement that the divergent positions it took on recognizing the new governments in Kampala and Phnom Penh reflected a blatant example of the selective application of principles. It was power politics that dictated that China condemn Vietnam for toppling a government that had committed mass murder against its citizens whilst turning a blind eye to its client's violation of the same rule.

---

[56] Evans and Rowley, *Red Brotherhood*, 192.
[57] Thomas, *New States, Sovereignty and Intervention*, 113.

The recognition of the new government in Kampala by over sixty states at the end of 1980 contrasts starkly with the decision of the UN General Assembly in Resolution 34/22 to deny recognition to the new government in Cambodia. This resolution had been pressed by ASEAN, which is guilty of double standards in its decision to recognize the Tanzanian-installed government in Kampala. At the same time as the five South-East Asian governments condemned Vietnam and backed the guerrilla army of Pol Pot as the legitimate government of Cambodia, they 'did not hesitate in accepting the Tanzanian intervention as legitimate and in recognizing the new regime. There was no hypocritical attempt to maintain that Amin still had to be recognized as the country's legal ruler.'[58] Unfortunately, neither Vietnam nor any of its supporters pointed out the basic contradiction in the position taken by the West, China, and ASEAN on the recognition of the governments in Kampala and Phnom Penh in the General Assembly debate on the Cambodian seat. It is interesting to speculate whether an exposure of these contradictions would have changed the voting pattern in the General Assembly.

Turning to the regional reaction, Tanzania was the first African state to recognize the new Ugandan Government, a move quickly followed by the front-line states of Zambia, Angola, Botswana, and Mozambique. Without legitimating Tanzania's intervention, the President of Zambia, Kenneth D. Kaunda, said that the defeat of Amin was 'a triumph for freedom, justice and human dignity'.[59] Within the next few days, Malawi, Rwanda, Gambia, Ethiopia, and Guinea also recognized the new Ugandan Government. Given that Tanzania had flouted the rules of the OAU, it is surprising that there was no condemnation of the Tanzanian action in the immediate aftermath of the overthrow of Amin.[60] Nevertheless, Tanzania was to come in for some criticism at the OAU Summit in Monrovia.

Nyerere had wanted the OAU to condemn Uganda for invading the Kegara Salient, and, in response to this, President Numeiry had taken the view that it was not possible for the organization to condemn a fellow member state. However, the outgoing OAU Chairman broke with all convention at the Heads of State Meeting held at Monrovia on 17–21 July and used his opening speech to attack Tanzania for its rejection of OAU mediation efforts. He told the 2,000 delegates that the 'Ugandan side showed readiness to co-operate',[61] but Tanzania was interested only in securing the OAU's condemnation of Amin. The clear implication was that Nyerere's intransigence was responsible

---

[58] Evans and Rowley, *Red Brotherhood*, 191.

[59] 'Invaders Establish Control in Kampala and Call on All Ugandans to Hunt Amin'.

[60] The exception was Morocco, where the pro-government paper *El Maghrib* on 12 April expressed regret at the 'silence of the OAU' and noted that this was the first time an African state had 'invaded its neighbour and taken its capital with impunity' (quoted in *Keesing's Contemporary Archives*, 22 June 1979, 29673).

[61] *African Contemporary Record*, 12 (1979–80), A61.

for the war, which Numeiry described as 'a sad precedent in Africa'.[62] Stressing that he was no defender of Amin's regime, he named Tanzania's use of force as a clear violation of 'our Organization's Charter, which prohibits interference in other people's internal affairs and invasion of their territory by armed force'.[63]

The Tanzanian President had the right to respond to the Sudanese President's bitter attack from the rostrum, but decided to reply from his seat. Even now, as Tanzania came under bitter attack from the outgoing Chair of the OAU, the Tanzanian President refused to defend his overthrow of Amin as a humanitarian intervention. Instead, he argued that the OAU should be condemning Uganda not Tanzania for its violation of the Charter in invading Tanzanian territory:

> We are asked to support the proposition that when one country has committed an act of aggression against another, has clearly violated the Charter of the OAU, has blatantly attempted the annexation of a piece of land of another country, that to appeal to the OAU to condemn that act of violation of the Charter is in itself a violation of the Charter ... I want to congratulate my brother, President Numeiry, in that he now wants this matter to be discussed. My only criticism is that he would like to see in the dock not the aggressor but the victim.[64]

The next day Nyerere flew home, having arrived at the summit only twelve hours earlier. A Tanzanian spokesperson claimed that his departure had no connection with his exchange with Numeiry, and that the President had planned to return home early to prepare for a visit by Queen Elizabeth. Before leaving Monrovia, Nyerere had circulated a seventeen-page statement, the so-called Blue Book setting out Tanzania's case. The statement described Amin as 'an abominable murderer of the people of Uganda', detailing the atrocities of his eight-year reign of terror. It also highlighted how far Tanzania's advance into Uganda was greeted as an act of liberation 'by the Ugandan people, who danced in the streets [and] generally celebrated'.[65] Whilst Nyerere must have hoped that documenting Amin's human rights abuses and stressing the liberating role played by Tanzanian soldiers would moderate any censure of Tanzania at the summit, at no point does the Blue Book justify Tanzania's action under the doctrine of humanitarian intervention. Nyerere had repeatedly argued for a change of the OAU Charter so that it did not protect tyrants like Amin. Monrovia provided an opportunity for the Tanzanian President to issue a direct challenge to the pluralist rules of the OAU by arguing that African governments that descend to the level of butchery seen in Uganda should forfeit protection of the Charter and expose themselves to forcible

---

[62] *African Contemporary Record*, 12 (1979–80), A61.
[63] Ibid.   [64] Ibid.
[65] The full text of the Tanzanian Blue Book is published in 'Tanzania and the War against Amin's Uganda', *Daily News*, 20 July 1979.

intervention by other African states. Although it was reported that Nyerere saw his intervention as an opportunity to press for such a change in the rules of the OAU,[66] the Blue Book persisted with the justification that Tanzania had acted in self-defence: 'The war between Tanzania and Idi Amin's regime in Uganda was caused by the Ugandan army's aggression against Tanzania and Idi Amin's claim to have annexed part of Tanzanian territory. *There was no other cause for it.'*[67]

What is significant about the Blue Book is that it was admitted for the first time that Kampala had fallen to a combined force of anti-Amin forces and the Tanzanian army. Tanzania made no apology for 'taking the war started by Uganda into Uganda', Amin's regime being 'a turbulent menace to the peace and security of East Africa'.[68] This was the closest Nyerere came to advancing the legal argument that Tanzania's overthrow of Amin was justified as an act of self-defence because it was proportional to the threat posed by Amin to Tanzania's security. The Blue Book also invoked a new justification to legitimate the action. Tanzania had been forced to take on the main burden of the war because of Libyan involvement, and this reason was now publicly used to justify the action. The Blue Book stated that Tanzania had made no public statement about Libyan intervention in the conflict, even though it had been supplying arms to Amin's forces and fighting alongside them during the war—the clear implication being that, without Libyan support, Amin would have been toppled by the intervention of the exile forces and an uprising of the Ugandan people.[69]

If Nyerere hoped that his early departure from the summit and the publication of the Blue Book would put an end to the argument, then he must have been disappointed the following day when Nigeria's Head of State, General Olusegen Obasanjo, reopened the question. The Tanzanian President justified intervention by pointing to Ugandan 'aggression', but Obasanjo turned this round and named Tanzania as the 'aggressor'.[70] He challenged the Tanzanian claim that Uganda was the first to violate the border, claiming that there had been interventions by Tanzania in support of Ugandan dissidents. Moreover, the Nigerian President argued that Uganda had taken retaliatory action only after notifying the UN and OAU, which had failed to act. By advancing this fictitious account of the history of the Ugandan–Tanzanian conflict, the Nigerian leader was seeking to make trouble for Nyerere.

Although it is easy to dismiss Obasanjo's distortion of the historical record as an attempt to place Tanzania on the defensive, there are other parts of his speech that speak directly to the legitimacy of humanitarian intervention. The Nigerian Head of State stated that his government had put pressure on

---

[66] See 'Bending the Rules to Get Rid of an African Barbarian', *Guardian*, 7 Apr. 1979.
[67] 'Tanzania and the War against Amin's Uganda'; emphasis added.
[68] Ibid.   [69] Ibid.
[70] *Africa Research Bulletin*, 1–31 July 1979, 5329.

Amin's regime to improve its human rights record, but the responsibility of African states to condemn domestic tyranny did not issue a licence for unilateral humanitarian intervention. Obasanjo set out Nigeria's view on the limits of guardianship of human rights in the society of states:

We saw our duty as being to condemn, to warn, and to bring together whatever pressure we could to bear on the constituted government of Uganda to curb its excesses and return to the path of morality and decency. We never saw it as our duty, and we did not see it as the duty of any other country, to forcibly effect a change in the government of another country on the grounds that we do not agree with the ideology, style or morality of that government and under any smokescreen.[71]

The significance of this passage is that one can hear in it the tension between pluralist and solidarist conceptions of international society. The contention that the human rights records of African states should be open to the legitimate scrutiny and censure of their peers is a retreat from a strict pluralist interpretation of the OAU Charter. However, the limits of this emergent solidarism can be seen clearly in the Nigerian Head of State's assertion that individual states do not have a 'duty' to use force to change the 'morality' of another government with which they disagree. His justification for this position is that the rules of sovereignty and non-intervention exist to protect cultural diversity and to shield the weak from the strong; any erosion of these rules risked placing 'the weaker and smaller nations of Africa' at the mercy of 'their powerful neighbours'.[72] In making this argument, Obasanjo was expressing the pluralist view that it was not possible for African states to reach a consensus on the moral principles that should govern a right of unilateral humanitarian intervention.[73] Here, the Nigerian leader echoed a view that his government had expressed two days before Tanzanian forces took control of Kampala. At that time, Nigeria had voiced its concern that Tanzania's intervention could trigger a 'chain reaction' in which 'a few militarily powerful nations would be able to determine the leadership of other states'.[74]

Faced with Obasanjo's mobilization of the legitimating principles of the OAU Charter against him, Nyerere could have instructed his delegation to

---

[71] *Africa Research Bulletin*, 1–31 July 1979, 5329. [72] Ibid.

[73] The realist argument that states will abuse a right of humanitarian intervention is also hinted at in the Nigerian President's concern about governments using moral justifications as a 'smokescreen'.

[74] 'A Victory for Tanzania, a Worry for Africa', *New York Times*, 16 Apr. 1979. Caroline Thomas interprets Obasanjo's argument about the dangers of 'powerful neighbours' as a veiled criticism of Tanzania's expansionist tendencies. She refutes this charge by arguing that Tanzania was not militarily superior to Uganda, concluding that Obasanjo's hidden motive for criticizing Tanzania was that Nigeria still harboured a grudge against Nyerere for his support of Biafra's attempted secession from Nigeria in the late 1960s. See Thomas, *New States, Sovereignty and Intervention*, 111. However, Obasanjo had other reasons for taking a tough line against Tanzania's intervention. Although Obasanjo was Nigeria's outgoing head of state, he was under pressure from some of his fellow Muslim officers in the military regime. They had used the paper *New Nigerian* to describe the Tanzanian intervention as 'immoral and damnable', and Nyerere's government as 'smug and self-virtuous'. See *African Contemporary Record*, 12 (1979–80), A63.

reveal at the summit the covert support that Obasanjo had given Tanzania during the war.[75] However, he did not want to enter into a dispute with Nigeria, placing considerable value on its support for the front-line states in their battle against South Africa. The Tanzanian Foreign Minister told reporters that Tanzania contested Nigeria's 'analysis' of the Uganda issue but 'would not answer back out of respect for General Obasanjo'.[76] This was a weak argument that masked Nyerere's desire not to alienate further those within the Nigerian Government who were already suspicious of Tanzania's action in overthrowing Amin.

Tanzania's reluctance to enter into a debate with Obasanjo can be contrasted with the position taken by the new Ugandan President, Godfrey Binaisa. Nyerere had rejected unilateral humanitarian intervention as a legitimating reason for Tanzania's use of force, indicating how the pluralist rules of the OAU Charter constituted the givens of discourse. However, Binaisa challenged the dominant interpretation of the rules prevalent at Monrovia, and the significance of his speech is that he defended Tanzania's use of force as a humanitarian intervention. He reinforced Tanzania's claim that it had acted in 'self-defence and security'[77] before going on to praise the action for bringing about the demise of Amin, whom he claimed had killed half a million people during his eight-year rule. He criticized the Sudanese and Nigerian Presidents for condemning a Tanzanian intervention that had been warmly welcomed by the Ugandan people.[78] In asking the OAU Assembly whether 'a Head of State [is] entitled to decimate the entire population behind the wall of non-interference',[79] Binaisa issued a direct solidarist challenge to the pluralist meanings that constituted the rules of the OAU Charter. The Ugandan President pointed to the contradictions between the atrocities of Amin's regime and the vision of the founders of the OAU that the organization would 'unite our continent in order to enhance the freedom and dignity of the sons and daughters of Africa'. The clear implication was that protection of the OAU's rules depended upon African governments upholding basic standards of human rights at home. Thus, Tanzania's action was not

---

[75] Obasanjo's relationship with Nyerere is a complex one, since it is claimed that it was 'Obasanjo himself who had given Nyerere the "green light" to move deeper into Uganda after Libya had entered the conflict'. (*African Contemporary Record*, 12 (1979–80), A62). There is, then, a clear contradiction between Obasanjo's criticism of Tanzania at Monrovia and his covert role in the Ugandan–Tanzanian conflict. Even if Obasanjo tacitly backed Nyerere against the Libyans, it does not follow from this that he was not worried about the precedent-setting effects of Tanzania's action. There is nothing in his speech, contra Thomas, to indicate that Obasanjo viewed Tanzania as a predatory state, and it might be speculated that his arguments were directed as much at his own successors in Lagos, who had the power forcibly to change every government in West Africa, as they were at Nyerere. Like all strong states, Nigeria had least to fear from an erosion of the OAU Charter and for this reason it is implausible to read Obasanjo's speech as an example of special pleading.

[76] *Africa Research Bulletin*, 1–31 July 1979, 5329.

[77] 'Eight Years of Terror', *Daily News*, 23 July 1979.

[78] 'Row on Tanzania's Toppling of Amin Dominates OAU', *Guardian*, 20 July 1979.

[79] 'Eight Years of Terror'.

a breach of the OAU Charter because Amin's bestial rule meant that Uganda forfeited its right to be treated as a legitimate sovereign.[80]

Natalino Ronzitti argues that Binaisa's speech is of little importance in assessing the legitimacy of humanitarian intervention, because his government had been installed by Tanzanian arms.[81] But, contra Ronzitti, it is significant that Binaisa advanced humanitarian claims, because the objection that he did so only to legitimize his accession to power fails to account for why he did not stick with Tanzania's defence in the Blue Book. Certainly, the new Ugandan Government's contestation of existing norms contrasts starkly with the position taken by the Heng Samrin government in Cambodia, which repeated the two-wars justification invoked by Vietnam.

Binaisa's solidarist claim was not publicly supported by any other government at Monrovia, and at the end of his speech Obasanjo, who was debate Chairman, said to the Ugandan President: 'You are on honeymoon now, but when it is over you will see reality.'[82] Since the Tanzanian intervention of Uganda was proving so divisive, the new Chairman of the OAU, President Tolbert of Liberia, took up the suggestion of President Ahmed Sekou Toure of Guinea that the matter be discussed in a private plenary session. There are no reports of what was discussed in closed session, but the OAU Assembly did not pass any resolution condemning Tanzania. With the exception of the outgoing Chairman of the OAU and the Nigerian Head of State, no other African state expressed public disapproval.

The OAU's reaction to Tanzania's toppling of Amin differed markedly from the response of ASEAN to Vietnam's overthrow of Pol Pot. Thomas considers that the 'general African consensus . . . seemed to settle at the level of tacit approval of Tanzanian action'.[83] Three key factors seem to explain the differing regional reactions to Tanzania's and Vietnam's use of force. The first is that there was considerable sympathy among African states for Tanzania's claim that Uganda had attacked first. Amin justified his intervention in the Kegara Salient in terms of territorial claims that existed prior to independence, and this set a dangerous precedent in a continent where the borders inherited at the time of independence are sacrosanct. During his eight-year

[80] In advancing this solidarist claim, Binaisa tried to undermine Obasanjo's criticism of Tanzania's action by reminding the Assembly that the Nigerian President had argued at the 1978 OAU summit that 'we must have courage to tell ourselves what is unjust and what is immoral so that we can ensure amongst ourselves certain minimum levels of decent leadership and good government for our people'. These remarks by the Nigerian President implied that it was possible for Africans to arrive at a shared understanding of what counts as unacceptable domestic conduct. Now this does not necessarily lead to the conclusion that states have a right or duty to use force to end cruelty and slaughter, but Obasanjo's argument at Khartoum in 1978 could be interpreted as legitimating the use of force in supreme humanitarian emergencies. Obasanjo's speech at the 1978 OAU Summit is quoted in 'Eight Years of Terror'.

[81] Ronzitti, *Rescuing Nationals Abroad*, 105.

[82] 'OAU Drops Invasion Dispute', *Daily Telegraph*, 20 July 1979.

[83] Thomas, *New States, Sovereignty and Intervention*, 112.

rule, Amin also made territorial claims against Kenya, the Sudan, and Rwanda. Little wonder then that, in recognizing the post-Amin government, the Ethiopian Government stated that Amin had 'despised all the rules governing international relations'.[84] Although Pol Pot was similarly dismissive of the post-colonial compact on borders, and the neighbours of the DK were clearly suspicious of its intentions, Cambodia's provocations of Vietnam were not perceived as justifying the removal of Pol Pot from power. Vietnam's use of force produced a positive humanitarian outcome, but, in acting to maintain its security, Hanoi was perceived by its neighbours as having decreased their security. Conversely, Tanzania's removal of Amin increased its own security without threatening wider regional security.

The second difference is that Vietnam was perceived by ASEAN as having installed a puppet government. Nyerere wanted to avoid the charge that he had invaded Uganda to restore his friend Obote to power. Consequently, he arranged for a conference of exile leaders to be held in the Tanzanian town of Moshi on 23–25 March in the hope that this could produce a provisional government for Uganda. Obote did not attend the conference, having been asked by Nyerere to stay away so as to avoid the impression that Tanzania was promoting him.[85] The Tanzanian Foreign Minister attended the conference throughout and emphasized in a statement that Tanzania stood by the post-colonial borders and respected the right of the Ugandan people to determine their own affairs.[86] As a consequence of the conference, Yusef Lule was elected head of the government-in-exile that came to power a few weeks later on 11 April 1979.

As Lule took the oath of office in Kampala, he was flanked by Tanzanian army commanders, symbolizing that his government, like that of the PRK, existed by virtue of force of arms. However, where ASEAN—especially Thailand—perceived a threat to their security in Vietnam's military presence in Cambodia, the vast majority of African states accepted that the Tanzanian military presence in Uganda did not reflect 'aggrandisement or imperialism' on the part of Nyerere.[87] Although a contrast is often made between the quick

---

[84] Ronzitti, *Rescuing Nationals Abroad*, 104.
[85] *African Contemporary Record*, 11 (1978–9), B434. [86] Ibid. B435.
[87] Thomas, *New States, Sovereignty and Intervention*, 118. The exception was Kenya, which viewed Tanzania's move into Uganda with considerable concern. Nyerere had asked President Moi to cut off oil and other supplies to Amin during the war, but Kenya had refused on the grounds that it had an obligation to allow trade with landlocked countries. Kenya feared that the new Ugandan Government would prevent it using Uganda, as it had under Amin, as a transit route for Kenyan exports to Rwanda, Zaïre, and Sudan. Moreover, Kenya was unhappy with what it saw as Nyerere's defiance of the principles of sovereignty and non-intervention. Parts of north-eastern Kenya are claimed by Somalia, and, whilst President Moi did not want to be seen defending Amin at Monrovia, it was reported that he felt 'privately bitter and vulnerable' that the OAU had not done more to sanction Nyerere for breaching the cardinal rules of the OAU. See 'Bending the Rules to Get Rid of an African Barbarian'. Further evidence of Kenya's concerns at Tanzania's policy in Uganda can be seen in Kenya's expression of concern at the Commonwealth Summit in August 1979 that Tanzania was too dominant a force in Ugandan political life. See Thomas, *New States, Sovereignty and Intervention*, 117.

withdrawal of Tanzanian forces and the prolonged occupation of Vietnamese ones, Tanzanian forces remained in Uganda for several years after the intervention. As I argued in the previous chapter, Vietnam's continued military presence in Cambodia can be justified on humanitarian grounds, and this is also the case with Tanzania's decision to maintain forces inside Uganda. After being replaced as President by Binaisa, Lule did accuse Nyerere of turning Uganda into 'a satellite state', claiming that he had rigged the new government with pro-Obote supporters.[88] But there is every reason to think that Nyerere would have liked to withdraw his forces as quickly as possible. The economic burden of sustaining approximately 40,000 troops in Uganda has been estimated at £500,000 pounds a day, and this on top of the economic costs of the war was imposing a massive strain on the Tanzanian economy. This crushing burden explains why Tanzania had asked Western states for financial support in June. Nyerere began pulling back half the force the week before the OAU Summit, presumably to defuse criticism of his intervention, but he was persuaded by the Ugandan Government to leave 20,000 troops, which would be withdrawn over the next two years.[89] Remnants of Amin's forces were still at large in the country, and there was no local police or security forces that had the trust of the Ugandan people.[90] The Tanzanian army had rescued the citizens of Uganda from mass killing and it remained the best guarantee of their security.

Conclusion

Tanzania's intervention in Uganda clearly meets the threshold requirements of a legitimate humanitarian intervention. Amin's terrible abuses against the people of Uganda produced a supreme humanitarian emergency where intervention was justified. Given the chronic insecurity that pervaded the country, indigenous forces were incapable of putting an end to the atrocities. The only prospect of ending these was external military intervention, and, as with Vietnam's *rescue* in Cambodia, the use of force was proportionate to the scale of the violations it ended. Without Amin's removal from power, there was no hope of ending the abuses and restoring the rule of law. There is no such thing as a cost-free humanitarian intervention, but, as with India's and Vietnam's actions, the costs in lives to Tanzanian soldiers and Ugandan civilians killed as

---

[88] *Africa Research Bulletin*, 1–31 July 1979, 5338.

[89] 'Tanzanians Anxious to Leave Uganda', *Guardian*, 13 July 1979. This account is contradicted by Lule's statement that he asked Nyerere at a meeting on 2 May when Tanzanian forces would be withdrawn following reports that Tanzanian soldiers were responsible for acts of rape, looting, and killing. According to Lule, Nyerere placed the blame elsewhere and said the troops would be removed after two years. See *Africa Research Bulletin*, 1–31 July 1979, 5338.

[90] Thomas, *New States, Sovereignty and Intervention*, 117–18.

a consequence of the fighting have to be set against the number of lives saved by Tanzania's intervention.

Hassan maintains that Nyerere's primary motive in using force was his obsessive desire to remove Amin and that Tanzania incurred the heavy economic costs of intervention only because of this motivation.[91] He argues that naming Tanzania's action as a humanitarian intervention ignores the fact that unilateral actions are always 'a phenomenon of *power* . . . the presence of the *realpolitik* in international law'.[92] Nyerere was determined to get rid of Amin after the Ugandan invasion of the Kegara Salient had convinced him that Tanzania would not have lasting security while Amin ruled Uganda. However, the existence of non-humanitarian motives undermines the humanitarian credentials of Tanzania's action only if these undermined a positive humanitarian outcome. Hassan's argument overlooks the fact that Nyerere's motives for removing Amin and securing the long-term safety of the Tanzanian state required actions that were compatible with the goal of ending human rights abuses inside Uganda.

A further criticism that can be levelled at Hassan's argument is that humanitarian reasons played an important part in Tanzania's decision to intervene. This is the position taken by Thomas, who argues that Nyerere's decision to use force indicates that the 'humanitarian impulse played a significant role'.[93] Nyerere was an outspoken advocate of humanitarian values on the African continent and had campaigned for a change of the OAU Charter to provide greater protection of human rights. Consequently, it might be argued that Nyerere had humanitarian motives for using force but felt unable to reveal these publicly because humanitarian justifications did not belong to the legitimating rules of international society.

Although Hassan and Thomas disagree on the nature of Tanzanian motives, they both assume that this factor is sufficient to explain Tanzania's decision to intervene in Uganda. The problem with this approach is that it ignores the importance of justification since this case supports Skinner's proposition that actions will be constrained if they cannot be legitimated. It is clear that, without Uganda's initial act of aggression, there would have been no question of using force against Amin or taking the war into Uganda. Nyerere made this clear in the statement he issued at Monrovia. The Blue Book stated that Tanzania 'had co-existed with Idi Amin for eight years and could have continued to do so' albeit with 'a consciousness of shame at the activities of this murderer of African peoples'.[94] Nyerere had issued protests against Amin's human rights abuses since his brutal regime first came to power, and he would have gone on campaigning on behalf of the Ugandan

---

[91] Hassan, 'Realpolitik in International Law', 897.
[92] Ibid. 911–12; emphasis in original.
[93] Thomas, *New States, Sovereignty and Intervention*, 116.
[94] 'Tanzania and the War against Amin's Uganda'.

people. However, his socialization into the rules of the OAU led him publicly to reject the legitimacy of a doctrine of unilateral humanitarian intervention. Amin's aggression opened up new possibilities for ridding Africa of a barbarian, and a factor in Tanzania's military support for the exile forces was surely Nyerere's desire to end the domestic excesses of the Ugandan regime. But even after Uganda had invaded Tanzania, the Tanzanian President remained reluctant to become too deeply involved in the overthrow of Amin. Certainly, he did not anticipate breaching the OAU Charter, because he expected intervention to be confined to the southern border areas, an action that could be justified in terms of self-defence. Nyerere's hatred of Amin and his humanitarian impulse to end the atrocities in Uganda were important determinants of Tanzania's action, but, without the public legitimating reason supplied by Ugandan aggression, intervention would not have been possible.

The reason why most African states tacitly accepted Tanzania's forcible removal of the Ugandan dictator was not because they accepted the legitimacy of a rule of unilateral humanitarian intervention; rather, it reflected the fact that Amin had broken all the rules of the OAU game. Moreover, these rules were the ones of sovereignty and non-intervention, because, as Nyerere himself admitted, had Amin confined his excesses to the domestic realm, there was no legal right for other African sovereigns to act as the conscience of humanity. Consequently, I disagree with Teson, who argues that the reason why Africa condoned Tanzania's use of force was its 'moral judgement that no rights of territorial integrity or political independence, no rule of non-intervention, can possibly shield tyrants like Amin'. He claims that the Tanzanian case is the 'the clearest in a series . . . which have carved out an important exception to the prohibition of article 2 (4)'.[95]

This claim that Tanzania's intervention establishes an important precedent for humanitarian intervention in customary international law is open to two critical objections. First, as discussed above, Tanzania's use of force became possible only because of a prior Ugandan attack. The OAU's toleration of Amin's atrocities through the 1970s indicates that, had he respected the rules of sovereignty and non-intervention, any use of force against his regime would have been strongly condemned.

The second problem with Teson's claim is that, with the exception of the new Ugandan Government, no other state legitimated Tanzania's use of force on humanitarian grounds. Although the voice of solidarism can be heard strongly in Godfrey Binaisa's speech, his argument that governments that massively violated human rights should be denied protection of the OAU Charter failed to elicit any support from other African states. If the Tanzanian intervention in Uganda is a case supporting a new rule of customary international law, then this should be evident in the moral reasoning of state leaders.

[95] Teson, *Humanitarian Intervention*, 174, 167–68.

As I argued in Part One, for a legal rule of humanitarian intervention to develop, there has to be a new practice and *opinio juris*: the vast majority of states have to argue that the new practice is permitted or required by the law. The Ugandan case fails to meet these requirements, because, when given the opportunity to defend Tanzania's action in terms of the legal claim of unilateral humanitarian intervention, African heads of state preferred to stay silent. They probably accepted that Tanzania had acted in good conscience and this made them willing to mitigate the action, but what they would not do was recognize it as a legitimate exception to the rules of the OAU Charter.

The only leader to speak out against Tanzania's action was General Obasanjo of Nigeria, who worried that if 'we sacrifice principles . . . Africa will be the worse for it'.[96] His argument against a duty of humanitarian intervention was the pluralist one that to permit this would jeopardize order on the continent given that African states were divided over questions of morality and justice. Set against this, Binaisa argued that it made a mockery of the principles of the OAU to believe that they were intended to shelter tyrants like Amin. He appealed to the shared values that had inspired the founding of the OAU in an effort to persuade African governments to accept that there had to be limits to the exercise of sovereign rights. An increasing number of African states were sympathetic to this argument, but what they rejected was Binaisa's claim that tyrants who 'decimate . . . behind the wall of non-interference'[97] expose themselves to legitimate interventions like Tanzania's toppling of Amin.

One of the positive outcomes of the summit was the decision of the OAU Assembly to begin work on an African Charter for the protection of human rights.[98] Nyerere had been arguing for years that the OAU should take a more intrusive role in monitoring states' human rights practices, and the decision of the Assembly to create such a legal instrument was a vindication of his efforts. However, he had never championed a right of unilateral intervention to defend human rights. By contrast, in applauding Tanzania's intervention as liberating the Ugandan people, Binaisa argued that Tanzania's use of force had set a good precedent for African states to follow in future cases where African governments committed mass murder against their citizens.

Precedent setting was the dominant objection raised by Western states against Vietnam's action, and this raises the question why this concern was

---

[96] 'Amin Killed 500,000 People', *Daily News*, 20 July 1979.

[97] 'Eight Years of Terror'.

[98] It was reported that Senegal, supported by a number of Francophone states, had sponsored a resolution in closed session giving greater power to the OAU to denounce human rights violations. This led to the Assembly setting up a commission of inquiry to investigate the question and to the subsequent adoption of the Banjul Charter on Human and People's Rights at the 1981 summit of the OAU. However, Robert Jackson argues that its apparent protections for the rights of African citizens are in fact 'a thin disguise for asserting the priority of sovereign rights over human rights in Africa' (Jackson, *Quasi-states*, 154).

not voiced by them in relation to Tanzania's action. Nyerere was not congratulated for ridding the world of a barbarian but neither was his government sanctioned for breaking the rules of the society of states as Vietnam had been. Consequently, it is hard to avoid the conclusion that the doctrinal arguments used against Vietnam were conveniently forgotten by Western states when it came to Tanzania. It might be argued that this divergence in response illustrates the realist dictum that states will always apply principles selectively depending upon self-interest. At first sight, this conclusion seems to run against the argument advanced in the previous chapter that Western states were not simply manipulating the objection of precedent setting to legitimate their condemnation of Vietnam. After all, if pluralism formed the background normative context against which these governments defined their interests, why did they not invoke the precedent-setting argument in the Tanzanian case?

The answer seems to be that Western governments were sufficiently worried about precedent setting to avoid legitimating Tanzania's action, but judged that the circumstances surrounding Tanzania's use of force justified a very different response from that of Vietnam: Tanzania had been attacked first; Amin's regime was one of the most brutal the century had seen; and, most importantly, Tanzania's intervention did not touch on vital superpower interests, as in the case of Vietnam. The cold-war enemies who were divided over recognition of the PRK government in Phnom Penh could unite in welcoming the new government in Kampala.

Realism does not rule out a moral dimension in foreign policy provided that this does not conflict with a state's vital security interests. In the case of Tanzania's overthrow of Amin, Western states welcomed the outcome and tacitly accepted the means by which this had come about. It can be agreed with Evans and Rowley that 'Uganda was an entirely different matter, not because of any point of law, but because the interests of the great powers were not involved'.[99] The same choice between human rights and international law was posed in this case as in the Cambodian one, but it was resolved in favour of humanity on this occasion because there were no vital security interests at stake. Selectivity in the application of principles is a major realist objection to humanitarian intervention, and it remains to be seen in the following chapters how far the society of states is vulnerable to this charge in its response to humanitarian crises in the 1990s.

---

[99] Evans and Rowley, *Red Brotherhood*, 192.

PART THREE

Humanitarian Intervention after the Cold War

5

A Solidarist Moment in International Society? The Case of Safe Havens and No-Fly Zones in Iraq

The paralysis of the Security Council during the cold war was the context for the interventions by India, Tanzania, and Vietnam. The point of departure for the four case studies in Part Three is the central role played by the Security Council in legitimating the threat or use of force in defence of humanitarian values. The other distinguishing feature of these cases is that the intervening states have all been Western ones and they have justified their actions on explicitly humanitarian grounds. Given that this argument was either rejected or not raised in the Bangladeshi, Cambodian, and Ugandan cases, the following chapters examine how far the humanitarian claims raised by Western states in the 1990s secured legitimacy in the society of states. In justifying their interventions in humanitarian terms, Western governments can be held accountable for how far their subsequent actions produced a positive humanitarian outcome. I argued in previous chapters that the society of states should have welcomed India's, Vietnam's, and Tanzania's acts of rescue, but can the same verdict be applied to those Western interventions that were justified as humanitarian?

This chapter examines the international response to the plight of the Kurds and Shiites in Iraq in 1991–3. The Kurds have wanted to establish their own state since the late nineteenth century, but have found themselves trapped within the borders of Iraq, Turkey, Iran, and Syria. The three to four million Kurds living in northern Iraq secured an important measure of autonomy under a 1974 decree, but this did not protect them from brutal Iraqi repression during the latter stages of the Iran–Iraq War. At a moment of Iraqi weakness, Kurdish rebels had seized the opportunity to challenge the Baath party's control of northern Iraq, resulting in massive Iraqi attacks against both rebel forces and civilians. Some commentators claim that the killing of the Kurds in 1988 constituted a genocide as Iraqi soldiers rounded up and killed as many as 100,000 people.[1] In March of that year, Iraqi air forces attacked

---

[1] J. E. Stromseth, 'Iraq', in L. F. Damrosch (ed.), *Enforcing Restraint: Collective Intervention in Internal Conflicts* (New York: Council on Foreign Relations, 1993), 81.

the city of Halabja with chemical weapons, and, after the signing of a cease-fire in August with Iran, Iraq continued to attack Kurdish towns and villages with chemical munitions.[2]

There was verbal condemnation of Iraq's appalling attacks against civilians, but no sanctions were imposed against the government of Saddam Hussein, and there was no international rescue of the Kurds.[3] This situation stands in stark contrast to the international intervention to save the Kurds in the immediate aftermath of the Gulf War. A 'no-fly' zone was set up over northern Iraq and Western military forces were deployed inside Iraq's borders to set up 'safe havens' to protect the Kurds, and this was followed a year later by the creation of a southern no-fly zone to protect the persecuted Shiites in the south. This chapter investigates the changed context that made Western intervention possible, and here there are essentially two conflicting interpretations: first, that this is a landmark case supporting a new customary rule of humanitarian intervention in international law; secondly, that the Iraqi case does not mark a change in normative practice because it took place in the specific circumstances of the Gulf War, which limits its value as a precedent.

The chapter opens with an examination of the conversation in the Security Council that produced Resolution 688, the key legitimating argument employed by Western states to justify their intervention. The significance of this resolution is that it generated an argument within the Council as to the limits of its interventionist role given Article 2 (7) of the UN Charter. It may be recalled that this question had arisen and been resolved against Security Council intervention in the Bangladeshi case. Next, I examine the decision by Western states to give teeth to Resolution 688 by providing armed protection for the Kurds inside northern Iraq. Initially, Western governments argued that forcible intervention was not an option, but within a matter of days this decision had been reversed. Western publics were bombarded with images of the human suffering of the Kurds trapped in the mountains of Northern Iraq, and I assess how decisive this media coverage was in leading Western governments to launch a rescue mission to save the Kurds.

Western states legitimated their intervention as being in conformity with Resolution 688, but concern was expressed by the UN Secretary General as to the legality of this action. Although no state that voted in favour of Resolution 688 disputed the legality of the safe havens, subsequent Western plans to replace their forces with armed UN guards were publicly contested by both UN officials and the Soviet Union as exceeding the authority of Resolution 688. Consequently, a key question raised by the West's creation of the safe havens is how far this action received legitimation in wider international society.

[2] Stromseth, 'Iraq', 81.

[3] The USA and France strongly condemned Iraqi action, but Stromseth argues that there was no concerted action because 'political and strategic considerations once again overrode humanitarian concerns' (ibid.).

The extent to which Western governments lived up to their humanitarian justifications is discussed in the final part of the chapter. Here, I consider how far the intervention in northern Iraq achieved a positive humanitarian outcome, as well as the charge of selectivity in relation to the different response to the plight of the Shiites in southern Iraq.

Resolution 688

The defeat of Iraqi forces by the US-led coalition created an unstable political situation inside Iraq that was seized on by the Kurds in the north and Shiite Muslims in the south. In early March, uprisings took place against Saddam Hussein, and the rebels were initially successful in controlling key cities. However, Iraqi Republican Guard units quickly responded by using helicopters and tanks against the rebels and unarmed civilians. Although Western pilots were overflying Iraq as part of their monitoring of Iraqi military activity, they had strict orders not to intervene to protect the Kurds and Shiites. Senior Iraqi military figures had persuaded Allied generals during ceasefire talks in early March that they needed to fly their helicopters to move troops around, and it was these that now proved so effective in suppressing the uprising. By the end of March, the rebellions had been brutally crushed and Iraqi forces had retaken control of the country. Fearing Iraqi retribution, hundreds of thousands of Kurds and Shiites fled into the mountains near the border with Turkey and Iran. It is estimated that between 400 and 1,000 were dying every day from hypothermia, exhaustion, and disease.[4] Stranded without food, shelter, or medicines, and vulnerable to Iraqi helicopter gunships, the Kurds were in a desperate plight.

Faced with this mounting humanitarian emergency, France and Turkey (which feared an exodus of refugees across its border) took the initiative on 5 April in bringing the issue before the Security Council. France had tried two days earlier to get a clause inserted into the Gulf War ceasefire resolution concerning Iraqi massacres of the Kurds, with President Mitterrand declaring that failure to protect the Kurds would severely affect 'the political and moral authority' of the Council.[5] The French Foreign Minister went even further, arguing that the fate of the Kurds should lead the society of states to recognize a 'duty of intervention' in cases where human rights are being massively violated. Roland Dumas claimed that 'justice can evolve', pointing to the example of the Nazi genocide against the Jews, which had led jurists to develop new laws, which named this practice as a 'crime against humanity'.[6]

---

[4] T. G. Weiss, *Military–Civilian Interactions: Intervening in Humanitarian Crises* (Oxford: Rowman & Littlefield, 1999), 50.   [5] 'UN Abandons Kurds', *Independent,* 4 Apr. 1991.
[6] 'Paris Calls for New UN Laws to Help Kurds', *Independent,* 5 Apr. 1991.

The solidarist claims raised by Mitterrand and Dumas reflected the demands of a growing constituency within French society that sovereignty should be no barrier to the relief of suffering. This conviction had inspired the founding of MSF by French doctors during the Biafran War of Independence, and the philosophy behind MSF could be found within the corridors of the French Government itself. In 1991 one of MSF's founding members, Bernard Kouchner, was Minister for Humanitarian Affairs, a role in which he was strongly supported by the President's wife, Danielle Mitterrand, who was outspoken in her criticism of Western governments for failing to rescue the Kurds.[7]

The humanitarian claims advanced by France for a 'duty of intervention' to protect the Kurds failed to secure support from other members of the Security Council, who were fearful that this would weaken the non-intervention rule.[8] However, it was increasingly apparent to many members of the Security Council that they had a responsibility to involve themselves in the humanitarian crisis inside Iraq. Turkey and Iran had requested in letters to the Security Council on 2 and 4 April respectively that international action be taken to prevent up to a million Kurdish refugees in the north and 500,000 Shiites in the south from seeking refuge inside their territorial borders.[9] They argued that a flow of refugees across borders on this scale posed a threat to the security of the region that was legitimately the subject of Security Council action. It was clear from the 'informal consultations' among members that this argument would be contested in the chamber itself.[10] Nevertheless, it

[7] In an interview with *L'Express*, Danielle Mitterrand said she was 'totally appalled' by the repression and that 'nobody [could] claim that they do not know what is happening there'. She described the Kurds as 'in the process of being exterminated', expressing her outrage at the fact that 'nobody is moving' (quoted in ibid.).

[8] 'UN Abandons Kurds'. Sir David Hannay, Britain's Permanent Representative on the Security Council at this time, states: 'We were all worried by that [the French proposal for a "duty of intervention"] because that elevated the whole thing into an issue of principle . . . If you had asked about one hundred and eighty-five members of the UN whether they agreed that there was a duty to intervene, one hundred and eighty-four would have said no. Because they would have seen it might happen to them' (interview with Sir David Hannay, London, Mar. 1999). What is noteworthy about Hannay's comments is his assumption that states defend the non-intervention rule as a protection against intervention by other states rather than a genuine commitment to this principle. Hannay's position, then, supports the view that actors are using this language strategically to further their interests.

[9] See letter to the President of the Security Council from UN Ambassador of Turkey, S/22435, 2 Apr. 1991, and letter from Iran's UN Ambassador, S/22447, 4 Apr. 1991.

[10] One of the characteristics of contemporary Security Council practice that developed in the 1990s, compared to that of the 1970s, was the 'informal consultations' that took place before going into the chamber to vote on resolutions. All fifteen Ambassadors met for lengthy discussions, where many of the compromises that appear in the final resolutions were hammered out. Unfortunately, minutes of these meetings were not made public and this prevented domestic publics, humanitarian NGOs, and wider global civil society from listening in on these informal consultations and holding governments accountable for the positions they took. Ivor (now Lord) Richard, Britain's Permanent Representative to the UN during the Cambodian and Ugandan cases, laments this development, believing that the practice of informal consultations has narrowed the scope for general discussion in the Security Council and produced a more stultifying atmosphere in debates. Interview with Lord Richard, House of Lords, Jan. 1999.

appeared that naming the transboundary consequences of Iraqi repression as a threat to 'international peace and security' would be sufficient to placate most members' worries about the legitimacy of Security Council action.

A draft resolution submitted by France and Belgium and co-sponsored by the UK and USA was adopted as Resolution 688 on 5 April 1991. Ten members voted in favour, three voted against (Cuba, Yemen, and Zimbabwe), and two abstained (China and India). It was the least widely supported of all the resolutions passed in response to Iraq's invasion of Kuwait.[11] This reflected the fact that it was not only an immediate response to the suffering of the Kurds but also the result of a process of argumentation within the Council as to the meaning to be given Article 2 (7) in the post-cold-war period. As Jane Stromseth points out, the participants knew that the draft resolution would set a precedent for future Security Council action.[12] Debate, then, focused on the central question as to whether the Security Council could legitimately address the humanitarian concerns raised by Iraq's repression without violating the ban on UN intervention in the 'domestic jurisdiction' of states in Article 2 (7) of the UN Charter.[13]

The only exception to Article 2 (7) is 'the application of enforcement measures under Chapter VII'.[14] Although Resolution 688 employed the language of a threat to 'international peace and security' (the key enabling move that activates the enforcement provisions of Chapter VII), it did not explicitly invoke the latter. Not surprisingly, the Iraqi Government in its testimony before the Council argued that the Security Council was acting in 'violation of Article 2 of the Charter'[15] by intervening in Iraq's internal affairs. Iraq was supported by Yemen, Zimbabwe, and Cuba in this claim. The Yemeni Ambassador argued that the humanitarian crisis inside Iraq did not pose a threat to international peace and security, and that therefore 'the whole issue is not within the competence of the Security Council'.[16] He expressed his concern that the draft resolution set a 'dangerous precedent' by circumventing the non-intervention rule of the UN Charter, and concluded his speech with the following words:

We have been told that one of the pillars of the new world order is respect for law and the rule of law. That statement has given us cause for hope. What we are witnessing, however, is in point of fact a gradual retreat from law and the rule of law and, in some cases, an attempt to circumvent the international rule of law for political ends.[17]

The Zimbabwe Ambassador also argued that the humanitarian crisis inside Iraq did not justify Security Council action. He recognized that the crisis posed problems for Iraq's neighbours, but argued that other organs of the UN

---

[11] Rodley, 'Collective Intervention', 29.   [12] Stromseth, 'Iraq', 86.
[13] Rodley, 'Collective Intervention', 29.
[14] Charter of the United Nations, Article 2 (7).
[15] SCOR, 2982nd Meeting, 5 Apr. 1991, 17.   [16] Ibid. 27.   [17] Ibid. 28–30.

were the appropriate ones to deal with the humanitarian situation and the question of the refugees. The Cuban Ambassador was equally emphatic that the Security Council 'simply has no right to violate the principle of non-intervention',[18] and that questions of a 'humanitarian nature'[19] raised by some members constituted a clear breach of the domestic jurisdiction rule in Article 2 (7). Like the Yemeni Ambassador, he claimed that the draft resolution turned the UN 'into a system dominated by an oligarchical group which attributes to itself powers that no one has given it and therefore imposes its will on the entire Organization'.[20] He argued that the constitutionally correct move was to place the issue before the UN General Assembly, a body that can make only non-binding decisions.

China abstained on Resolution 688, with its Ambassador expressing his government's concern that the draft resolution should not violate Article 2 (7). China recognized that there were 'international aspects' but considered that these should be settled through the appropriate channels. India, which also abstained, argued that the Security Council was competent to address the issue of the plight of the Kurds only if it could be shown that Iraq's use of force resulted 'in a clear threat to international peace and security'. The Indian Ambassador stated that under no circumstances should the Council act in ways that breached the 'cardinal principle in international relations'[21] of upholding the sovereignty and territorial integrity of states.

The ten states that supported Resolution 688 relied crucially on the argument that the transboundary implications of Iraq's repression posed a threat to international security, thereby legitimating Security Council action. The first operative paragraph 'condemns the repression of the Iraqi civilian population in many parts of Iraq . . . the consequences of which threaten international peace and security in the region'. This view was stressed by Britain, France, the Soviet Union, and six of the non-permanent members of the Council (Austria, Belgium, Ecuador, Romania, Zaïre, and the Côte d'Ivoire).

Although Nigel Rodley argues that the emphasis in Resolution 688 'is clearly on the internal repression, rather than its external consequences',[22] the resolution would not have passed the Council in the absence of this legitimating argument. From reading the speeches of the six non-permanent members and those of the USA and Soviet Union, it is clear that they were very anxious not to set a precedent that might legitimize Security Council intervention on humanitarian grounds alone. For example, Romania argued that, whilst Iraqi repression was 'a legitimate concern of the international community', it was important not to 'create a precedent that could be used— or, rather, misused—in the future for political purposes'. The Romanian Ambassador considered the Iraqi situation to be 'a special case in the after-

---

[18] SCOR, 2982nd Meeting, 5 Apr. 1991, 46.   [19] Ibid.
[20] Ibid. 47.   [21] Ibid. 63.
[22] Rodley, 'Collective Intervention', 31.

math of the Gulf war'.[23] Ecuador's Ambassador argued that the Security Council had a legitimate right to act, given the threat posed to international security by the refugee flows, but was equally emphatic that his government would not have supported the resolution had it been 'dealing solely with a case of violation of human rights by a country within its own frontiers'.[24] Similarly, Zaïre, Austria, Belgium, the Côte d'Ivoire, and the Soviet Union all emphasized that their support for Resolution 688 did not represent a weakening of their commitment to the non-intervention rule in the society of states. The Soviet Ambassador stated that the 'sovereignty, territorial integrity and political independence of Iraq must be ensured'.[25] This position was echoed by the US Ambassador in his statement that 'it is the Council's legitimate responsibility to respond to the concerns of Turkey and the Islamic Republic of Iran . . . The transboundary impact of Iraq's treatment of its civilian population threatens regional stability.'[26]

The only states to raise explicitly humanitarian claims during this meeting of the Security Council were Britain and France. The former argued that Article 2 (7) did not apply to human rights because they were 'not essentially domestic'. Britain's Ambassador, Sir David Hannay, pointed to the precedent of South Africa, where the Security Council had invoked Chapter VII of the Charter to enforce a mandatory arms embargo against the Apartheid state. Not surprisingly, given its stance over the previous few days, France also pressed humanitarian claims arguing that the Security Council had a duty to protect human rights inside Iraq. The French Ambassador, Rochéreau De La Sablière, argued that 'violations of human rights such as those now being observed become a matter of international interest when they take on such proportions that they assume the dimension of a crime against humanity'. In addition, having passed fourteen resolutions designed to restore peace and security in the region, the Security Council 'would have been remiss in its task had it stood idly by, without reacting to the massacre of entire populations, the extermination of civilians, including women and children'.[27]

These solidarist claims appear to have played no part in persuading members of the Security Council to adopt Resolution 688, since they were raised after the vote had been taken. It is customary for permanent members to speak after the vote and what happened in the British case was that Sir David Hannay was sent instructions from London that he should employ the South African precedent in defence of Britain's position. According to Hannay, this argument was never raised in the 'informal consultations', which were dominated by the transboundary argument.[28] Indeed, Hannay

[23] SCOR, 2982nd Meeting, 5 April 1991, 24–5. [24] Ibid. 36.
[25] Ibid. 61. Sir David Hannay claims that the transboundary argument 'was the one that enabled the Russians to vote for Resolution 688' (interview with Sir David Hannay, Mar. 1999).
[26] SCOR, 2982nd Meeting, 5 Apr. 1991, 58. [27] Ibid. 53.
[28] Interview with Sir David Hannay, Mar. 1999.

concluded his speech by stressing the threat to international peace and security posed by the 'huge surge of refugees'.[29]

Twenty-four hours prior to the adoption of Resolution 688, the French Foreign Minister had called for a 'duty of intervention' to save the Kurds, the clear implication being that the Security Council should legitimate the use of force to save the Kurds. This plea had not received any support from members, and it is clear that, had the draft resolution made any mention of military enforcement action, it would not have secured the necessary votes and would have been vetoed by the Soviet Union and China.[30]

Although Resolution 688 did not authorize military enforcement action, it was the first time—other than the case of South Africa—that the Security Council had collectively demanded an improvement in the human rights situation of a member state as a contribution to the promotion of international security.[31] Paragraph two of Resolution 688: '*Demands* that Iraq, as a contribution to removing the threat to international peace and security in the region, immediately end this repression and expresses the hope in the same context that an open dialogue will take place to ensure that the human and political rights of all Iraqi citizens are respected.' The use of the word 'demand' places it very close to the Chapter VII end of the spectrum, and it can be agreed with Rodley that the Security Council was most interventionist in paragraph three when it 'insists that Iraq allow immediate access by international humanitarian organizations to all those in need of assistance in all parts of Iraq and to make available all necessary facilities for their operations'.[32] Nevertheless, the resolution was not adopted under Chapter VII and it falls between the stools of Chapter VI (pacific settlement of disputes where the Security Council recommends actions) and full-blown enforcement action under Chapter VII. By naming the consequences of Iraq's repression as a threat to international security, the door was open to move to military-enforcement action. Yet it is clear from the arguments raised in the Security Council during the adoption of Resolution 688 that anything stronger than the draft resolution would have failed to secure the required number of votes in the Council. The question was whether Resolution 688 would be enough to persuade the Kurds and Shiites that they would be protected if they returned to their homes. And, if Resolution 688 proved insufficient to address their humanitarian needs, what other steps were open to the society of states to save these victims of Iraqi repression?

[29] SCOR, 2982nd Meeting, 5 Apr. 1991, 53.

[30] Sir David Hannay claims that the main reason why there are no enforcement provisions for military action in Resolution 688 is that 'the Russians would not allow this' (interview with Sir David Hannay, Mar. 1999).

[31] Rodley, 'Collective Intervention', 32.

[32] Ibid. 31.

The Safe Havens

It could be argued that Security Council action to protect Iraqi civilians came far too late, and that there should have been intervention in defence of the Kurds and Shiites when they were challenging Saddam's control in March 1991. For example, coalition forces could have armed the Kurds, attacked Republican Guard units, and shot down Iraqi helicopters. Had this happened, it is conceivable that the rebels would have been successful in overthrowing the Iraqi leader. President Bush was accused of failing to support rebellions that he had actively encouraged,[33] with leading Democrats challenging the administration to take action to stop the killing of innocent civilians. For example, Congressman Lee Hamilton, Democratic Chairman of the House subcommittee on Europe and the Middle East, said that Iraqi helicopters 'are now creating a blood bath'[34] that must be stopped.

The Bush Administration justified its decision to leave the Kurds and Shiites to their fate by representing the violence taking place inside Iraq as an 'internal struggle' or 'civil war' that the Iraqi people had to resolve for themselves. The President declared, 'We're not going to get sucked into this by sending precious American lives into this battle.'[35] Bush and his advisers believed that this position would be legitimated by an American public that wanted to celebrate its Gulf War victory over Saddam, and was wary of any intervention that risked turning into another Vietnam.[36] Speaking on the day that Resolution 688 was passed in New York, Bush said, 'I feel frustrated any time innocent civilians are being slaughtered . . . But the United States and those other countries with us in this coalition did not go there to settle all the internal affairs of Iraq.'[37]

There is no reason to question the sincerity of this public rationale for the US policy of non-intervention. However, the Administration had another less public reason for staying out of Iraq's internal affairs. It was under pressure from its coalition partners in the Gulf, especially Saudi Arabia and Turkey, not to allow Iraq to break up. The spectre of an independent Kurdistan haunted Turkey, which was fighting an armed secessionist movement among its own Kurdish minority, and, whilst Saudi Arabia feared Saddam Hussein, it also

---

[33] On 15 Feb. 1991, President Bush had declared 'there's another way for the bloodshed to stop, and that is for the Iraqi military and the Iraqi people to take matters into their own hands to force Saddam Hussein the dictator to step aside and to comply with the United Nations resolutions and then rejoin the family of peace-loving nations' (quoted in L. Freedman and D. Boren, ' "Safe Havens" for Kurds', in N. S. Rodley (ed.), *To Loose the Bands of Wickedness* (London: Brassey's, 1992), 46).

[34] 'Bush Rejects Call for US Intervention in Iraq', *Financial Times*, 2 Apr. 1991.

[35] 'Bush: No Obligation to Kurds', *International Herald Tribune*, 6–7 Apr. 1991.

[36] 'Rebels have No Hope in Bush', *Independent*, 4 Apr. 1991.

[37] 'US and the Kurds: A Perfect Dilemma', *International Herald Tribune*, 5 Apr. 1991.

worried that the disintegration of Iraq could lead to the emergence of an Iranian controlled Shiite state hostile to its interests.[38]

These public and private reasons for inaction were held strongly by the Bush Administration, but within less than two weeks of the President's defence of a policy of non-intervention the USA was deploying military forces inside northern Iraq to create safe havens for the Kurds. How did this change of policy become possible?

The origins of the safe-havens idea was a speech by Turkey's President on 7 April, when he declared that 'We have to get [the Kurds] better land under UN control and to put those people in the Iraqi territory and take care of them'.[39] Turkey opened its borders to some of the refugees but was not prepared to accept the influx of hundreds of thousands of Kurds. The only solution was the creation of protected areas inside Iraq.[40] Turkey's initiative coincided with US Secretary of State James Baker's visit to the region, which was a crucial turning point in US thinking on the crisis. The Secretary of State spent fifteen minutes with the refugees at Uzumlu in Turkey and was shocked by the scenes he witnessed. He declared that 'these people must be free from the threats, persecution and harassment that they have been subjected to by that brutal regime in Baghdad'.[41] Baker repeated that the USA would not allow itself to be dragged into a 'civil war' but was well aware that the administration could not be seen to be leaving the Kurds to die on the mountains of northern Iraq.[42]

Those reporters and camera crews that had covered the Gulf War now relayed live pictures of the terrible agony of the Kurds into the homes of millions in the West. Moreover, as Martin Shaw points out in relation to British television coverage, the footage was 'overlaid . . . with an unremitting commentary pinning responsibility simply and directly on Western leaders, especially Bush and Major'.[43] The British Prime Minister tried initially to deny any responsibility for the plight of the Kurds, commenting sarcastically that he could not 'recall asking the Kurds to mount this particular insurrection'.[44]

---

[38] 'Bush Rejects Calls for US Intervention in Iraq'. This fear on the part of Turkey and the Arab states that Iraq would be divided into separate spheres of influence was confirmed by Sir David Hannay in my interview with him.

[39] Quoted in Freedman and Boren, ' "Safe Havens" ', 52.

[40] Turkey feared that the influx of Kurds would strengthen the Kurdish separatist movement within Turkey itself. The Marxist Kurdistan Workers' Party (Partiya Karkeren Kurdistan (PKK)) was involved in a guerrilla war with the Turkish army, and the Turkish army, which had the task of dealing with the Kurds, was determined to prevent massive numbers of refugees entering Turkey who might swell the ranks of the PKK. See Freedman and Boren, ' "Safe Havens" ', 49–50.

[41] Quoted in ibid. 52.

[42] One senior State Department official was reported to have said privately that 'the word came down that there should be an all-out effort, that money and organization didn't matter . . . Baker said "Find the money, find the organization" ' (quoted in 'Haven from the Hell-Holes', *Sunday Times*, 21 Apr. 1991).

[43] M. Shaw, 'Global Voices', in T. Dunne and N. J. Wheeler (eds.), *Human Rights in Global Politics* (Cambridge: Cambridge University Press, 1999), 229.

[44] Quoted in 'After Victory Comes Betrayal', *Independent*, 10 Apr. 1991.

In more diplomatic language, Foreign Secretary Douglas Hurd justified Britain's policy of non-intervention on the grounds that there was no legal mandate to intervene inside Iraqi borders.[45] Nevertheless, Prime Minister Major was clearly affected by the television coverage of the Kurdish crisis, and was also stung by criticism from his predecessor that Britain should be doing more to save the Kurds. Mrs Thatcher had met a Kurdish delegation on 3 April and afterwards told reporters, 'it is not a question of standing on legal niceties . . . The people need help and they need it now.'[46]

Five days later, on his way to an EC Summit in Luxembourg, Major decided that he had to respond to the growing pressures for action to save the Kurds. They would not come down from the mountains because they feared Iraqi retribution, and to address this the Prime Minister proposed the creation of 'safe enclaves' (as they were originally called) inside northern Iraq. This plan received the endorsement of other EC governments; the fact that Major had not discussed the idea with the USA helped convince the French Government that it was a genuinely European initiative.[47] Speaking at a news conference after the summit, Major said his proposal would require two stages: 'The immediate aim will be to get the Kurds and the other refugees actually down from the mountains and into a safe area. The second stage is to get them back home.'[48]

The initial US response to the enclaves idea was not enthusiastic, with White House spokesman Marlin Fitzwater considering that the proposal had 'some merits in terms of a possible solution'.[49] This lukewarm response partly reflected the fact that Major had not consulted Bush before announcing his idea.[50] The more important consideration was the administration's fear that the creation of enclaves for the Kurds could lead to the break-up of Iraq, embroiling the USA and its allies in a protracted commitment. One senior Pentagon official was reported to have said privately that the British plan 'had Vietnam quagmire written all over it'.[51] In an attempt to meet US concerns about maintaining Iraq's territorial integrity and the dangers of a long-term Allied commitment, Major took up Sir David Hannay's suggestion that the term enclave be substituted by that of 'safe haven'. From discussions at the UN it was clear to Hannay that the term enclave would cause trouble because it suggested a redrawing of national borders.[52] This was no part of Major's

---

[45] 'Government Resists Calls to Help Kurds', *Guardian*, 2 Apr. 1991.
[46] 'Haven from the Hell-Holes'.   [47] Ibid.
[48] 'UK Urges Kurdish Enclave', *Financial Times*, 9 Apr. 1991.
[49] Freedman and Boren, ' "Safe havens" ', 53.
[50] 'Haven from the Hell-Holes', and 'Bush Agrees in Principle with Kurd Havens Plan', *The Times*, 11 Apr. 1991.
[51] 'Haven from the Hell-Holes'.
[52] Hannay reflected: 'Enclave is a geographical term. Therefore, it implies some support for a splitting-up of Iraq. Because if you have an enclave it has to be drawn on a map and it's an enclave from what? From Iraq. So, it has a connotation that implies that you're prepared to tolerate the breaking-up of Iraq. Well that was not the policy of the British, or American, or French or any other

plan and he was emphatic in his attempts to build international support for the safe havens that there was no question of establishing an independent Kurdish state.[53]

Although the Bush Administration was not ready at this stage to send troops to save the Kurds, it was stepping up its efforts to protect the humanitarian relief effort in northern Iraq. Resolution 688 insisted that Iraq allow humanitarian relief agencies to operate inside Iraq, and, in ensuring Iraqi compliance with this, the USA found itself increasingly involved in the provision of relief. Iraq was instructed on 11 April not to send military forces north of the 36th parallel as 'coalition officials would be operating in those areas to distribute humanitarian assistance to the Kurdish population'.[54] This military exclusion zone was justified in terms of protecting US personnel engaged in relief efforts, but it also provided protection for the Kurds from Iraqi military forces. Despite growing US involvement, the problem remained how to get the Kurds to come down from the mountains. One senior American official was reported as saying: 'This was an instant education service for us. Every day that went by, the more we got educated on what the international organizations couldn't do, how much the Kurds fear going back, how hard it is to get in there.'[55]

Bush had defended a non-interventionist policy fearful that intervention could suck US troops into another Vietnam. This was the advice he was receiving from the Pentagon and he took this military concern very seriously.[56] In a speech on 12 April he continued to represent the situation inside Iraq as a 'civil war' rather than a humanitarian emergency caused by Iraqi repression. He declared that, 'I'm not going to involve any American troops in a civil war in Iraq'.[57] However, Bush's position became increasingly untenable as public and Congressional opinion in the USA swung decisively against non-intervention. In relation to the latter, Claiborne Pell, Chairman of the Senate Foreign Relations Committee, declared on 9 April that the USA had 'a moral obligation to do what we can to stop Saddam from killing those who have the courage to resist'.[58] And Senator Sam Nunn, an influential member of the Senate Armed Services Committee, named Iraqi repression an act of 'genocide'. By interpret-

government. All strongly believed that Iraq's territorial integrity must be maintained. And so it was a very dangerous term, in my view. And it was a very dangerous term because it raised a whole number of issues which wouldn't have got through in New York and which would arouse huge opposition. Whereas the term safe haven was a purely humanitarian term, since there wasn't a line drawn on a map' (interview with Sir David Hannay, Mar. 1999). See also 'Haven from the Hell-Holes'.

[53] 'Haven from the Hell-Holes'.

[54] Quoted in Freedman and Boren, ' "Safe havens" ', 53.   [55] 'Haven from the Hell-Holes'.

[56] Secretary of Defence Dick Cheney and Colin Powell, Chairman of the Joint Chiefs of Staff, were very concerned about becoming involved in Iraq's internal affairs, fearing that this could become a quagmire. See 'Mission of Mercy', *Time*, 29 Apr. 1991, 18, and 'Haven from the Hell-Holes'.

[57] 'Bush will not be Drawn into a Civil War', *Daily Telegraph*, 12 Apr. 1991.

[58] 'US Cautious over Plan for Kurds' Haven', *Independent*, 10 Apr. 1991

ing events in northern Iraq as a 'genocide' rather than a 'civil war', the Senator legitimated a much more interventionist policy. And picking up on an argument raised by the French in the debate over Resolution 688, Nunn argued that the USA had a responsibility for the Kurds, since 'anytime you get into a conflict like this, there are certain obligations that flow from it'.[59]

The State Department estimated that 1,000 Kurds were dying every day, and, with pictures of their suffering being beamed into American living rooms, the President was persuaded by his Secretary of State that he had to change course. Baker was all too well aware that this human disaster could become a political one for the Bush Presidency, and he telephoned the President, who was fishing in Alabama, to report the growing pressure from Congress and the allies to save the Kurds.[60] His advice proved critical in persuading Bush to overrule the Pentagon and send US soldiers into northern Iraq to protect the Kurds.[61] On 16 April Bush announced that he had

directed the US military to begin immediately to establish several encampments in northern Iraq where relief supplies for these refugees will be made available in large quantities and distributed in an orderly manner . . . adequate security will be provided at these temporary sites by US, British and French air and ground forces . . . I want to underscore that all we are doing is motivated by humanitarian concerns. We continue to expect the government of Iraq not to interfere in any way with this latest relief effort. The prohibition against any Iraqi fixed or rotary-wing aircraft flying north of the 36th parallel thus remains in effect.[62]

Bush reiterated that the USA was not going to be drawn into a 'Vietnam-style quagmire' and stressed the temporary nature of the operation by declaring that the 'administration of and security for the sites' would be handed over 'as soon as possible to the United Nations'.[63]

The initial plan of 'Operation Provide Comfort' was to build, administer, and guard six camps that would shelter around 60,000 refugees. The camps were to be protected by airpower and ground troops as well as rapid reaction forces that would fly in from Turkey. Five thousand US troops were involved in the plan, with Britain sending another 2,000 and France 1,000, as well as a smaller contingent of Dutch forces.[64] Although the initial objective was to

---

[59] Ibid.

[60] Baker reportedly told Bush that the Turkish Government was particularly worried about the scale of the catastrophe and President Ozal confirmed this in a telephone conversation on Monday, 15 Apr. See 'Mission of Mercy', 19.

[61] It is reported that Bush met his national security advisers on 15 April and National Security Adviser Robert Gates was given the job of coming up with a plan with officials from the State Department, the Pentagon, and the Central Intelligence Agency (CIA). Gates reported to Bush later that day with a plan that, after telephoning Prime Minister Major, French President François Mitterrand, and Turkish President Turgut Ozal, Bush announced the following afternoon. See 'Mission of Mercy', 18, and 'Haven from the Hell-Holes'.

[62] Quoted in Freedman and Boren, ' "Safe Havens" ', 54.   [63] Ibid. 55.

[64] 'US Troops Move in to Set up Safe Havens', The Times, 18 Apr. 1991, and Freedman and Boren, ' "Safe Havens" ', 56.

create protected areas within confined zones, the logic of the safe havens was to 'establish Western military authority over a substantial area of Iraq'.[65] If the Kurds were to return to their homes in safety, then it was necessary to secure the withdrawal of Iraq's military forces and its paramilitary and police units.[66] It was made clear to Iraq that failure to pull back all those forces south of the 36th parallel would be met with the use of force, and this threat persuaded the Iraqis to comply.[67]

The safe havens provided a response to the immediate threat of death and starvation facing the Kurds. However, the action raised two crucial questions: first, how far did Western states have legal authority for their intervention and what was the reaction of other states to the deployment of Western military forces inside Iraq's borders? Secondly, there was the question of how to ensure that the Kurds could return in safety to their homes. Bush had justified US involvement as a temporary measure, but achieving this required putting in place a security framework that would protect the Kurds in the absence of Western forces. It was hoped that the UN would take over this security role, but achieving this raised a number of legal and operational difficulties.

Legitimating Short- and Long-Term Intervention in Iraq

In announcing the US decision to send military forces to rescue the Kurds, Bush stated that this was 'consistent with United Nations Security Council resolution 688'.[68] The British Government had argued in early April that there was no legal mandate for intervention, but Resolution 688 was claimed to have changed all that. In justifying the safe-havens idea on 9 April, Major claimed that such an intervention was legally provided for in Resolution 688. Speaking the next day on BBC Radio, Douglas Hogg, Minister of State at the Foreign Office, stated that, 'We have, I think, the authority of the UN in the last resolution [Resolution 688] in order to ensure the safety of the Kurds and this is a method of devising that, delivering that.'[69]

Questioned on whether a Western military presence in northern Iraq could be established under UN authority without Iraqi consent, Perez de Cueller responded: 'No. No. No. We have to be in touch first of all with the Iraqis.'[70]

---

[65] Freedman and Boren, ' "Safe Havens" ', 57.   [66] Ibid.
[67] Ibid. 58–9.   [68] Ibid. 54.
[69] 'Major's Enclave Plan for Kurds Runs into Trouble', The Times, 10 Apr.1991. The UN Secretary General's Special Envoy to northern Iraq took a different view. Eric Suy stated that Iraq's consent to the safe havens would be a 'fundamental principle and this appears not to be the case. So I assume that such a zone, to be controlled and created by the United Nations, will likely not be attainable' ('UN Envoy Pours Cold Water on Kurd Refugee Plan', The Times, 10 Apr. 1991).
[70] 'UN Clashes with West over Forces for Northern Iraq', The Times, 18 Apr. 1991.

He declared that for the safe havens to be created without Iraq's consent but under the 'aegis of the United Nations, consent would have to be obtained from the Security Council'.[71] Although there were reports in the press to the contrary, Sir David Hannay claims that Britain never tried to secure a new Security Council resolution authorizing the safe havens.[72] Resolution 688 had been a close vote, given the concern that nothing should be done to weaken Article 2 (7) of the Charter, and a new resolution authorizing protection of the Kurds would have been viewed by many members as too much of an erosion of the principle of non-intervention.

Although the UN Secretary General was sensitive to the legal questions involved, he acknowledged the importance of acting from a 'moral and humanitarian point of view'.[73] Moreover, he considered that 'if the countries involved do not require the United Nations flag, then that is quite different'.[74] At no point, then, did he argue that the creation of the safe havens was illegal under Resolution 688. Sir David Hannay considers that Perez de Cueller could live with Western intervention in northern Iraq because the UN was not being asked to do anything illegal, but this begs the question whether Britain, France, and the USA were breaking international law in creating the safe havens.[75]

The basis for the claim that Resolution 688 provided sufficient legal authority for the safe havens is paragraph six of the resolution, which *'appeals to all Member States and to all humanitarian organizations to contribute to these humanitarian relief efforts'*. Rodley argues that the declared intention to hand the relief operation over to the UN meant that Western intervention fell within the parameters of Resolution 688.[76] Going further than Rodley, Marc Weller claims that the resolution 'gives states the right to ensure the

---

[71] 'West and UN Shamed into Aiding the Kurds', *Independent*, 18 Apr. 1991.

[72] It was reported in the press that Hannay initiated discussions in New York on a new resolution to authorize the setting-up of the safe havens on 12 Apr. but that it became apparent during informal consultations among members of the Security Council that a new resolution would not receive the necessary support. It is reported that the draft resolution drawn up by Britain was framed in terms of providing humanitarian assistance to the Kurds, but, as Peter Jenkins pointed out at the time, such a resolution would have 'created a fresh mandate for the ultimate use of force, this time to enforce the observance of fundamental human rights'. Not surprisingly given its absolutist defence of the non-intervention rule, China privately expressed strong opposition to this move. And even without the threat of a Chinese or Soviet veto, it is doubtful that the resolution would have secured the necessary nine votes. See 'UN Says Iraq must Endorse Haven', *The Times*, 12 Apr. 1991, and 'That Slippery Slope', *The Economist*, 13 Apr. 1991 The Peter Jenkins quote is cited in 'Major Puts the UN on the Spot', *Independent*, 10 Apr. 1991. Hannay denies any recollection of trying to secure a new resolution (interview with Sir David Hannay, Mar. 1999).

[73] 'Allies Embark on an Uncharted Path', *Independent*, 18 Apr. 1991.

[74] 'West and UN Shamed into Aiding the Kurds'.

[75] According to Sir David Hannay, 'Perez de Cueller was ready to do it because he knew it was his duty to do it [assist the relief effort as required under Resolution 688] . . . Resolution 688 instructed him to use all the means available to him to get humanitarian aid to the refugees . . . He wasn't asked to do anything that was illegal. He was not asked to use force' (interview with Sir David Hannay, Mar. 1999).

[76] Rodley, 'Collective Intervention', 32.

implementation of the humanitarian aid programme by military means'.[77] The problem with both of these legal arguments is that the threat to use force in defence of the relief effort is certainly not mandated in Resolution 688. Had the draft resolution tabled on 5 April had provisions in it authorizing the threat or use of force in defence of humanitarian assistance or human rights, it would have been killed by a Soviet veto. It was this awareness that the Security Council could not be persuaded to go beyond Resolution 688 that led Western governments to refrain from putting forward a new resolution authorizing the creation of the safe havens.

At best, Resolution 688 provided meagre legal cover for Western military intervention in Iraq. How, then, are we to account for the fact that no Security Council member who voted for this resolution publicly challenged the West's legal right to create the safe havens?[78] One answer is that, while members would not authorize enforcement action in defence of humanitarian purposes, they were prepared tacitly to legitimate Western action.[79] This leads Stromseth to argue that:

resolution 688's open-endedness was both a necessity and a virtue—a necessity because of the unwillingness of the Security Council to provide a more definitive authorization, and a virtue because it permitted the allies to take action during this period of evolving norms while not forcing the hand of the Chinese and others who were willing to tolerate actions de facto that they would not authorize de jure.[80]

This argument of tacit legitimation is supported by the fact that—in contrast to the case of Uganda—the Western powers publicly justified their action in humanitarian terms. Thus, the lack of criticism from other states could be taken as setting a precedent for similar action in future cases. Yet, if the safe havens set a precedent for humanitarian intervention, it was a very limited one. There was strong opposition in the Security Council to any steps that undermined the principles of sovereignty and non-intervention, and Western military intervention was accepted only because it quickly became clear that this was a temporary measure with Western forces withdrawing within a matter of months.[81] Although the relief operation was backed by the threat of force, the world's media focused on the key role played by Western militaries in bringing aid to the needy. The Soviet Union, China, and the other non-Western States on the Security Council were anxious about the precedent set by Western action in northern Iraq, but none of these states wanted to be exposed publicly as opposing a rescue mission that was saving lives and they were shamed into silence.[82] Acquiescence, then,

---

[77] 'New York Resolution Opens Way for Use of Force', *The Times*, 10 Apr. 1991.
[78] Rodley, 'Collective Intervention', 33.
[79] 'West and UN Shamed into Aiding the Kurds'.
[80] Stromseth, 'Iraq', 100.
[81] Interview with Sir David Hannay, Mar. 1999.
[82] 'West and UN Shamed into Aiding the Kurds'.

rather than tacit legitimation captures the response of those governments to Western intervention.

Having avoided a bitter dispute over the legality of the safe havens, the next question facing Western governments was how to hand the operation over to the UN so that Western forces could withdraw from northern Iraq. One of the reasons why UN officials were cautious about Western plans to set up safe havens was their concern that this could jeopardize the UN's own humanitarian relief efforts. In fact, it was Western military intervention that compelled Iraq to accept the levels of humanitarian access for UN and other aid agencies demanded by Resolution 688. The Western powers were keen to ensure that their intervention did not become a prolonged one, and, as Freedman and Boren point out, 'this too was the Iraqi preference. If it had to have a foreign presence on its soil it much preferred this to be civilian UN workers rather than Western soldiers.'[83] To secure the removal of Western forces from its soil, Iraq agreed to unprecedented levels of access for humanitarian aid organizations. As Ramsbotham and Woodhouse put it, 'Saddam Hussein's agreement to the MOU [Memorandum of Understanding] . . . and his general acquiescence in the UN programme . . . were elicited under duress.'[84]

On 18 April, a MOU was reached by Eric Suy and Prince Sadruddin Aga Khan (the Secretary General's Representative for Humanitarian Affairs in Iraq), with the Iraqi Government permitting the establishment of a 100 civilian-run humanitarian centres throughout Iraq. The purpose of these centres was twofold: first, to deliver aid in conjunction with the International Committee of the Red Cross, regional and Iraqi Red Crescent Societies, and other non-governmental aid agencies. The second goal was to create conditions of security that would persuade the Kurds in the north and Shiites in the south to return to their homes. The MOU covered the whole of the country, as required by Resolution 688, and its philosophy was 'that humanitarian assistance is impartial and that all civilians in need, wherever they are located, are entitled to receive it'.[85]

Both Iraq and the Western powers were anxious that the UN take over the running of the safe havens as soon as possible, but the problem was how to convince the Kurds that their long-term security would be protected after the Western powers had departed.[86] In a letter to the UN Secretary General on 2 May, Prime Minister Major proposed that allied forces be replaced by a UN police force, and this plan received backing from the USA and the EC.[87] Western governments claimed that Resolution 688 provided sufficient

[83] Freedman and Boren, ' "Safe Havens" ', 61.
[84] Ramsbotham and Woodhouse, *Humanitarian Intervention*, 82.
[85] Text from Memorandum of Understanding quoted in ibid. 81.
[86] Freedman and Boren, ' "Safe Havens" ', 60.
[87] Ibid. 62, and 'Britain Urges UN to Police Iraq', *Independent*, 30 Apr. 1991.

authority for such a force, but, as with the legality of the safe havens, this was questioned by the Secretary General's Special Envoy to Iraq. Eric Suy declared that deploying UN forces would require a new resolution 'otherwise it will be an intervention and that will smell like Operation Desert Storm'.[88] This view was echoed by Sir Brian Urquhart, former under-Secretary General for Special Political Affairs, who expressed concerns about 'a small powerful minority' of Western states imposing their ideas on the UN.[89] Perez de Cueller hoped that any disagreement over the legal question could be avoided by persuading Iraq to accept the presence of a UN police force. However, on 11 May he announced that he had received 'a very clear rejection from the Iraqi Government. They do not want a United Nations police presence.' The key obstacle to an agreement was Iraq's insistence that UN policeman should not carry arms.[90] In the absence of Iraqi consent, Perez de Cueller argued that any deployment would require explicit authorization by the Security Council.[91]

Although the USA took the view that Resolution 688 provided the legal authority for a UN police force, Bush stated on 16 May that the USA was considering returning to the Security Council 'to get further authority'.[92] However, it was clear from discussions in New York that the Soviet Union and China might veto any such move. In a meeting with the US Secretary of State, the Soviet Foreign Minister emphasized his government's concerns with deploying armed UN police to protect civilians without the consent of the Iraqi Government. He stated that a 'thin line . . . separates the necessity for humanitarian support and the concerns for the sovereignty of a country . . . And it is a very intricate balance.'[93] China was equally sensitive about setting a precedent that might erode the non-intervention principle, and, given these political obstacles, the Western powers made no attempt to introduce a new resolution in the Security Council.[94]

The failure of Major's UN police plan faced the Western powers with the scenario they had feared from the outset—being drawn into a protracted commitment to protect the Kurds. But realizing that a UN presence in northern Iraq was the price of getting rid of allied forces, Iraq gave the Western powers the exit strategy they were seeking by agreeing to the deployment of up to 500 UN guards. This was significantly less than the deployment originally envisaged by Major, and the guards were allowed to carry only personal weapons like handguns. According to Prince Sadruddin Aga Khan, the guards' mandate was 'to protect the precious human and material assets deployed in

---

[88] Freedman and Boren, ' "Safe Havens" ', 60.

[89] 'Questions Hang over UN Police Force Plan', *Independent*, 27 Apr. 1991.

[90] Freedman and Boren, ' "Safe Havens" ', 62.

[91] 'Bessmertnykh is Cool to UN Police Force in Iraq', *International Herald Tribune*, 14 May 1991, and Stromseth, 'Iraq', 91.

[92] Quoted in Freedman and Boren, ' "Safe Havens" ', 62.

[93] 'Bessmertnykh is Cool to UN Police Force in Iraq'.

[94] Interview with Sir David Hannay, Mar. 1999.

the humanitarian operation'.[95] There was no mention in the agreement with Iraq of police protection for the Kurds, but, making the best of a bad situation, the UN claimed that the guards were a 'visible presence' that would monitor and report on the humanitarian and security situation inside Iraq. The idea was that these reports could act as the trigger for further UN action, but it was clearly hoped that the guards' presence would be sufficient to deter Iraqi attacks against the Kurds. Not surprisingly, Kurdish leaders were not convinced that the UN guards were reliable guardians of the Kurds' security. Jalal Talabani, the leader of the Patriotic Union of Kurdistan (PUK), expressed grave concerns about the security afforded by UN protection, fearing that the Kurds might return to the mountains.[96] These concerns are understandable, given that 21,700 highly trained troops were being replaced by 500 lightly armed UN guards whose normal function was to protect UN buildings in New York and Geneva.[97]

The British Prime Minister had first pressed the idea of a UN police force to protect the Kurds, and ministers were coming under increasing pressure from critics in Parliament and the media for what was seen as their abandonment of the Kurds.[98] Responding to these pressures, the British Foreign Secretary told reporters that Britain, France, the Netherlands, and Italy had agreed not to end their operations in northern Iraq whilst the Kurds remained at risk.[99] This put the Europeans on a collision course with the USA, which was eager to withdraw its forces as soon as possible. However, any disagreement over the timing of allied withdrawal was smoothed over when it was agreed by the coalition partners that a residual multinational force would remain in the region to protect the Kurds. Turkey agreed to base a rapid reaction force of air and ground forces on its territory, and this was to be backed up by US carriers based in the eastern Mediterranean. By mid-July, Western troops began leaving Iraq and it was made clear to Saddam Hussein that the no-fly zone in the north remained in operation and would be policed by Western air forces. The residual force was called 'Operation Poised Hammer' and it was a clear signal to Iraq that any future attacks against the Kurds risked allied retaliation.

---

[95] 'Give the United Nations Guards a Chance in Iraq', *International Herald Tribune*, 13 June 1991.

[96] 'Major's Haven Plan in Tatters', *Independent*, 17 June 1991.

[97] Freedman and Boren, ' "Safe Havens" ', 63. A different view is expressed by Hannay, who considers that 'the local people were terrified because they had just been through a very traumatic experience and it was very important to them and it was very important above all to the objective of getting the Iraqi Kurds back out of Turkey and back to their homeland that they saw somebody in uniform who looked as if they might give them a bit of security and that's the role that the UN guards played. And that was why, in the end, we persuaded Perez de Cuellar to deploy the UN guards. Perez de Cuellar persuaded the Iraqis to acquiesce in the deployment of UN guards and the Iraqi Kurds found the presence of these UN guards comforting and went back in larger and larger numbers, so it was highly successful' (interview with Sir David Hannay, Mar. 1999).

[98] Ann Clwyd, Labour Shadow Minister for Overseas Development, called on the Prime Minister to 'honour his promise' to the Kurds. See 'Prince Flies in to Plead for Kurds', *Independent*, 19 Nov. 1991, and 'A Retreat from Responsibility', *Independent*, 4 June 1991.

[99] 'Europeans Agree not to Desert Kurds', *Independent*, 18 June 1991.

The Humanitarian Success of Western Military Intervention in Iraq

Saving the Kurds in northern Iraq in 1991 depended upon meeting three objectives: first, bringing humanitarian aid to refugees dying on the mountains; secondly, getting the Kurds down from the mountains and into the safe havens; and, finally—the most difficult task of all—creating a security environment that made it possible for the Kurds to return to their homes. There can be no doubt that Western military intervention saved thousands who would otherwise have perished. As US Secretary of State Baker put it, the Western powers intervened 'because we did not feel that anyone else was in a position to do what had to be done to save lives'.[100] Although the USA and Britain congratulated themselves on the success of their intervention in northern Iraq,[101] any assessment must take into account how far it addressed the underlying political causes that had given rise to Iraqi repression and the Kurds' subsequent exodus into the mountains.

Iraq's oppression of the Kurds was the root cause of the humanitarian emergency in northern Iraq and there were two possible solutions to the challenge of securing long-term protection of human rights for the Kurds. The first, and most radical, was to give the Kurds their own state under some form of international protection. This was never contemplated by Western states and any proposal along these lines would have sent shock waves through those governments in the region that had large Kurdish minorities. Moreover, legitimating secession would have established a dangerous precedent that would have placed at risk the constitutive rules of sovereignty, non-intervention, and territorial integrity in the society of states.

With statehood ruled out, the second option was for Kurdish leaders to negotiate a new autonomy deal with Saddam Hussein that would be backed by international guarantees. Resolution 688 had expressed the Security Council's view that a dialogue should take place aimed at ensuring respect for the 'human and political rights of all Iraqi citizens'. As soon as Western forces began deploying inside northern Iraq, the leaders of the two Kurdish parties, Massoud Barzani and Jalal Talabani, began negotiating a new agreement with the Iraqi Government. The Kurdish leaders wanted the Security Council to pass a resolution guaranteeing any new autonomy agreement in the belief that this would put pressure on Iraq to comply. However, Western governments

---

[100] Quoted in 'Bessmertnykh is cool to UN Police Force in Iraq'.

[101] The US Department of Defence described the operation in northern Iraq as 'an outstanding success' (quoted in Freedman and Boren, ' "Safe Havens" ', 76). Similarly, the British Minister for Overseas Development, Lynda Chalker, told the House of Commons that the operation of getting the Kurds down from the mountains had been successfully completed. See 'Europeans Agree not to Desert Kurds'.

took the view that there could be no question of the Security Council standing as guarantor, since the negotiation between Iraq and the Kurds was an
'internal arrangement . . . miles out of UN territory'.[102]

Iraq was strongly opposed to any form of international guarantees, and
there were further disputes at the autonomy talks over Kurdish demands for
democratic elections throughout Iraq; the territory to be included in the
autonomous region; and Kurdish claims for a share in the oil revenues from
Kirkuk. Negotiating a new deal was not helped by the fact that the Kurdish
leaders themselves were divided and talks came to an end when Talabani's
party pulled out in September 1991.[103] Iraq was quick to exploit these divisions and in late 1991 Saddam Hussein imposed an internal economic block-
ade against the Kurds, blocking supplies of food, medicines, and fuel.[104]
Growing Iraqi pressure on the Kurds reflected Saddam Hussein's calculation
that Western interest in protecting the Kurds was waning. Western air forces
based in Turkey continued to overfly northern Iraq, but air patrols could 'do
little to challenge police-inspired terrorism on the ground'.[105] Although the
UN guards had been deployed to provide a visible symbol of reassurance to
the Kurds that they could return to their homes, they were increasingly
unable to protect themselves, fellow UN aid workers, or the Kurds against
Iraqi terrorist attacks.[106]

Iraqi terrorist action threatened the human rights of the Kurds, but this
level of threat compared favourably with their terrible predicament in
March–April 1991, or their suffering at the hands of Saddam Hussein in the
late 1980s. Resolution 688 called upon the Iraqi Government and the Kurds to
enter into a new dialogue, but this did not happen. Instead, sheltering under
allied air protection, the Kurds rejected Iraq's offers of new autonomy talks and
established their own parliamentary system of government.[107] The Iraqi leader
did not test Western resolve in the 1990s by launching military attacks against
the 3.5 million Kurds living north of the 36th parallel, but this cannot be ruled
out in the future. The Kurds have experienced periods of relative autonomy
before only to see these followed by appalling violations of their human rights.
Maintaining and enhancing their security depends crucially on the future
evolution of the Iraqi state, but it also rests on the willingness of Western

[102] 'Via Telegram towards a Kurdish Compromise', *Independent*, 30 Apr. 1991. Sir David Hannay
claims that he has no recollection of this issue ever being raised in New York (interview with Sir
David Hannay, Mar. 1999).

[103] 'Iraq Attacks Kurds and Defies Sanctions in Challenge to UN', *Independent*, 13 Sept. 1991.

[104] Stromseth, 'Iraq', 92.

[105] 'Kurdish "Safe Haven" Braces itself for Saddam's Wrath to Come', *Observer*, 17 Jan. 1993.

[106] D. Keen, 'Short-Term Interventions and Long-Term Problems', in J. Harriss (ed.), *The Politics of
Humanitarian Intervention* (London: Pinter, 1995), 171. Sir David Hannay admits that, after their
initial success in providing a symbol of reassurance, the guards came under pressure and 'there were
a few bad incidents'. However, he maintains that the guards continued to function in a security role
for quite a long time. Interview with Sir David Hannay, Mar. 1999.

[107] 'Kurds Enjoy Taste of Freedom under Dual Embargo', *Financial Times*, 2 Apr. 1998.

states to defend the Kurds in the event of any future Iraqi attacks against them.

Any assessment of the success of Western humanitarian intervention in northern Iraq cannot ignore the fact that there was no armed rescue of the Shiites in the south. As Kurdish refugees sought safety in the mountains of northern Iraq, an estimated 500,000–850,000 Shiites fled into the marshlands of southern Iraq, where they were vulnerable to Iraqi artillery fire.[108] The UN accepted responsibility for providing aid to the refugees who were dying of famine and disease, but the Secretary General did not believe that the 1,440 UN peacekeepers sent to patrol the demilitarized zone in southern Iraq should take on the role of protecting the Shiites.[109] Iran accepted some of the refugees, as did Saudi Arabia, but Kuwait refused to allow them to enter its territory. The MOU between Iraq and the UN ensured that some humanitarian aid was getting through to the refugees trapped in the marshlands, but access was not easy and relief efforts were hampered by the presence of Iraqi military forces.[110] The refugees feared for their safety and were desperate for UN protection.

The Foreign Office did issue a statement on 12 June 1991 stating that 'action by the Iraqi government against the Shiites would be in contravention of Security Council Resolution 688 . . . and would have very serious consequences'.[111] Iraq's response to this warning was further to obstruct UN aid efforts by suspending convoys and blockading the marshlands.[112] As reports increased of Iraqi attacks against the Shiites, the UN Human Rights Commission appointed a Special Rapporteur to report on Iraq's compliance with Resolution 688. The former Dutch Foreign Minister, Max van der Stoel, spent months investigating Iraqi human rights abuses, reporting that Shiite refugees were being bombarded by Iraqi artillery and air attacks, and that Iraqi generals had been instructed to 'wipe out' specified tribes who had lived for centuries in the marshlands. The report claimed that Iraq was forcibly relocating the tribes in an operation that it likened to Iraq's destruction of the Kurds in the late 1980s.[113]

The Special Rapporteur's findings made a mockery of British claims in June 1991 that Iraq would face 'severe consequences' if it attacked the Shiites. Pressure from the media and public opinion had shamed Western governments into creating safe havens for the Kurds. Unfortunately for the Shiites,

---

[108] Weiss, *Military–Civilian Interactions*, 51.

[109] Freedman and Boren, ' "Safe Havens" ', 69, and 'UN Role in Helping Shiites and Troops is Uncertain', *Independent*, 19 Apr. 1991.

[110] UN sources said that the refugees were being shelled by the Iraqi army. See 'UN may Free Trapped Shia Refugees', *Independent*, 9 July 1991. For discussion of the plight of the refugees and their desire for protection, see Freedman and Boren, ' "Safe Havens" ', 69, and 'UN Role in Helping Shiites and Troops is Uncertain', *Independent*, 19 Apr. 1991.

[111] Quoted in Freedman and Boren, ' "Safe Havens" ', 70.   [112] Ibid.

[113] 'Iraq Trying to Wipe out Marsh Arabs', *Independent*, 1 Aug. 1992.

their cries for help in 1991 received little media attention and governments were not forced into taking the actions they had taken on behalf of the Kurds. One proposal suggested at the time was to create safe havens in the south, an idea pressed by the Iranian Government, which highlighted the West's selective treatment of the Kurds and Shiites. There were three objections to creating safe havens in southern Iraq: first, the Western powers and their Gulf War allies remained sensitive about actions that might lead to the break-up of Iraq, with Saudi Arabia particularly fearful of the emergence of an Iranian-backed Shiite state in the south. Secondly, there was the legal objection that setting up safe havens in the south would require a new resolution from the Security Council. Finally, there was the practical question of whether it was possible to deploy ground forces to protect the Shiites without Iran's consent. Despite proposing the idea of safe havens in the south, it is highly unlikely that the Iranian Government would have allowed US forces to pass through its territory. The reason why the operation was possible in the north was because allied forces could operate from Turkey, which was a NATO ally.[114] Even if such an operation had been logistically feasible, there would have been no enthusiasm among Britain, France and the USA to take on protection of the Shiites having only recently extracted their forces from northern Iraq.

There was no question of the Security Council being able to take action on the basis of the Special Rapporteur's investigation into human rights abuses in southern Iraq, the reason being that those members who were sensitive to any erosion of the sovereignty rule would have rejected any attempt to use a report, produced by a representative appointed by the General Assembly, as the basis for Security Council enforcement action.[115] Instead, Belgium, which was President of the Security Council for August, succeeded in persuading members that they should discuss the report. In a meeting on 12 August, the Security Council condemned Iraq's repression of the Shiites and Marsh Arabs, but there was no support for any form of enforcement action inside Iraq's borders. The former Dutch Foreign Minister wanted the Council to send human rights monitors to southern Iraq to investigate and report on human rights abuses,[116] but even this limited step failed to secure approval by the Council. The same doctrinal concerns that had prevented non-Western members from authorizing enforcement action in Resolution 688 continued to constitute the boundaries of acceptable action.

The failure once again to secure Security Council authorization for tougher action against Iraq's human rights violations forced Western states to act on their own. With ground forces clearly ruled out, Western governments relied on extending the no-fly to southern Iraq. They argued that protection of the Shiites and Marsh Arabs required a ban on Iraqi fixed-wing

---

[114] Interview with Sir David Hannay, Mar. 1999.

[116] 'Iraq Trying to Wipe out Marsh Arabs'.

[115] Ibid.

planes and helicopters.[117] Although this action was not expressly provided for in Resolution 688, Britain argued that it was in support of the resolution's demand that Iraq end its repression and cooperate with UN humanitarian relief efforts. In response to a question on BBC Radio 4 that the operation was not legal because of the lack of specific authorization in Resolution 688, the Foreign Secretary, Douglas Hurd, replied:

But we operate under international law. Not every action that a British Government or an American Government or a French Government takes has to be underwritten by a specific provision in a UN resolution provided we comply with international law. International law recognizes extreme humanitarian need. No-one who has looked at the report which the UN . . . received the other day . . . [the Special Rapporteur's report] can doubt extreme humanitarian need. In support of the UN resolution—it happens to be 688—which enjoins Saddam Hussein not to commit these acts of aggression against his own people we are clear—the French are clear, the Americans are clear—we are on strong legal as well as humanitarian ground in setting up this 'No-fly' zone.[118]

The US, British, and French Governments announced the imposition of the no-fly zone on Iraqi fixed- and rotary-wing aircraft south of the 32nd parallel on 26 August 1992. In a joint statement the coalition partners stated that, given Iraq's 'failures to comply with UNSCR 688, the coalition has concluded that it must itself monitor Iraqi compliance with UNSCR 688 in the South'.[119] There was no discussion of the southern no-fly zone in the Security Council, and no government, apart from Iraq, publicly challenged the legality of the operation.

This international acceptance of the zone reflected the fact that no one wanted to be seen criticizing an action that was directed against a government that was guilty of appalling human rights abuses. Yet this acquiescence left Western forces free to shoot down Iraqi fixed- and rotary-wing aircraft if they entered the zone. Such actions clearly exceeded the terms of Resolution 688, and this is implicitly acknowledged in Douglas Hurd's suggestion that not every action has to be 'underwritten' by a UN resolution. It is plausible to read into the British Foreign Secretary's defence of the southern no-fly zone a legal justification grounded in the argument that there exists a right of humanitarian intervention in customary international law provided that this supports existing Security Council resolutions.[120] This legal argument begs

---

[117] See British Foreign Secretary Douglas Hurd's interview on the BBC World Service, 20 Aug. 1992.

[118] FCO text, quoted in The British Yearbook of International Law 1992 (Oxford: Oxford University Press, 1993), 824.

[119] Quoted in D. Sarooshi, The United Nations and the Development of Collective Security: The Delegation by the UN Security Council of its Chapter VII Powers (Oxford: Oxford University Press, 1999), 231. Four days earlier Prime Minister Major had argued that a no-fly zone was intended to prevent 'genocide' ('Back to the Gulf', The Economist, 22 Aug. 1992).

[120] Christopher Greenwood argues that Western states were 'asserting a right of humanitarian intervention of some kind' (C. Greenwood, 'Is there a Right of Humanitarian Intervention?', The World Today, 49/2 (1993), 36).

the further question as to what is permitted in terms of the use of force under such a rule? The British Foreign Secretary acknowledged in a BBC radio interview on 21 August that the Security Council would need to be consulted if the coalition's human rights monitoring in southern Iraq indicated that 'further steps need to be taken'.[121] This implied that Security Council authority would be necessary for the use of force against Iraqi ground targets, but, given the sensitivities of the Security Council on enforcement action to defend human rights inside state borders, it was clear that securing such a resolution was a non-starter.[122]

One of the criticisms of the southern no-fly zone is that it stopped at Iraqi fixed- and rotary-wing aircraft. An editorial in the *New York Times* posed the question: 'Why stop at planes?', arguing that the failure to attack Iraqi military forces on the ground would have the effect of setting the Shiites 'up for further slaughter'.[123] The British Government's justification for not instructing its planes to attack Iraqi artillery shelling the Shiites and Marsh Arabs was that this exceeded the permissible limits of Resolution 688. Interviewed on BBC Television on 24 August 1992, Douglas Hurd in response to a question about whether RAF planes could attack military targets inside Iraq replied: 'No, we do not believe that that would be within the scope of the existing legal basis of Security Council resolutions.'[124] For the British Government, then, there were clear limits to the exercise of a right of humanitarian intervention in customary international law.

The southern no-fly zone was justified on grounds of extreme humanitarian need, but, since it did little to stop the human rights violations taking place on the ground, it is easy to conclude that it failed to live up to its humanitarian justifications. Compared to the plight of the Kurds, the suffering of Iraqi civilians in the south attracted very little media coverage in the West. Consequently, Western governments were not under the same domestic pressure to act on their behalf. Humanitarian considerations clearly played a role in the actions of state leaders in setting up the no-fly zone, but a key motive was to put pressure on Saddam Hussein for his non-compliance with UN weapon inspectors, who were mandated under the Gulf War ceasefire resolution to verify the disarmament of Iraq's weapons of mass destruction. By limiting his authority over another part of Iraq, the allies were determined to show Saddam Hussein that there was a price to be paid for his continuing non-cooperation.[125]

The first point to make here is that the existence of this non-humanitarian

---

[121] 'Hurd Agrees that UN would be Consulted before Allied Action', *Guardian*, 22 Aug. 1992.
[122] British Shadow Foreign Secretary Jack Cunningham argued that even the creation of a southern no-fly zone required a new Security Council resolution. See 'Hurd Agrees that UN would be Consulted before Allied Action'.
[123] 'No to the No-Fly Zone', *International Herald Tribune*, 29 Aug. 1992.
[124] FCO text, quoted in *The British Yearbook of International Law 1992*, 820–1.
[125] Interview with Sir David Hannay, Mar. 1999.

motive does not weaken the humanitarian claim behind 'Operation Southern Watch', unless it can be shown that this 'off-the-board' reason undermined the humanitarian benefits of the no-fly zone. The reason why the latter failed to protect Iraqi civilians in the south was not because of any hidden motives behind the creation of the zone; rather, it reflected the limitations of the no-fly zones as a means of humanitarian intervention. Why did allied planes, for example, not attack Iraqi ground targets? In justifying the character of the means employed, Britain argued that it could not attack Iraqi ground forces responsible for human rights abuses because of the constraints imposed by Resolution 688. Military strikes against Iraqi ground targets would have stretched still further the coalition's already strained interpretation of what this resolution permitted, but there were two 'off-the-board' reasons that led Western governments to set strict limits to the use of force within the zone: first, they were determined to avoid any commitment that might become protracted or risk lives; secondly, they were sensitive to the concerns expressed by Arab states in the region. Many of the latter have large Shia populations and feared that support for the cause of the Iraqi Shiites might encourage their own Shiites to become more restive. This explains the reluctance of Arab states to welcome the southern no-fly zone in contrast to the support they had given to the northern one. It was easy to support actions to save the Kurds because none of the Arab states had large Kurdish populations to worry about.[126] From a Western point of view, Operation Southern Watch was a delicate balancing act between, on the one hand, putting pressure on Saddam Hussein to comply with Western demands and, on the other, not alienating the Gulf War allies in the region by encouraging the Iraqi Shiites. Consequently, these hidden reasons led the allies to select military means that were incapable of protecting the human rights of the Shiites. The negative relationship between humanitarian means and outcomes in this case disqualifies Operation Southern Watch as a legitimate humanitarian intervention.

Conclusion

How far did the international response to Iraq's repression of its minorities represent a change of norm on the legitimacy of humanitarian intervention in international society? The voice of solidarism had been excluded from the dialogue of states in the 1970s, but this changed in response to the suffering of the Kurds. Western states advanced new humanitarian claims that

---

[126] 'Policy on Air Shield for Shias', *Independent*, 27 Aug. 1992.

contested dominant understandings of pluralist rules and the ensuing conversation changed the boundaries of permissible state action.

Britain and the USA initially excluded military action to rescue the Kurds as being illegitimate, but this decision was quickly reversed and action taken to protect the Kurds. What, then, explains this shift of policy? The most commonly cited explanation for Major's and Bush's U-turn is that 'media coverage compelled intervention by the Western powers'.[127] The initial response of politicians in Britain was to hide behind the non-intervention rule, while Bush represented intervention as risking another Vietnam. These pluralist and realist considerations ruled out any armed rescue mission to save those dying on the mountains in northern Iraq. The argument is that this position became untenable as the media—especially television—pinned moral responsibility on Western leaders for their abandonment of the Kurds after inciting them to rise up and overthrow Saddam Hussein. In James Mayall's words, action was taken only 'because the attention devoted by the Western media to the plight of the Kurds threatened the political dividends Western governments had secured from their conduct of the war itself'.[128] The Kurds were rescued because Major and Bush realized that to leave them to their fate would be unacceptable in the eyes of public opinion.

This contention that television coverage of the Kurds' suffering was responsible for intervention relies on a causal link between real-time images of human suffering and Western foreign-policy responses; yet, as I discuss in Chapters 7 and 8, appalling pictures of human suffering in Rwanda and Bosnia were not sufficient to compel Western intervention. Without media coverage of the Kurds, desperate plight, there would have been no safe havens, but it does not follow from this that the media caused the intervention. Martin Shaw's claim that television forced Major to reposition 'himself as the saviour of the Kurds'[129] implies that the Prime Minister had no choice over how to respond to the growing media pressure. However, there was nothing inevitable about Major's response to the crisis. Other leaders might have chosen to ride out the storm of media criticism and not take the political risks of leading on the safe havens, which raised complex legal and operational questions, and relied on US military support, which could not be guaranteed.

In an interview with Nik Gowing in 1994, Major said that he had been 'personally moved' by the images of Kurdish refugees, and that it was this that had led him to run with the safe-havens option.[130] As his advisers in the

---

[127] M. Shaw, Civil Society and Media in Global Crises (London: Pinter, 1996), 156.

[128] J. Mayall, 'Non-Intervention Self-Determination and the "New World Order" ', International Affairs, 67/3 (July 1991), 426.

[129] Shaw, 'Global Voices', 229.

[130] N. Gowing, 'Real-Time Television Coverage of Armed Conflicts and Diplomatic Crises: Does it Pressure or Distort Foreign Policy Decisions?', Joan Shorenstein Barone Centre, the John F. Kennedy School of Government, Harvard University, Working Paper, June 1994.

Foreign Office pointed out, this was risky, since the USA was keen to get its troops home after the Gulf War and was worried about becoming drawn into another Vietnam-style commitment.[131] The gamble paid off and Major was able to bounce the Americans into following Britain's lead, although a key factor in this was Baker persuading Bush to overrule the advice of the Pentagon and support the British and EU initiative on safe havens. Again, other Presidents might have responded differently and followed the Pentagon's advice not to become involved. Major and Bush clearly realized that there were political benefits to be had from saving the Kurds, but, while television coverage might have ensured domestic legitimacy for the safe havens, it did not determine this interventionist response.

The question as to the role played by the media in determining intervention in northern Iraq overlooks the critical significance of Resolution 688 in reconstituting the possibilities for Western action. In early April, the Foreign Secretary and Prime Minister had justified Britain's non-intervention policy on the grounds that there was no legal mandate to intervene in Iraq's internal affairs. Although there is controversy over whether Resolution 688 legally permitted the safe havens and no-fly zones, it provided legitimating arguments that could plausibly be stretched to cover these actions. Moreover, the Western power's reliance on Resolution 688 was not *post facto* rationalization; instead, it enabled intervention internationally, just as media coverage did domestically.

Given that Britain and the USA justified the safe havens as permitted by Resolution 688, it is fascinating to speculate whether the safe havens would have been possible in the absence of this. The argument advanced in this book is that state actions are inhibited if they cannot be legitimated, and this raises the question as to whether the Western powers could have justified the safe havens in the absence of Resolution 688. Given the strong defence of the rules of sovereignty and non-intervention expressed by non-Western members of the Security Council during the adoption of this resolution, it is reasonable to suppose that Western military intervention in Iraq would have been condemned as a violation of the UN Charter. Having just fought a war against Iraq in the name of upholding the principles of sovereignty and non-intervention, and having argued that there was no legal mandate for intervention to save the Kurds and Shiites, Western governments would have had a tough time legitimating the safe havens internationally. At the very least, their actions would have appeared incompatible with the principles that they claimed had motivated them in going to war against Iraq.

Without the legitimating reason supplied by Resolution 688, it would have been much more difficult to intervene, but I am not arguing that without this there would have been no intervention. Set against the problem of securing

---

[131] 'Coming to the Rescue of the Kurds', *The Times*, 10 Apr. 1991.

international legitimacy is the fact that any action by Britain, France, and the USA would have been legitimated domestically. Thus, Major and Bush might have decided that domestic pressures required them to go against the traditional rules and accept that their actions would lack the stamp of international legitimacy. At this point, the best legal minds in the Foreign Office and State Department would have been called upon to supply as convincing a legal defence as possible. This would presumably have had to rely on the claim that there is a right of humanitarian intervention in customary international law. In fact, this very legal justification for the safe havens was proffered in December 1992 by Anthony Aust, Legal Counsellor to the Foreign and Commonwealth Office (FCO), in reply to a question about the legal authority for UN operations from a member of the House of Commons Foreign Affairs Committee. Mr Aust stated that 'the intervention in northern Iraq . . . was in fact not specifically mandated by the United Nations, but the states taking action . . . did so in exercise of the customary international law principle of humanitarian intervention'. Asked to specify the definition of such a right, he argued that it covered cases of 'extreme humanitarian distress', which could be alleviated only by an outside intervention 'limited in time and scope'.[132]

Although Iraq argued that the safe havens and no-fly zones violated Article 2 (4), this was denied by Western governments, who at no time publicly claimed that they were breaching Iraq's sovereignty on humanitarian grounds. The Legal Counsellor's reasoning cited above supports the view of those international lawyers who argue that humanitarian intervention is permitted under Article 2 (4). Western military intervention in northern Iraq met these requirements: it was temporary, did not lead to a regime change or territorial adjustments, and was in conformity with the purposes laid down in Resolution 688.[133] In acquiescing to Western states deploying military forces inside the borders of another state without the consent of that sovereign government or explicit authorization in a supporting resolution, Pierre Laberge argues that those members of the Security Council who had voted for or abstained on Resolution 688 acknowledged by their silence that customary international law may develop 'by precedents of omission'.[134]

This proposition is rejected by Adam Roberts and Robert Jackson, who argue that Operation Provide Comfort does not mark a shift in normative practice, because it became possible only in the circumstances surrounding the immediate aftermath of the Gulf War. Western actions were tolerated by

---

[132] Quoted in *The British Yearbook of International Law 1992*, 827–8.

[133] This position is also advanced by Howard Adelman, who argues that the intervention was permissible under Article 2 (4) because Britain, France, and the USA did not use force '*against* . . . [Iraq's] territorial integrity or . . . political independence' (H. Adelman, 'Humanitarian Intervention: The Case of the Kurds', *International Journal of Refugee Law*, 4 (1992), quoted in P. Laberge, 'Humanitarian Intervention: Three Ethical Positions', *Ethics and International Affairs*, 9 (1995), 31.

[134] Laberge, 'Humanitarian Intervention', 31.

international society because they emerged out of a context where Iraq had violated its neighbour's sovereignty and then been defeated in war. The Security Council had authorized in Resolution 678 the use of 'all necessary means' to reverse Iraq's invasion of Kuwait, and, as the French argued in the debate over Resolution 688, the Security Council could not wash its hands of responsibility for the plight of Iraqi civilians. Moreover, having been vanquished in war, Iraq was exposed to the customary law right of victors to make claims 'in respect of a defeated country for whose condition they have some responsibility, and over whose future they wish to have some say'.[135] By violating the cardinal rules of the society of states, Iraq temporarily forfeited its sovereign rights, and this recognition can be seen in the reluctance of other states to endorse its view that the safe havens and no-fly zones violated its sovereignty and territorial integrity. This leads Robert Jackson to conclude that it 'would therefore be misleading to claim that the Coalition intervention in Iraq to protect the Kurds signals a fundamental normative change in the direction of a new armed humanitarianism in international relations'.[136]

How, then, are we to decide between these competing interpretations of the Iraqi case? The Kurds had suffered Iraqi repression in the late 1980s, including the gassing of Kurdish towns and villages, and no armed intervention had been forthcoming. To save the Kurds in the late 1980s required going to war against Iraq and no coalition of states could have been mobilized for a humanitarian intervention that would have cost soldiers' lives and risked escalating to a superpower conflict, given that Iraq was a client of the Soviet Union. In this respect, Roberts and Jackson are right that the intervention would have been inconceivable in any other circumstances than the aftermath of a war that had seen Iraq defeated militarily.

On the other hand, Resolution 688 and the safe havens altered the normative boundaries of legitimate intervention in international society. The significance of this resolution in setting a precedent for UN humanitarian intervention is that the Security Council recognized for the first time that a state's internal repression could have transboundary consequences that threatened 'international peace and security'. India had argued in 1971 that the exodus of refugees across its borders posed a threat to international security, but this claim had been rejected by the Security Council on the grounds that Pakistan's repression of the Bengalis was an internal matter. Although Cuba, Yemen, and Zimbabwe pressed the same argument in relation to Iraq's repression of its citizens, the majority of the Council argued that the prohibition on Security Council action in Article 2 (7) did not apply, since Iraq's repression posed a threat to international security. Nevertheless, the sensitivity of members on the question of Article 2 (7) ensured that the Council did

[135] A. Roberts, 'Humanitarian War: Military Intervention and Human Rights', *International Affairs*, 69/3 (1993), 437.
[136] R. J. Jackson, 'Armed Humanitarianism', *International Journal*, 48 (Autumn 1993), 594.

not pass Resolution 688 under Chapter VII of the Charter. As became apparent when Britain, France, and the USA tried to secure Security Council backing for the safe havens, and later for a UN police force to take over the allied operation, the Security Council was not ready to cross the normative rubicon of authorizing the threat or the use of force to protect human rights inside state borders.

The significance of the safe havens is that this action pushed against these normative constraints. For the first time a group of states publicly justified the use of force in terms of enforcing compliance with a Security Council Resolution that demanded respect for human rights. In doing so, Western states challenged dominant understandings of the sovereignty rule that hitherto prohibited even as limited an intervention as Operation Provide Comfort. By justifying the safe havens as in conformity with the humanitarian purposes laid down in Resolution 688 and not a breach of Iraq's sovereignty, Western governments argued that a new meaning should be given to the rules of sovereignty and non-intervention. The right of humanitarian intervention asserted was a limited one, in that it required a supporting Security Council resolution[137] and it was restricted to bringing '*relief* and redress in human rights emergencies'.[138] But these caveats do not alter the fact that the safe havens marked a solidarist moment in the society of states. It is claiming too much to argue that the silence that greeted Western action supports a new custom of humanitarian intervention, since international law requires that there be supporting *opinio juris*. Yet, by raising new humanitarian claims, the language of safe havens entered the normative vocabulary of the society of states, and with it, as Jane Stromseth notes, 'expectations that similar responses will be forthcoming in other conflicts'.[139] Having broken with the traditional interpretation of the sovereignty rule, the question was whether, contra Roberts and Jackson, similar departures would follow in the future, and whether these would be legitimated rather than acquiesced in by the society of states.

The first test came in southern Iraq, but, for a mix of logistic and political reasons, there were no safe havens for the Shiites and Marsh Arabs, and nor were there air attacks against those Iraqi military forces shelling them. The media did not try to pin responsibility on Bush and Major for the plight of the Shiites, as they had done with the Kurds. The result was that the West's selective treatment of Iraq's persecuted minorities never became an issue upon which governments were challenged. This fact of selectivity does not disqualify the intervention in the north as humanitarian, but if, as I have

---

[137] Adam Roberts argues that 'no right of purely national intervention on humanitarian grounds, without Security Council authority, was recognized' (Roberts, 'Humanitarian War', 437).

[138] This phrase is taken from Perez de Cueller's final report to the General Assembly in September 1999 and it captures well the spirit of Operation Provide Comfort. Quoted in Stromseth, 'Iraq', 99.

[139] Ibid. 103.

argued here, Western governments could have done more to stop the human rights abuses against the Shiites, it weakens the humanitarian credentials of the safe havens.

How well, then, does Operation Provide Comfort satisfy the threshold tests of a legitimate humanitarian intervention? The plight of the Kurds constituted a supreme humanitarian emergency and without outside military intervention hundreds of thousands would have died from hypothermia and exhaustion. Crucially important here was the logistic capability of the US military, which, according to Thomas Weiss, 'was simply the only option at the onset of the crisis'.[140] The threat to use force if Iraqi military and paramilitary forces did not withdraw was clearly commensurate with the gravity of the humanitarian crisis. The decision by Major and Bush to launch the safe havens reflected a mix of humanitarian and non-humanitarian motives, but what matters is that, even if it is argued that Major and Bush acted only to appease domestic public pressures for intervention, this non-humanitarian motive did not conflict with the declared humanitarian purpose of the operation. Finally, we come to the success of the operation as a *rescue* and in addressing the underlying political causes of Iraq's repression of the Kurds.

In the words of the UN High Commissioner for Refugees, Sadako Ogata, the safe havens were a 'case of successful humanitarian intervention'.[141] This assessment is an apposite one in terms of the success of the action in getting the Kurds into the safe havens and later back to their homes. Unfortunately, it is less apt when applied to the achievement in creating a political context that would provide for their long-term safety. Stromseth argues in relation to this intervention that 'humanitarian relief alone will not solve deep-seated problems'[142] and Freedman and Boren that 'humanitarian intervention which fails to address the underlying dispute which has led to the crisis in the first place is liable to conclude without guarantees of no recurrence'.[143] The assumption that human rights abuses always have political causes underpins a solidarist conception of humanitarian intervention, but the society of states failed to address these causes in its response to this humanitarian emergency.

The most that the Security Council would do was to call upon the parties to have a dialogue to ensure that human rights were respected. Recognizing that the lack of a lasting political solution left the Kurds exposed to future Iraqi attacks, the Western powers wanted to deploy armed police to provide long-term protection for the Kurds. This failed because, in attempting to secure Security Council authorization for such a force to take over the running of the safe havens, Western power bumped up against the resistance of pluralist rules. The Security Council was prepared to demand humanitarian access, but it was not ready to back this up with enforcement action.

---

[140] Weiss, *Military–Civilian Interactions*, 64.   [141] Quoted in ibid. 68.
[142] Stromseth, 'Iraq', 99.   [143] Freedman and Boren, ' "Safe Havens" ', 81.

It can be agreed with Weiss, then, that 'the longer-term benefits of the intervention remain fundamentally ambiguous'.[144] Allied air forces policing the skies of northern Iraq provided guarantees for the Kurds against a full-scale Iraqi attack, but this presence could do little to deal with covert attacks by Iraqi security forces who infiltrated into Kurdish-controlled territory. The UN guards were ill equipped to cope with this threat, which required a substantial presence of armed UN police or peacekeepers on the ground. The refusal of non-Western states on the Security Council to back such a deployment indicated the limits of the inroads that solidarism had made into a society of states that remained stubbornly pluralist.

By late 1992 the media spotlight had shifted from the plight of Iraqi civilians to other conflicts, notably the war in the former Yugoslavia and the famine in Somalia. In the case of the latter, the Security Council broke new ground by authorizing armed intervention on humanitarian grounds. How this became possible and what it signified for the legitimacy of humanitarian intervention in international society is the subject of the next chapter.

[144] Weiss, *Military–Civilian Interactions*, 68.

6

From Famine Relief to 'Humanitarian War': The US and UN Intervention in Somalia

For those who thought that Western intervention to save the Kurds was a one-off response, which had to be located in the context of the immediate aftermath of the 1991 Gulf War, the US intervention in Somalia in December 1992 suggested that humanitarian intervention was securing a new legitimacy in post-cold-war international society. It seemed that an era might be dawning in which Western governments, freed from the constraints of the cold war, would use their armies to save strangers in places far away from home. The US intervention in Somalia is historic, because it is the first time that the Security Council authorized a Chapter VII intervention—without the consent of a sovereign government—for explicitly humanitarian reasons. If Somalia is the site where humanitarian intervention broke new boundaries, it also marked a turning of the tide against such endeavours. As I show in the next chapter, the débâcle of the loss of the US Rangers in October 1993 had tragic consequences, since it was the ghost of Somalia—a mirror of that earlier ghost of Vietnam—that led the Clinton Administration to stand by and watch Hutu militias and Rwandan security forces slaughter over a million Rwandan civilians between April and July 1994.

This chapter examines the changing fortunes of humanitarian intervention following its ambivalent emergence in the response of the society of states to Iraq's oppression of the Kurds. I begin by examining the background to the collapse of the Somali state into civil strife, which led to the terrible famine that gripped the country in 1992. All the humanitarian organs of the UN failed to act quickly and effectively to stop the deaths of hundreds of thousands from malnutrition and starvation. By the summer of 1992 the UN was finally beginning to respond to the emergency in Somalia, and this was in no small measure due to the skill and dynamism shown by the Secretary General's Special Envoy, Mohammed Sahnoun. His sophisticated understanding of Somali culture and his commitment to dialogue facilitated the delivery of humanitarian aid. He also began to establish the bases for a more permanent peace settlement between the warring parties. However, Sahnoun's strategy of dialogue was abruptly replaced by the UN Secretary General with a more forcible approach, and crucial to this was a sea change in the Bush Administration's handling of the Somali crisis. The President was coming under increasing domestic pressure to act to save Somalia, and the second part of the chapter examines how far this determined the US military response. Here, I consider how far the Bush Administration's motives for acting were different from its humanitarian justification. The previous chapter argued that Resolution 688 supplied an important legitimating reason for action, and I investigate how far Resolution 794 served the same function.

The focus then turns to a detailed analysis of the significance of Resolution 794, which was adopted unanimously. There was none of the controversy over the legal competence of the Security Council to act in relation to Somalia that had characterized members' arguments in the Iraqi case. Nor was there any opposition to giving the USA a Chapter VII mandate for military enforcement action in Somalia, a ground-breaking decision by the Security Council given its previous reluctance to cross this normative rubicon. This raises the question how far the Security Council's response represents the first genuine case of UN authorized humanitarian intervention.

The final part of the chapter focuses on how far the US and later the UN intervention in Somalia met the requirements of a legitimate humanitarian intervention. Here, I apply the now familiar tests of necessity, proportionality, and a positive humanitarian outcome, asking the following questions: how far had non-violent means of humanitarian intervention and conflict resolution been exhausted before US forces were sent to Somalia? How successful was intervention in the short term in rescuing the victims of starvation and in the longer term in establishing the political conditions that would prevent a return to the cycle of civil war and famine in Somalia? Finally, by examining how the noble UN Security Council-authorized mission of rebuilding Somalia as a law-governed polity collapsed into the 'humanitarian' intervenors using force against Somali civilians, I consider how far this case supports the proposition that the threat and use of force cannot serve humanitarian ends.

The International Response to the Humanitarian Crisis in Somalia in 1991–1992

The humanitarian tragedy that engulfed the Somali people in 1991–2 was a result of the civil war and subsequent disintegration of the state that followed the fall of the government of Siad Barre in January 1991. The latter came to power in the late 1960s and had ruled Somalia in a brutal and discriminatory

fashion. To understand Somali politics it is necessary to appreciate the importance of the clan system. Somalis are ethnically and linguistically homogenous, fiercely independent, and have a strong sense of superiority *vis-à-vis*
other cultures.[1] However, they are divided into an elaborate system of clans
and sub-clans. Barre maintained power by both manipulating clan loyalties
and employing violence—tactics that eventually culminated in an uprising of
the Issk clan in the north-west of the country precipitating a nationwide
rebellion against his dictatorial rule.[2]

The United Somali Congress (USC), formed in spring 1989 and based on
an alliance between two leading members of the Hawiye clan, General
Mohamed Farah Aidid and Ali Mahdi, drove Siad Barre from the capital in
January 1991. Any hope that Somalis would form a government of national
reconciliation quickly evaporated as the forces that had defeated Barre
divided along sub-clan lines.[3] By November 1991 full-scale war had erupted
between Aidid and Ali Mahdi, and, with the country awash with weapons
owing to US and Soviet arms transfers during the cold war, Somalia disinteg-
rated into violence and destruction on a scale never experienced before.[4]
According to Lewis and Mayall, the 'conflict, which split Mogadishu into two
armed camps, polarised along clan lines, quickly engulfing what was left of
the city in a protracted blood bath, killing an estimated 14,000 people and
wounding 30,000'.[5] Somalia's descent into civil war in 1991 devastated agri-
cultural and livestock production, and it was this, compounded by drought,
that produced the famine that killed between 300,000 and 350,000 people
during 1992.[6]

The question, then, is could UN bodies, national governments, and
humanitarian NGOs have done more in 1991–2 to stop the suffering of the
victims of civil war and starvation? The worst of the fighting between the
warlords Aidid and Ali Mahdi took place between November 1991 and March
1992, when a UN-brokered ceasefire was finally agreed. During this period,
the UN's humanitarian agencies withdrew from Somalia because of fears for
the security of UN personnel, and they did not return until late 1991.
Moreover, even when the UN returned, its programmes were often ineffective
in meeting the needs of the Somali people. Alex de Waal gives the example of
Somali hospitals running out of essential drugs, whilst the United Nations

---

[1] I. Lewis and J. Mayall, 'Somalia', in J. Mayall (ed.), *The New Interventionism 1991–1994: United
Nations Experience in Cambodia, Former Yugoslavia and Somalia* (Cambridge: Cambridge University
Press, 1996), 101–3.

[2] A penetrating analysis of these events is provided in T. Lyons and A. I. Samatar, *Somalia: State
Collapse, Multilateral Intervention, and Strategies for Political Reconstruction* (Washington: Brookings
Institute, 1995), 14–21.

[3] The Issk clan and sub-clans in the north declared their region independent.

[4] Lewis and Mayall, 'Somalia', 105–6.   [5] Ibid. 106.

[6] Weiss, *Military–Civilian Interactions*, 78, J. Clark, 'Somalia', in L. F. Damrosch (ed.), *Enforcing
Restraint: Collective Intervention in Internal Conflicts* (New York: Council on Foreign Relations, 1993),
213, and Lewis and Mayall, 'Somalia', 107.

Children's Fund (UNICEF) kept supplies in a warehouse.[7] The International Committee of the Red Cross (ICRC) was so disappointed by the UN's humanitarian role in Somalia that it took the rare step in late 1991 of publicly condemning its operations in Somalia.[8]

Growing criticism of the UN's role led the Secretary General to begin to galvanize the organization into greater involvement in the deepening humanitarian emergency. This took two forms: Security Council enforcement action and the negotiation of the March ceasefire between the warring parties. The Security Council had taken no action to stop Somalia's descent into chaos through 1991; it was too preoccupied with the Iraqi crisis and the developing war in the former Yugoslavia to busy itself with civil war in a small African state that had ceased to have any strategic significance at the end of the cold war. Given that the superpowers were primarily responsible for flooding Somalia with arms, it was ironic that the Security Council's first action was to establish an arms embargo—a classic case of closing the door after the horse has bolted. Resolution 733, unanimously adopted on 23 January, declared that the internal conflict in Somalia constituted 'a threat to international peace and security', a finding that enabled the Council to authorize an arms embargo under Chapter VII of the Charter. The resolution called upon the Secretary General to increase humanitarian assistance, and to work with the OAU and Arab League to achieve a ceasefire.

After some difficult negotiations in Somalia between UN Special Envoy James Jonah and Aidid and Ali Mahdi, the principles of a ceasefire were agreed at UN headquarters on 3 March. There were two possible ways of viewing this limited breakthrough: first, as a means of supporting the provision of humanitarian aid; and, secondly, as the basis for a politics of national reconciliation that would not only address the immediate crisis of starvation but also put in place a new structure of civil authority based on the rule of the law.[9] There was no interest among Security Council members in taking on the massive and open-ended commitment of helping Somalis to construct a legitimate polity, and the ceasefire was valued because it promised to ensure that the aid supplied by international donors would begin to reach those most in need.

---

[7] Alex de Waal's observation is discussed in Ramsbotham and Woodhouse, *Humanitarian Intervention*, 200. The UN withdrawal from Somalia in January 1991 stands in stark contrast to the decision of humanitarian international non-governmental relief organizations to continue working in Somalia. The International Committee of the Red Cross (ICRC) in conjunction with the Somali Red Crescent Society, MSF, Save the Children Fund (UK), the International Medical Corps, and SOS-Kinderdorf delivered humanitarian aid despite the deteriorating security situation. Indeed, the ICRC was even forced to take the unprecedented step of hiring its own armed guards to protect its aid convoys.

[8] Clark, 'Somalia', 218. Also see 'UN under Attack for Somalia bungling', *Independent*, 16 Jan. 1992. Unlike the UN, the ICRC, along with the relief agencies World Vision, CARE, Save the Children, and MSF, maintained operations throughout 1991–2. Weiss estimates that the activities of the ICRC and the other NGOs in early 1992 'averted 50,000 deaths and an additional 40,000 between September and December 1992' (Weiss, *Military–Civilian Interactions*, 80–1).

[9] Lyons and Samatar, *Somalia*, 31.

Unfortunately, this hope proved overly optimistic as Mogadishu collapsed into a state of general lawlessness. The militias might have agreed a fragile truce in their battle for territory and resources, but this did not stop looting and extortion by the armed gangs who roamed the streets of Mogadishu in their vehicles mounted with heavy guns. These groups, mostly outside the control of the warlords, demanded a share of the incoming aid as the price for providing aid agencies with security against attack. And, in the absence of international armed protection, there was no escape from this protection racket for those humanitarian international non-governmental organizations (INGOs) determined to deliver aid to the victims of the famine.

The deaths of hundreds of thousands of Somalis in 1992 was not because of a lack of aid; rather, it was because aid could not be distributed quickly enough because of the chronic lawlessness that prevailed in Mogadishu and in the countryside. The Security Council's paltry response to the emergency was to authorize the sending of fifty unarmed observers to monitor the cease-fire, and to agree in principle to the deployment of 500 peacekeepers to assist with the delivery of humanitarian aid provided that the militias consented to this. At this stage, there was no question of the Security Council acting without the consent of the most powerful Mogadishu warlords. Paradoxically, given its armed intervention in Somalia later in the year, the USA was a strong opponent at this time of sending a large peacekeeping force to Somalia because it feared that it would end up bearing the financial burden.[10]

A humanitarian emergency of catastrophic proportions, combined with a deteriorating security environment for the delivery of relief, was the situation that confronted the UN's new special representative, the former Algerian diplomat Mohammed Sahnoun, when he arrived in Somalia on 1 May. In contrast to previous UN envoys to Somalia, Sahnoun was culturally sensitive and worked hard to establish good relations with the warlords, especially Aidid, who needed considerable persuading of the UN's good offices in Somalia.[11] In addition to negotiating with the warlords, Sahnoun travelled into the interior, where he was successful in enlisting the authority of the local elders in reducing the fighting and allowing food deliveries.[12] Sahnoun was perceptive enough to see 'that the clan system, however complex and shifting, diluted power, and must form the basis for enduring peace'.[13] And, by securing the support of the clan elders, he strengthened his bargaining

---

[10] Ramsbotham and Woodhouse, *Humanitarian Intervention*, 203, Lewis and Mayall, 'Somalia', 108, and 'UN Plans to Escort Food to Somalis', *Guardian*, 23 Apr. 1992. For a critical view of the US position, see 'Casualties in Somalia Put at 41,000', *Guardian*, 27 Mar. 1992, and 'Somalia, Too, Needs Help', *International Herald Tribune*, 13 May 1992.

[11] J. Stevenson, 'Hope Restored in Somalia?', *Foreign Policy*, 91 (1993), 146. Aidid was deeply suspicious of the UN Secretary General, dating back to the latter's time as Egyptian Foreign Minister when Aidid had suspected that Egypt had territorial designs against Somalia.

[12] M. M. Sahnoun, 'Prevention in Conflict Resolution: The Case of Somalia', *Irish Studies in International Affairs*, 5 (1994), 10.

[13] Ramsbotham and Woodhouse, *Humanitarian Intervention*, 203.

leverage with the warlords. After long negotiations, Aidid, Ali Mahdi, and the other faction leaders finally agreed at the beginning of August to the deployment of the 500 peacekeepers that the Security Council had mandated in March.

Sahnoun incurred the displeasure of his political masters in New York by publicly criticizing the failures of the UN in Somalia, but it was this frankness coupled with his sensitivity to local Somali traditions that earned him the respect of many Somalis.[14] He recognized that Somalia's best hope for lasting peace and security lay in the promotion of new leaders in local communities within the regions, a 'grassroots process' that was 'well under way' and which served to weaken the hold of the Mogadishu warlords.[15] To strengthen this process, Sahnoun proposed that UN relief operations be decentralized to the regions. But, to his frustration, the UN continued to concentrate relief operations in Mogadishu, a situation that bolstered rather than weakened the bargaining power of the Mogadishu warlords.[16]

Having secured the agreement of the faction leaders to the deployment of the 500 peacekeepers, Sahnoun is critical of the fact that they did not arrive until mid-September. He claims that the early deployment of this force 'would have made an appreciable difference' to the security situation. As it was, the peacekeepers had not even arrived when the Secretary General announced that the UN was sending 3,000 troops to Somalia with or without the consent of the faction leaders. The Security Council on 28 August had authorized in Resolution 775 the deployment of a 3,500-strong peacekeeping force to provide protection for humanitarian relief supplies, and Sahnoun had set about persuading the warlords and elders to accept this increased deployment. Consequently, Boutros Boutros-Ghali's announcement massively undermined Sahnoun's efforts and led to his resignation. As he later reflected, 'this statement was made without informing the UNOSOM [United Nations Operation in Somalia] delegation in Mogadishu . . . and, worse still, without consulting the Somali leaders and community elders as we had done before'.[17]

The Secretary General wanted quicker results in Somalia and was pushing for a more forcible response to the crisis. However, the consequences of the announcement to deploy UN forces without consent were negative for the humanitarian relief operation. Aidid, ever suspicious of the UN, 'threatened to send the soldiers home in body bags, and lost interest in keeping the port [Mogadishu] open and safeguarding relief operations'.[18] And when the 500 Pakistani peacekeepers were eventually deployed in mid-September, Aidid refused to protect them. The Pakistanis did take control of Mogadishu airport with the agreement of the clan controlling it in early November, facilitating

[14] Ibid.   [15] Sahnoun, 'Prevention in Conflict Resolution', 9.
[16] Ibid. 10.   [17] Ibid. 11.
[18] Quoted in Ramsbotham and Woodhouse, *Humanitarian Intervention*, 205.

the US airlift of humanitarian aid that had begun in late August (see below). However, UNOSOM I was attacked at the airport and the Pakistani soldiers, who were equipped only for self-defence, did not venture from the airport until the arrival of the US-led intervention force in December.

The resolution authorizing the deployment of the 3,500 peacekeepers was passed under Chapter VII of the Charter, but there was no specific mandate permitting the use of force. Nevertheless, the Security Council's proposal to deploy UN forces without the consent of the parties represented a decisive shift from the previous strategy of negotiating with the armed militias who were blocking humanitarian relief efforts. The door was now open to enforce the delivery of humanitarian aid by the threat or use of force. The problem was that, having dispensed with Sahnoun's strategy of negotiations, no force was available to implement such an ambitious mandate. As Lewis and Mayall argue, 'the UN lacked the organisational resources and its members the political interest or will to fashion a coherent strategy for Somalia'.[19]

Two months later the situation changed radically when the USA asked the UN for a mandate to send 30,000 of its troops to Somalia to provide armed protection for relief operations. Given that the Bush Administration had opposed the sending of a UN peacekeeping force to Somalia in March 1992, what accounts for the US decision forcibly to intervene in Somalia in December 1992? How did US military intervention become possible in a faraway African country of which the American people knew very little?

The Bush Administration and 'Operation Restore Hope'

After the fall of Siad Barre, the USA, in the words of ex-Ambassador T. Frank Crigler, 'turned out the light, closed the door and forgot about Somalia'.[20] Certainly, senior officials in the Bush Administration were too preoccupied with the situation in Iraq, the disintegration of the Soviet Union, and the collapse of the former Yugoslavia to give much attention to the plight of Somalis. However, other officials in the government were exercised by the deepening humanitarian crisis. Andrew Natsios, Director of the Office of Foreign Disaster Assistance (OFDA), declared in January 1992 that the famine in Somalia was 'the greatest humanitarian emergency in the world',[21] and the State Department's African bureau tried to put Somalia on Secretary of State Baker's agenda. Had there been the media focus on Somalia that accompanied

[19] Lewis and Mayall, 'Somalia', 109.
[20] Quoted in J. Pilger, 'The US Fraud in Africa', New Statesman and Society, 8 Jan. 1993, 10.
[21] Quoted in Clark, 'Somalia', 212.

the Kurdish crisis, the Bush Administration might have acted sooner to save lives, but press briefings given by OFDA and the State Department in the first six months of 1992 failed to generate significant media interest.[22]

The turning point in US responses to the deepening Somali emergency came in the form of an emotional telegram from the US Ambassador in Kenya that described the starvation in the Somali refugees camps along the Kenyan border. The Democratic challenger in the election campaign, Bill Clinton, was criticizing Bush for his alleged foreign-policy failures over both Bosnia and Somalia, and this coupled with Bush's personal reaction to the stories of suffering Somalis galvanized the President to act decisively on the Somali issue. He used the opportunity of the Republican Party Convention to announce a US military airlift of food to Somalia. The President, who had fiddled whilst Somalia descended into the abyss of lawlessness and famine, now declared that 'starvation in Somalia is a major human tragedy' and that the USA would provide food for 'those who desperately need it'.[23] As Jeffrey Clark points out, the 'timing of the announcement . . . more than five months after the March cease-fire and eight months after relief chief Natsios had described the famine as the world's greatest humanitarian emergency— evoked a high degree of cynicism among many observers'.[24]

Livingstone and Eachus argue that it was Bush's announcement of the airlift on 13 August that 'finally sparked the sort of intense media attention usually associated with the CNN [Cable News Network] effect'.[25] With the benefit of hindsight it is easy to see how Bush's humanitarian rationale for the airlift generated the expectations among media and public opinion that were a key determinant of the President's decision to send US soldiers to Somalia. In August, however, officials in the White House and Pentagon opposed any further US involvement in the run-up to an election in which Bush was being accused by his opponents of focusing too much on foreign policy.

The problem was that, having made Somalia an issue for the media, it was not easy for the administration to control the subsequent coverage, which focused on the fact that over 1,000 Somalis were dying daily. Reflecting in 1996 on Bush's decision to intervene in December 1992, Natsios claimed that 'sustained media coverage of the anarchy and starvation in Somalia certainly contributed mightily to the Bush administration's decision to deploy Operation Restore Hope, but that contribution postdated Washington's decision to initiate a robust relief'.[26] And Lawrence Eagleburger, who was

---

[22] A. Natsios, 'Illusions of Influence: The CNN Effect in Complex Emergencies', in R. I. Rotberg and T. G. Weiss (eds.), *From Massacres to Genocide: The Media, Public Policy, and Humanitarian Crises* (Washington: Brookings Institute, 1996), 159.

[23] Quoted in Pilger, 'The US Fraud in Africa'.   [24] Clark, 'Somalia', 227.

[25] Quoted in S. L. Carruthers, *The Media at War* (London: Macmillan, 1999), 220. This is also the argument in L. Minear, C. Scott, and T. G. Weiss, *The News Media, Civil War and Humanitarian Action* (Boulder, Colo.: Lynne Rienner, 1996), 54.

[26] Natsios, 'Illusions of Influence', 159.

Secretary of State during the Somali crisis, opined in 1994 that 'television had a great deal to do with President Bush's decision to go in. I was one of those two or three that was strongly recommending he do it, and it was very much because of the television pictures of these starving kids [and] substantial pressures from the Congress that come from the same source.'[27]

The pictures of starving Somalis in late 1992 contrasted unfavourably with Bush's promise in August that the USA would provide food for 'those who desperately need it'. One Pentagon official was reported as saying that Bush felt he had to act and 'would not leave office with 50,000 people starving that he could have saved'.[28] The reason given by the media for the starvation was that warlords and armed gangs were holding up the delivery of humanitarian aid that could save thousands of lives. This representation struck a powerful chord with a US public that wanted the administration to ride shotgun into Mogadishu and rescue the victims of lawlessness and starvation. As with the case of the Kurds, media coverage enabled humanitarian intervention by ensuring domestic legitimacy, but it did not determine a forcible response to the Somali emergency. There are three other key reasons that explain Bush's decision to launch Operation Restore Hope.

The first is the humanitarian impulses of the President and his senior policy advisers. Natsios recalls a meeting he attended between Bush and Phil Johnson, who was President of CARE-US and UN Director of Humanitarian Operations in Somalia.[29] Bush described a visit that he, the First Lady, and Johnson had made to a CARE shelter for starving children in the Sudan during the Sahelian famine in the mid-1980s. He declared that memories of the suffering he had witnessed there 'had clearly affected his decision to send troops into Somalia'.[30] Similarly, having opposed a greater US military commitment to Somalia for months, the Chairman of the Joint Chiefs of Staff, Colin Powell, argued that the suffering in Somalia had reached a critical point where the USA should intervene in a massive military operation.[31]

The second set of motivations relates to the fact that Somalia was perceived as a relatively risk-free and short-term operation. The National Security Council (NSC) Deputies Committee (a group of senior staff below cabinet level) convened four times between 21 and 26 November to consider a variety of military options, and it was during this process that the interagency group came up with the proposal of using US ground forces.[32]

[27] Quoted in Minear *et al. The News Media,* 54–5.

[28] Reported in 'White House "Steamrollered" into Intervention', *Independent,* 10 Dec. 1992.

[29] Johnson was a vigorous advocate of armed intervention in Somalia. See Alex de Waal, 'African Encounters', *Index on Censorship,* 6 (1994), 19–20, and Ramsbotham and Woodhouse, *Humanitarian Intervention,* 204.   [30] Natsios, 'Illusions of Influence', 168.

[31] Powell's change of heart on intervention is discussed in 'Waiting for America', *US News and World Report,* 7 Dec. 1992, 26–8, and in J. L. Hirsch and R. B. Oakley, *Somalia and Operation Restore Hope: Reflections on Peacemaking and Peacekeeping* (Washington: United States Institute of Peace, 1995), 42.   [32] Ibid. 42–3.

According to Lewis and Mayall, Powell was prepared to support forcible intervention to protect relief supplies provided that the following conditions were met: the operation was restricted to protecting the delivery of humanitarian aid; it was confined to the geographical regions of Mogadishu, Berbera, and Baidoa, which were most devastated by the famine; and US troops would hand over to a UN peacekeeping force shortly after the new President came to office.[33] If these conditions were agreed, then the Pentagon chief 'favoured intervening with sufficient force and fire-power to overawe any Somali opposition and minimise casualties'.[34] The latter was a crucial consideration for US policy-makers, and it was the conviction that the mission could be carried out with little or no risk to soldiers' lives that led the President at an NSC meeting with his senior advisers on 25 November to back the use of force. Eagleburger recalled in 1994 that he had argued at the time that 'we could do this . . . at not too great a cost and, certainly, without any great danger of body bags coming home'.[35] It was the fear of 'body bags' and being drawn into a protracted commitment that led the administration to oppose President-elect Clinton's calls for the use of force in the Bosnian conflict.

There can be little doubt that a further reason for the intervention in Somalia was Bush's desire to deflect attention from his inaction over Bosnia.[36] Having lost the election campaign, Bush viewed a humanitarian intervention in Somalia as showing his critics that his vision of a 'new world order' was not just empty rhetoric. And employing US military power to save dying Somalis appealed to a President who wanted to leave office with a last foreign-policy success and who saw the USA as having a responsibility for international leadership.[37] Speaking on 6 December 1992, Eagleburger tried to justify publicly the administration's differing responses to Somalia and Bosnia:

But the fact of the matter is that a thousand people are starving to death every day, and that is not going to get better if we don't do something about it, and it is in an area where we can affect events. There are other parts of the world where things are equally tragic, but where the cost of trying to change things would be monumental. In my view, Bosnia is one of those.[38]

Realists argue that selectivity of response is a major objection to the legitimacy of particular humanitarian interventions, but Eagleburger's reply is that the moral impulse to save lives has to be balanced against the costs and risks involved.

The final issue to be addressed in understanding how Operation Restore Hope became possible is the importance of UN authorization. Lewis and

---

[33] Lewis and Mayall, 'Somalia', 111.   [34] Ibid.
[35] Quoted in Minear *et al.*, *The News Media*, 55.
[36] Hirsch and Oakley, *Somalia*, 42–3.
[37] Natsios, 'Illusions of Influence', 161.
[38] Quoted in Roberts, 'Humanitarian War', 442.

Mayall argue that the USA was 'prepared to act unilaterally',[39] but White House spokesman Marlin Fitzwater stated that the USA would intervene only as part of a UN mission and Pentagon sources were reported as saying that, 'until we get word from the UN, our plans are nothing more than drafts'.[40] The implication was that, in the absence of UN Security Council authority, the USA would not have intervened. This is supported by John Hirsch and Robert Oakley, who claim that, at the NSC meeting on 25 November, 'the president decided that if the Security Council concurred, then US ground forces would lead a rescue mission'.[41] Given that all the participants at the NSC meeting were agreed that the UN had to take over the operation after a limited US involvement, any deployment without UN authorization jeopardized this exit strategy. Public opinion was clamouring for US action, but should this turn into a protracted and messy commitment, as had happened in Vietnam and the Lebanon, domestic support for US intervention would quickly ebb away. It was not so much concerns about international legitimacy that constrained US actions; rather, UN legitimation was vital in securing Bush's objectives for the mission, and hence in maintaining domestic legitimacy for it.

Resolution 794: A New Collective Norm of Humanitarian Intervention?

A day before Bush had decided to go ahead with military intervention in Somalia, the Secretary General had written to the Security Council detailing the deteriorating situation. His report concluded that the only way to stop the deaths of up to two million Somalis was to break the 'cycle of extortion and blackmail' and establish 'security conditions that will permit the distribution of relief supplies'.[42] In a statement to the Security Council following his report, Boutros Boutros-Ghali expressed his view that force would be necessary to ensure the delivery of aid in Somalia. After this meeting the Security Council's President for December, André Erdos of Hungary, stated that 'the situation went too far to be tolerated and too far to use the same practices and methods that we have been using so far'.[43] The Security Council asked the Secretary General to prepare a report on possible options, and it was against this background that Eagleburger flew to New York the following day with the

---

[39] Lewis and Mayall, 'Somalia', 111.

[40] 'US Offers Military Guard for Somali Aid', *Sunday Times*, 29 Nov. 1992, and 'US Troops Await Vote on Somalia', *Independent*, 3 Dec. 1992.

[41] This is based on interviews with senior figures who were at this key NSC meeting with Bush. See Hirsch and Oakley, *Somalia*, 43.

[42] 'US Offers Troops for Somalia', *Guardian*, 27 Nov. 1992.   [43] Ibid.

US offer to provide up to 30,000 US troops to protect the delivery of humanitarian aid in Somalia.

The Secretary General reported to the Security Council on 29 November,
setting out five possible courses of action: speed up the deployment of
UNOSOM I as envisaged in Resolution 775; abandon all efforts to use peacekeeping forces to protect humanitarian aid supplies, leaving humanitarian
relief agencies to their own efforts; change the mandate of UNOSOM I so that
it could use force to assist in the delivery of humanitarian aid, but restrict this
to Mogadishu; an enforcement mission under UN command and control that
would cover the whole country; and a nationwide enforcement mission by an
authorized group of states, whose forces would be under national command
and control. Boutros Boutros-Ghali favoured the last option because
Eagleburger had made it clear that Bush's offer was conditional upon US
forces remaining under national command and control.

In advocating the forcible option to the Security Council, the Secretary
General argued that, since no government existed in Somalia, the Council
would have to authorize the use of force under Chapter VII of the Charter.
Boutros Boutros-Ghali wrote:

At present no government exists in Somalia that could request and allow such use of
force. It would therefore be necessary for the Security Council to make a determination
under Article 39 of the Charter that a threat to the peace exists, as a result of the *repercussions* of the Somali conflict on the entire region, and to decide what measures should
be taken to maintain international peace and security.[44]

Although the Secretary General's justification for Security Council action
was an attempt to make the Somali case fit the pluralist rule governing
Chapter VII enforcement action, it is apparent from the debate in the Security
Council that led to the adoption of Resolution 794 that the key reason for
acting was humanitarian.[45] Indeed, this resolution, passed unanimously on 3
December 1992, declared in the preamble that the reason for invoking
Chapter VII of the Charter was that 'the magnitude of the human tragedy
caused by the conflict in Somalia, further exacerbated by the obstacles being
created to the distribution of humanitarian assistance, constitutes a threat to
international peace and security'.

The Security Council had to find a threat to 'international peace and security' to legitimate Chapter VII enforcement action, but, as Christopher
Greenwood points out, the resolution is ground-breaking because it authorizes the use of force on the grounds that the human suffering inside Somalia
constitutes a threat to 'international peace and security'.[46] In the case of the
Kurds, the Security Council had found a threat to international security in the

---

[44] Quoted in Roberts, 'Humanitarian War', 440; emphasis added.
[45] Ibid.
[46] Greenwood, 'Is there a Right of Humanitarian Intervention?', 38.

external consequences of Iraq's repression, but it had not identified the human rights abuses themselves as legitimating Chapter VII action, nor had it authorized any form of enforcement action. By contrast, in operative paragraph 10 of Resolution 794, the Security Council, 'acting under Chapter VII of the Charter [authorized] the Secretary-General and Member States . . . to use all necessary means to establish as soon as possible a secure environment for humanitarian relief operations in Somalia'.

It might be ventured that, given the flow of refugees to neighbouring countries, the Security Council had some justification in making a Chapter VII determination. Yet, on the floor of the Council, only the US and Cape Verdean Ambassadors stressed the transboundary implications of the Somali conflict. Cape Verde was the only government to echo the Secretary General's argument that the Somali conflict had 'repercussions' for wider regional security.[47] Instead of focusing on the regional dangers posed by the conflict, the USA argued that, by providing a secure environment for the delivery of humanitarian relief, 'the Council has once again taken an essential step to restore international peace and security'.[48] The US Ambassador considered that the case of Somalia demonstrated that international society was faced in the post-cold-war period with a new kind of threat to that which had confronted it during the cold war. But no explanation was given as to how the humanitarian emergency in Somalia posed a threat to international security, and it can be agreed with Adam Roberts that, while the Council's finding of a threat to 'international peace and security' was not wholly fictitious, 'it in no way concealed the centrality of the humanitarian rationale for the Somalia operation'.[49]

It was what they perceived as the illegitimate stretching of Chapter VII to permit Security Council action to protect Iraqi civilians that had led Cuba, Yemen, and Zimbabwe to vote against Resolution 688. The latter was the only one of this group still serving on the Security Council, but, in a case where the justification for invoking Chapter VII and authorizing the use of force was much more tenuous than in the case of northern Iraq, there was no opposition from Zimbabwe—or any other member—to the legal competence of the Security Council to act in this matter. It was humanitarian reasons that were invoked by the Zimbabwean Ambassador to justify his support of the resolution. He declared that 'we cannot countenance this untold suffering of innocent men, women and children from starvation and famine',[50] while the Moroccan Ambassador claimed that the 'Security Council [was] the only hope' of saving thousands whose daily plight had 'aroused the universal conscience'.[51] In accounting for the position taken by the African states on

[47] S/PV.3145, 3 Dec. 1992, 19–20.   [48] Ibid. 38.
[49] Roberts, 'Humanitarian War', 440.   [50] S/PV.3145, 3 Dec. 1992.
[51] Ibid. 44.

the Security Council, Sir David Hannay considers that 'you have to understand the depth of shame of the Africans at what was happening in Somalia.
A feeling that Africa was being found wanting and that every African solution
that had been tried had failed.'[52]

Britain and France had been most forthright in pressing humanitarian claims
in the Iraqi case and it is, therefore, not surprising that they enthusiastically
supported Security Council enforcement action on humanitarian grounds. The
French Ambassador argued that his government viewed the resolution as of
'major importance' because it 'is part of the principle of establishing access to
victims and of the right to emergency assistance'.[53] The claim that the victims
of oppression and famine have a right to emergency assistance begs the question
as to which agent bears the correlative moral duty: individuals, governments, or
international organizations? Security Council members had not responded positively to France's argument at the outset of the crisis in northern Iraq that the
UN Charter should be rewritten to incorporate a 'duty to intervene', but several
members argued in December 1992 that the Security Council had a responsibility or obligation to intervene to rescue the Somali people.

The different position taken by Ecuador in the cases of northern Iraq and
Somalia is instructive in this regard. Ecuador had supported Resolution 688
only because of the impact of Iraq's oppression on wider regional security,
being emphatic that the Security Council did not have the legal authority to
intervene inside Iraq's borders to protect human rights. In this case, however,
it considered that the Security Council could not 'remain impassive in the
face of human tragedy' and that it had 'ineluctable responsibilities' to save
the Somali people.[54] Similarly, the Venezuelan Ambassador stated 'that the
current state of affairs in Somalia constitutes an affront to the dignity and
conscience of the international community',[55] and Russia, which had
strongly opposed the use of force to protect the Kurds, argued that it was the
'international community's obligations to put an end to the human tragedy'
and that this 'requires the use of international armed forces under the
auspices of the Security Council'.[56]

In unanimously passing Resolution 794, it might be thought that the
Security Council had significantly changed the normative context of legitimate intervention. For the first time, humanitarian claims were being
advanced and legitimated by members as justification for the use of force,
and, in contrast to Resolution 688, there was no disagreement over the legal
competence of the Security Council to deal with a humanitarian crisis inside
the borders of a sovereign state. Equally ground-breaking was the view
expressed by several members that the Security Council had a moral responsibility to save the victims of famine and civil strife.

---

[52] Interview with Sir David Hannay, Mar. 1999.   [53] S/PV.3145, 3 Dec. 1992, 29.
[54] Ibid.   [55] Ibid. 39–40.   [56] Ibid. 26–7.

Set against this, there are good reasons for thinking that many members interpreted the Somali case as a special one that warranted exceptional action. Thus, immediately prior to noting the relationship between human suffering and the threat to 'international peace and security', the resolution recognizes 'the unique character of the present situation in Somalia and *mindful* of its deteriorating, complex and extraordinary nature, requiring an immediate and exceptional response'. The Somali case was 'exceptional' because, in Roberts's words, it was 'not a case of intervention against the will of the government, but of intervention when there is a lack of government'.[57] This 'unique' character of the Somali intervention was emphasized by those states on the Security Council that had been most sensitive about eroding the rules of sovereignty and non-intervention in relation to the Kurds. India, speaking after the vote, emphasized that the resolution had been adopted against the background of an 'extraordinary situation, with no Government in control'.[58] China, which, had abstained on Resolution 688, reluctantly supported Resolution 794, stressing the 'chaotic situation resulting from the present lack of a Government in Somalia'.[59] China initially indicated that it was going to abstain on the resolution, expecting that the African states would object to the resolution because of concerns about sovereignty.[60] However, when it became apparent that African governments were fully behind the proposed US action, China, which had a policy of supporting African states in the Security Council, found itself in the difficult position of supporting the resolution. Certainly, the Chinese did not want to be left out in the cold abstaining on a resolution that was the best hope for saving Somalis from starvation.[61]

The insertion of the words 'unique', 'extraordinary', and 'exceptional' into the resolution was a concession to China's and India's concerns that this case should not be seen as setting a precedent for humanitarian intervention.[62] Thus, after the Security Council meeting that adopted Resolution 794, the Chinese Ambassador, Li Dayou, declared that Somalia was 'an exceptional case'.[63] By arguing that Security Council action was possible only because no government existed, those states most fearful of weakening a pluralist interpretation of the sovereignty rule could claim that no such precedent had been set. However, the ambiguity inherent within this position was made clear by the Zimbabwean Ambassador when he acknowledged that, while 'Somalia is a unique situation that warrants a unique approach', the responses 'adopted

---

[57] Roberts, 'Humanitarian War', 440.   [58] S/PV.3145, 3 Dec. 1992, 49.

[59] Ibid.

[60] Interview with Sir David Hannay, Mar. 1999. The claim that China was planning to abstain is supported in 'UN Votes to Send US-Led Force to Protect Somalia Famine Aid', *Guardian*, 4 Dec. 1992.

[61] Interview with Sir David Hannay, Mar. 1999.

[62] Ibid.

[63] Quoted in 'UN Votes to Send US-Led Force to Protect Somalia Famine Aid'.

create of necessity a precedent against which future, similar situations will be measured'.[64]

The argument that the Somali case is an 'exceptional' one because the government had collapsed might have persuaded China and India not to challenge Resolution 794's permissive interpretation of what counts as a threat to 'international peace and security', but it becomes problematic when the legal character of the non-intervention rule is scrutinized. It can be sustained only if one of the following lines of reasoning is pursued: first, that the non-intervention rule did not arise in the Somali case because the government had collapsed and that as a result the Security Council could not be violating the UN's non-intervention rule in Article 2 (7). The problem with this argument is that states and not governments are recognized in international law as the bearers of rights and duties. A more convincing version of this argument is predicated upon the claim that the non-intervention rule was not at stake because the state had ceased to exist. This identifies the correct subject of rights and duties, but, applied to the statements in the Security Council, it is tantamount to arguing that the state had collapsed because the government had collapsed. However, it is clear from the customary law relating to state recognition that government and state are not synonymous, with the former being a criterion for, but not wholly constitutive of, statehood. Consequently, it is by no means certain that the collapse of the Somali Government meant that the Somali state had ceased to exist in a juridical sense.[65]

Given that international recognition of a state's sovereignty is the defining mark of membership of the society of states, the question of whether Somalia existed in a juridical sense depended upon the collective judgement of the society of states. The Security Council would have exceeded its legal competence had it tried to justify enforcement action on the grounds that Somalia had ceased to exist in a juridical sense, hence the requirement to find a threat to 'international peace and security' in the consequences of the human suffering. Nevertheless, China and India justified their support for the resolution on the grounds that this was an exceptional case in which governmental authority had collapsed, and this argument was not challenged by other members. China and India were prepared to go along with the application of the Chapter VII rule to this case because they could maintain that Security Council action did not weaken the principle of 'domestic jurisdiction' in Article 2 (7) of the Charter. In short, they signed up to Resolution 794—in contrast to Resolution 688—because it did not set a precedent for the breach of the rules of sovereignty and non-intervention because there was no sovereign state against which to intervene.

---

[64] S/PV.3145, 3 Dec. 1992, 8–10.
[65] I owe this formulation to Justin Morris.

Humanitarian Outcomes in Somalia

Operation Restore Hope and the subsequent UNOSOM II mission were justified in humanitarian terms and the final part of this chapter examines how far these interventions achieved their humanitarian purposes. There are three key issues that require investigation here: first, there is the question as to whether the Secretary General and the Security Council were right to believe that there was no alternative to the threat or use of force in saving the Somali people from starvation. Secondly, was the level of force employed proportionate to the harm it was aimed at redressing? Finally, how far did the US and UN military interventions in Somalia succeed in both rescuing the Somali people from the immediate emergency and establishing the political conditions that would prevent a future collapse into civil war and famine?

In his report to the Security Council on 26 January 1993, the Secretary General claimed that the Unified Task Force (UNITAF), headed by the USA (thirty other states provided contributions of men and equipment to the mission), had fulfilled its mission of ensuring that humanitarian aid reached those most in need. This point is bolstered by Roberts, who, writing in early 1993, considered that 'countless lives have been saved'.[66] Similarly, Terrence Lyons and Ahmed I. Samatur judge that UNITAF 'prevented massive starvation and clearly represented a major accomplishment of the international intervention'.[67] UNITAF, then, was a necessary and successful response to an urgent humanitarian crisis that could not be addressed by non-forcible means.

This rosy picture of US humanitarian intervention is challenged by Alex de Waal, who forcefully argues that Operation Restore Hope was the wrong response to a famine that had passed its worst point by December 1992 and where the real killer had become disease and not starvation. De Waal rejects the claims in the Secretary General's letter of 24 November that 80 per cent of the aid was being looted, and that two million Somalis faced imminent death from starvation. Contra the dominant UN view, he asserts that life-threatening hunger had largely been banished by July, and that death rates had been falling in Baidoa, one of the worst affected parts of the country since September.[68] This leads de Waal to conclude that 'Operation Restore Hope was flawed in its conception; it was aimed at supplying massive food aid to a region that no longer needed massive food aid . . . it neglected the most pressing relief needs: a programme against malaria and effective measles vaccination. There is in fact no evidence that the intervention had any impact on mortality rates at all.'[69]

---

[66] Roberts, 'Humanitarian War', 441.   [67] Quoted in Lyons and Samatar, *Somalia*, 39.
[68] A. de Waal, 'Dangerous Precedents? Famine Relief in Somalia 1991–93', in J. Macrae and A. Zwi (eds.) *War and Hunger* (London: Zed Books, 1994), 152.
[69] A. de Waal, 'African Encounters', 20.

How, then, should we decide between these competing views? Thomas Weiss argues that, even if it is accepted that the worst of the famine was over, 'UNITAF hardly hurt Somalia', since it opened up distribution networks and provided 'security for humanitarian relief so that those who had not already died could leave camps and plant crops, and those without resources could receive food aid'.[70] Most commentators would concur with the findings of a report by the Refugee Study Group in November 1994, which estimated that some four million Somalis faced food insecurity and an increased risk of disease in 1992–3. Out of this number, '330,000 . . . were at imminent risk of death . . . Of those at imminent risk, 110,000 lives were sustained (deaths averted) due to health, food, and other interventions that reached over one million Somalis.'[71]

The next issue in assessing the legitimacy of Operation Restore Hope concerns the question of the relationship between short-term and long-term humanitarian outcomes. From the outset, Boutros Boutros-Ghali wanted UNITAF to disarm the warring factions, but this was opposed by the USA, which saw its mission as the much more limited one of facilitating the delivery of humanitarian aid.[72] Moreover, in implementing this goal, UNITAF depended upon the cooperation of the armed militias, which were responsible for Somalia's descent into lawlessness and famine. Resolution 794 empowered UNITAF to 'use all necessary means' to create a secure environment for the delivery of humanitarian aid. However, the respected US diplomat Robert Oakley, whom Bush had appointed as his Special Envoy, and who had served in Vietnam, recognized that the success of the mission depended upon securing the consent of the warlords. Oakley has been criticized for giving too much legitimacy to warlords such as Aidid and Ali Mahdi, but he appreciated that their support was vital in protecting US soldiers' lives and in ensuring the speedy delivery of aid.[73] Oakley was not afraid to threaten force and when he visited Baidoa the day before the marines arrived—his practice was to visit areas and negotiate access prior to the arrival of UNITAF forces—he is reported to have told the militia leaders 'that the best thing to do is not to screw with us'.[74] As a result of these tactics, many of the heavy weapons were removed

---

[70] Weiss, *Military–Civilian Interactions*, 94.

[71] Quoted in ibid. This view is supported by Oliver Ramsbotham and Tom Woodhouse, who, after judiciously assessing the evidence, conclude that 'UNITAF undoubtedly succeeded in improving food distribution in the areas it controlled, and, at any rate initially, in breaking the extortion rackets' (Ramsbotham and Woodhouse, *Humanitarian Intervention*, 208).

[72] See the Secretary General's Report on 'The Situation in Somalia', S/24992 (1992), 19, and 'US and UN at Odds over Somalia', *Independent*, 12 Dec. 1992.

[73] Reflecting on the question of whether UNITAF should have pursued a policy of general disarmament, Hirsch, who was a political adviser to UNITAF, and Oakley wrote in 1995 that, had 'UNITAF pursued a policy of full-scale disarmament, it would have needed a much greater force for the mission and would almost certainly have become embroiled in a series of local clashes, both small-scale and with large militias such as the SNA, SNF and SSDF' (Hirsch and Oakley, *Somalia*, 104).

[74] Quoted in Lyons and Samatar, *Somalia*, 40.

outside Baidoa, and the US marines were able to take control and ensure that food aid continued to reach a region that had been terribly hit by the famine.

In justifying Operation Restore Hope to the American people the day after Resolution 794, Bush had stated that the mission might require the use of force against the warlords: 'Our mission is humanitarian, but we will not tolerate armed gangs ripping off their own people, condemning them to death by starvation. General Hoar and his troops have the authority to take whatever military action is necessary to safeguard the lives of our troops and the lives of Somalia's people.'[75] Despite this rhetorical pronouncement, the President's desire to transfer the operation over to the UN as soon as possible, so that he could get the troops home before Clinton's inauguration, ensured that UNITAF restricted itself to the protection of humanitarian aid. Disarming the warlords and establishing the rule of law were crucial in preventing Somalia from falling back into civil war and famine. But helping Somalis to create the institutions of an independent police and judiciary required a long-term commitment of soldiers and resources; it certainly could not be achieved in the time frame that the Pentagon had established for the operation.[76] Nor could it be done without risking soldiers' lives and this was totally unacceptable to the administration. Consequently, Oakley told the warlords that they could keep their heavy weapons if they moved them out of Mogadishu or into UN monitored containment areas.[77]

In their assessment of Operation Restore Hope, Walter Clarke (who was Deputy Chief of Mission at the US Embassy in Somalia during Operation Restore Hope) and Jeffrey Herbst argue that the failure to disarm the warlords was a 'tragic mistake' and that the USA 'simply postponed the problems that logically followed from the intervention'.[78] Having intervened in Somalia's internal affairs, the USA had a responsibility to tackle the underlying causes of the conflict; it was best placed to do this, given its overwhelming firepower, and failure to do so merely passed the question of restoring law and order to the less respected and weaker UNOSOM II. There are two problems with this argument: first, it overlooks the context in which Operation Restore Hope became possible. Had there been any question of a protracted US commitment involving casualties, it is clear that Bush would not have launched an intervention that was designed to end the Presidency with a glittering humanitarian success.

The second problem relates to the character of any disarmament process among rival militias. Clarke and Herbst write as if the factions' weapons were the underlying source of the security problem rather than the symptom of a deeper malaise. It is true that accumulating weapons feeds insecurity and

---

[75] Quoted in W. Clarke and J. Herbst, 'Somalia and the Future of Humanitarian Intervention, *Foreign Affairs*, 75/2 (1996), 74–5.   [76] Ibid.

[77] Ibid. 75, and Lyons and Samatar, *Somalia*, 41–2.

[78] Clarke and Herbst, 'Somalia', 75.

mistrust between enemy groups, but trying to disarm one warlord without disarming all the others at the same time risked being seen as partisan and this was likely to place at risk the disarming troops as well as prolonging the civilwar.[79] Yet achieving general and comprehensive disarmament in a situation where guns could easily be hidden required a prior political reconciliation among all the factions as the basis for rebuilding legitimate state institutions. Otherwise, the departure of the intervening forces would merely bring the guns back onto the streets.

The difficulty for outsiders in helping Somalis to demilitarize their society was that this crucially depended upon marginalizing the militia leaders or persuading them to give up their weapons in favour of a commitment to constitutional processes. Although UNITAF is criticized for not taking on the disarmament mission, Oakley realized, as Sahnoun had done, the importance of shifting power away from the warlords, and he tried to give a voice to leaders committed to a politics of non-violence.[80] This was welcomed by those Somalis eager to develop a law-governed society. As one commented, 'for the past two years, most of the social forces—like women, intellectuals, wise men—they were silenced by the gun. With the arrival of the [UN] forces, the social forces can now talk. They can reorganize themselves.'[81] On the other hand, Oakley's reliance on the militias in implementing UNITAF's mandate undercut this strategy of giving a voice to civil society by making it more difficult for those committed to peace to challenge the power of the gunmen.[82]

A vivid illustration of this problem was Boutros Boutros-Ghali's attempts in January 1993 to establish a new framework for rebuilding the institutions of the Somali state. At the first meeting at Addis Ababa in January 1993, the Secretary General stated that the purpose of the talks was 'to make Somalis feel they are participating in their own national rehabilitation and that the thousands of soldiers and relief workers in their country are not an army of occupation'.[83] The problem was that the dominant players at the conference were the militia leaders and not the clan elders and other leaders of civil society, who were virtually excluded from the process.[84] The outcome of this meeting was a formal ceasefire and disarmament agreement among the fourteen groups invited to the conference, and the setting up of a 'ceasefire monitoring group', which would take control of all the heavy weapons. Boutros Boutros-Ghali's assumption was that UNITAF would be heavily involved in

---

[79] Hirsch and Oakley point out that US political and military leaders in Somalia were very aware of the lesson that the USA had learned so tragically in the Lebanon in 1983, which is ' "Don't take sides, and proceed carefully" . . . UNITAF, it was agreed, would not "pick a winner", would try hard not to play favorites, and would de-emphasise coercion' (Hirsch and Oakley, Somalia, 156).

[80] Hirsch and Oakley write that UNITAF 'planned to maintain a dialogue with all, remaining vigilant and ready to respond if attacked but pushing the factions to turn gradually away from the use of force and toward pursuing more peaceful political paths to power' (ibid. 156–7).

[81] Quoted in Lyons and Samatar, Somalia, 47.   [82] Ibid. 48.

[83] Ibid. 44.   [84] Ibid. 45.

this process. This was the dreaded 'mission creep' that frightened Oakley and his political masters in Washington.[85]

Despite the signing of a ceasefire agreement at Addis Ababa, fighting broke out in Mogadishu and the port of Kismayu in late January. Bush's hopes that the troops would be home by January were dashed as UNITAF found itself trying to police the ceasefire agreement. US Cobra gunships attacked forces loyal to the militia leader General Morgan, and Oakley justified this by stating that US forces 'took care of Morgan for not respecting the cease-fire, continuing to move south after we told him to stop, and for general misbehaviour'.[86] The deteriorating security situation led UNITAF to increase its policing role on the streets of Mogadishu, leading to the disarmament of Somalis carrying weapons and raids on houses in search of weapons. This forcible policing of the militias saw the US teetering on the edge of a slippery slope down which the USA was to slide, radically departing from its limited humanitarian mission, which had been the rationale for Operation Restore Hope.

Given the growing tensions between UNITAF and the militias, it was timely that a second conference met in Addis Ababa under UN auspices on 11–13 March. In addition to the participants from January, invitations were also sent to those groups in civil society who had been excluded from the first conference. UN officials hoped that by broadening the base of participation it might be possible to come up with a solution that would have widespread legitimacy, but in the end the UN reached an agreement with the fourteen warlords. The peace process nearly came off the rails when Aidid walked out in protest over Morgan's attack on his ally Jess, and his relations with UNITAF were not helped by the fact that US Quick Reaction Forces (QRFs) had prevented Jess from counter-attacking against Morgan.[87] Eventually, UN negotiators persuaded the fourteen leaders to sign a far-reaching agreement that held out the promise of disarmament and the rebuilding of a new state in Somalia. The agreement signed on 27 March called for a Transitional National Council (TNC) that would provide representation for all the factions, a rotating presidency to serve as a national executive, and a network of regional and district councils that would have varying degrees of autonomy. As Oakley remarked, the agreement was 'an important step forward but its not the end of the process'.[88]

The agreement called for disarmament within ninety days, but no mechanism was established as to how this was to be achieved. The most that the parties would agree to was that UN forces should apply 'strong and effective sanctions against those responsible for any violation of the ceasefire agreement of January 1993'.[89] If the UN was to support the Somalis in building the

---

85 Lewis and Mayall, 'Somalia', 113–14.   86 Quoted in Lyons and Samatur, *Somalia*, 93.
87 Ibid. 50.   88 Quoted in ibid. 51.
89 Quoted in Lewis and Mayall, 'Somalia', 115.

constitutional state promised in the Addis Ababa agreement, then it would require a very different mandate from that which the Security Council had given to UNITAF. The latter was only authorized to use force to assist with the delivery of humanitarian aid. It did not have a mandate to police ceasefires, disarm factions, and ensure that Somalia did not collapse back into the lawless anarchy that had existed prior to UNITAF's arrival in late 1992.

The Secretary General had advocated that the UN take on the role of rebuilding failed states in his 1992 *Agenda for Peace*, and he saw Somalia as a test case for this conception of post-cold-war intervention. Boutros Boutros-Ghali wrote to the Security Council on 3 March to request that it authorize a new force under Chapter VII to replace UNITAF and support the peace-building efforts of the Somali people. The Clinton Administration was eager to hand over the Somali operation to the UN as soon as possible, but it took a further three weeks before the Security Council adopted Resolution 814. This delay reflected the Secretary General's attempts to secure a strong US commitment in terms of financial, political, and military support before finally accepting UN responsibility for the mission. Hirsch and Oakley comment that the 'U.S.–UN dialogue on this resolution resembled bargaining in a bazaar. In the end, the United States provided more support than had been planned, and the secretary-general agreed that the UN should take over from the U.S.'[90]

Resolution 814 was unprecedented in UN history, because it authorized UN forces under Chapter VII to use force to implement the following mandate: to create a secure environment throughout Somalia; to promote political reconciliation; to establish the rule of law; to ensure compliance by all Somali parties, including movements and factions, with the commitments they had undertaken in signing up to the Addis Ababa accords, especially in relation to the implementation of the ceasefire and disarmament provisions; and to assist in the repatriation of refugees and the resettlement of displaced persons. This was the most ambitious mandate ever entrusted to a UN mission and it reflected the heady optimism of the Secretary General and members of the Security Council. The USA was particularly committed to the resolution and its Ambassador, Madeleine Albright, declared that it 'aimed at nothing less than the restoration of an entire country as a proud, functioning and viable member of the community of nations. This is an historic undertaking. We are excited to join it and we will vigorously support it.'[91]

No member of the Security Council spoke out against the operation, although Morocco, Spain, and especially China emphasized that it was an 'exceptional' case. In the case of the latter, the Chinese Ambassador did feel it necessary to emphasize that the unprecedented character of the authorization under Chapter VII 'is based on the needs of the unique situation in Somalia and should not constitute a precedent for United Nations

---

[90] Hirsch and Oakley, *Somalia*, 111.   [91] S/PV.3188, 26 Mar. 1993, 19.

peace-keeping operations'.[92] This caveat aside, it is clear from the speeches of members that the resolution was viewed as a 'historic one'[93] and that the UN was entering the uncharted waters of taking on the responsibility of assisting the Somali people to rebuild the institutions of the rule of law and civil society.

To achieve this goal, the Security Council agreed to dispatch 20,000 UN peacekeepers and 2,000 civilians to replace UNITAF by 1 May. The US contribution to the twenty-nine-nation UNOSOM II force was 8,000 logistical troops and a QRF of 1,200 men, as well as providing a third of the initial estimated cost of $800 million. The logistical forces came under UN command and control, but the QRF (and the Delta Force and Army Rangers that arrived in Somalia in August 1993) were outside the formal UN command structure. The Rangers took their orders from US Central Command in Florida, and all their subsequent operations against Aidid were approved by senior military officials in Washington.[94] The man placed in charge of UNOSOM II was the retired Admiral Jonathan Howe (a former Deputy National Security adviser to Bush), who was the Secretary General's Special Representative.

By the time UNOSOM II took over on 4 May, the security situation was deteriorating in Mogadishu as the factions manoeuvred for power. UNOSOM tried to support the implementation of the Addis Ababa agreement, but it was accused by Aidid of interfering in Somalia's internal affairs. He threatened that, if the Somali National Alliance (SNA) did not control the regional and district councils, then he would use force to interfere with the process.[95] Aidid had not forgiven the UN for what he perceived as its partisan support for his rival Morgan in the battle over Kismayu in March, and his radio station broadcast anti-UN statements during April and May. There was a widespread view among Somalis that UNOSOM II would be much weaker than UNITAF, despite continuing US military participation, and it seemed only a matter of time before the SNA would test its resolve.[96]

The denouement came on 5 June, when Pakistani peacekeepers were killed after they had conducted an inspection of a UN-sanctioned SNA arms depot, which was located next to Aidid's radio station. At the same time, other Pakistani patrols that were distributing food aid on the other side of Mogadishu were attacked. An independent Commission of Inquiry called for by the Security Council in Resolution 885 concluded in February 1994 that Aidid's men had 'orchestrated the attacks' that had killed twenty-four

---

[92] S/PV.3188, 26 Mar. 1993, 22.

[93] This phrase was employed by the British Representative Mr Richardson (Ibid.).

[94] Clarke and Herbst, 'Somalia', 73.

[95] Lyons and Samatar, Somalia, 55.

[96] Hirsch and Oakley, Somalia, 115. Aidid had respected the US marines and been reluctant to challenge them, but, according to Richard Dowden, Somalis 'despised' the Pakistanis, East Europeans, and Asians who made up the bulk of the multilateral UNOSOM II force, making them 'easy targets for the fighters' ('The Sheriff and the Warlords', Independent, 14 June 1993).

Pakistanis and wounded fifty-seven but could find no 'conclusive evidence' that the attacks were 'pre-planned and pre-meditated'.[97] According to the report, an SNA official was given an ultimatum on 4 June that an inspection would take place using force if necessary, and he strongly opposed this, but UNOSOM proceeded without further consultation. Hirsch and Oakley point out that Deputy Force Commander Montgomery had made preparations for an attack by providing the Pakistani patrols with twenty-two armoured personnel carriers and discussing the dangers with Pakistani commanders. However, the Pakistanis claimed they had been taken by surprise and no one anticipated that the SNA would interpret 'interference with the radio station as a casus belli'.[98]

Although the subsequent inquiry provided a more sober interpretation of events, the immediate response in New York was to blame Aidid for the premeditated killing of twenty-four UN peacekeepers. This was what Boutros Boutros-Ghali reported to the Security Council, and, with Pakistan demanding that action be taken against Aidid, the Security Council on 6 June unanimously adopted Resolution 837, which condemned the 'unprovoked armed attacks' and authorized 'all necessary measures against all those responsible'. The SNA was named in the resolution (Pakistan had wanted to name Aidid as responsible but was persuaded to remove his name on the grounds of inadequate evidence) and this put the UN and Aidid on a collision course.[99]

Admiral Howe, acting in an idiom more suited to the Wild West than the complex task of peace and security building in Somalia, offered a reward of $25,000 for the capture of Aidid. The US construction of the Somali conflict in black-and-white terms with Aidid as the 'thug'[100] who had to be punished for his bad behaviour led in early June to US air attacks against the clans and sub-clans allied to the SNA. Cobra helicopters attacked arms dumps and AC-130H cargo planes mounted with canons and guns destroyed Aidid's radio station and other key installations. It is reported that over 100 Somalis, including women and children, were killed as a result of these attacks against SNA forces. The USA had been welcomed as rescuers by the Somali people when they had landed in December 1992; now they were greeted by

---

[97] Commission of Inquiry Established by Security Council Resolution 885, 24 Feb. 1994, 29–30. Hirsch and Oakley point out that the Commission of Inquiry concluded that 'the June 5 inspection [was] highly provocative and unwise, though it did fall within the mandate of Security Council Resolution 814' (Hirsch and Oakley, *Somalia*, 18).

[98] Ibid. 118. A contrary interpretation is suggested by the Commission of Inquiry, which notes that the letter from UNOSOM commanders notifying Aidid of the inspection was handed to a member of 'Aidid's security' (it was addressed to Ambassador Alim, an adviser to Aidid who was not present), who in the Commission's words 'commented to the effect that the SNA needed time to respond and that if UNOSOM insisted on conducting the inspections as planned that would lead to war' (Commission of Inquiry, 17).

[99] Hirsch and Oakley, *Somalia*, 118.

[100] The US Secretary of State named Aidid as a 'thug' in an op-ed piece. See 'Yes, There is a Reason to be in Somalia', *New York Times*, 10 Aug. 1993, quoted in Lyons and Samatar, *Somalia*, 58.

hundreds in the streets chanting 'Down with the UN . . . Down with USA'.[101] Speaking on 14 June, the President of the Security Council, Juan Antonio Yanez-Barnuevo of Spain, argued that restoration of law and order was vital if the process of humanitarian assistance, national reconciliation, and disarmament was to move forward.[102] Howe justified the mission in characteristically blunt terms, declaring that there 'are clearly too many illegal arms . . . So today we have started a disarmament process . . . Disarmament had begun in earnest today.'[103] The irony of having to use force to disarm was apparently lost on the Admiral.

Aidid's attack against UN peacekeepers clearly posed a major dilemma for the organization. On the one hand, the UN had thousands of peacekeepers serving in trouble spots all over the world and the Secretary General feared that a failure to respond to Aidid's attack could place in jeopardy the lives of other Blue Berets.[104] This was also the view of Clinton, who argued that military action against Aidid was necessary to strengthen the credibility of 'UN peacekeeping in Somalia and around the world'.[105] However, was the response of using US gunships to destroy SNA weapon sites, radio stations, and command and control facilities in the knowledge that Somali civilians would be killed as a consequence of these attacks compatible with the *jus in bello* requirement of proportionality? UNOSOM tried in the early weeks of June to minimize civilian casualties by illuminating the target buildings from the air and instructing their occupants to leave by loudspeakers before commencing the attacks. Nevertheless, as the Commission of Inquiry pointed out, 'even the most careful targeting and precision bombing *cannot* avoid collateral damage'.[106]

The fundamental problem was that the hunt for Aidid not only prevented UNOSOM II from fulfilling its mission of political reconciliation; it also fundamentally contradicted the humanitarian rationale that had led to the initial US intervention in December 1992. For example, only one dollar in ten of the UN's 1993 budget for Somalia was allocated to relief programmes, and aid agencies complained that their work was threatened by the UN strategy of singling Aidid's faction out for punitive strikes.[107] In terms of their political consequences, the US attacks alienated the Somali people, strengthened political support for Aidid, and were criticized by wider international public opinion.[108]

Moreover, there was growing criticism of this strategy from within

---

[101] 'Enter the Terminator', *Sunday Times*, 13 June 1993.
[102] Quoted in Samuel M. Makinda, *Seeking Peace from Chaos: Humanitarian Intervention in Somalia* (Boulder, Colo.: Lynne Rienner, 1993), 81.
[103] 'Enter the Terminator'.   [104] Clarke and Herbst, 'Somalia', 80.
[105] Quoted in Makinda, *Seeking Peace*, 81.
[106] Commission of Inquiry, 37–8; emphasis added.
[107] 'Aid for Somalia Running out', *Guardian*, 9 July 1993, and Hirsch and Oakley, *Somalia*, 123.
[108] Ibid.

UNOSOM II by some troop-contributing governments, particularly the Italians, who worried about the civilian casualties and the increasing risk to UN peacekeepers. The Italians favoured a more conciliatory approach and felt that this had achieved results in the Italian sector. Consequently, they had protested on 22 June when the US-led UNOSOM II force command had initiated attacks against SNA weapon sites without prior consultation.[109] As the conflict escalated though July–September, and Italy lost three of its soldiers in clashes with the SNA, Italian military commanders refused to follow the orders of UN commanders in Mogadishu, preferring to operate through negotiations with factional leaders, including Aidid. After a battle in which it was reported that the US QRF had killed over 100 people, most of them women and children, the Italian Defence Minister Fabio Fabbri stated that to 'shoot women and children is the antithesis of a humanitarian mission'.[110] Writing in early 1993 in relation to Operation Restore Hope, Adam Roberts had presciently observed that 'a military intervention in the name of humanitarianism may come to involve a range of policies and activities which go beyond, or even conflict with, the label "humanitarian" '.[111] This was clearly the tragic fate that befell UNOSOM II in the summer of 1993.

As tensions escalated between the UN and the SNA, the US QRF on 12 July employed helicopter gunships in a raid against the Abdi house that was suspected to be Aidid's command and control centre. However, in contrast to previous raids, no warning was given; eliminating the SNA command centre and its occupants depended upon maintaining the element of surprise, whatever the civilian deaths as a result of this change in policy. UNOSOM estimated the number of Somalis killed at twenty, the SNA had the number killed at seventy-three, while the ICRC had figures of fifty-four dead and 161 injured.[112]

This operation was planned by UNOSOM force commanders and was approved up the entire US chain of command to the President. Hirsch and Oakley maintain that this US raid spelt the end of any hopes of accommodation between the UN and Aidid. They quote a report in the *Washington Post* that claimed that Aidid took the decision after this raid to 'kill American soldiers'. SNA leaders were aware of the lessons of Vietnam and Lebanon, and calculated that US casualties were the Achilles heel of US involvement in Somalia.[113] The SNA responded to the 12 July attacks by killing four US soldiers with a remote-controlled bomb on 8 August, and, when six more

---

[109] Commission of Inquiry, 23.

[110] 'Clans and UN Fight in Somali Capital', *Independent*, 11 Sept. 1993.

[111] Roberts, 'Humanitarian War', 448.   [112] Commission of Inquiry, 24.

[113] The cardinal rule of UNITAF had been to avoid taking sides, but Hirsch and Oakley point out that SNA spokesman Abdi Abshir Kahiye said after the 12 July air strikes, 'there was no more United Nations, only Americans. If you could kill Americans, it would start problems in America directly' (quoted in K. B. Richbug, 'In War on Aidid, UN Battled Itself', *Washington Post*, 6 Dec. 1993, quoted in Hirsch and Oakley, *Somalia*, 121–2).

Americans were wounded by a landmine on 22 August, Clinton took the fateful decision to send in the Delta Force and Army Rangers.

As the USA began to incur casualties, there was, as Aidid had hoped, a strong backlash in the Congress. There were growing pressures for a US pull-out by the end of October from a bipartisan group of senators, but this was rejected by the Senate, which asked the administration to report by 15 October. By mid-September it was clear to the Clinton Administration that it had to change course if it was to maintain domestic legitimacy for a US presence in Somalia.[114] Defence Secretary Les Aspin heralded this change of policy with a speech on 27 August that called for less focus on the military side of UNOSOM II and a renewed emphasis by the UN and the OAU to restart negotiations with all the parties.[115] The shift towards a political approach was supported by the US Secretary of State, Warren Christopher, who wrote to the Secretary General on 20 September challenging the military focus of UNOSOM II, and National Security Adviser Anthony Lake told the President in late September that he was working up options to promote a process of political reconciliation.[116] Powell had also expressed reservations about US search and destroy missions against the SNA, but the short-term problem of protecting US forces against the SNA convinced Powell of the need to support the decision in late August to send the élite forces. As the policy began to change in Washington towards exploring the possibilities of dialogue, the Rangers continued to implement their orders of hunting down Aidid, and it was this that led to the October 3 débâcle.[117]

Intelligence indicated that Aidid was meeting his senior advisers at the Olympic Hotel and the Rangers launched a daylight helicopter raid that ended in disaster. Two Blackhawks were shot down by SNA forces and the Rangers found themselves trapped and surrounded by SNA forces. In the ensuing sixteen-hour firefight that killed over 500 Somalis, eighteen US Rangers were killed, eighty-four were wounded, and one helicopter pilot was captured. Within hours, video footage appeared on US television networks of a dead Ranger being dragged through the streets of Mogadishu. Clinton was reported to be 'very angry',[118] and there were thousands of telephone calls to Senators from citizens demanding to know why American soldiers were sacrificing their lives in Somalia.[119] The American people had strongly supported sending American soldiers to save the lives of emaciated Somalis, but, as the *New York Times* put it, 'they were understandably shocked to find them in house-to-house combat'.[120] The subsequent funer-

---

[114] Lyons and Samatar, *Somalia*, 59, and Hirsch and Oakley, *Somalia*, 124–5.
[115] Ibid. 125.
[116] 'U.S. Changes Strategy over Somali Warlord', *International Herald Tribune*, 29 Sept. 1993.
[117] Hirsch and Oakley, *Somalia*, 125.   [118] Quoted in Carruthers, *The Media*, 223.
[119] 'Horror Comes Home', *Independent*, 13 Oct. 1993, Minear *et al.*, *The News Media*, 55, and 'TV Brings Grim News of Mogadishu', *Independent*, 7 Oct. 1993.
[120] Quoted in Lyons and Samatar, *Somalia*, 59.

als in Arlington cemetery, interviews with relatives, and publication of the last letters home evoked painful memories in an American public that once again questioned the wisdom of foreign entanglements on behalf of distant strangers.[121]

To stem the growing pressure from the public and Congress for a speedy exit from Somalia, Clinton announced that in the short term he was building up US forces as a protective measure, but that all US forces would be withdrawn by 31 March 1994. The President argued that US forces should remain in Somalia because it was important to give the UN and Somalis 'a reasonable chance' to rebuild the country and to show that the USA 'will have lived up to the responsibilities of American leadership in the world . . . addressing the problems of a new era'.[122] Clinton was determined that the débâcle in Somalia should not send a signal to the rest of the world that the USA could not function militarily, and was convinced that a hasty withdrawal would weaken the credibility of American power in the world.[123] Nevertheless, a firm timetable had been set for US withdrawal and the hunt for Aidid was over. As US and other European forces began pulling out in early 1994, they were replaced by forces from India, Pakistan, Malaysia, and Egypt. These forces did not try to prevent the armed gangs returning to the streets, leading one journalist to despair: 'In the 18 months since the first UN troops were sent to Somalia to protect humanitarian supplies at the height of the country's war-induced famine, UNOSOM has failed either to disarm the factions or provide an alternative to the gun.'[124]

An alternative, and more optimistic, view of the success of UNOSOM II intervention is provided by Malcolm Harper, Director of the United Nations Association in the UK, in a report based on his visit to Somalia in early 1994. Harper concluded a year before the final UN withdrawal that the operation, especially the work of UNICEF, was making an important contribution to alleviating malnutrition and disease in the country. He also considered that, in the vital role of restructuring the police force and the courts, UNOSOM II was doing 'very well for the most part',[125] and that progress was being made in setting up district and regional councils to administer the country. Harper's conclusion in March 1994 was that UNOSOM had achieved some successes, but that the media focus on the UN's hunt for Aidid had distracted attention from these. What was needed was a continuing UN commitment to the rebuilding of Somalia. We will never know what might have been achieved had the UN followed Harper's policy recommendations and invested new energy and resources into the Somali operation.[126] Instead, there was no

---

[121] 'Horror Comes Home'.   [122] Quoted in Hirsch and Oakley, *Somalia*, 129.

[123] 'Anatomy of a Disaster', *Time*, 18 Oct. 1993, 42.

[124] Quoted in Lyons and Samatar, *Somalia*, 60.

[125] M. Harper, 'Back to Somalia: A Report on his Visit to Somalia', United Nations Association, UK, Mar. 1994.   [126] Ibid.

enthusiasm to continue with UNOSOM II, and by February 1995 the UN had withdrawn from Somalia, leaving that country once again to its own devices.

Conclusion

The significance of Resolution 794 in the evolution of the Security Council's thinking on the legitimacy of humanitarian intervention is that it was the first time that it had authorized the use of force under Chapter VII to deliver humanitarian aid when this was being obstructed by armed warlords. The closest parallel is Resolution 770, adopted in August 1992, which authorized the use of force to assist with the delivery of aid to civilians in the former Yugoslavia. However, as I discuss in Chapter 8, this resolution is less significant in terms of a change in the pluralist rule structure of the society of states, because it was consented to by a sovereign state, in this case Bosnia-Hercegovina. The problem that confronted the Security Council in its deliberations over Somalia was that the government had collapsed and its existing rules were inadequate to cope with this challenge. The Secretary General felt compelled, in Adam Roberts's words, 'to make the awkward facts of a crisis fit the procrustean bed of the UN Charter'[127] by arguing that the consequences of the human suffering threatened regional security. Resolution 794 makes such a finding, but this move lacked plausibility and was undermined by the fact that most members justified the Security Council's action in explicitly humanitarian terms. It is tempting to argue that the absence of contestation over the legitimacy of Security Council action reflected a new intersubjective understanding among members that, when governments had collapsed into lawlessness and starvation, the UN had a moral responsibility to intervene to provide security for the citizens of that state. This changed understanding of the Security Council's responsibilities under Article 39 of Chapter VII, marking a major departure from the pluralist interpretative framework that had hitherto governed the application of this rule.

Whatever the attractions of this evolutionary view of the Security Council's moral practices, it fails to take into account the fact that some members—notably China and India—repeatedly emphasized that the Somali case was 'unique', 'extraordinary', and 'exceptional'. There is no mention of Article 2 (7) in Resolution 794, as there was in Resolution 688, and this reflected the fact that these states took the view that the Security Council's action did not breach the non-intervention rule, because the Somali government had ceased to exist. This placed it in a different category from the Iraqi case, where the dispute was over the Security Council's right to intervene against an existing government that was grossly abusing human rights.

[127] Roberts, 'Humanitarian War', 154.

Resolution 794 provided international legitimacy for US intervention in Somalia and it was also crucial to the Bush Administration in maintaining domestic legitimacy for the action. Bush was determined that the UN should take over the operation in Somalia, and, without this assurance in the form of Resolution 794, he would not have launched Operation Restore Hope. Thus, the resolution was a critical enabling condition of action; the other key enabling condition was media coverage of the plight of Somalis, which made the US public very supportive of humanitarian intervention. After months of inaction over Somalia, the timing of Bush's decision to send the marines suggests that the mission was well named, because it was aimed at giving 'hope' to Americans whose consciences were troubled by pictures of dying and malnourished Somalis. The media's power to stir the conscience of US public opinion was a key determinant of US action, but the existence of this public legitimating reason coupled with that supplied by Resolution 794 did not determine US intervention. This would be to make the opposite error of those who assume that the justifications of actors are irrelevant in understanding decision-making. The public legitimating reasons of US action were a necessary condition of the intervention, but they were not a sufficient one. It required the following motives to turn the enabling factors into a decision to intervene: Bush's strong moral sense that he should act; his desire to end the Presidency on a glittering high note; and, most importantly, the belief of Bush and his senior advisers that there was a clear exit strategy and no great risk of losing soldiers' lives.

In arguing that the Bush Administration's humanitarian justifications for Operation Restore Hope belied a complex set of humanitarian and non-humanitarian motivations, I am not arguing that this case, any more than the Iraqi one, is an illustration of the realist objection of abuse. There is no evidence that the USA had any hidden power-political reasons for intervening that contradicted the declared humanitarian purposes of Operation Restore Hope. This leads Martha Finnemore to argue that US intervention in Somalia poses a significant problem for realist theory because it was 'undertaken in a state of little or no strategic or economic importance to the principal intervener'.[128] Her contention is the constructivist one that realists fail to recognize that changing norms of legitimate intervention reconstitute state interests, making possible intervention on behalf of humanity rather than in the service of strategic or economic interests. There are three problems with this claim in relation to the Somali case that lead to the conclusion that the retreat from realism was a very limited one.

The first is that the humanitarian rationale for US action would carry greater moral force had US policy-makers responded earlier to the plight of Somalis. There were arguments raised within the administration for more

---

[128] Finnemore, 'Constructing Norms', 154.

decisive action at an earlier stage, and opportunities arose during the first half of 1992, when an outside force with an enforcement mandate might have facilitated the peace-building process and the delivery of humanitarian aid. Lyons and Samatar argue that the UN should have deployed peacekeeping forces to bolster the ceasefire agreement in March 1992, and it is generally accepted that Sahnoun's strategy would have borne even greater fruit had the Security Council ensured that troops had arrived in Somalia by the beginning of September. The failure of the USA to take the lead at the UN and stop Somalia's slide into the chaos from which it subsequently tried to rescue it weakens the humanitarian credentials of Operation Restore Hope.

Secondly, although there was a debate within the US foreign-policy establishment as to whether intervention in Somalia promoted the national interest, administration officials would not have taken the decision to intervene had they believed that this weakened US strategic or economic interests. Indeed, as Eagleburger admitted, the attraction of Somalia compared to Bosnia was that the USA could do good without any of the attendant costs and risks associated with intervention in the Balkans. Moreover, as realists are at pains to point out to those who will listen, there is nothing in their tradition that precludes states from having an interest in the promotion of moral goals.[129] What realists cannot accept, according to Michael Desch, is 'intervention that undermines a state's security or economic interests'.[130] Given that Bush would have ruled out Operation Restore Hope had he believed that this threatened US security interests, Desch argues, contra Finnemore, that Somalia does not pose a serious 'puzzle' for realist theory.[131]

The final reason why US intervention in Somalia does not significantly challenge realist theory is that, when the USA experienced a relatively low number of casualties, it announced its intention to withdrawl. As I discussed in Part One, realists argue that states should not risk soldiers' lives to save non-citizens if this is likely to lead to casualties. The problem is that, whilst some realists specify the threshold of unacceptable losses as one death, others talk of moderate casualties. Haunted by the memories of Vietnam, and the more recent loss of 300 marines in the Lebanon in 1983, the Bush Administration's conception of this threshold was very low, and a key determinant of US intervention in Somalia was the conviction that there was little risk of casualties. Henry Kissinger, then, was exaggerating when he penned the following words:

The new approach [in Somalia] claims an extension in the reach of morality . . . 'Humanitarian intervention' asserts that moral and humane concerns are so much a part of American life that not only treasure but *lives* must be risked to vindicate them;

---

[129] S. Forde, 'Classical Realism', in T. Nardin and D. R. Mapel (eds.), *Traditions of International Ethics* (Cambridge: Cambridge University Press, 1992), 81–2.
[130] M. Desch, 'Culture Clash: Assessing the Importance of Ideas in Security Studies', *International Security*, 23/1 (1998), 144.   [131] Ibid. 140.

in their absence, American life would have lost some meaning. No other nation has ever put forward such a set of propositions.[132]

Kissinger's bold contention restates the classic thesis of American exceptionalism. But before we celebrate this case as an example of the locomotive of US solidarism pulling the society of states towards the destination of humanitarian intervention, it is important to recognize—contra Kissinger—that the limits of the US 'reach of morality' were shown in the Clinton Administration's response to the loss of the Rangers in October 1993. Michael Walzer argues that, if US soldiers are fighting for a noble cause in which it has been decided that soldiers might die, 'we cannot panic when the first soldier or the first significant number of soldiers . . . are killed in a firefight'.[133] This is the 'new approach' that Kissinger talks of, but Somalia was chosen as the place for US intervention only because it was believed that the mission would not result in 'body bags'.

This proved a fallacious assumption, raising the question as to whether international intervention in Somalia was doomed from the outset. The conventional wisdom is that UNITAF was a humanitarian achievement because it ended the famine and restricted itself to the delivery of humanitarian relief, and that things started to go badly wrong when the UN changed the character of the mission to rebuilding a legitimate Somali state. The first problem with this interpretation is that it assumes that military intervention was the appropriate response to the supreme humanitarian emergency facing the Somali people. However, it could be argued that the best approach was the one pursued by Sahnoun, which sought to weaken the power of the warlords by enlisting the cooperation of the clan elders. Ramsbotham and Woodhouse call this type of strategy 'non-forcible humanitarian intervention' and it is fair to conclude that it was drawn to a close—for US domestic political reasons— just as it was beginning to produce results. US intervention, then, arguably fails the test of necessity or last resort because non-violent means of conflict resolution were producing results. Moreover, there is the further objection that UNITAF arrived too late to provide the relief that would have kept many more people alive had it arrived a few months earlier, and that by the time US forces landed in Mogadishu the real killer was disease. These criticisms suggest that the short-term consequences of the intervention were not as positive as is often claimed, but they do not detract from the fact that UNITAF saved lives. The methodological conundrum in judging the success of forcible humanitarian intervention against other peaceful approaches to the humanitarian emergency is that we will never know how many more lives would have been lost in the absence of the deployment of US forces with a Chapter VII mandate in December 1992.

---

[132] H. Kissinger, 'Thin Blue Line for a World Cop', *Guardian*, 16 Dec. 1992.
[133] M. Walzer, 'The Politics of Rescue', *Dissent*, 42/1 (1995), 38.

The balance sheet of US military intervention is inevitably coloured by the disastrous UN mission that followed it. This raises the fundamental question as to whether the non-humanitarian reasons that led Bush to launch Operation Restore Hope undermined the chances of a successful humanitarian intervention in Somalia. In short, could UNITAF have done more to lay the groundwork for a successful UN mission? Rescuing the victims of starvation is a laudable achievement, but, by refusing to engage with the underlying political causes of that suffering, UNITAF did nothing to prevent a repeat of the cycle of lawlessness and starvation. The major area of controversy here concerns the means of US humanitarian intervention. Should the USA have disarmed the warring factions and made greater efforts to establish the institutions of an independent police and judiciary? The fundamental problem is that securing this positive humanitarian outcome required a long-term commitment and an acceptance of casualties; this was unacceptable to an administration that had intervened only because it believed it could avoid these costs and risks.

With the failure of the USA to take on the task of removing the gun from Somali politics, the burden fell upon UNOSOM II, which was mandated in Resolution 814 to rebuild a viable law-governed polity. The significance of this resolution is that it was an attempt to address the underlying political causes of the humanitarian emergency in Somalia by sponsoring a dialogue between the militias and widening this to bring in other groups within Somali society committed to restoring human rights. The purpose of this dialogue was nothing less than the rebuilding of a legitimate state with the institutions of police, judiciary, and a network of district and regional councils ensuring participation at all levels in Somali society. Boutros Boutros- Ghali tried hard to persuade suspicious Somalis, like Aidid, that this was not an imperialist project and that the purpose of UNOSOM II was to work with Somalis and not against them. This justification echoes Bhikhu Parekh's concern that humanitarian intervention should not be a new form of imperial control, but a political act 'intended to help create conditions conducive to the creation of a structure of civil authority acceptable to the people involved'.[134] The problem with Parekh's view, as applied to the Somali case, is that there was ambiguity from the beginning of Operation Restore Hope through to UNOSOM II as to who the 'people' were. Was intervention aimed at stripping the militias of their power both politically and militarily or was it aimed at socializing the warlords into non-violent forms of conflict resolution?

UNOSOM II's political strategy was to facilitate the emergence of new leaders committed to rebuilding a legitimate government, and the implementation of the ceasefire and disarmament provisions of the Adis Ababa accords were pivotal to this. The problem was that this process threatened the power

---

[134] Parekh, 'Rethinking Humanitarian Intervention', 55–6.

base of leaders like Aidid, and he was prepared to challenge the UN, given an opportunity. The decision by UNOSOM to carry out its first inspection of SNA weapon sites provided such an opening, and, in the context of the rising tension between UNOSOM and the SNA, this was clearly going to be viewed as a provocative move. Aidid's action in killing the Pakistani peacekeepers was intolerable, but the decision by the Security Council and the White House to give authority to UNOSOM II to launch attacks against the clans and sub-clans in the SNA was a profound mistake. The use of force by US QRF forces was simply not commensurate with the goal of bringing Aidid to justice and reducing the danger posed by the SNA to UN forces by reducing its military capacity. There was no moral justification for conducting search and destroy missions with the increasing disregard for the lives of Somali civilians that characterized US missions during the summer of 1993.[135] This was the legacy of the memories of Vietnam, a Weinberger–Powell doctrine that sanctioned force only where US casualties could be minimized by overwhelming the enemy with superior firepower, and where concerns about civilian deaths were secondary to the protection of US military personnel. Madelaine Albright may have been right to call Aidid a 'thug', but others could have been forgiven for thinking he was not the only one as they watched American forces on their television screens killing Somali civilians in their attempt to punish Aidid and destroy his military forces.

The UN Secretary General should have worked with the Security Council to put a stop to these military operations as soon as it became clear that the hunt for Aidid was leading to civilian deaths on such a horrific scale.[136] The problem was that, whilst the UN Security Council had authorized in Resolution 837 'all necessary measures' against those responsible for the attacks on the Pakistani peacekeepers, it failed to exert effective control over military operations, especially those launched by the USA. Several Security Council members had emphasized the importance of maintaining effective UN command and control of UNOSOM during the adoption of Resolution 814, but, as the Commission of Inquiry pointed out, many 'major operations undertaken under the United Nations flag and in the context of UNOSOM's mandate were totally outside the command and control of the United Nations, even though the repercussions impacted crucially on the mission of UNOSOM and the safety of its personnel'.[137]

The fundamental mistake of the UN Security Council in the aftermath of Aidid's outrageous killing of the peacekeepers was its failure to take the lead in displaying cultural sensitivity. Sahnoun argues that the UN should have

---

[135] Falk, 'Hard Choices'.

[136] Citing John Sommers' estimates in *Hope Restored? Humanitarian Aid in Somalia, 1990–1994* (Washington, D.C.: Refugee Policy Group, 1994), 72, Weiss gives figures of 1,500 Somali fatalities and 6,000–8,000 wounded during UNOSOM II. See Weiss, *Military-Civilian Interactions*, 93.

[137] Commission of Inquiry, 39.

gathered all the information relating to Aidid's guilt, and then persuaded the elders and other clan leaders of the importance of cooperating with the UN in bringing him to justice. He claims that this 'would have worked in Somalia because Somali tradition itself requires stern measures for slaughter and places the highest priority on collective undertaking in the matter'.[138] A further example of this lack of cultural sensitivity is that one of the worst insults in Somali society is to show your shoe to someone, and it did not foster good relations when Somalis could see the boots of US soliders facing down on them as US helicopters flew their low-level search and destroy missions over Mogadishu.

Greater cultural sensitivity is essential to any future international interventions aimed at rebuilding failed states like Somalia, but the troubling question raised by the experience in Somalia is whether the threat or use of force can ever promote conflict resolution in situations where societies are plunged into lawlessness as a consequence of civil war and the disintegration of state structures. The Somali case is different from all the ones considered so far because the cause of the suffering was not governments murdering their citizens; instead, it was the breakdown of civic authority. In the cold-war cases, it was relatively straightforward for a neighbouring army to knock out a murderous regime, as Tanzania and Vietnam did in their interventions in Uganda and Cambodia respectively. In the Somali case, interveners confronted a situation where, as Walzer puts it, the source of the violence was deeply rooted in social structures, and, in seeking to change this, the UN found itself using violence in ways that beget even greater levels of violence. Do the adjectives 'force' and 'humanitarian' go together or does the oxymoron 'humanitarian war' hide a tragic contradiction?

Even if Aidid had not decided to test the resolve of UNOSOM II, there would surely have come a point when one of the factions directly challenged the disarmament and political provisions of the Addis Ababa agreement. At that point, UNOSOM would have confronted the fateful decision as to whether to use force to enforce the agreement. It is reassuring to think that Somali civilians trapped in the web of interclan war and famine would welcome outsiders using violence against militia leaders who frustrated the peace process. However, it is crucial that any such use of force be discriminate and have the widest possible legitimation among those groups in wider civil society committed to non-violent conflict resolution. Neither of these conditions were satisfied in the case of UNOSOM II. If governments do take on the burden of using force to ensure agreements are complied with, then it is also vital that this is coupled with a commitment to provide help with wider political, economic, and social reconstruction. This requires a commitment to stay the course. It is no good providing armed protection to groups in civil society

<hr>

[138] Sahnoun, 'Prevention in Conflict Resolution', 13.

who want to challenge the rule of the gun, if, after experiencing casualties, interveners head for the sign marked exit. Had the USA started out in December 1992 with a commitment to creating a UN trusteeship for Somalia, and not engaged in such ill-thought out knee-jerk responses as the hunt for Aidid, the story might have turned out differently. The militias had expected the USA to disarm them in December, and this strategy, coupled with the Addis Ababa process, might have won the confidence of Somalis and enabled them to create a nationwide police force and judiciary that would have had the trust of all the clans and sub-clans.

The problem was that the USA was not prepared to pay the price of nation building and was eager to hand over to the UN as soon as possible. The Security Council recognized the need to build a bridge between the short-term response to the humanitarian emergency and the longer-term problem of restoring legitimate authority to Somalia, but within months the UN's first experiment in rebuilding failed states lay in ruins. This leads Weiss to ask whether it is 'inadvisable to intervene to save lives, even if there is no stomach for nation-building',[139] but the deeper concern here is the imperial arrogance lurking behind the whole idea of nation building. Michael Ignatieff argues that the idea of UN trusteeship is a hangover of the West's imperial past that leads to the belief that the rich and powerful states have the capacity to tame the natives and bring them into the orbit of civilized behaviour.[140] Certainly, the haunting question raised by Somalia is whether humanitarian intervention that tries to combine both the short-term and long-term goals of rescuing victims from starvation and lawlessness, and restoring legitimate authority, is *always* doomed to end in a humiliating exit.

---

[139] He does not answer the question, considering that it 'is a morally uncomfortable hypothesis to recommend testing' (Weiss, *Military–Civilian Interactions*, 96).

[140] Ignatieff, *The Warrior's Honour*, 94.

7

Global Bystander to Genocide: International Society and the Rwandan Genocide of 1994

The killings in Rwanda in 1994 confronted the society of states with the first case of genocide since the Holocaust, and this chapter charts the abject failure of international society to honour humanity's promise to the Jews of 'Never Again'. It shows how limited were the claims made for a new doctrine of UN-authorized humanitarian intervention that had gained currency in the aftermath of the interventions in Iraq and Somalia. As I pointed out in the previous chapter, Somalia represented the high point of UN humanitarian intervention in the 1990s, but few could have predicted that, as a consequence of disaster and failure in one African country, the Security Council would become a bystander to genocide in another.

The most important question that can be asked of the Rwandan genocide is whether it could have been prevented by early and decisive action on the part of the UN. The first part of the chapter briefly maps the history of violent conflict between the Hutus and Tutsis in Rwanda, identifying the background factors that led Hutu extremists to plan the extermination of Rwanda's Tutsi minority. The warning lights were flashing at least a year before the genocide began and the UN received intelligence reports in early 1994 warning of the risk of genocide. This raises two questions: what could the UN have done to prevent the genocide and why were such actions not taken?

Having failed to prevent the outbreak of mass killing in Kigali, the UN Security Council was confronted with the decision of whether it should reinforce the UN forces deployed in late 1993 to monitor the ceasefire between the government and the forces of the Tutsi-dominated Rwandan Patriotic Front (RPF). The second part of the chapter opens with the Council's decision on 21 April to withdraw UN forces who had taken on the role of protecting civilians. This decision condemned Rwandans to their fate. There were alternative courses of action open to the Council, and the force commander in Kigali, General Romeo Dallaire, requested the deployment of additional forces with air support to halt the genocide. He has subsequently argued that the deployment of such a force in the first few weeks of the genocide could have saved hundreds of thousands of lives. Why, then, did no member of the Security Council come forward with the offer of forces and why did the Council fail publicly to name Rwanda a genocide? Does the failure of those Western states—crucially the USA—with the military capacity to act demonstrate the continuing grip of the statist paradigm on the moral imagination of state leaders? Under the 1948 Genocide Convention, signatories have a legal obligation to prevent and punish the crime of genocide. Having failed to intervene to stop the genocide, Western governments avoided naming Rwanda as a genocide. I examine how far this reflected the recognition that to employ this language would be to expose themselves to the charge that they had failed to live up to their responsibilities under the Genocide Convention.

As the enormity of the killings became apparent through growing media coverage, the Security Council reversed its earlier decision and agreed to send a larger force to Rwanda. Although several African states offered to contribute troops, this force did not deploy until late August, owing to the failure of Western states to provide the necessary logistical support. When the inferno of genocide had almost burned out, France requested a mandate from the Security Council to provide humanitarian protection for Rwandans who had been displaced by the genocide and the renewal of the civil war.

The Security Council authorized the French action under the Chapter VII provisions of the Charter, but many members were concerned that its humanitarian justifications were a cloak for the pursuit of selfish interests and that French action would jeopardize the efforts to deploy a new UN force. In keeping with the theme of previous chapters, I examine the humanitarian credentials of French action and the extent to which these arguments can be heard in the debate within the Security Council over the legitimacy of French intervention.

Could the Rwandan Genocide have been Prevented?

It is comforting for those of us who live in the West to think that what happened in Rwanda was the result of ancient tribal hatreds; that the orgy of violence that consumed Rwanda is an African phenomenon that we could do very little about. However, this image, which is replete with Conradian overtones of Africa as *The Heart of Darkness*, is simply wrong. The fact is that this genocide, like that of the Holocaust, was the product of deliberate political design. To understand how the majority Hutu population came to believe the extremists' propaganda that their survival depended upon the physical elimination of the Tutsis it is necessary to examine how identities became constructed during the era of Belgium's colonial rule. After the First World War, the colonial administration, according to Philip Gourevitch, 'sought out those features of the existing civilization that fit their own ideas of [racial] mastery and subjugation and bent them to fit their purposes'.[1] The Tutsis were the traditional political and economic élite because they owned cattle whereas the Hutus cultivated the fields (although these distinctions were not hard and fast), but Hutus and Tutsis spoke the same language and inter-married, and the differing social and economic power between the two groups had not generated violent intra-group conflict. What changed this context was Belgium's decision to designate the Tutsis as 'civilized', in oppo-sition to the Hutus, who were designated as an inferior race. By politicizing the differences between Hutus and Tutsis in racial terms and explicitly privi-leging the Tutsi as its favoured ruling group, Belgium's contribution was to ensure that all subsequent struggles for the scarce resources of land and live-stock became framed in these 'ethnic' terms.[2]

Resentful at the political power exercised by the Tutsi monarchy under Belgian colonial rule, the Hutu rebelled in 1959, leading to a violent conflict that resulted in the overthrow of the Tutsi monarchy after the withdrawal of Belgium forces in 1961. The Hutu came to power following a UN supervised referendum in 1961 and the country remained under UN trusteeship until it became independent in July 1962. During the 1959 uprising, it is estimated that 20,000 were killed and 160,000 fled to neighbouring states.[3] Moreover, after a failed attempt by Tutsi émigrés to retake power in 1963, there were widespread reprisals against the Tutsi minority that Bertrand Russell described as 'the most horrible and systematic human massacre we have had occasion to witness since the extermination of the Jews by the Nazis'.[4]

The Party of the Movement and of Hutu Emancipation Parhehuith led by Grégoire Kayibanda ruled Rwanda from 1962 to July 1973, when Major General Juvenal Habyarimana came to power in a *coup*. The new leader's power base was among the northern Hutu and the military takeover took power away from the southern Hutu. In contrast to their southern brethren, the northern Hutu had few contacts with the Tutsi and there was little inter-marriage among the two groups. Instead, they constructed the Tutsi as an inferior other and were determined that they would never share power with them.[5]

---

[1] P. Gourevitch, *We Wish to Inform you that Tomorrow we will be Killed with our Families: Stories from Rwanda* (London: Picador, 1998), 55.

[2] A striking manifestation of this colonial imposition of a racial ideology was the decision in 1933–4 to issue identity cards that registered the ethnic identity of Rwandans as either Hutu or Tutsi. The significance of this, as Gourevitch points out, was that it became 'virtually impossible for Hutus to become Tutsis, and permitted the Belgians to perfect the administration of an apartheid system rooted in the myth of Tutsi superiority' (ibid. 56–7).

[3] These figures are quoted in P. J. O'Halloran, 'Humanitarian Intervention and the Genocide in Rwanda', *Conflict Studies*, 277 (1995), 3.   [4] Quoted in ibid. 3.

[5] R. Lemarchand, 'Rwanda: The Rationality of Genocide', *Issue: A Journal of Opinion*, 23/2 (1995), 9.

The immediate causes of the 1994 genocide can be traced to fears among extremist elements within Habyarimana's governing party, the Mouvement National pour la Révolution et le Développement (MNRD), that the President was going to share power with moderate Hutus and the Tutsis. The President's natural instincts were to support the doctrine of Hutu superiority, a position to which his wife and in-laws were strongly committed. However, there were two key factors pushing the President in a more conciliatory direction. The first was that his government was embroiled in a civil war with the RPF, which was made up of exiled Tutsis (and some Hutus) who had fled to Uganda after the 1959 uprising. The RPF wanted recognition of the social and political rights of Tutsi refugees and a power-sharing agreement. The RPF was supported by neighbouring Uganda and on 1 October 1990 it had invaded Rwanda. This action was repelled by the Rwandan army with military support from French, Belgium, and Zaïrian forces.

The second factor influencing the President's calculations was that the RPF invasion took place in the context of growing international pressure on the Rwandan Government to democratize. International aid donors indicated that future economic aid would be conditional upon constitutional change and improved respect for human rights. The Habyarimana government was particularly vulnerable to this type of conditionality, owing to the collapse of coffee prices, coffee being the mainstay of Rwanda's foreign exports. The President reluctantly agreed to a new multi-party constitution, which came into force in June 1991. Three key political parties emerged to challenge the ruling MNRD and all were committed to bringing the RPF into a power-sharing agreement. Given this changing domestic context and under increasing pressure from African states and the OAU, Habyarimana entered into negotiations with the RPF in June 1992 that eventually culminated in the signing of the peace agreement in the Tanzanian town of Arusha in August 1993.

The reason it took so long to reach an agreement was that Habyarimana was fearful of the implications for his own position of negotiating with the RPF. Eventually, international pressure from France, Belgium, the USA and African states, coupled with the active mediation efforts of the OAU and the UN, forced the Rwandan President to sign up to the accords. On the surface, the agreement reached at Arusha was a textbook success of preventative diplomacy and conflict management. The right of return was granted to Rwandan refugees and the power-sharing agreement provided equal representation for the RPF and Habyarimana's former ruling party (five ministers each out of a cabinet of twenty-one). The result of this was that the balance of power was held by the smaller parties that had been established after 1991 and which were committed to working with the Tutsis. Most controversially of all, the composition of the army was to be divided 50 : 50 at the officer level with only a 60 : 40 advantage to the government in overall troop numbers.[6] To monitor the implementation of the ceasefire and the movement to a transitional government, the Security Council agreed on 5 October in Resolution 872 to establish the United Nations Assistance Mission for Rwanda (UNAMIR). The 1,458 troops to be deployed in phase 1 would rise to 2,548 in the second phase of the mission, which was to oversee the process of demobilization and the creation of a new integrated army.

The peace process was doomed from the outset, since its implementation depended upon the extremists within Habyarimana's clique compromising with the RPF. The response of the extremists was to begin a campaign of killing Tutsi, since, as Réné Lemarchand points out, the 'wanton killing of Tutsi civilians . . . became the quickest and most "rational" way of eliminating all basis for compromise with the RPF'.[7] As the President negotiated away the bases of the ruling élite's power, and the international community failed to respond to massacres of Tutsi civilians, the idea of a 'final solution' to the problem of the Tutsi became thinkable. During 1992 the virulently anti-Tutsi Coalition pour la Défense de la République (CDR) was set up, and behind the scenes the organizational machinery of genocide was being created. This centred on four key elements: the architects of the 'final solution', which included members of the President's own family and trusted advisers; the rural organizers, who were drawing up lists of Tutsi and moderate Hutu for extermination; the armed militias (the *interahamwe* and the *impuzamugambi*), who were the youth wings of the MNRD and the CDR recruited predominantly from disaffected Hutus who eyed Tutsi wealth with envy;[8] and the Presidential Guard, which would support the death squads where necessary.[9] By the time that Arusha was signed, the regime had put in place a chillingly effective organizational structure that would implement the political plan of genocide more efficiently than was achieved by the industrialized death camps in Nazi Germany.

By agreeing to the Arusha accords, Habyarimana, in Fergal Keane's words, literally signed his own 'death warrant'.[10] There was too much at stake to give up power to the Tutsi, and the extremists were further emboldened by events in neighbouring Burundi, where a democratically elected Hutu President, Melchior Ndadaye, had been assassinated by the Tutsi army in a *coup*. As Lemarchand argues, 'the message conveyed by Ndadaye's assassination came through clear and loud: "Never trust the Tutsi!" '[11] One important consequence of events in Burundi was the influx of some 200,000 Hutu refugees into the south and central regions who were ripe for political mobilization in

[6] C. Clapham, 'Rwanda: The Perils of Peacemaking', *Journal of Peace Research*, 35/2 (1998), 203.

[7] Lemarchand, 'Rwanda', 10.

[8] G. Prunier, *The Rwanda Crisis: History of a Genocide* (London: Hurst & Co., 1995), 128–9.

[9] These four elements are set out in Lemarchand, 'Rwanda', 10. For more details, see Prunier, *The Rwanda Crisis*, 224.

[10] F. Keane, *Season of Blood: A Rwandan Journey* (London: Penguin, 1996), 27.

[11] Lemarchand, 'Rwanda', 10.

areas of the country where the architects of mass extermination feared most resistance to their policy. The spark that lit the tinder box of genocide was the shooting-down of Habyarimana's plane on 6 April 1994. Although it remains unclear who exactly downed the plane, it is hard to avoid the conclusion that the extremists had decided that the President had outlived his usefulness and that it was time for a more reliable set of Hutu politicians to eliminate the problem of the Tutsi once and for all.

As soon as Habyarimana's jet was shot out of the skies, 'one hundred days of genocide had been launched'.[12] Within one hour the killing machine had swung into operation in Kigali. Road blocks were set up and the militias and the Presidential Guard began crossing Tutsi off their lists, as well as Hutu politicians and civil servants who stood in the way of the extermination process. A key tool in the battle to win ordinary Hutus to the cause of geno-cide was the radio station. For most Rwandans, radio is the only source of information, and thus control of the airwaves is critical to mobilizing popu-lar support. During 1993 members of Habyarimana's inner circle had set up Radio Télévision Libre Mille Collines (RTLMC), which broadcast messages of hate in the national language, as against Radio Rwanda, which broadcast in French. As soon as the killings began, RTLMC began broadcasting incitements to kill Tutsi and, within the next few hours, it issued instructions to the killers. For example, the radio declared that: 'You have missed some of the enemies in this or that place. Some are still alive. You must go back there and finish them off . . . The graves are not yet quite full. Who is going to do the good work and help us fill them completely.'[13]

The international response to the mass killing unleashed in the days after Habyarimana's death is the subject of the next section. Before turning to this, it is necessary to address two questions: first, what responsibility should be attached to the Arusha peace process in bringing about the genocide, and, secondly, how far did the UN ignore warnings of the 'final solution' that was being prepared for the Tutsi?

Accepting that the vast majority of mediators acted in good faith, Christopher Clapham argues that they 'carry a substantial measure of respons-ibility for making possible the genocide that followed'.[14] He makes the impor-tant point that external efforts to resolve conflicts such as the civil war in Rwanda inevitably involve actions that change the balance of advantage between the parties. In this context, the result of the Arusha process was to exclude the extremists and to allocate a key role to the smaller parties. However, since the latter had no control over territory or the armed forces, and their level of popular support was unknown, the power-sharing agree-ment was a façade that bore little or no reality to the facts of power on the

---

[12] Keane, *Season of Blood*, 27.
[13] Quoted in Prunier, *The Rwanda Crisis*, 224.
[14] Clapham, 'Rwanda', 204.

ground.[15] Moreover, whilst the British and especially the French governments were critical of the Arusha process for marginalizing the extremists, it is clear that involving them in the talks would have stopped the peace process in its tracks, given their implacable opposition to compromise with the RPF. In contrast to Clapham, Bruce Jones does not charge the negotiators of the Arusha accords with any specific responsibility for the genocide, but he does claim that the 'tragic' result of this experiment in preventative diplomacy was the transformation of 'a civil conflict which had claimed 6,500 lives into a power struggle between old and new guards: the old guard then chose to claim the lives of a million Rwandans rather than surrender its power'.[16] It has become an accepted truism to claim that preventative diplomacy is always better than a belated intervention when things start to go wrong. However, the lesson of the Arusha process is that outside intervention aimed at averting a civil war can have unintended consequences that produce human wrongs on an unimaginable scale.

The most difficult question raised by the peace agreement is whether it could have succeeded had it been enforced by the society of states against the Hutu extremists. Here, I disagree with Clapham, who argues that a stronger UN force could not have ensured the implementation of the peace settlement.[17] It is true that, given the extremists' doctrine of racial superiority and their complete opposition to any accommodation with the RPF, the implementation of the peace process depended upon neutralizing those who wanted to wreck what had been achieved at Arusha. However, it does not follow from this that the only option for the UN was to remain 'neutral',[18] since the Security Council could have decided to intervene decisively against the extremists.

Speaking at a press conference in September before the UN had authorized the deployment of UNAMIR, Habyarimana claimed that the UN forces would 'be there to provide security to everyone'.[19] To live up to this expectation, UNAMIR required a very different mandate and force structure to the peace-keeping one that the Security Council had given it in Resolution 872. This authorized UNAMIR to monitor the ceasefire and oversee the implementation of the accords; there was no question of it acting in a peace-enforcement role to impose the agreement or to protect human rights. As the force commander General Dallaire put it in February 1994: 'the minute there is a significant ceasefire violation by either side . . . my mandate does not exist here any more.'[20] If there was a general expectation among Rwandans committed to

---

[15] Clapham, 'Rwanda', 205.

[16] Bruce D. Jones, '"Intervention without Borders": Humanitarian Intervention in Rwanda, 1990–94', *Millennium: Journal of International Studies*, 24/2 (1995), 248.

[17] Clapham, 'Rwanda', 206.   [18] Ibid.

[19] A. J. Kuperman, 'The Other Lesson of Rwanda: Mediators Sometimes Do More Damage than Good', *SAIS Review*, 16/1 (1996), 236.

[20] Quoted in ibid.

the peace process that UNAMIR would neutralize the extremists by disarming their militias, then the peacekeeping mandate given to UNAMIR indicated that this conception was not shared by the Security Council.

The UN was seriously overstretched and preoccupied with operations in Bosnia and Somalia. Indeed, only two days before the Council discussed whether to send a peacekeeping force to Rwanda the eighteen US Rangers had been killed in Somalia. This created a powerful backlash in the USA against participation and support for UN operations. According to Linda Melvern, the USA argued in the Council's informal consultations that Congress would not pay for any new operations and that the UN was in danger of becoming over-committed.[21] African members countered that there was a moral duty to assist Rwanda in its transition to democracy and after some discussion it was agreed to create UNAMIR. In supporting Resolution 872 in the Council the USA established the condition that continuing support for the force would depend upon progress in implementing the peace agreement and keeping costs under control.[22] From the outset, then, the force was deprived of the funds and support to make it a viable mission and a good example of this is that General Dallaire's force had armoured cars but no spare parts or mechanics.[23]

An underfunded UN force that had a mandate only to monitor the cease-fire sent a powerful signal to the extremists that they could act with impunity. RTLMC was filling the airwaves with hate propaganda and arms were being widely distributed on the streets of Kigali.[24] General Dallaire set up an unofficial intelligence unit within UNAMIR to collate information on the activities of the extremists. This information, which pointed to a deliberate plan to destroy the peace process, was forwarded to UN Headquarters and to Belgium, whose forces made up the bulk of UNAMIR I. The most critical piece of intelligence came from a high-level informer who told Colonel Luc Marchal of UNAMIR the chilling news that the extremists planned to precipitate the withdrawal of UNAMIR by killing Belgian soldiers and Tutsi in Kigali at an estimated rate of 1,000 every twenty minutes using militia units.[25] The credibility of this information was confirmed when UN forces found secret caches of weapons at sites disclosed by the informant.

On 11 January, Dallaire cabled the UN's Department of Peacekeeping Operations (DPKO) with this warning and requested that he be allowed to seize the weapons.[26] The DPKO turned down the force commander's request

[21] L. Melvern, 'Genocide behind the Thin Blue Line', *Security Dialogue*, 28/3 (1997), 335.

[22] S/PV.3288, 5 Oct. 1993, 23.   [23] Melvern, 'Genocide', 335.

[24] A. J. Klinghoffer, *The International Dimension of Genocide in Rwanda* (London: Macmillan, 1998), 35.

[25] Howard Adelman, 'Preventing Post-Cold War Conflicts: What Have We learned? The Case of Rwanda', paper presented to the International Studies Association Conference at San Diego, California, 17 Apr. 1996, 8.

[26] Ibid. 12–13, and Klinghoffer, *The International Dimension*, 36.

to act unilaterally and insisted that he was permitted to act only in support of government forces. Since the extremists controlled the gendarmerie and the army, the instruction to act with the consent of the government ensured that there would be no operation to seize the militias' weapons. When asked to justify this decision on BBC's Panorama programme in December 1998, Iqbal Riza, a senior member of the DPKO at the time, stated that, although the warning from Dallaire was 'alarming', the DPKO view was 'not Somalia again'.[27] After the débâcle in Somalia, no one in the UN wanted to cross the 'Mogadishu-line' of peace enforcement in Rwanda. It was an article of faith among members of the Secretariat that, were the UN to suffer another disaster like Somalia with more peacekeepers being killed, the organization would suffer a possibly fatal blow to its credibility.[28]

With the benefit of hindsight, it is clear that the DPKO's response to the force commander's request was a crucial turning point in the story of the Rwandan genocide. Senior officials in the DPKO claim that they shared the warning with 'key members of the Security Council'[29] and that Dallaire was instructed to inform the French, Belgian, and US embassies, so that they could take the issue up with Habyarimana. In addition to the warning that Dallaire communicated to New York, the US State Department received an analysis from the CIA that concluded that should the Arusha Process collapse, half a million people would die in Rwanda.[30] Moreover, given its very close political, military, and economic links with the Habyarimana government, and the fact that its soldiers had played a critical role in training the militias, France must have been 'aware of the potential for genocide'.[31] Yet at no point did the USA or France try to convene the Security Council to discuss the warnings and Melvern claims that the Secretariat failed to share the intelligence with non-permanent members.[32] Boutros Boutros-Ghali did warn the Security Council on 30 March about the deteriorating security situation in Rwanda, but this was framed solely in terms of UNAMIR having to withdraw in the event of a breakdown of the ceasefire[33]—the implication being that the

[27] Quoted in 'When Good Men do Nothing', BBC Panorama programme, Dec. 1998. The Secretary General was particularly wary of getting into the business of disarmament again, given that he was personally associated with pushing the disarmament strategy that had led to disaster in Somalia. Interview with Sir David Hannay, Mar. 1999.

[28] This mindset among UN officials is captured well in M. N. Barnett, 'The UN Security Council, Indifference, and Genocide in Rwanda', *Cultural Anthropology,* 12/4 (1997), 551–578.

[29] Adelman, 'Preventing Post-Cold War Conflicts', 13.

[30] Melvern, 'Genocide', 337.

[31] Lemarchand, 'Rwanda', 11, and D. Kroslak, 'Evaluating the Moral Responsibility of France in the 1994 Genocide in Rwanda', paper presented to the British International Studies annual conference, University of Sussex, 14–16 Dec. 1998.

[32] Melvern, 'Genocide', 338. It was not only the non-permanent members who were kept in the dark, since, according to Sir David Hannay, Britain was not informed about the warning from Dallaire. Interview with Sir David Hannay, Mar. 1999.

[33] In reflecting on how the DPKO handled Dallaire's warning, it has to be remembered that less alarmist reports were coming from the Secretary General's Special Representative in Rwanda, Jacques Roger Booh-Booh. He had arrived in Rwanda in November 1993 and was closely associated

parties to Arusha were to blame for this, when, as Howard Adelman points out, the peace was in danger because of the activities of the extremists.[34]

A day before the genocide began, the Security Council met to discuss whether UNAMIR's mandate should be renewed for a further six months. There was considerable controversy as to whether UNAMIR should withdraw, with the USA arguing that the mission should end unless the transitional government was created immediately, as required by the peace agreement. The majority of Council members argued that the Arusha process should be given more time and that additional UN resources should be provided. But under US pressure it was agreed in Resolution 909 that the UN would pull out in six weeks unless the transitional government was created. It is one of those cruel ironies that Rwanda was a member of the Council at this time and hence its Ambassador was well aware of the reluctance of the USA to support the continuation of UNAMIR.

Even a cursory glance at Resolution 909 would have done nothing to make the extremists think that the UN was prepared to intervene forcibly against them. Indeed, given the warning of genocide and the legal and moral responsibility of signatories under the 1948 Genocide Convention to act to prevent this crime, what is striking about the Security Council's deliberations is the absence of any discussion of the role that UNAMIR could play in protecting civilians in Rwanda in the event that the warning proved correct. We cannot know how the Security Council would have responded had it been briefed by officials in the DPKO on the warning received from Dallaire, but, as New Zealand's Ambassador, Colin Keating, who was President of the Council for April, told Linda Melvern, we 'were kept in the dark . . . The situation was much more dangerous than was ever presented to the Council.'[35] Keating concluded from this that the Secretariat must improve the circulation of information to the non-permanent members, who often lack the intelligence capabilities of the major players on the Council. He claims that, had the non-permanent members been exposed to the warning of genocide, the Council 'might have proceeded quite differently'.[36]

It is incumbent upon those who argue that the Security Council could have prevented the genocide to show how this alternative could have been realized. The vital prerequisite for any preventative intervention was a change of mission from peacekeeping to enforcement action to protect civilians.[37] This required neutralizing the extremists by seizing their secret stockpiles of

---

with Habyarimana. Melvern points out that his reports focused solely on the risks of the conflict being renewed and never once mentioned the possibility of mass killing or genocide. Instead, he provided 'optimistic assessments of the President's intentions' to implement the Arusha process in the reports he sent to Riza and the Secretary General. See L. Melvern, *A People Betrayed: The Role of the West in Rwanda's Genocide* (London: Zed Books, forthcoming).

[34] Adelman, 'Preventing Post-Cold War Conflicts', 14.
[35] Quoted in Melvern, 'Genocide', 338.   [36] Quoted in ibid.
[37] Adelman, 'Preventing Post-Cold War Conflicts', 14.

arms, breaking up the militias, and closing down the sources of hate propaganda. This type of enforcement action clearly crosses the 'Mogadishu-line' and required a larger force than UNAMIR I, supported with helicopters and tanks. Yet, if such a UN force had been operational on the streets of Kigali, it is difficult to believe that the extremists would have launched or been successful in carrying out their 'final solution'.

The idea of changing the mandate of UNAMIR from peacekeeping to preventative humanitarian intervention was never discussed in the Security Council. But, even if such a change of mandate had been raised during the period from January to April, two powerful objections would have stood in the way. The first is the legal one of how to justify such an infringement of Rwanda's sovereignty.[38] Given the Security Council's sensitivities in relation to Western enforcement action in northern Iraq, would members have been persuaded that preventative humanitarian intervention fell within the legitimate purview of Chapter VII action? Set against this, the Genocide Convention states that any contracting party can 'call upon the competent organs of the United Nations to take such action under the Charter . . . as they consider appropriate for the prevention and suppression of acts of genocide'.[39] Consequently, the Security Council could have determined under Article 39 of the Charter that the risk of genocide in Rwanda constituted a 'threat to the peace' that justified the triggering of the Chapter VII enforcement provisions of the Charter. It can only be speculated whether this solidarist argument would have been received favourably by members, but what can be stated with greater certainty is that there is no legal precedent for this use of Chapter VII, and no member raised this claim in the Security Council in the months and weeks preceding the outbreak of the genocide. The clear implication of Keating's argument cited above is that, had the non-permanent members been aware of Dalliare's cable, this would have changed the context of the Security Council's decision-making in the weeks leading up to the outbreak of the genocide.

The second problem with preventative humanitarian intervention in Rwanda is who was going to shoulder the burden of enforcement action against the extremists? The USA was licking its wounds after the loss of its soldiers in Somalia and it is doubtful that the existing troop-contributing countries of UNAMIR would have been eager or capable of taking on a peace-enforcement role. Despite the antagonism of the RPF towards France for its military support of the Habyarimana government, it was the only realistic candidate for leading such an intervention. France had the capability in the form of its rapid reaction force based in the region quickly to deploy in support of UNAMIR. Moreover, since French military advisers had trained the

---

[38] Kuperman, 'The Other Lesson of Rwanda', 236.

[39] See Article VIII of the Convention on the Prevention and Punishment of the Crime of Genocide.

Presidential Guard and the militias, who better to close down the radio station, confiscate the weapons, and police the streets of Kigali. This would have sent a clear signal to the architects of the genocide that their plan of mass extermination would not be tolerated by their former friends in the French Government and military. As it was, when French paratroopers deployed into Rwanda six days after the outbreak of the genocide, it was only to rescue their own and other foreign (that is, Western) nationals, key members of Habyarimana's clique, and the embassy dog. It was revealing of the French Government's attitude to the crisis that the paratroopers left to their fate the Tutsi employees in the French embassy.

The Security Council's Response to the Genocide

As the killing began on the streets of Kigali, the targets of the Presidential Guard, gendarmie, and militias were not restricted to Tutsis. On 7 April, government soldiers murdered the Hutu Prime Minister, Ms Uwilingiyimana, and the ten Belgium peacekeepers protecting her.[40] Five days later the Belgium Government announced that it was withdrawing its contingent from UNAMIR, justifying its decision on the grounds that UNAMIR's existing mission was 'pointless within the terms of its present mandate' and that its soldiers were being exposed 'to unacceptable risks'.[41] Bangladesh, which had 900 soldiers serving in Rwanda, also expressed concern about the safety of its personnel, given that UNAMIR was being drawn into the crossfire between the RPF and government forces. With the departure of the Belgians, UNAMIR's strength was being significantly depleted at the same time as its peacekeeping mandate was in ruins. On 10 April, Dallaire was told by the Secretary General's special political adviser, Chinmaya Gharekhan, to prepare for withdrawal. The UNAMIR commander was very unhappy with this decision, since his force was protecting thousands of civilians in Kigali. According to Linda Melvern, he requested reinforcements and a 'show of force' to convince the militias that the UN was serious about halting the massacres.[42]

At the request of the Security Council, the Secretary General prepared a report setting out three alternatives for UNAMIR, but nowhere in this document is there any discussion of protecting civilians, as advocated by Dallaire. Instead, the importance of this report is that it represented the violence and

[40] Later that day the Security Council condemned all the killings in Kigali, including that of the UN soldiers. See Statement by the President of the Security Council, S/PRST/1994/16, 7 Apr. 1994.

[41] Letter from the Permanent Representative of Belgium to the President of the Security Council, S/1994/430, 13 Apr. 1994. See also 'UN Rwandan Role in Doubt as Belgians Quit', *Financial Times*, 15 Apr. 1994.

[42] See Melvern, 'Genocide', 339, and 'Rwandan Blood Flows as Foreign Forces Depart', *Guardian*, 16 Apr. 1994.

suffering solely in terms of the breakdown of the Arusha peace process. Boutros Boutros-Ghali's most ambitious proposal was a massive deployment of troops and a change of mandate so that it could coerce the parties into a ceasefire, restore law and order, and put an end to the killings.[43] He recognized that this would require thousands of additional troops and a Chapter VII mandate. The next option was to scale down UNAMIR to a force size of around 270, which would be charged with negotiating with the parties and assisting with humanitarian relief efforts. The final option, which the Secretary General did not favour, was the complete withdrawal of UNAMIR. The Secretary General concluded his report by stating that it is the parties to the Arusha agreement who must 'bear the responsibility' for the current situation.[44]

There is no reason to question the sincerity of the Secretary General in holding this interpretation, but there were alternative constructions of the killing both inside and outside the UN system of which he should have been aware. With regard to the former, why was there no mention in the report of Dallaire's secret cable of 8 April stating that the killing was based on 'ethnic origin', that UNAMIR camps had become safe havens for Rwandan civilians, and requesting reinforcements to protect human rights?[45] Further evidence of the genocidal nature of the killing was supplied in a letter to the Security Council by the US-based Human Rights Watch, which stated that as many as 100,000 people might have been killed during the previous two weeks.[46] By excluding these alternative constructions of the killing in favour of the narrative of a 'tribal war', Boutros Boutros-Ghali's list of options presented themselves as the only available courses of action. Given that the non-permanent members relied on the Secretariat for their information, they were in no position to challenge the Secretary-General's interpretation of the situation.[47] For those states such as France, Britain, and especially the USA that had the military capabilities to respond to Dallaire's request for rein-

---

[43] Special Report of the Secretary General on UNAMIR, S/1994/470, 20 Apr. 1994.

[44] According to Melvern, this reflected the intelligence that the Secretary General and his officials were receiving from Booh-Booh, who was a close personal friend of Boutros Boutros-Ghali. She cites a cable from Dallaire on 8 April that described the killings as 'very well planned, organized, deliberate and conducted campaign of terror initiated principally by the Presidential Guard since the morning after the death of the head of state'. Yet in the same cable, Booh-Booh attributes the killings to the 'fighting between the Presidential Guard and the RPF' (quoted in Melvern, *A People Betrayed*). A similar interpretation was proffered by the *Washington Post* in an editorial when it claimed that responsibility for what was happening in Rwanda rested with the political class and that when 'a fire of Rwandan dimensions breaks out, it means that the country has utterly failed' (repr. in the *International Herald Tribune*, 18 Apr. 1994).

[45] See BBC Panorama programme 'When Good Men Do Nothing', Dec. 1998. Michael Barnett, who served in the US mission in New York during this period, considers that the reason why the Secretariat did not communicate Dallaire's request to the Security Council was that 'it feared becoming embroiled in a conflict that spelled failure' ('The UN Security Council, Indifference, and Genocide', Barnett, 573).

[46] 'UN Force Begins Rwanda Pullout', *International Herald Tribune*, 21 Apr. 1994.

[47] Barnett, 'The UN Security Council, Indifference, and Genocide', 559.

forcements to protect human rights, the Secretariat's naming of the violence as a civil war and not a genocide legitimated their decision not to intervene to stop the massacres.

The Security Council met informally on 20 April to discuss the Secretary General's report. According to Melvern, who has obtained a copy of what was discussed in private, Britain's Ambassador, Sir David Hannay, opposed reinforcing UNAMIR, reminding members to 'think back to Somalia and think about what you would ask these troops to do'. He opposed intervention, on the grounds that it would mean contesting the forces of both the RPF and the Rwandan Government.[48] Britain advocated the Secretary General's second option of withdrawing UNAMIR whilst leaving a small force behind to try and negotiate a ceasefire. The only opposition to this plan came from Ambassador Gambari of Nigeria, who worried that none of the options would protect the '14,000 people presently sheltering under the UN flag. Was the UN to do nothing to help civilians?'[49] The Council went into recess that evening and a group of Ambassadors from the non-permanent members were briefed by the Secretary General's Canadian military adviser, Maurice Baril. He had been in constrant touch with Dallaire and described the terrible conditions under which the peacekeepers were operating. In an interview with Melvern, Baril stated that there 'was not a military commander in the world who would leave an army exposed in such a way . . . they were "exhausted, confused and questioning the responsibility of their superiors" and constantly in fear'.[50]

This briefing had a profound impact on the thinking of the non-permanent members and the Security Council unanimously agreed the following day in Resolution 912 to reduce UNAMIR to 270. No member challenged the interpretation of the causes of the killing in the Secretary General's report, and nor did Nigeria or any other state publicly argue for strengthening UNAMIR and changing its mandate to protect civilians. Instead, members expressed their concern about the safety of UN forces in such a dangerous situation, and consensus settled on the alternative of retaining a much reduced force that could work to negotiate a new ceasefire and provide humanitarian relief efforts. Reflecting on the decision, Keating said that it 'was not a resolution that went forward with any enthusiasm on my part. But I am still convinced it was the only decision.'[51]

This justification stands in sharp contrast to the verdict of Howard Adelman, who claims that the decision to withdraw UN soldiers 'must go down in history as one of the most ignominious actions of the international community in general and the Security Council in particular'.[52] The appalling

---

[48] Melvern, *A People Betrayed.*   [49] Ibid.   [50] Ibid.
[51] Quoted in Melvern, 'Genocide', 340.
[52] Adelman, 'Preventing Post-Cold War Conflicts', 9. The options of withdrawing UNAMIR or significantly reducing it had been strongly opposed by the OAU Secretary General, Salim Ahmed Salim, in a letter to the UN Secretary General dated 21 Apr. 194. In this letter the Salim Ahmed Salim

moral consequences of this decision can be seen in the fact that, as soon as the bulk of UNAMIR troops left Kigali, many of the civilians being protected by them were immediately killed. In a sense, both Adelman and Keating are right in their judgements about Resolution 912, since it all depends upon the context in which the decision is located. To leave the UNAMIR soldiers on the ground with their existing force structure and mandate was to place peace-keepers in an intolerable position. Reflecting on the bureaucratically driven arguments that he and his colleagues in the US mission employed at this time, Michael Barnett claims that any 'more peacekeeping fatalities . . . would undoubtedly mean more criticism and fewer resources for the UN' and this became 'the moral equation and the justification for inaction'.[53] However, it is hard to escape the conclusion that this was a convenient argument that masked the fact that no state on the Security Council was prepared to risk its soldiers to save Rwandan civilians. The Secretariat and Security Council had a moral responsibility to protect the UNAMIR soldiers and this had to be weighted against the protection they were providing for Tutsis and moderate Hutus, but this agonizing moral choice could have been avoided by a change of mandate and the deployment of an effective fighting force.

Adelman's argument that the Security Council bears the responsibility for failing to volunteer the forces that could have protected civilians overlooks the fact that the Secretariat never informed members of Dallaire's request for reinforcements. Would such a briefing have changed the decision in Resolution 912? Michael Barnett suggests that it might have done so 'quite significantly', because it would have undermined the argument that there was no alternative but to withdraw the force or massively reinforce it. He writes: 'There is no doubt that a strong *démarche* from the Secretary General that included both a realistic military proposal coupled with a forceful moral imperative . . . would have undermined the argument in favor of withdrawal. Boutros Boutros-Ghali's failure to make the case meant that there was no real-istic alternative to the option of withdrawal.'[54] Yet, even if members had been aware of Dalliare's request for reinforcements, it is by no means clear that this would have been sufficient to persuade them to provide additional troops.[55] And, without this, there really was no alternative to the decision in

---

had argued that such a decision would be seen 'as a sign of indifference or lack of sufficient concerns for African tragic situations'. Indeed, he made a veiled reference to the Council's double standards in focusing on other conflict regions to the exclusion of Africa. It is likely that the OAU Secretary General had Bosnia in mind where only six days later the Council was to authorize in Resolution 914 the sending of a further 6,500 peacekeepers. The OAU Secretary General's letter is cited as Document 50 in *The United Nations and Rwanda 1993–1996* (New York: UN Department of Public Information, 1996), 226. See also Klinghoffer, *The International Dimension*, 49. Oxfam and Christian Aid also condemned the UN decision to pull out. See 'Aid Agencies Condemn UN Pull-Out from Rwanda', *Guardian*, 23 Apr. 1994.

53 Barnett, 'The UN Security Council, Indifference, and Genocide', 575.
54 Letter to the author from Michael Barnett, 21 June 1999.
55 Interview with Sir David Hannay, Mar. 1999.

Resolution 912, given that UNAMIR was collapsing as troop-contributing countries desperately sought an exit from the deteriorating security situation in Rwanda.[56]

The UNAMIR force commander is cited by Senators Paul Simon and James Jeffords of the Senate Committee on Foreign Relations in a letter to Clinton on 13 May 1994 as believing that a force of '5,000 to 8,000 troops . . . [could] stop the senseless slaughter . . . [and] effectively achieve the desired result'.[57] The Canadian General had been asking for reinforcements since 10 April, and the implication is that a quite limited military intervention in the second or third week of April could have saved hundreds of thousands of lives. Three years after the genocide the Carnegie Commission on Preventing Deadly Conflict, the Institute for the Study of Diplomacy at Georgetown University, and the US Army undertook a project to assess the validity of Dallaire's judgement. An international panel of senior military leaders was convened to discuss Dallaire's military assessment. In his report to the Carnegie Commission based on the discussions at the conference, Scott Feil points out that there was a consensus among the panel that Dallaire's assessment was an accurate one and that a force of 5,000 operating with air support, logistics, and communications, and deployed with a Chapter VII mandate, 'could have averted the slaughter of a half-million people'.[58] There was also agreement that 'U.S. participation would have been essential—to lead in supplying resources, carrying out critical functions, and achieving mission goals'.[59]

The window for deploying such a force was between 7 and 21 April, because during this period 'the political leaders of the violence were still susceptible to international influence' and would have altered their political calculations in the face of a determined rescue mission.[60] The reason for the time frame of 7–21 April is that deploying any later 'would have required massive amounts of force because the situation had expanded to the countryside'.[61] The implication of this is that intervening to stop a genocide that had spread throughout the country would militarily be a much more difficult

[56] As Sir David Hannay puts it, 'the situation the Security Council was facing [in deciding on Resolution 912] almost immediately was the complete collapse of the peacekeeping force; it wasn't the Council that cut it back, they marched with their feet. The Belgians were out within two days after the murder of their detachment . . . the Bangladeshis went within a short time. We were left with one battalion . . . we didn't cut it back they voted with their feet'. Hannay opposed the American view that the force should be completely withdrawn because the conditions for a peacekeeping operation were gone. Against this, Hannay argued that it would be 'desperate' to take away the battalion willing to stay there and that the force should be consolidated. Interview with Sir David Hannay, Mar. 1999.

[57] Letter from Senators Simon and Jeffords to President Clinton, 13 May 1994. I am grateful to Linda Melvern for making this letter available to me.

[58] Carnegie Commission, *Preventing Deadly Conflict: Final Report With Executive Summary of the Carnegie Commission on Preventing Deadly Conflict* (New York: Carnegie Commission on Preventing Deadly Conflict, 1997), 6, and S. R. Feil, *Preventing Genocide: A Report to the Carnegie Commission on Preventing Deadly Conflict* (New York: Carnegie Corporation, 1998), 27.

[59] Feil, *Preventing Genocide*, 27.   [60] Ibid. 26.

[61] Ibid. 22.

operation, with a significantly increased risk to soldiers lives. Consequently, the assumption driving Feil's study is that US forces, under effective command and control, and backed by air power, could have protected Rwandan civilians with little or no risk to US soldiers.[62]

It can only be speculated how the Clinton Administration would have reacted to events in Rwanda had this been the President's first African humanitarian crisis. As it was, the ghost of the eighteen Rangers lost in the Somali firefight haunted the US Government, with the President ruling out any options that placed US personnel in harm's way. In response to the Somali débâcle and Congressional concerns that the USA was acting as the world's policeman, the President agreed Presidential Decision Directive (PDD) 25, which was made public at the beginning of May. This attempted to establish strict limits to US participation in future UN peacekeeping operations by stating that the USA would contribute to operations only where its national interests were engaged and that its soldiers would always remain under national command and control. Although several commentators have suggested that the Tutsis were the first to suffer the consequences of Clinton's PDD 25,[63] the document is sufficiently indeterminate to have been invoked by the administration to justify sending US soldiers to Rwanda. As Ramsbotham and Woodhouse point out, the directive states that it is in the US national interest to support peace-enforcement operations where 'there is a threat to or breach of international peace and security ... defined as one or a combination of the following: international aggression; or urgent humanitarian disaster coupled with violence ... or gross violation of human rights coupled with violence; or threat of violence'.[64] Consequently, the Clinton Administration could have defended forcible humanitarian intervention in Rwanda in the first two weeks of April on the grounds that halting genocide was both a moral duty and in the national interest. Unfortunately the President—who on his trip to Rwanda four years later apologized for the international community's failure to save Rwanda—was not prepared to take the lead in arguing the case at home that US soldiers should be put at risk in defence of common humanity. Indeed, having decided against intervention, the Clinton Administration mobilized against those governments, NGOs, and media that wanted to name Rwanda a genocide. The administration reportedly

---

[62] Although it is recognized in Scott Feil's report that the intervention would have encountered varying degrees of resistance from Rwandan government forces, the militias, and perhaps even from the RPF, a weakness of the report is that there is no explicit assessment of the likely cost in soldiers' lives.

[63] For example, Alain Destexhe, 'The "New" Humanitarianism', in A. J. Paolini et al. (eds.), *Between Sovereignty and Global Governance: The United Nations, the State and Civil Society* (London: Macmillan, 1998), 97.

[64] PDD 25 Executive Summary, 4, quoted in Ramsbotham and Woodhouse, *Humanitarian Intervention*, 141.

issued a secret directive to officials that they were not to use the word genocide, because this would raise the awkward legal question as to whether the
USA was obliged to intervene under the 1948 Convention.[65] Convention or
no convention, the administration had no intention of becoming
embroiled in Rwanda's nightmare.[66]

If the power of naming Rwanda a 'genocide' frightened the Clinton
Administration, then it was exactly the normative power of the Convention
to enable intervention that some members of the Council and several NGOs
were trying to enlist to save the victims of the genocide. Having been exposed
to only one interpretation of the killing in the weeks leading up to the fateful decision in Resolution 912, New Zealand as Council President and
Czechoslovakia took the lead in acting in Barnett's words, as the 'conscience
of the Council'.[67] On 25 April Keating was briefed by a doctor from MSF who
had been in Rwanda and who told him that a genocide was taking place
against the Tutsi.[68] Three days later the British aid agency Oxfam warned that
the lives of up to half a million Tutsi were in danger in a 'pattern of systematic killing' that amounts to 'genocide'.[69] By the end of April the extermination of the Tutsis was finally beginning to attract serious media coverage, as
journalists who had been preoccupied with the historic election of a Black
President in South Africa parachuted into Rwanda on their way home. This
was the first time we saw the horrifying television images of mutilated bodies,
thousands of them floating down blood-soaked rivers, and pictures of a terrible human exodus as up to half a million fled across the Tanzanian border in
search of safety. At the same time the Secretary General was receiving reports
from UN officials in Kigali that government forces and militias were systematically killing Tutsi in an 'attempt to eliminate them'.[70]

Against this background of growing evidence that a genocide was taking
place, the Security Council was embarrassed that its only response had been
to reduce UNAMIR. Under pressure from the Secretary General and the New
Zealand and Czech governments, the Security Council met informally on 28
and 29 April to discuss the situation. The Czech Ambassador, Karel Kovanda,
had been so shocked by the reports of genocide that he had sought a briefing
from Alison des Forges, a consultant for Human Rights Watch/Africa.

---

[65] Gourevitch, *We Wish to Inform you*, 152.

[66] The BBC Panorama programme 'When Good Men Do Nothing' interviewed Tony Marley, who
was Political/Military adviser to the State Department at the time and he claimed that the administration was worried that to name Rwanda a genocide and then be seen to have done nothing whilst
genocide took place would cost the President in the forthcoming Congressional elections.

[67] Barnett, 'The UN Security Council, Indifference, and Genocide', 572.

[68] Melvern, '*Genocide*', 341.

[69] 'Oxfam Warns of Rwanda Genocide', *Financial Times*, 29 Apr. 1994. A few days later Oxfam
condemned the Security Council's decision to cut back UN forces to a skeletal force of 270 and
pointed to the selectivity of this action in comparison with its decision to send additional forces to
Bosnia-Herzegovina. See 'Oxfam Accuses UN of Inconsistency', *Independent*, 3 May 1994.

[70] 'It's Genocide, says UN, as Rwandan Butchery Continues', *Guardian*, 29 Apr. 1994.

Kovanda gathered together a number of the non-permanent members in the Czech mission to hear des Forges's stories of the suffering that had been inflicted on her friends and associates in Rwanda.[71] The Czech diplomat was so moved by what he heard that he appealed to the Security Council to declare that a genocide was taking place. Kovanda's family were survivors of the Holocaust and his words must have carried considerable moral force when he likened the UN's current approach as 'rather like wanting Hitler to reach a ceasefire with the Jews'.[72] Kovanda was supported by Keating, who proposed the following day that the Council issue a statement condemning the killings as 'genocide'. This was supported by Spain and Argentina, but there were strong objections from China, the USA, and especially Britain. Hannay stated that, were the Council to use this word, it would become a 'laughing stock'.[73] His argument was that, having failed to find any troops for intervention, the Security Council would lack all credibility if it was then to name Rwanda a genocide.[74] The debate went on for several hours and eventually Keating used what Melvern describes as the 'somewhat desperate measure' of threatening the Council that, if there was no agreement, he would table a draft resolution supporting his statement. This would require a vote and would expose members' positions to the glare of world public opinion.[75] A compromise was finally found whereby a Presidential Statement was issued that used words from the Genocide Convention but did not explicitly invoke the word genocide.[76]

The Security Council's Presidential Statement of 30 April reflected its response to the growing international demand from domestic publics and humanitarian NGOs for action to stop the killings. Media coverage of the genocide finally galvanized the UN into action, and the Secretary General in a major volte-face had written to the Council the day before its Presidental Statement to express his growing concern about the security of civilians in Rwanda. He requested the Council to reconsider its decision in Resolution 912, because this did not give UNAMIR a mandate to protect civilians. Rather than locating responsibility for the violence in the breakdown of the peace process, the Secretary General now blamed armed groups of civilians who had taken advantage of the complete breakdown of law and order. This analysis still betrayed a reluctance to accept that a genocide was taking place, but his recommendation that the Security Council consider authorizing member states to use force 'to restore law and order and end the massacres' indicated

---

[71] Des Forges's meeting with the Ambassadors in the Czech mission is described in Linda Melvern, *The Ultimate Crime: Who Betrayed the UN and Why* (London: Allison & Busby, 1995), 11.

[72] Melvern, 'Genocide', 341.   [73] Melvern, *A People Betrayed.*

[74] Interview with Sir David Hannay, Mar. 1999.   [75] Melvern, *A People Betrayed.*

[76] The Statement declared that the 'Security Council recalls that the killing of members of an ethnic group with the intention of destroying such a group in whole or in part constitutes a crime punishable under international law'. Melvern claims that this compromise reflected 'the drafting ability of British diplomats'. See Melvern, 'Genocide', 341, and S/PRST/1994/21, 30 Apr. 1994.

that the Secretary General was at last seized of the urgent need to rescue Rwandan civilians.[77]

Following up on its Presidential Statement, the Security Council requested that the Secretary General provide a report setting out how an expanded UNAMIR force could alleviate the deepening humanitarian crisis that had displaced over two million Rwandans. The Security Council began informally to debate the question of an intervention force' and New Zealand proposed a draft resolution on 6 May supported by the other non-permanent members to create a new UN force to protect civilians.[78] It will never be known whether the fate of Rwandans would have been different had New Zealand possessed the capabilities to intervene forcibly, but the only states that had the military means to save civilians rejected this option. The political difficulty that faced New Zealand and its allies on the Council was that they wanted to volunteer the soldiers of other states for UN intervention when they were not prepared to put forward any forces of their own. As Barnett puts it having observed the Council at work, 'i was suspicious that when other states evoked the "international community", they were, in fact, pointing to the United States . . . the United States should take the lead.'[79]

A week later Boutros Boutros-Ghali reported back to the Security Council and recommended that it create a force of 5,500 troops to be deployed in phases to create safe conditions for displaced persons and other groups and assist relief organizations with the delivery of humanitarian aid. In contrast to the draft New Zealand resolution, the Secretary General's plan did not envisage enforcement action, believing that the mission would operate through 'deterrence', but if this failed, then the force should be mandated under Chapter VII to take action in self-defence against any threats to its mission.[80]

Three days later the Security Council formally met to discuss the Secretary General's report and adopted Resolution 918, which authorized an increase in UNAMIR to 5,500 troops with a mandate to provide humanitarian assistance. However, there was disagreement over how quickly and where the new force should be deployed, with the USA arguing that deployment in Kigali required the consent of the warring parties. The most the USA would agree to in Resolution 918 was the immediate dispatch of an 850-member Ghanaian force to secure Kigali airport and the transfer of 150 UN observers to the interior.[81] Reflecting the Clinton Administration's determination to avoid a repeat of Somalia, its Ambassador stated that 'it is critical that all parties

[77] Letter from the UN Secretary-General to the President of the Security Council, S/1994/518, 29 Apr. 1994.

[78] Melvern, 'Genocide', 341.

[79] Barnett, 'The Un Security Council, Indifference, and Genocide', 572.

[80] Report of the Secretary General on the situation in Rwanda, S/1994/565, 13 May 1994.

[81] 'Rwanda Stand Reflects New U.S. Caution', International Herald Tribune, 19 May 1994.

respect absolutely the inviolability of United Nations personnel and peace-keepers'.[82] The reason why the Clinton Administration wanted to base the expanded UN operation outside Kigali was that it did not want American transport planes landing under fire at Kigali airport.[83] Concerns for the safety of US aircrew and ground personnel had led the administration to propose the creation of 'protective zones' on the borders of Tanzania and Zaïre.[84] By making the deployment in Kigali of the five battalions envisaged in phase two of the Secretary General's plan dependent upon a ceasefire, the Clinton Administration demonstrated its determination that Rwanda would be a casualty-free operation for US forces.[85]

New Zealand voted in favour of Resolution 918, but Keating expressed his concern that it had too limited a mandate to provide the protection of civilians that was so desperately needed. He reminded the Security Council that his government had proposed a draft resolution on 6 May to send forces to Rwanda to 'make a start on the task of protecting civilians at risk in various locations in the interior of Rwanda'.[86] Supporting Keating was Kovanda, who was the only member publicly to describe the killings as 'genocide'.[87] Neither Keating's nor Kovanda's arguments were sufficiently compelling to push the Security Council into a more robust response and the matter was left that the Secretary General would report back to the Council on how phase two of UNAMIR II should be implemented.

Testifying before the House Foreign Affairs Subcommittee, US Ambassador Albright justified the US decision to go slow on an expanded UNAMIR by arguing that it would have been 'folly' for the USA to venture too quickly into this African 'maelstrom'.[88] She said, 'We want to be confident that when we do turn to the UN, the UN will be able to do the job.'[89] The US Ambassador argued that it was essential that the UN did not overreach itself in Rwanda and jeopardize its future credibility. Reflecting Congressional pressures for greater US restraint in UN peacekeeping, Albright made Rwanda the first test of PDD 25.[90] As I argued earlier, this National Security Council directive could

---

[82] S/PV.3377, 16 May 1994, 13

[83] 'US Veto Holds Back Rwanda Peace Force', *The Times*, 18 May 1994, and interview with Sir David Hannay, Mar. 1999.

[84] Ambassador Albright argued the 'protective-zone' idea would require fewer troops than the 5,500 envisaged by the Secretary General and would be 'less complex logistically' ('US Proposes Refugee Zone for Rwandans', *The Times*, 12 May 1994). Melvern records that US military advisers arrived at the UN to discuss details of their plan with officials in the DPKO and this dragged on through May. Melvern cites an interview with Keating in July 1994 where he stated: 'It was almost surreal . . . while thousands of beings were hacked to death every day, ambassadors argued fitfully for weeks about military tactics (quoted in Melvern, 'Genocide', 342).

[85] See S/PV.3377, 16 May 1994, 13. Set against this US position, some members of the Security Council during the debate over Resolution 918 expressed regret that it authorized only a modest first phase of an expanded UNAMIR. For example, see the statements of the New Zealand and French Ambassadors in the Council in S/PV.3377, 16 May 1994, 11–12.

[86] See S/PV.3377, 16 May 1994, 12.   [87] Ibid. 16.

[88] 'Rwanda Stand Reflects New U.S. Caution', *International Herald Tribune*, 19 May 1994.

[89] Ibid.   [90] Ibid.

have been used by senior administration officials to justify putting US soldiers at risk in Rwanda by making the case that moral obligation and national interest required the USA to take the lead in ending the scourge of genocide. In a clear sign of how far the Somali débâcle had shaken the earlier US confidence in liberal internationalism, no member of the House Committee challenged Albright by arguing that the USA was failing to live up to its responsibilities under the Genocide Convention.[91]

Editorials in the *New York Times* during this period did invoke the language of 'genocide', but the paper strongly opposed US intervention on the grounds that there were no clear political and military objectives.[92] The President felt sufficiently confident about the prevailing mood of US public opinion that he went further than the *New York Times* and explicitly argued on 25 May that the USA had no vital interests in Rwanda and that US military personnel could not be sent to every trouble spot where Americans were 'offended by human misery'.[93]

In the absence of Western intervention, the only alternative was for African states to take the lead. In its Presidential Statement of 30 April the Security Council had requested the Secretary General to investigate this possibility. In response to Boutros-Boutros Ghali's requests, Ghana, Ethiopia, Senegal, Nigeria, Zimbabwe, Zambia, Congo, Mali, and Malawi came forward with offers of troops for phase two of the deployment of UNAMIR II. In doing so they made it clear that they would need equipment, heavy lift support, and their costs underwritten by the UN. Given the UN's budgetary crisis, financing UNAMIR II depended upon Western states. The difficulties of securing even this level of support can be seen in the haggling that the USA entered into with the Ghanaians over bringing their existing forces up to battalion strength. The USA had agreed to provide the necessary equipment and vehicles but the deployment was delayed as the Pentagon tried to supply the fifty armoured personnel carriers (APCs) as cheaply as possible and arguments raged between the UN and the USA as to who was to cover the costs of transport.[94] The result of all this was that the APCs did not arrive in Uganda until the end of June and it then took a further month for the vehicles to arrive in Kigali, by which time it was too late for the hundreds of thousands of Rwandans who had perished in the previous weeks.

Given the delay in implementing phase one of the UNAMIR II deployment, the Secretary General wrote to the Council on 31 May to request that the four mechanized battalions be deployed immediately with or without a ceasefire. In closing his report the Secretary General for the first time described the situation as a genocide and placed 'overwhelming responsibility' for the killings

---

[91] Ibid. For a discussion of the *New York Times* coverage, see Klinghoffer, *The International Dimension*, 98.   [92] See ibid.
[93] Quoted in ibid. 97.   [94] Ibid. 93.

on 'Rwandan government forces'.[95] He welcomed the offer of troops by African governments but emphasised that the success of UNAMIR II depended upon 'the proper equipment [being] ... provided by other Governments'.[96] Boutros Boutros-Ghali grimly reflected that, nearly two months after the killings began,

the international community appears paralysed in reacting ... even to the revised mandate established by the Security Council. We all must recognize that, in this respect, we have failed in our response to the agony of Rwanda, and thus have acquiesced in the continued loss of human lives. Our readiness and capacity for action has been demonstrated to be inadequate at best, and deplorable at worst, owing to the absence of the collective political will.[97]

In response to the Secretary General's criticisms and the offer of troops from African states, the Council met on 8 June and passed unanimously Resolution 925, which authorized the deployment of the 5,500 troops first called for in the Secretary General's report of 13 May.[98] What is noticeable about this meeting is that there was less hesitancy on the part of several members to name Rwanda a genocide.[99] Given all the reports in the media about the scale of the butchery of civilians, the Council recognized that it could not be seen, in the words of the Djibouti Ambassador, to allow 'Rwanda to burn while the United Nations fiddles'.[100]

Having finally authorized the full-scale deployment of UNAMIR II to provide protection for civilians and support for humanitarian relief operations, there was still the question of securing the necessary equipment to enable the troops to deploy. It was anticipated by the Secretary General that, given the reluctance of member states to supply this, it would be necessary to seek the services of a civilian contractor. As a result, UNAMIR might not be in a position to fulfil its mandate for at least another three months.

The carnage was continuing on a daily basis through June and it was against this background that France offered to lead a multinational rescue mission that would serve as an interim measure until UNAMIR II was fully deployed. Given the growing pressure on the UN to do something to stop the genocide, a humanitarian intervention by the French had the merit that the UN would finally be seen to be responding to the genocide. However, there were other less comfortable aspects that went with this offer, which cast considerable doubt on the legitimacy of any French action in Rwanda.

---

[95] Report of the Secretary General on the situation in Rwanda, S/1994/640, 31 May 1994.
[96] Ibid.   [97] Ibid.
[98] S/PV.3388, 8 June 1994.
[99] See the statements by the Ambassadors for the Czech Republic, Britain, the Russian Federation, Spain, and New Zealand. S/PV.3388, 8 June 1994, 3–4, 6–8, 10.
[100] S/PV.3388, 8 June 1994, 3.

Operation Turquoise and the Politics of Gesticulation?

The justification given by French ministers for intervention in Rwanda was to save lives. Having floated the idea on Radio France Internationale, Foreign Minister Alain Juppé wrote in the daily *Liberation* on 16 June that France had 'a real duty to intervene in Rwanda . . . to put an end to the massacres and protect the populations threatened with extermination'.[101] France wanted other states to participate in this rescue mission and the issue was discussed at a meeting of the nine-member Western European Union (WEU). However, there was no enthusiasm among other European states for such a venture. Senegal and Chad provided token support to their French ally, but this was very much an independent French operation. To secure domestic and international legitimacy for its proposed action, the Prime Minister, Édouard Balladur, identified five preconditions in a speech to Parliament on 21 June: the operation must have UN Security Council authorization; all operations should be limited to humanitarian actions; troops should remain near the border with Zaïre; they should not enter into the heart of Rwanda or become embroiled in war with the RPF; and, finally, the mission should be limited to a maximum of two months before France handed over to UNAMIR II.

In justifying the action in these terms, the Prime Minister established a normative framework against which subsequent French actions could be judged. Particularly significant in this respect was his commitment that France would act only with explicit Security Council authorization. In making this move, Balladur probably hoped that securing UN legitimacy would head off any criticisms that France was too implicated in the actions of the Habyarimana regime to play the role of a rescuer in Rwanda. Yet it probably also reflected the belief of ministers that they required a legal mandate from the Council to intervene forcibly in Rwanda. The day before the Prime Minister's speech, the French Ambassador at the UN, Jean-Bernard Mérimée, had written to the Secretary General requesting a Chapter VII mandate to provide the 'legal framework' for French action. The interim Rwandan government that had installed itself as Habyarimana's successor and which was responsible for orchestrating the genocide remained the *de jure* government. It could have exercised its sovereign prerogative by inviting French intervention, but, since most of the territory of Rwanda was under the *de facto* control of the RPF (which many states recognized as the only legitimate government of Rwanda) and the Rwandan Government was almost universally condemned as a perpetrator of genocide, this legal claim would have strained credibility. More ominously, it would have fuelled accusations that were gaining currency in the French press that the real purpose of the

---

[101] Quoted in Prunier, *The Rwanda Crisis*, 280.

'humanitarian' mission was to save its client government that was losing the war with the RPF.

The Security Council met to discuss the French request for authorization and, although ten states voted in favour of the operation in Resolution 929, there were five abstentions (China, Brazil, New Zealand, Pakistan, and Nigeria). This reflected the unease that members had about the humanitarian credentials of Operation Turquoise. However, since the Security Council had acted during the previous two months as a global bystander to genocide, no one felt able publicly criticize to a French mission that was justified in terms of saving lives.[102] The Russian Ambassador described the French action as an 'imperative' and the Djibouti Ambassador captured the enabling power of France's humanitarian rhetoric when he said that 'the rest of humanity probably feels at this point that anything would be better than what is'.[103] Those members who abstained on the vote publicly defended their position on the grounds that French energies and resources would be better devoted ensuring that the strengthened UNAMIR arrived in Rwanda as soon as possible. The difficult position that France's proposal placed members in can be seen in Keating's attempt to undercut the operation without directly raising the question as to whether France was cloaking self-interest in the guise of humanitarianism. He said that he respected France's 'humanitarian motivation' but questioned whether the operation would save the victims of the genocide. Fearing that the French action might undermine the efforts to deploy UNAMIR II, the New Zealand Ambassador drew on his interpretation of the lesson of Somalia:

Somalia has shown us that even where we have the best of humanitarian intentions, if we do not employ the right means, tragedy can be the result. We have already seen the evidence. Trying to run two separate operations in parallel with different command arrangements does not work and, in the long run, those whom we set out to save can be those who suffer. The Security Council must learn from history.[104]

Although no member felt able to challenge the humanitarian rationale of Operation Turquoise, there was no similar reticence on the part of the Western media and human rights organizations, which identified two key reasons for doubting its humanitarian credentials. First, French actions in the immediate period following the death of Habyarimana were highlighted when it did nothing to stop the massacres and voted along with the rest of the Security Council to cut back UNAMIR. One Paris source is quoted as saying: 'We just want to gesticulate . . . We said nothing during the massacres . . . but now the killing is mostly over, we suddenly find a burning desire to save lives.'[105] And, having voted effectively to neutralize UNAMIR at the

---

[102] 'French Press on with Rwanda Mission', *Independent*, 21 June 1994.
[103] S/PV.3392, 22 June 1994, 4.   [104] Ibid. 7.
[105] 'French Press on with Rwanda Mission'.

beginning of the genocide, France was now censured by the media and NGOs for acting in ways that undermined UNAMIR II. For example, Oxfam publicly expressed its disappointment with the Security Council decision, asking how it was that the French force could be mobilized within a matter of days when Western governments had refused to provide logistic support for UNAMIR II.[106] This was similar to the concern that some states had raised in the Security Council during the debate over Resolution 929. For those journalists who did not have to worry about the diplomatic niceties, the reason for France's independent operation was clear. Stripped of its humanitarian rhetoric, the purpose of Operation Turquoise was to prop up a failing French ally.[107]

This leads into the second and related reason for questioning France's humanitarian claims, which is that French policy-makers were determined to stop the triumph of the 'Anglophones' in what they viewed as their part of Africa. It will be recalled that the French had propped up the one-party state of Habyarimana and had intervened against the RPF from 1990 onwards. Given the changed context of the summer of 1994, with France's old ally accused of genocide, it was not possible for Paris to install the old regime in Kigali. Instead, the mission was to maintain what was left of French influence by securing the power base of those Hutu refugees who were fleeing from the victorious RPF.[108] And, in the face of the success of the Ugandan-backed RPF, strategists in the African cell of the Elysée focused their attention on strengthening Francophone Zaïre. As Gérard Prunier points out, changing geopolitical calculations had turned President Mobuto's dictatorial regime from being beyond the pale to one that would receive active French support.[109] Given the loss of its Rwandan client, it became urgent in French perceptions to demonstrate to Africa and the rest of the world that France was no paper tiger and that it could project power rapidly on the continent.[110]

These hidden motivations of *realpolitik* became increasingly apparent when on 4 July France declared the existence of a 'safe humanitarian zone' (SHZ) in the south-western part of Rwanda. France tried to justify the zone created around the districts of Cyangugu and Gikangoro and the southern

---

[106] 'Hutus Cheer French at the Border', *Independent*, 24 June 1994.

[107] See S. Smith, 'L'Armee française malvenue au Rwanda', *Libération*, 20 June 1994; J. Chatain, 'Polémique sur les responsabilités françaises', *L'Humanité*, 20 June 1994. I am grateful to Daniela Kroslak for bringing these references to my attention.

[108] This *realpolitik* view of the French action was not surprisingly expressed by Jacques Bihozagara, the RPF's representative in Europe, when he stated that the RPF would treat the French as 'aggressors' and that this 'so-called humanitarian action' is motivated by 'reasons other than humanitarian'. He added: 'The regime which is massacring today has been helped, supported and armed by France. Now we think that France's action is aimed at prolonging its aid to this crumbling regime' quoted in 'Paris troops' Mission "to Last Two Months" ', *Independent*, 24 June 1994.

[109] Prunier, *The Rwanda Crisis*, 279.

[110] M. McNulty, 'France's Rwanda Débâcle: The First Failure of Military Intervention in France's African Domain', 6 Aug. 1998, *http://www.kcl..ac.uk/kis/schools/hums/war/Wsjournal/rwanda.htm*, 13, and Jones, ' "Intervention without Borders" ', 231.

half of the district of Kibuye (some 20 per cent of Rwandan territory), as necessitated by the mass exodus of refugees that was becoming increasingly uncontrollable. It argued that the zone would protect the fleeing population from the fighting and that this was in conformity with Resolution 929. The difficulties with this contention are twofold: first, the Security Council had been explicit in providing authorization for Operation Turquoise that it should be 'impartial', and several members made clear in their statements on Resolution 929 that they were not supporting an 'interposition' force between government forces and the RPF. Yet, in declaring the zone the French Government and its commanders on the ground made clear that the RPF would not be allowed to enter the zone.

The second reason for doubting the humanitarian justifications for the SHZ is that the zone provided a sanctuary for the retreating Rwandan armed forces and militias who had been responsible for the genocide. There is considerable evidence that elements in the French military with the knowledge of government officials were secretly supplying arms to the Rwandan army and militias during the genocide.[111] This had failed to turn the tide of war against the RPF and the strategists in the Elysée hoped to use French intervention to create a secure base for the rump government and its forces to regroup. It is no coincidence that the zone was set up on the day that the RPF took Kigali. As Mel McNulty points out, France's continuing support for the perpetrators of genocide can be seen in the fact that French commanders refused to arrest suspected war criminals, prevent the looting of towns in the zone, or close down the radio station that continued to broadcast hate propaganda, thereby encouraging the Hutu refugees to eliminate any Tutsi living in the zone.[112]

It is clear from the above that, if the legitimacy of humanitarian intervention is defined in terms of the primacy of humanitarian motives, then French intervention fails the test. However, I have argued that there are two key reasons for rejecting an exclusive focus on motives. The first is that motives become significant only if it can be shown that they undermined a positive humanitarian outcome. President Mitterrand claimed that French intervention had rescued 'tens of thousands of lives'.[113] However, Prunier, who was brought into the decision-making on the implementation of Operation Turquoise, considers that at best 'Turquoise might have saved 13,000 or 14,000 lives'.[114] The problem was that the French safeguarded those Tutsi refugees who were in large concentrations, such as the 8,000 near Cyangugu, but they did little for the Tutsi being hunted in the bush.[115] Indeed, Prunier records

---

[111] Kroslak, 'Evaluating the Moral Responsibility'.
[112] McNulty, 'France's Rwanda Débâcle', 13.
[113] Quoted in Prunier, The Rwanda Crisis, 297.
[114] Ibid. 297.
[115] Ibid. 292.

that when soldiers did encounter fleeing Tutsi they often lacked the trucks and lorries to rescue them and would tell them that they would return the next day. But by the time the French returned next morning the Tutsi were usually dead.[116]

In highlighting these limits of the French rescue mission in Rwanda, it is apparent that what was lacking, as Keating had feared in the Security Council debate authorizing the operation, was the 'right means'. The means employed were not consistent with French humanitarian justifications and this severely compromised the outcome in humanitarian terms. And, if we ask why these military means were selected, then the answer is that the French Government's priority was not to save lives but to demonstrate to Africa and the rest of the world that France could still rapidly project military power. It was this non-humanitarian motive behind Operation Turquoise that shaped the ill-suited means of humanitarian intervention—the deployment of a well-armed and equipped fighting force at the expense of the logistics needed for a successful *rescue* mission.

The second reason for rejecting a narrow focus on motivation is that it ignores how changes in normative context enable new possibilities for state action. The motives-first approach interprets French humanitarian justifications as window dressing to disguise selfish reasons for acting. What is missing from this account is how French intervention became possible when it had been ruled out only a few weeks previously. Speaking on 10 May, Mitterrand stated that 'the international community could not act as a global police force and send peacekeepers to all the places where people fight'.[117] This position was supported by Prime Minister Édouard Balladur and Defence Minister François Léotard, who took the view that France could no longer assume the role of a hegemonic power in Africa.[118]

This position became increasingly untenable as abhorrent television pictures of the killings and lobbying by NGOs generated growing domestic pressure on the French government to act. Mitterrand, like Major in the case of the Kurds, recognized an opportunity to seize the moral high ground and repositioned himself as an advocate of humanitarian intervention in Rwanda. Under the legitimating cover supplied by humanitarian justifications, France could act to stop the triumph of the 'Anglophones' by protecting the rump Hutu forces and the Mobuto regime. Against a background of growing media pressure, the Prime Minister, Defence Minister, and especially the Foreign Minister all swung behind the President's growing advocacy of military intervention.

---

[116] Ibid. 293.

[117] Interview with President Mitterrand on French television (A TF1 Et France 2), 10 May 1994. I am grateful to Daniela Kroslak for bringing Mitterrand's statement to my attention.

[118] P. V. Jakobsen, 'National Interest', Humanitarianism or CNN: What Triggers Un Peace Enforcement after the Cold War', *Journal of Peace Research*, 3312 (1996), 210.

French policy-makers would have found it very difficult to legitimate French intervention in the absence of support from public opinion. This raises the question as to why France became so engaged with the suffering in Rwanda when other Western publics had been exposed to similar levels of media coverage without this generating similar pressures for intervention. The reason seems to be that, thanks to the efforts of MSF and high-profile figures in the French humanitarian movement like Bernard Kouchner, there is strong public support in France for Le Devoir d'Ingérence.[119] This is the idea that individuals in distress have a right to humanitarian assistance and that this creates a correlative duty on the part of the international community to deliver it.[120] This is the philosophy behind MSF's practice of bringing humanitarian assistance to victims even in situations where the sovereign government has prohibited access. As I noted in Chapter 5, MSF was born during the Biafran civil war, when a number of doctors working for the ICRC became dissatisfied with the implications of its core principle that aid operations depended upon the consent of the sovereign government. Breaking with this practice, the doctors charted planes and flew into those areas under the control of the secessionist forces. Despite not always respecting the sovereignty rule, MSF always employs non-violent methods. At the same time, it has always opposed forcible intervention, because states cannot be trusted to act for noble purposes. However, the Rwandan genocide so shocked MSF that the organization made a historic call for armed intervention to stop the killing.[121] MSF would have preferred France not to have been involved, because it worried that this would be viewed as partisan by the RPF and serve only to exacerbate further the conflict.[122] Set against this, it recognized that, after weeks of inaction by the UN, a government was finally taking the initiative to save the Tutsi. The mixed feelings of the French doctors are well captured by the then Secretary General, Alain Destexhe. He commented: 'It's a dilemma . . . At least some action is being taken and it is what we have called for. But it may not be the right kind of action.'[123]

If a normative commitment to humanitarian intervention was more deeply rooted in French society than in other Western states, then the reason why the government was so responsive to these public pressures was that the media coverage of the genocide emphasized the government's links with the Habyarimana regime and its responsibility for arming and training the killers. In the same way that British and American journalists pinned specific

---

[119] 'French Aim in Rwanda is to Save Lives', *Guardian*, 20 June 1994, and Jakobsen, 'National Interest', 210.

[120] For a discussion of this idea, see B. Bowring, 'The "Droit et Devoir d'Ingérence": A Timely New Remedy for Africa', *African Journal of International and Comparative Law*, 7/3 (1995), 493–510, and Jakobsen, 'National Interest', 210.

[121] It made this call for armed intervention on 18 June 1994.

[122] 'Paris Troops' Mission 'to Last Two Months'.

[123] 'Hutus Cheer French at the Border'.

responsibility for the plight of the Kurds on Major and Bush, French newspaper and television coverage highlighted France's specific responsibility for the genocide. As a result, the policy of non-intervention lost whatever legitimacy it enjoyed through April and May and it became necessary for the government to act 'in the hope of washing off any genocidal bloodspots in the baptismal waters of "humanitarian" action'.[124] It is necessary to state the now familiar point that this changing normative context enabled new state actions, but it did not determine that Operation Turquoise would be launched. In this case, the public clamour that 'something must be done' fitted in well with Mitterrand's desire to support Francophone interests in Africa. Although French commentators pointed to the glaring contradictions between the humanitarian rhetoric and French actions before and during the genocide, the majority of the public focused on the gratifying pictures of French soldiers rescuing Tutsis, convinced that France had discharged its duty to common humanity.

A key precondition for Security Council approval of Operation Turquoise was a timetable for the withdrawal of French troops. The government had established 21 August as the final deadline, but its forces began leaving Rwanda at the end of July. As they did so, French actions worsened the escalating refugee crisis that had seen a million people cross over into Zaïre to escape the advancing RPF. In makeshift camps around Goma, militia leaders and government soldiers found themselves without food or medicines living side by side with their Tutsi victims. Cholera broke out in the camps and killed thousands in a matter of days and it was television images of this human misery that finally galvanized the USA and Britain into a humanitarian rescue mission with President Clinton sending in US transports and soldiers to assist with the delivery of humanitarian aid.[125] The French provided logistic support for the relief operations in the camps, but their intention to leave on the 21 August created panic in the SHZ, as thousands of Hutus chose to take their chances in the camps in Zaïre rather than stay and face the RPF.[126]

Sensitive to the criticism that Operation Turquoise had only temporarily saved lives, Defence Minister Leotard claimed that 'we did all that was possible to stabilise and reassure the population . . . It is now up to the RPF to make the necessary gestures.'[127] With over half a million refugees leaving the SHZ for Zaïre; with an estimated 30,000 killed by cholera in the camps during July; and with perhaps as few as 13,000 rescued against over a million killed during the previous three months, Operation Turquoise represented a dismal response on the part of the society of states to the Rwandan genocide.

---

[124] Prunier, *The Rwanda Crisis*, 296. This is also the argument of Bruce Jones, who writes that the intervention was 'a humanitarian exercise . . . to downplay the negative publicity of France's support for the Habyarimana regime' (Jones, ' "Intervention without Borders" ', 231).
[125] Prunier, *The Rwanda Crisis*, 304.   [126] Ibid. 311.
[127] Quoted in ibid. 310.

Conclusion

History will record that, in the months leading up to the genocide, the Security Council never even considered changing the mandate of UNAMIR from peacekeeping to preventative humanitarian intervention. Given that the force commander on the ground and human rights NGOs had alerted the Council to the growing risk of mass killing, it stands indicted for its failure to act decisively to protect civilians. Strategists are right to caution us against the dangers of worst-case forecasting in international relations. However, when it comes to responding to warning signals on genocide, it is surely better to assume the worst, given the intolerable consequences of getting it wrong. In early 1994 the Security Council could have changed UNAMIR's mandate by determining that the threat of massive human rights violations constituted a 'threat to the peace' under Article 39 of the UN Charter. This argument would have met considerable resistance from those members sensitive to any erosion of Article 2 (7). But what is clear is that any future development of the Security Council's capacity for preventative humanitarian intervention depends upon such a broad and dynamic interpretation of Article 39.

Having failed to prevent the genocide, the Security Council could have determined that the violations of human rights justified enforcement action under Chapter VII. Indeed, it could have taken the unprecedented step of invoking the Genocide Convention as the basis for such a finding. This was the argument pressed by New Zealand and Czechoslovakia, but their position was open to the rebuttal that neither of these states volunteered forces for intervention. Similarly, whilst a number of African states condemned the UN's decision to cut back UNAMIR in Resolution 912, none of these governments was prepared to mount any intervention in the critical days following the shooting-down of the Presidential jet. In the face of genocide in Rwanda, no African state argued that this was a matter of internal affairs, but neither did anyone come forward to lead an intervention force in those crucial weeks after the genocide began.

With African states unwilling and ill equipped to stop the genocide, responsibility passed to those Western states that had the military capability to bring about a rapid end to the killing. In the cases of northern Iraq and Somalia, media coverage played a critical role in cajoling Western policy-makers into intervention. But even after sustained media coverage of the genocide in late April and May, there was no equivalent public pressure on the Clinton Administration or its allies to intervene to end the genocide. The Western media described what was happening in Rwanda as a genocide, but there was no attempt to pin specific responsibility on Western policy-makers for the killings or to demand military intervention to stop them. Representative of this stance were the editorials in the *New York Times*, which acknowledged that a genocide was taking place, but argued in support of the administration's view that there were no clear political and military objectives that justified risking American soldiers' lives. Although it is clear that an earlier deployment of UNAMIR II would have saved lives, the real time for action was the first two to three weeks after the start of the killings in Kigali— for the tragic fact is that hundreds of thousands had already been killed by the beginning of May, with the genocide spreading like wildfire into the interior of Rwanda.

The only exception to this stance of Western indifference was the French Government, which sought to appease growing public criticisms of its role in supporting and arming the Habyarimana regime by launching an intervention that was justified in humanitarian terms. Governments that lay claim to the humanitarian mantle have a responsibility to live up to these claims and Operation Turquoise failed on this score. The criticism is not that France failed to act earlier to stop the genocide, since this charge could also be levelled at India, Vietnam, and Tanzania in the 1970s, interventions that I have argued qualify as humanitarian. Instead, the accusation is that the non-humanitarian motives behind the French intervention led to means being employed that conflicted with its humanitarian purposes. It might be replied here that there is no convincing basis upon which to differentiate between the legitimacy of the Vietnamese intervention in Cambodia and the French one in Rwanda. It is simply a matter of historical accident that the relationship between motives, means, and outcomes played out positively in the Cambodian context and negatively in the Rwandan one.[128] The problem with this argument is that it overlooks the fact, discussed in detail earlier in the book, that Vietnam never tried to justify its intervention in humanitarian terms. In seeking to occupy the moral high ground, France set itself a more demanding test of legitimacy, and thereby risked having further to fall. This is the basis upon which the solidarist framework developed in Part One distinguishes between the two cases. While it is true that Operation Turquoise saved lives, the solidarist theory of humanitarian intervention does not rely on a strict consequentialist judgement. Instead, it crucially investigates how far there is a contradiction between the motives and means of intervention on the one hand, and a positive humanitarian outcome on the other. In the case of the French intervention in Rwanda, the point is not that lives were saved but that *more lives could have been saved* had France selected military means that were appropriate to its humanitarian claims.

The moral ambiguities of French intervention in Rwanda could have been avoided had Western governments intervened in the days and weeks after 7 April. Accepting that such an intervention depended crucially upon US leadership and capabilities, the buck stops at the door of Clinton's White House.

---

[128] This point was prompted by a conversation with Jack Donnelly.

The President could have decided that the loss of US soldiers in Somalia should not be allowed to stand in the way of sending American soldiers to stop the killing in Rwanda. He would have encountered resistance at home from Congress and public opinion, but Presidents surely have a moral responsibility to lead public opinion and to enlarge their moral imaginations. Clinton should have sought to persuade the American people that here was a cause worth dying for, but, having experimented so disastrously with humanitarian intervention in Somalia, Clinton preferred to argue that the USA had no interests at stake. In doing so, he squandered a golden opportunity to make the case that the moral obligation to protect human rights in Rwanda was in conformity with an enlightened view of US national interests. Instead of setting up human rights and national interest as opposed values, Clinton should have argued that a failure to stand up for justice in Rwanda would risk a contagion that would eventually come to undermine the values that Americans cherish. It is one of those cruel ironies of history that, when Clinton stepped foot on Rwandan soil for the first time on 25 March 1998, his expression of regret for the world's failure to stop the genocide emphasized the dangers of states acting as bystanders. The President asserted that the lesson of Rwanda was that 'each bloodletting hastens the next, and as the value of human life is degraded and violence becomes tolerated, the unimaginable becomes more conceivable'.[129]

Stopping genocide requires a willingness to use force and to risk soldiers' lives and it was this that was completely lacking in the Clinton Administration in April 1994. I referred in the previous chapter to Michael Desch's argument that the initial US intervention in Somalia did not violate the realist canon because it did not pose a risk to core US interests. However, what Desch overlooks is that the critical precondition for this action was the conviction that the risk to soldiers' lives was minimal. In the end, this assessment proved tragically wrong, as the USA lost soldiers in the summer of 1993. As a result of this, when it came to decisions on Rwanda, it was the spectre of more body bags that haunted the administration. Indeed, an important indicator of this was its opposition to the rapid deployment of UNAMIR II, because it did not want to land US transports into Kigali airport under fire. This would have placed US air and ground crew at some risk, but it would have made possible a deployment that could have saved the thousands of lives lost through late May. This illustrates the severe limits on the US willingness to sacrifice for those who find themselves in danger in parts of the world that are peripheral to US security interests.

The arrival of a multinational rapid reaction force led by the USA and including other NATO states such as Britain and Canada could, as Dallaire pleaded at the time, have stopped the Hutu killing machine in its tracks. In

---

[129] Quoted in Gourevitch, *We Wish to Inform you*, 351.

risking soldiers' lives to stop a genocide where no direct strategic or economic interests were involved, Western intervention would have sent a clear signal to other would-be perpetrators of this crime that the world was finally ready to back up the 1948 Convention with the threat and use of force. It was the refusal of Western governments to accept this cost that was the obstacle to humanitarian intervention in Rwanda.

Had Western states decided to act over Rwanda, they would have secured a Chapter VII mandate. It is inconceivable that the Security Council would have blocked this, given the way it responded to the French request for a mandate, despite considerable misgivings about the humanitarian character of Operation Turquoise. In April and May 1994, members would have been only too happy to authorize African or Western states to intervene to end the killing. Certainly, no member of the Security Council wanted to be publicly exposed as blocking military intervention out of doctrinal concerns for Article 2 (7) of the Charter. This echoes the argument I advanced in relation to the Iraqi case which is that a growing awareness of the pressures of world public opinion can shame the Security Council into adopting resolutions that push out the boundaries of legitimate intervention in the society of states.

This claim is further supported by the final case study of the book, which examines how a Security Council that was overprotective of the sovereignty rule at the beginning of the war in the former Yugoslavia came, with the important exceptions of Russia and China, to legitimate NATO's use of force against the Government of the Federal Republic of Yugoslavia in March 1999.

8

The Limits of Humanitarian Intervention from the Air: The Cases of Bosnia and Kosovo

The question of humanitarian intervention in the former Yugoslavia preoccupied policy-makers, human rights activists, journalists, and academics through the 1990s. Despite repeated calls for armed intervention to stop 'ethnic cleansing'[1] in Croatia and Bosnia-Hercegovina, Western governments refused to commit their ground forces in anything other than a peacekeeping role. There was no question of sending troops to protect civilians besieged in the towns and cities of the former Yugoslavia, victims of a virulent form of Serbian and Croatian nationalism. Instead, the Clinton Administration argued that the horrors could be stopped by the use of Western air strikes and the arming of the Bosnian Government army. NATO, acting with Security Council authority, did initiate widespread air strikes against Bosnian Serb targets in 1995, and it is claimed that this action was decisive in persuading the President of the rump Yugoslav state, Slobodan Milosevic, to negotiate a peace settlement under US auspices at Dayton, Ohio, in 1995. The lesson many concluded from the endgame of the Bosnian War was that the use of force had worked to induce Serbian compliance. The belief that Milosevic would back down in the face of a credible threat became the article of faith that was put to the test when NATO went to war against the Federal Republic of Yugoslavia (FRY) in March 1999.

From the perspective of this book, the significance of NATO's bombing campaign is immense: for the first time since the founding of the UN, a group of states explicitly justified their use of force against another state on humanitarian grounds in a context where there was no explicit Security Council authorization. Moreover, NATO's action was for the most part greeted with either approval or acquiescence by the society of states. Given the ground-breaking

---

[1] The term has been defined by the UN Commission of Experts as 'rendering an area ethnically homogeneous by using force or intimidation to remove from a given area persons of another ethnic or religious group' (quoted in M. Kaldor, *New and Old Wars: Organized Violence in a Global Era* (Cambridge: Polity Press, 1999), 33).

character of NATO's use of force, the purpose of this chapter is to map the changing context that led NATO to raise humanitarian claims, and to examine how it was that seven members of the Security Council came to vote with NATO against a Russian draft resolution calling for a cessation of hostilities.

The chapter focuses on two key questions that structure its chronological ordering: first, how far did Western intervention in the Bosnian war establish new precedents for humanitarian intervention? Did the deployment of peacekeeping forces to protect humanitarian relief convoys, the 'safe-areas' policy, and the use of air power against Serb targets in 1994 and 1995 push out the boundaries of intervention in ways that rivalled the cases of Iraq and Somalia? Or, is it NATO's intervention in Kosovo that marks the crucial turning point in changing the normative context of humanitarian intervention in the former Yugoslavia?

The second question is whether Western intervention was successful in promoting humanitarian values. Western governments justified their actions in Croatia and Bosnia on the grounds that placing their soldiers in harm's way would not have stopped the ethnically motivated violence, but how persuasive were these rationales? Did they mask a deeper reluctance on the part of Western governments to become engaged in armed rescue when no vital interests were perceived to be at stake? The strong inhibitions in Western capitals against committing ground troops was evident in NATO's reliance on air power in Bosnia, and especially during the war over Kosovo. Air power is attractive to policy-makers because it holds out the promise of 'casualty-free' humanitarian intervention, but it failed to stop the atrocities and mass expulsion of civilians in both Bosnia and Kosovo. In the case of the latter, the means of humanitarian intervention was the deeply problematical one of bombing. This resulted in civilian casualties, raising the question, as in the Somali case, whether violent means can ever serve humanitarian ends. It also revealed the profound gap between the moral rhetoric of Western leaders and their commitment to sacrifice for non-citizens in danger.

International Responses to the Serb–Croat War, June 1991–April 1992

The international dimension of the Yugoslav crisis was triggered by the Croatian and Slovenian declarations of independence on 25 June 1991. The background to these decisions has been extensively dealt with elsewhere, but what is important for our purposes is that these actions placed two of international society's legitimating principles at loggerheads with each other: the principle of maintaining the territorial integrity of states and the right of peoples to self-determination. The Yugoslav state was made up of six constituent nations (Serbs, Croats, Slovenes, Montenegrins, Macedonians, and, later, Bosnian Muslims) and was politically and administratively organized on the basis of republics in a federal system of government that had a rotating Presidency. After the founding of the Yugoslav state at the end of the first World War, the Croats found themselves increasingly excluded by the Serbs, who controlled the government, army, and economy of the infant state. This deepening conflict culminated in many Croats and Serbs taking opposing sides during the Second World War. The Usashe state installed in Croatia by the Nazis was responsible for the killing of at least 300,000 Serbs.[2] After the war, Tito, a Croat who had led the Partisans against the Nazis, became leader of the new Yugoslav state. He tried to heal the scars of the civil war by creating a new socialist identity for all his people as 'Yugoslavs'. Tito's project of nation building was an attempt to pacify the ethnic enmities unleashed during the Second World War. He achieved some success in this ambitious project, as different national groups intermarried and lived peacefully if not harmoniously together. The death of Tito in 1981 and the growth of the 'Serbian Renewal Movement' in 1986 spelt the end of Tito's attempt to forge a new Yugoslav identity. This revival of Serb nationalism frightened Slovenes and Croats, who responded with their own brand of ethnic nationalism.

The key architect of the demise of the Yugoslav ideal was the Serbian leader, Slobodan Milosevic, who had taken power in 1987 and who seized the opportunity to forge an alliance with Serb nationalists who dreamed of a 'Greater Serbia'.[3] Milosevic's first target was the autonomous provinces of Kosovo and Vojvodina, which had been granted powers under the 1974 constitution that enabled them to have their own courts, police forces, and territorial defence. There was growing dissatisfaction with this state of affairs on the part of the Serb minority living in Kosovo, which felt that it should have greater privileges and faced growing economic hardships. Many emigrated to Serbia, and this, coupled with the Albanians, high birth rate, meant that the total Serb population fell below 10 per cent. Those who stayed faced a general climate of hostility and this provided grist for the Serbian propaganda mill in Belgrade.[4] Milosevic exploited the Serbs' resentment and

---

[2] There were two independent studies carried out in Croatia and Serbia in the 1980s that came to the conclusion that 480,000 Serbs were killed in total during the Second World War. Ivo Banac estimates that 120,000 of all nationalities were killed in the concentration camps run by the Ustashe. See M. Tanner, *Croatia: A Nation Forged in War* (London: Yale University Press, 1997), 152. I am grateful to Alex Bellamy for drawing these figures to my attention.

[3] C. Cviic, *An Awful Warning: The War in Ex-Yugoslavia* (London: CPS Policy Study No. 139; Centre for Policy Studies, 1994), 8.

[4] See T. Judah, *The Serbs: History, Myth and the Destruction of Yugoslavia* (London: Yale University Press, 1997), 149–64. Alex Bellamy reveals that it was not just Serbs who left Kosovo. He cites an independent Pristina newspaper as showing that 300,000 Albanians left the province. See A. J. Bellamy, 'If you Tolerate this . . . Two Decades of Human Wrongs in Kosovo', *International Journal of Human Rights*, 4/3–4 (2000), n. 74.

stripped the Albanians of their rights under the 1974 constitution.[5] At a rally in June 1989 held at Kosovo Polje (the scene of the battle where the Serbs had been 'gloriously' defeated by the Turk 600 years earlier and which has gone into Serbian folklore as a symbol of Serb defiance in the face of enemies), Milosevic told the crowds that Kosovo had been restored to its rightful place at the heart of the Serbian nation.

With hindsight, the rally marked the beginning of a decade-long struggle between the West and the policies pursued directly and indirectly by Milosevic. In retrospect it is easy to argue that international society should have reacted to the crackdown in Kosovo. There were moves in the US Congress to cut off financial aid to the federal government in Belgrade in the hope that the latter might prevail on Milosevic, now leader of the Serbian republic, to stop his repression of the Kosovars. US bilateral aid was quite limited, but some members of Congress wanted the Bush Administration to push for the withdrawal of IMF and World Bank finance from Yugoslavia. However, Bush accepted the Yugoslav President's plea that the people of Yugoslavia should not be made to suffer for Milosevic's abuse of human rights, and that denial of IMF loans might push the ailing economy further into crisis, thereby increasing the risks of civil war.[6] Whatever the practical difficulties in imposing sanctions on Milosevic for his treatment of the Kosovo Albanians, it is clear that an opportunity was missed that might have served to foster a more moderate republican leadership in Belgrade; or, at the very least, put Milosevic on notice that there was a high price to pay for human rights abuses.

The Slovenian and Croatian declarations of independence provided an ideal opportunity for the ethnic nationalists in Belgrade to continue their campaign of achieving a 'Greater Serbia'. Slovenia was a sideshow because it was ethnically homogenous and its population was well armed and committed to independence. Croatia, however, was very different, since the 600,000 Serbs living there feared for their political future in an independent Croatian state. Milosevic's accomplices were on hand to remind the Serb minority of what had happened to them at the hands of the Croats during the Second World War and the Jugoslavenski Narodna Armija (JNA) (Yugoslav Peoples Army) was ready to provide arms to enable them to defend their land. There can be no doubt that the Croatian government of Franjo Tudjman could have done much more to reassure the Serbs that their rights would be protected. Certainly, the crass insensitivity displayed by the ruling Hrvatsja Demokratska Zajednica (HDZ) (Croatian Democratic Union) party played an important part in pushing the Serbs to use force to secede from the Croatian

    [5] See Bellamy, 'If you Tolerate this'; M. Vickers, *Between Serb and Albanian: A History of Kosovo* (London: Hurst & Co., 1998), 231–40; L. Silber and A. Little, *The Death of Yugoslavia* (London: Penguin for the BBC, 1995), 60–73.
    [6] J. Gow, *Legitimacy and the Military: The Yugoslav Crisis* (London: Belhaven Press, 1992), 306.

state. Having said that, it was the Croatian Serbs who bear the greatest responsibility for what followed, since, by resorting to force to protect their rights, they lit the powder keg of a decade of war and destruction.[7]

During the summer of 1991, Serb paramilitaries and JNA forces conducted a military campaign aimed at controlling the so-called Krajina region, which was economically and strategically important to any future Serb statelet in Croatia. The international response was to condemn the violence while issuing statements in support of maintaining the territorial integrity of Yugoslavia. The Conference on Security and Cooperation in Europe (CSCE) and the EC tried to broker ceasefires' and this was backed up by the sending of EC monitors to oversee any agreements negotiated on the ground. But, as the Serb campaign of ethnic cleansing continued relentlessly through the summer, it must have been very clear to Milosevic and his loyal generals in the JNA that there was going to be no military response from the West. There was some discussion of this option in the WEU in July and September 1991. France supported by Germany, the Netherlands, and Italy proposed that the WEU send a force to impose peace. However, this was opposed by the UK, which, with its experience of Northern Ireland in mind, argued that a force could not be sent if there was no peace to keep. Two months later, when under pressure from Labour MPs for naval action to relieve the siege of Dubrovnik, Prime Minister Major argued in the House of Commons that Western intervention 'would extend the fighting perhaps to Bosnia, Macedonia, or elsewhere'.[8] The problem with the British position was that it revealed to the Belgrade leadership that Western diplomacy lacked the will to escalate to the use of force and this provided the Serbs with no incentive to stop their campaign of violence.[9] Moreover, Major's argument that Western military intervention would serve only to escalate the war is open to the objection that the West's failure to act in Croatia only emboldened the Serbs to believe that they could extend their campaign to Bosnia.

There were alternative strategies open to the Western powers that might have stopped the Serbian military machine in its tracks. However, acting upon these would have required Western states to push out the boundaries of humanitarian intervention. The first move in a more robust interventionary strategy would have been to recognize the secessionist republics as sovereign states, thereby turning the conflict into an interstate war. Next, the West

---

[7] This argument finds support in Mark Thompson's account based on an interview with Tudjman's foreign policy adviser, Mario Nobilo. In reply to the question as to whether the Croatian Government could have done more to reassure the Serbs, Mr Nobilo replied: 'There *might* be fewer Serbs manning the blockades if we had taken better account of their reactions to our emotional explosion when we won the elections . . . If we had celebrated for three months less . . . But in my opinion it woundn't change the problem because Belgrade's policy would have been the same' (quoted in M. Thompson, *A Paper House: The Ending of Yugoslavia* (London: Vintage, 1992), 279). I am grateful to Alex Bellamy for bringing this to my attention.

[8] 'EC Troops May Go to Yugoslavia', *Independent*, 13 Nov. 1991.

[9] Cviic, *An Awful Warning*, 25.

could have promised to arm the secessionist republics if the JNA and the Serb paramilitaries did not cease their aggression. This could have been backed by a threat of air strikes against Serbian military targets and supply lines. None of this would have required a ground commitment by Western troops and the use of air power would have sent a powerful signal to Milosevic that the West would not tolerate a redrawing of Yugoslav's internal borders by force. If, as Christopher Cviic argues, the Belgrade political and military leadership was deeply worried about the West's reaction to its plan to create 'Greater Serbia', then there are good grounds for thinking that Milosevic might have backed down in the face of a determined Western threat to use force.[10] However, what if this strategy had failed to stop the advance of Serb forces? Having committed Western aircraft to battle, could Western governments have stood by whilst ethnic cleansing took place? Or, would the pressure to send ground troops have become irresistible, with Britain and France spearheading a European force to fight alongside the Croats?

Although the West would have justified any use of force against the Serbs as a defence of Croatian sovereignty, this would have been viewed with considerable suspicion by a society of states fearful of setting precedents that might unleash a wave of secessionist movements. For states like the Soviet Union, China, Romania, and India, who were all members of the Security Council at this time, there could be no question of recognizing Croatia and Slovenia as sovereign states, since this might have implications for their own restive nationalities. Instead of arming the Croats and Slovenes, Western powers tried to keep the lid on the conflict by imposing a mandatory arms embargo on the former Yugoslavia, and this was agreed by the Security Council in Resolution 713, adopted on 25 September 1991. What emerges clearly from the Security Council's discussion is its considerable sensitivities on the sovereignty question. The arms embargo was justified by Western states as a measure contributing to 'international peace and security', and several non-Western states were explicit that their support for this action in no way implied any erosion of the sovereignty rule.[11] Consequently, it is apparent, that had Western governments armed the Croats or, more significantly, employed air strikes against Serbian targets in late 1991, this would have been interpreted by many Council members as interference in the internal affairs of a sovereign state.

---

[10] Ibid. 26.

[11] For example, Zimbabwe stated that it insisted 'on the sovereignty of nations, big or small, and even if a country is in grave difficulties, as Yugoslavia is, we would not like to see its interests being trampled underfoot'. Moreover, India went to the heart of what was permitted by Article 2 (7) when it stated: Let us therefore note here today in unmistakable terms that the Council's consideration of the matter relates not to Yugoslavia's internal situation as such, but specifically to its implications for peace and security in the region.' This position was strongly supported by China, which emphasized the fact that the Yugoslav Government had consented to the arms embargo. See S/PV.3009, 25 Sept.1991.

Having carved out ethnically pure Serbian enclaves in Croatia, Milosevic was ready to agree terms and this led to the deployment of a UN peacekeeping force in January 1992. At the same time, international society reluctantly acknowledged the demise of Tito's Yugoslavia by recognizing Croatia and Slovenia as independent. Some months earlier, the EC had set up an Arbitration Commission chaired by the French constitutional lawyer, Robert Badinter, to investigate the criteria under which recognition might be given to the former republics of the Socialist Federal Republic of Yugoslavia (SFRY). The problem that faced Badinter was how to reconcile international society's commitment to the principles of both self-determination and territorial integrity: if nations were to be given the right to self-determination, then Serbia could legitimately claim that Serbs outside Serbia also had this right. This argument legitimated the majority Serb population living in the Krajina seceding from an independent Croatia. Not surprisingly, the EC's Arbitration Commission decided that this was a can of worms that was best left unopened, since accepting this right to self-determination challenged territoriality as the basis of claims to statehood in the society of states. Instead, the Badinter Commission applied the principle of *uti possidetis juris* in reaching its legal judgment on the right of self-determination. This rule emerged out of the process of decolonization and establishes that self-determination applies to the existing borders at the time of independence. In applying *uti possidetis* to the case of the former Yugoslavia, the EC accepted Badinter's recommendation that the inter-republican borders become the legally recognized borders of the new states.[12]

The implication of the EC decision was that Serbs living outside Serbia would have to accept the status of a minority group. The Badinter Commission proposed that recognition be conditional on the republics providing constitutional guarantees for their minorities. But this was not acceptable to those Serbs committed to the vision of a 'Greater Serbia'. In their submission to the Commission, the Serbs rejected the principle of *uti possidetis* on the grounds that they were a constituent nation of the Yugoslav federation, which had an equal right to self-determination as the other nationalities.[13] The flaw in this legal argument was that the Badinter Commission was not according a right of self-determination to Croats and Slovenes on the basis of their nationality; instead, it was according the right to the republics of Croatia and Slovenia on the basis of their territorial claims to statehood.

Having failed to win the legal argument, those Serbs committed to ethnic nationalism decided to contest the EC's decision by force of arms. The test

[12] The legal issues raised by the Badinter Commission are discussed in M. Weller, 'The International Response to the Dissolution of the Socialist Federal Republic of Yugoslavia', *American Journal of International Law*, 86/3 (1992), 569–607.

[13] Ibid. 590–1.

came in Bosnia, where the EC's offer of recognition confronted the Serbs with the prospect of living in a state dominated by Muslims and Croats.

Protecting Humanitarian Values by Force in Bosnia, 1992–1995

The EC decision to recognize the republics as independent states was a permissive cause of the war in Bosnia, but the local actors, especially militant Serbs, had been preparing for a showdown since the outbreak of the war in Croatia. The JNA had been planning since late 1991 for a campaign of annexation and conquest and it had been covertly arming Bosnian Serb forces loyal to Radovan Karadzic, the leader of the main Serbian party the Srpska Demokratska Zajednica (SDS) (Serbian Democratic Party).[14] The Bosnian Government held a referendum on independence in early 1992 that was boycotted by those Serbs who followed Karadzic. Of the 64 per cent who voted in the referendum, 99 per cent supported independence.[15] It is important to realize that the SDS vision of Serb identity was contested by thousands of Serbs who lived in the cities and voted in the referendum. These citizens saw no conflict between their identities as both Serbs and Bosnians, and, believing in a Bosnia committed to the values of toleration and multiculturalism, they strongly opposed Karadzic's form of ethnic nationalism.

The SDS argued that the referendum was unconstitutional and on 27 March Karadzic proclaimed the existence of a Bosnian Serb republic. More ominously, General Blagoje Adzic, the head of the JNA, declared on 30 March that his army would protect the Serbs.[16] Although the main responsibility for Bosnia's descent into hell must lie with the SDS forces and its backers in Belgrade, the new Muslim government of Alija Izetbegovic responded to the escalation of threats by making its own preparations for war.

Standing against this growing radicalization of Serb and Muslim groups was the commitment of the urban and educated citizens of Bosnia to a secular and pluralist state. Fearing the worst, 50,000–100,000 people marched through Sarajevo on 5 April to demand a resignation of the Bosnian government and the imposition of an international protectorate to prevent the slide into war.[17] The war began when Serb snipers fired on the demonstrators and the fighting quickly spread to other parts of Bosnia as the JNA and paramilitaries seized control of arms factories and communications centres. The next day the EC and the USA recognized Bosnia, but, at the very moment that the

---

[14] Cviic, *An Awful Warning*, 32.   [15] Ibid.   [16] Ibid.
[17] Kaldor, *New and Old Wars*, 43–4. She reports that thousands more came in buses but could not enter the cities because of Serb and Muslim barricades.

outside world acknowledged its sovereignty, the citizens of Bosnia found themselves in a situation where the rule of the gun had replaced the rule of law.

Reflecting on the lessons of the Bosnian War, Mary Kaldor argues that the cardinal mistake made by Western governments was to see the attacks against civilians as 'a side-effect of the fighting, not as the goal of the war'. She claims that the defining character of the Bosnian war was that the violence 'was directed not against opposing sides, but against civilian populations'.[18] By interpreting the killing and mass expulsion of civilians as a result of civil war, Western governments failed to understand that this was a war fought against civilians. Examples of this framing of the conflict are Prime Minister Major's statement to the House of Commons in June 1993 that the war was caused by the re-emergence of 'ancient hatreds in the old Yugoslavia' and Acting US Secretary of State Lawrence Eagleburger's comment in August 1992 that Bosnia was 'a civil war based on 500 to 1,000 years of history'.[19] The implication was that outsiders could do little to stop the carnage, and any commitment of troops would lead to them becoming bogged down in a Vietnam-style quagmire. British Defence Secretary, Malcolm Rifkind, speaking on a visit to Bosnia in early 1993, stated that imposing peace in a 'civil-war' by the use of force would be 'inappropriate', because it would require over 100,000 troops and the 'commitment would be open-ended . . . could last for very many years and there would be the certainty . . . of significant casualties'.[20]

By the end of 1992, the Bosnian Serb army had ethnically cleansed its way through large tracts of Bosnian territory. In this context, reversing Serb gains would have required a willingness to take on forces supported by JNA heavy artillery and organized and supplied by Belgrade. It is not surprising that governments on both sides of the Atlantic baulked from such a commitment, and the lesson to be drawn from this is that military intervention should have come earlier, before the violence broke out in April 1992. Although not without risks and costs, the society of states should have imposed an international protectorate in early 1992. The purpose of such a protectorate would have been to protect civilians from ethnic cleansing and to establish a framework of law and order in which the different political groups could arrive at a lasting settlement. This would have necessitated a long-term policing role, and there would have been the risk of casualties from extremist groups determined to wreck the creation of a law-governed multiethnic state. The costs

---

[18] Ibid. 58, 50. Kaldor recognizes that there were pockets of fighting around key strategic points, like the Brcko corridor, which linked Serb territories in Croatia and Bosnia, but the key strategy was the ethnic cleansing of towns and villages.

[19] Major's statement is cited in T. Barber, 'Bosnian Guilt: Ancient Hatreds or Wicked Leaders?', *Independent*, 14 Mar. 1991, and Eagleburger's comment is cited in 'UN may Back Force in Bosnia, *Financial Times*, 10 Aug. 1992.

[20] 'Rifkind Puts on a Show in the Snow', *Independent*, 9 Dec. 1992.

and risks of this preventative humanitarian intervention have to be set against the subsequent carnage of the Bosnian War and the fact that Western forces eventually took on such a policing role in Bosnia through the Implementation Force (IFOR) and the Stabilization Force (SFOR).[21] Christopher Cviic argues that such a solution would have attracted support from Muslims, Croats, and Serbs in early 1992 and that it would have served to neutralize the influence of the extremists.[22]

Would the creation of an international protectorate in early 1992 have secured international legitimacy? The West could have acted unilaterally, but the success and legality of any such venture would have been greatly improved had the Russians supported it. Without Russian support—ideally this would have involved Russian troops working alongside NATO forces, as subsequently occurred in Bosnia and Kosovo—Security Council authorization might have been blocked by the threat or use of the Russian veto. In addition, without Russian cooperation there was the risk that Moscow might view such an intervention as an extension of the Western sphere of influence into the Balkans. It will never be known how Russia would have reacted to a Western offer to join it in policing the former Yugoslavia, since the precondition for a protectorate was US political and military leadership, and the Bush Administration was adamant that it would not send ground forces to Bosnia.

As Western publics were increasingly exposed to media coverage of the atrocities of the war, a key turning point being the discovery by journalists and television reporters of a Serb detention centre for Muslim prisoners in August 1992, the British and French governments proposed to send armed escorts to protect the relief convoys of the office of the United Nations High Commissioner for Refugees (UNHCR). Both governments were determined to avoid deploying ground troops in a combat role, but at the same time neither felt that it could be seen to be doing nothing in the face of the worst abuses of human rights in Europe since the end of the Second World War. Although the consent of the Bosnian Government could have been argued to provide sufficient legal justification for the deployment of armed escorts, Britain and France preferred to work through the Security Council. There was growing pressure from Muslim states on the Council for tougher action against the Serbs. This resulted in Resolution 770, adopted on 13 August 1992 by twelve votes and three abstentions.[23] This resolution crossed the rubicon on the use

---

[21] IFOR was given the mandate to implement the military aspects of the Dayton peace agreement (Annex 1A) by Resolution 1031. A NATO-led multinational force began its mission on 20 Dec. 1995 with a one-year mandate. After the Bosnian elections in 1996 IFOR completed its mandated mission, but it was clear that the political environment in Bosnia-Hercegovina remained unstable, necessitating a continued foreign military presence. The North Atlantic Council carried out a lengthy study, which culminated with the activation of SFOR on 20 Dec. 1996. According to Council Resolution 1088 (12 Dec. 1996), SFOR has the same robust rules of engagement enjoyed by IFOR.   [22] Cviic, *An Awful Warning*, 35.

[23] China abstained on the grounds that it could not agree to the authorization of force contained in the resolution, arguing that the resort to force would only escalate the conflict in Bosnia. India

of force in Bosnia, authorizing member states under Chapter VII of the Charter to 'use all necessary means' to deliver humanitarian aid to the civilians of Bosnia.[24] Since this action was warmly welcomed by the internationally recognized government, the Security Council was not setting a radically new precedent for humanitarian intervention. However, it was the first time that states had been authorized by the Council to use force to deliver humanitarian aid (the US intervention in Somalia came four months later) and it marked the beginning of a greater engagement by the Security Council with the suffering of civilians in Bosnia.

Yet, when it came to drawing up rules of engagement for their soldiers in the United Nations Protection Force (UNPROFOR II), the French and British governments restricted their forces to a classic peacekeeping mission of only using force in self-defence. Lord Owen, who was the EU's lead negotiator in Bosnia from 1992 to 1995 argues that it was critical that the UN was seen to be impartial in Bosnia, because the route for aid convoys crossed miles of Serb territory, where the convoys were vulnerable to attack from the surrounding mountain ranges.[25]

During the winter of 1992–3, when hundreds of thousands of Bosnians were at risk from starvation, there can be no doubt that the UN operation played an important part in keeping people alive. However, critics argue that, even if the UN prevented starvation by feeding people in besieged towns and cities, it did little or nothing to stop the Bosnian Serbs from shelling these areas and ethnically cleansing them of Muslims. During the 1992 Presidential election campaign, Governor Clinton and his advisers pressed the case for lifting the arms embargo against the Bosnian Government and using NATO air power to reverse Serbian ethnic cleansing. Air strikes were strongly opposed by Britain and France, who feared for the safety of their military personnel on the ground and that of UN aid workers. Speaking in the House of Commons on 2 December 1992, the Prime Minister set out his position on the use of air power in the Bosnian War. Major stated that those 'who talk glibly about bombing from the air really should consider the risk of retaliation to our own troops, there at present, delivering humanitarian aid'.[26] To be fair to the advocates of air strikes in the Clinton Administration, they recognized that the precursor to this policy would have to be the withdrawal of UNPROFOR. If air strikes could have saved civilians from Serb attack, then this strategy had much to recommend it. But, as Lord Owen argued at the time, the best strategy for protecting the safe areas was to deploy ground troops to protect

and Zimbabwe both expressed reservations that the resolution authorized member states to use force, but did not establish any procedures by which member states could be held accountable to the Security Council for their actions. See statements by the Indian, Zimbabwean, and Chinese Ambassadors to the Security Council in S/PV.3106, 13 Aug.1992, 11–18, 49–50.

[24] Resolution 770 (13 Aug. 1992).

[25] D. Owen, *Balkan Odyssey* (London: Indigo, 1996), 388.

[26] 'British Military Intervention in Bosnia Ruled Out', *Independent*, 4 Dec. 1992.

these.[27] However, Clinton ruled out from the beginning the deployment of US troops into a combat environment, believing that the risks of an open-ended commitment were too high, and that the American public would not support the spilling of American blood to stop Bosnians killing Bosnians.

The debilitating effects of this major constraint on Western strategy can be seen in the débâcle of the so-called safe-areas policy. The origins of this attempt by the UN Security Council to apply the precedent of safe havens in Iraq to Bosnia can be traced to Serb attacks against Srebrenica in April 1993. The commander of the Bosnian Serb army, General Mladic, was putting pressure on Muslim-dominated towns in eastern Bosnia by heavy shelling, which was resulting in large numbers of civilian casualties. As part of this strategy of putting the squeeze on the Muslims, Mladic refused access to UN humanitarian relief convoys.[28] Clinton's advisers, especially UN Ambassador Madeleine Albright, were keen to interdict Bosnian Serb supply lines from the air and to lift the arms embargo on the Bosnian Government.[29] This was opposed by Britain and France, who feared that air strikes would lead to retaliation against their soldiers and UN aid workers trying to deliver relief aid to the eastern enclaves.[30] They also opposed lifting the arms embargo, fearing, in Douglas Hurd's widely quoted phrase, that this would only serve to escalate the conflict by creating a 'level killing field'.[31]

The safe-areas policy developed from two key impulses: first, it was an attempt to defuse American pressure for 'lift and strike' by declaring the towns under threat in eastern Bosnia as under UN protection;[32] secondly, the idea was attractive to the non-aligned group on the Council (Venezuela, Cape Verde, Djibouti, Morocco, and Pakistan), who were shocked by television coverage of the heavy shelling of Muslim towns in Bosnia.[33] The first step was Resolution 819, which declared on 16 April 1993 that Srebrenica was a safe area.[34] To give substance to this, the UN deployed 147 Canadian peacekeepers to reassure General Mladic that the Bosnian army would not be allowed to use Srebenica as a base for operations against his forces.[35] A month later in

---

[27] Owen, *Balkan Odyssey*, 388–9.

[28] J. Gow, *Triumph of the Lack of Will: International Diplomacy and the Yugoslav War* (London: Hurst & Co., 1997), 142, and M. R. Berdal, 'The Security Council, Peacekeeping and Internal Conflict after the Cold War', *Duke Journal of Comparative International Law*, 7/1 (1996), 79.

[29] Berdal, 'The Security Council', 79–80.   [30] Owen, *Balkan Odyssey*, 145

[31] The Hurd comment is cited in S. L. Woodward, *Balkan Tragedy: Chaos and Dissolution after the Cold War* (Washington: Brookings Institute, 1995), 306. In early May, US Secretary of State Warren Christopher visited European capitals in an effort to secure backing for the Clinton Administration's policy of so-called lift and strike but the discussions revealed the deep disagreements among the allies over the use of air power in the Bosnian war. See Berdal, 'The Security Council', 80.

[32] See Berdal, 'The Security Council', 80.

[33] Ibid. 81. The Venezuelan, Cape Verde, and Djibouti Ambassadors all confirmed the key role played by the non-aligned group in the adoption of Resolutions 819 and 824 in their statements to the Security Council supporting Resolution 836. See S/PV.3228, 4 June 1993, 15, 34–5, 37.

[34] See J. W. Honig and N. Both, *Srebrenica: Record of a War Crime* (London: Penguin, 1996), 5.

[35] Gow, *Triumph*, 144.

Resolution 824 the Security Council followed up its declaration on Srebrenica by adding Bihac, Tuzla, Sarajevo, Zepa, and Gorazde to the list of safe areas. Resolutions 819 and 824 were both passed under Chapter VII of the UN Charter, but neither resolution provided for enforcement action in the event that any of the parties violated the Council's demand that these towns 'be free from armed attacks and from any other hostile act'.[36] After a short-lived ceasefire had collapsed in late May, there was a further increase in attacks against civilians, and the Security Council responded by finally authorizing military enforcement action in defence of the safe areas.[37]

Resolution 836 passed on 4 June 1993 with two abstentions, extended UNPROFOR's mandate in operative paragraph 5 'to deter attacks against the safe areas', and in paragraph 9 it empowered UNPROFOR, 'acting in self-defence, to take the necessary measures, including the use of force, in reply to bombardments against the safe areas . . . or to armed incursion into them'. To fulfil this new mandate, member states, acting nationally or through regional organizations, were empowered to take: 'under the authority of the Security Council and subject to close coordination with the Secretary-General and UNPROFOR, all necessary measures, through the use of air power, in and around the safe areas in the Republic of Bosnia and Herzegovina, to support UNPROFOR in the performance of its mandate set out in paragraphs 5 and 9 above. It is clear from statements in the Security Council that members interpreted this mandate as being restricted to close air support in defence of UNPROFOR personnel.[38] In order to protect the eastern enclaves of Bosnia, it was necessary for the UN to accomplish two tasks: first, it had to signal to the attacking Serb forces that any attacks would be repelled, and this could most effectively be done by deploying ground forces with close air support. Secondly, given that the UN was determined to continue its mission of delivering relief aid in Serbian-controlled areas, it was vital that it was not perceived by the Serbs as taking sides in the war, since this would risk the humanitarian relief mission. To reassure the Serbs that the safe areas would not be used by the Bosnian Government as a secure base for offensive operations, it was vital that these were demilitarized.[39] Consequently, what was required was a significant increase in UN troops on the ground, and, three days after the passing of Resolution 836, the Secretariat reported that to defend and demilitarize the safe areas would require an additional 32,000 troops.[40] In the end, fewer than 3,500 additional troops were sent to Bosnia and this was palpably insufficient either to disarm the safe areas or to deter Mladic from attacking them.

---

[36] Cited in Honig and Both, *Srebrenica*, 5.   [37] Berdal, 'The Security Council', 81.

[38] As James Gow points out, this interpretation of the mandate is clearly reflected in the statement by the North Atlantic Council (NAC) on 10 June, when it stated that air attacks would be authorized only in defence of UNPROFOR troops protecting the safe areas. See Gow, *Triumph*, 136.

[39] In the case of Gorazde, the Bosnian Government forces even maintained a weapons factory inside the town. See 'Dustbin for a World of Dirty Politics', *Independent*, 6 May 1994.

[40] Berdal, 'The Security Council', 82.

The Security Council, then, was faced with a major dilemma, since its peacekeepers in the safe areas were at risk, as was its promise to protect civilians. The only military option available to the UN was NATO air strikes and these produced mixed results. On the positive side, NATO's air attacks against Bosnian Serb forces attacking Gorazde in April 1994 halted the offensive and brought an important measure of relief to the civilian population.[41] The pressure was stepped up in August 1994, when NATO attacked Serb forces around Sarajevo as part of enforcing a UN-imposed exclusion zone against heavy weaponry.[42] Moreover, the air campaign was significantly intensified after a Bosnian Serb attack against Sarajevo in August 1995 that killed thirty-seven people. NATO and UNPROFOR (which had been reinforced by a mobile rapid reaction force based on the British-led 24 Air Mobile Brigade) launched massive air and artillery strikes for three days against Serb heavy weapons on Mt Igman.[43] This was followed by two weeks of massive NATO air strikes against Serb ammunition dumps, command and control, armament factories, and fuel supplies.[44] Hitherto, NATO air strikes had been employed only against Serb forces directly threatening the safe areas, and this escalation in NATO strategy inflicted serious damage on the Bosnian Serb war machine.

However, in a story that was to be repeated in Kosovo four years later, NATO's degrading of Serb military capability from the air did nothing to save those civilians trapped in the safe areas. The enclaves of Zepa, Bihac, and Srebrenica all fell in 1995. In the case of the last, at least 7,414 Muslim men were systematically rounded up and killed by Mladic's forces in the worst war crime of the whole war.[45] The failure of air power to deliver the Security Council's promise to protect the safe areas proved yet again that air power is no substitute for an effective force on the ground. One immediate consequence of NATO air strikes was to confirm British and French fears that the Serbs would respond to such attacks by hostage taking. NATO air strikes placed the UN clearly in the role of a combatant, and the response of the Bosnian Serbs after the attacks against Pale in May 1995 was to take UN soldiers hostage and to overrun the towns of Srebrenica and Zepa.

There was a further adverse consequence of NATO's air strategy in Bosnia and that was its impact on relations with Russia. Although the internationally recognized Bosnian Government had been advocating NATO bombing of the Bosnian Serbs since the war began, Russia disputed that NATO had the authority to launch air strikes on the scale that was done in late 1995. The Russians were prepared to support the use of air power in a close support role,

---

[41] Gow, *Triumph*, 150.

[42] J. Gow, 'Coercive Cadences: Yugoslav War of Dissolution', in L. Freedman (ed.), *Strategic Coercion: Concepts and Cases* (Oxford: Oxford University Press, 1998), 15.

[43] Owen, *Balkan Odyssey*, 357.

[44] According to Lord Owen, '3,400 air sorties, of which about 750 were attack missions', were flown against Serb targets. Ibid. 363–4.

[45] For an authoritative analysis of this case, see Honig and Both, *Srebrenica*.

but they were very unhappy with what they viewed as NATO's unilateral decision to expand the range of targets. The UN Secretary General endorsed NATO's argument that its air strikes were permitted under Resolution 836, but Russia argued that the scale of these strikes exceeded the authority that the Security Council had given member states in June 1993. In a warning that foreshadowed the confrontation to come four years later over NATO's bombing against the FRY, President Yeltsin warned on 9 September 1995 that this was the 'first sign' of how an enlarged NATO would act.[46] Two days later the Russians tried to secure support in the Security Council for a draft resolution condemning NATO air strikes. It was clear from the informal consultations that the resolution would not secure widespread support and Russia refrained from putting it to the vote. The non-aligned group on the Security Council were desperate for action to protect Muslims in Bosnia and were not prepared to weaken the authority behind the only organization capable of bringing the Bosnian Serbs to heel.

Although NATO air strikes failed to protect the safe areas, and opened up a worrying split with the Russians, there is considerable controversy over the role they played in producing the final settlement negotiated at Dayton. Clinton's and Blair's faith in air power as the only means to prevent a humanitarian catastrophe in Kosovo followed directly from their interpretation of the endgame of the Bosnian War, which was that NATO air strikes had compelled Milosevic to end hostilities. The problem with this argument is that it risks drawing a general lesson about the efficacy of air strikes in humanitarian crises on the basis of a particular experience where air strikes were a significant but not decisive factor.

Richard Holbrooke, the chief US negotiator at the peace talks in Dayton, describes the two weeks of bombing by NATO aircraft in September 1995 as making 'a huge difference' to the negotiations. For example, Milosevic immediately accepted the principle of a joint negotiating team for the FRY and Bosnian Serbs that he would speak for (previously he had denied that he had any control over the Bosnian Serb representatives).[47] It is unwise, however, to attribute the final settlement solely to Operation Deliberate Force. Equally significant factors are that, despite the arms embargo, the Croats and Muslims were better armed than ever and were cooperating in attacks that was reversing the gains of the Bosnian Serbs. Finally, 'Operation Storm', the Croatian offensive that expelled the Serbs from the Krajina, fundamentally changed the balance of power on the ground. The new Yugoslav Army (Vojska Jugoslavije (VJ)) had stood by whilst its Serb brethren were ethnically

---

[46] Cited in Owen, *Balkan Odyssey*, 361.

[47] R. Holbrooke, *To End a War* (New York: Random House, 1998), 104–5. Holbrooke claims that the negotiations were not calibrated with the bombing, but that Operation Deliberate Force greatly facilitated the peace process. I am grateful to Alex Bellamy for drawing this point to my attention.

cleansed and this showed Karadzic and Mladic that Milosevic placed securing a deal at Dayton before defending Serb territorial gains.[48]

Consequently, as both Lord Owen and Richard Holbrooke point out, it was the combination of air strikes *and* the changing balance of military forces on the ground that produced the final settlement. In his judicious assessment of the role played by NATO air strikes, Lord Owen claims that they 'sapped its [Bosnian Serb army's] confidence', whilst at the same time emboldening the Croat and Muslim armies. Holbrooke concurs, claiming that, in his negotiations with Milosevic, 'we were struck by the change in his tone. Clearly, the Croat-Muslim offensive in the West and the bombing were having a major effect on the Bosnian Serbs.'[49] It was this combination of air and ground forces that had been so cruelly lacking in the previous years in Bosnia and that was to be missing yet again in NATO's response to Milosevic's human rights violations in Kosovo.

Operation Allied Force as a Humanitarian War

If Dayton closed a terrible chapter of human rights violations in Croatia and Bosnia, then it was also the prelude to Milosevic's war against the Kosovo Albanians. Since the Serbian President had stripped Albanians of their constitutional rights under the 1974 constitution, tensions had been steadily rising in the province. The Serbian minority dismissed Albanians from their posts, excluded them from the state school system, and treated them as a virtual colonial population.[50] Indeed, the strict segregation policies imposed by the Serbs on the Albanians amounted to the creation of 'an apartheid system in Kosovo'.[51] The Albanian response to this campaign of repression was to form the Democratic League of Kosovo (LDK) under the leadership of Ibrahim Rugova. In September 1991, the LDK organized an underground referendum claiming that, of the 87 per cent of voters who had taken part, over 99 per cent supported independence from Serbia.[52] Nevertheless, Rugova took the view that any divorce from Serbia would have to be negotiated with Belgrade, since to do otherwise would produce a terrible Serb backlash against the Albanians.[53]

---

[48] I owe this point to Alex Bellamy.

[49] Owen, *Balkan Odyssey,* 373, and Holbrooke, *To End a War,* 148.

[50] E. Biberaj, 'Kosovo: The Balkan Powder Keg', *Conflict Studies,* 258 (1993), 5–9, and 'Serbs Terrorize Ethnic Albanians', *Guardian* 19 Sept. 1994, which was based on a report by Amnesty International that documented a pattern of arbitrary detention, killing, and torture by Serbian police. This followed an earlier report by US Human Rights Watch, which described Kosovo as a police state run by brute forces and intimidation. International Helsinki Federation for Human Rights, *From Autonomy to Colonization: Human Rights in Kosovo 1989–93* (Vienna: International Helsinki Federation, 1993).   [51] Biberaj, 'Kosovo', 13.

[52] A. J. Bellamy, 'Lazar's Choice Deferred: Serbs, Albanians and the Contact Group at Rambouillet', unpublished Paper (University of Wales, Aberystwyth, 1999), 4.

[53] See 'Meet Kosovo's Number One Man', *Independent,* 31 Jan. 1999. Miranda Vickers quotes Rugova as saying in 1992: 'we have nothing to set against the tanks and other modern weaponry in

He persuaded Albanians that they should pursue a Ghandian-style politics of non-violence that centred around the creation of parallel state institutions. Funded by Albanian businessmen in Kosovo and among the Albanian diaspora, the LDK set up a separate government, education system, and health-care provision.[54] The success of the LDK as the legitimate expression of Albanian nationalism depended upon Rugova delivering on his claim that the strategy of non-violence would persuade the international community to place Kosovo on the agenda of any peace settlement in the Balkans. Dayton, then, was a terrible blow to Rugova, since, having argued for four years that the international community would take the concerns of Kosovo Albanians seriously, he watched as human rights violations in Kosovo did not even figure in the discussions or final text.

The betrayal at Dayton led to Rugova being marginalized in favour of more radical approaches to the national question.[55] The crucial turning point came in February 1996, when the Ushtria Clirimatare e Kosoves (UCK) (Kosovo Liberation Army) literally exploded onto the political scene with a campaign of bombing against Serb targets. Between 1996 and 1998 the UCK employed clandestine tactics, but by early 1998 it had gained in confidence and was sufficiently well equipped to launch an offensive against the Serbs in the Drenica Valley.[56] Serbian security forces responded by launching attacks against the UCK, and, with the use of heavy weapons and air power, they drove the movement out of the urban areas in central and western Kosovo. In a dry run of what was to happen on a much greater scale in 1999, Serb forces burnt villages and drove hundreds and thousands of Kosovars from their homes.

The Clinton Administration moved swiftly to condemn this forced expulsion of Kosovars. Secretary of State Albright stated in March 1998 that 'we believe that in 1991 the international community stood by and watched ethnic cleansing [in Bosnia] . . . We don't want that to happen again this time.'[57] The implication was that the Clinton Administration would defend

Serbian hands. We would have no chance of successfully resisting the army. In fact the Serbs only wait for a pretext to attack the Albanian population and wipe it out. We believe it is better to do nothing and stay alive than to be massacred' (Vickers, *Between Serb and Albanian*, 264).

[54] The best account of this is ibid. 259–64. But see also Biberaj, 'Kosovo', 13, and Bellamy, 'Lazar's Choice Deferred', 4–5.

[55] See H. Clark, 'Radicalization of Kosovo Albanians and parallel organizations', *New Routes* (1998), 4, 'A Balkan *intifada* in Kosovo', *IISS Strategic Comments*, 4/2 (1998), and, 'The Kosovo Liberation Army', *IISS Strategic Comments*, 4/7 (1998). Prior to Dayton, the UCK, which had been formed in 1993 and which was committed to armed resistance, had been opposed by most Albanians. However, after being cut out of the Dayton peace process, the UCK had gained in support, and the collapse of order in Albania in March 1997 had led to arms being available in the army barracks that were smuggled across the border. The funding for the UCK came from radical Albanians living in Germany and Switzerland. For further background on the development of the UCK, see Tim Judah, 'War by Mobile Phone, Donkey and Kalashnikov', *Guardian Weekend*, 29 Aug. 1998.

[56] A. J. Bellamy, 'Lessons Unlearnt: Why Coercive Diplomacy Failed at Rambouillet', *International Peacekeeping*, 7/3 (forthcoming).

[57] Cited in J. Steele, 'Learning to Live with Milosevic', *Transitions*, 5 (1998), 19.

the human rights of Kosovars, but, owing to Russian sensitivities, the furthest the Contact Group would go in its statement on 9 March was to condemn both the Serbs and the UCK for the violence and to demand a cessation of hostilities.[58]

This position was reinforced by the Security Council in Resolution 1160, which was adopted on 31 March 1998 and demanded an end to violence on both sides whilst openly supporting the path of non-violence followed by Rugova and the LDK. The Security Council acted under Chapter VII of the Charter determining that the conflict constituted a threat to 'international peace and security'. No member voted against this resolution, but several, notably Russia and especially China (who abstained), expressed their reservations about Security Council intervention in what they viewed as matters within the 'domestic jurisdiction' of the FRY. The Russian Ambassador stated that his government viewed 'recent events in Kosovo as the internal affair of the Federal Republic of Yugoslavia' and China supported this in its statement that, were the Security Council to intervene in ethnic issues within states 'without a request from the country concerned, it may set a bad precedent and have wider negative implications'.[59] Contrary to this position, the majority of members emphasized that human rights violations in Kosovo constituted a clear threat to peace and security in the Balkans. However, no state on the Security Council supported secessionist claims on the part of the Kosovar Albanians and the resolution reaffirmed the territorial integrity of the FRY.

Despite these international pressures on the Belgrade Government, the Serbs began a new offensive in May against Albanian villages in the area around Decani. Jonathan Steele argues that 'the Serbs did not go for all-out murder . . . [and] not every home was destroyed',[60] indicating that Milosevic might have had one eye on the dangers of provoking a forceful response from the Western powers. However, the scenes of over 100,000 refugees leaving Decani shocked the Blair Government, which began to prepare public opinion for a tougher response. In the case of the safe havens in Iraqi Kurdistan, it was media pressure that had pushed the Major Government into responding. In the case of Kosovo, there was no equivalent media interest and it was Prime Minister Tony Blair and Foreign Minister Robin Cook who took the lead in arguing that Britain and the Alliance had to be prepared to use force to stop Serbian ethnic cleansing in Kosovo.[61]

There were two major difficulties in going down the road of military action. The first was NATO's determination that, in the reported words of one planner, it did not 'become the [UCK's] air force'.[62] The battlefield situation was complicated in late June and early July because the UCK was beginning

---

[58] Statement of the Foreign Ministers of the Contact Group on Kosovo, London, 9 Mar. 1998.
[59] See S/PV.3868/Corr.2, 31 Mar. 1999, 10–12.
[60] Steele, 'Learning to Live', 20.
[61] Ibid. 19.
[62] Quoted in ibid. 21.

to achieve some successes against Serbian forces and NATO did not want to act to support the cause of secessionism in Kosovo.[63] However, the scale of the Serb counter-attack against Albanian villages in their drive to wipe out the UCK led to growing pressure within the Alliance for action against the Serbs. US Defence Secretary William Cohen stated at a NATO meeting of defence ministers in September that, if the Serbs do not cease their attacks, 'we shall act'.[64] There were divisions within NATO on the wisdom of threatening to use force, with Greece, Italy, and Germany hesitant about this option. One question that particularly concerned these governments was the issue of whether the Alliance should act without explicit Security Council authorization. This was the second obstacle that loomed large in the calculations of Britain and the USA as they prepared other members of NATO, and domestic publics, for military action.

In early June, Robin Cook had stated that 'we will need a mandate from the UN. We are looking for that mandate and will certainly be explaining to the Russians why it is so important they do not stand in the way.'[65] The implication was that any NATO action would be inhibited by the lack of an explicit Security Council resolution authorizing the use of force. Whatever Cook's hopes in June, it had become apparent by September that the Security Council would not support such a resolution. On 23 September, the Security Council adopted Resolution 1199 by fourteen votes, with China abstaining, in response to the growing civilian casualties in Kosovo. The resolution was passed under Chapter VII, with the Security Council determining that the threat to peace and security in the region stemmed from the 'deterioration of the situation in Kosovo'. In operative paragraphs 1–4, it demanded that the FRY and the Albanian leadership cease hostilities and take urgent steps to 'avert the impending humanitarian catastrophe'. Although the Security Council was acting under Chapter VII, and hence the resolution is legally binding, its demands were not backed up by the threat of military action. Instead, members reaffirmed their previous commitment to the sovereignty and territorial integrity of Yugoslavia, making clear that the solution to the Kosovo problem had to be found within the context of greater autonomy within the Yugoslav state. Having demanded a cessation of hostilities and negotiations between the FRY and the Albanians to solve the problem, the Security Council considered that, in the event of non-compliance, it would consider what further action might be taken.

---

[63] It has been claimed that Western governments refrained from condemning the Serbian counterattack in July because they wanted to see the UCK weakened *vis-à-vis* Rugova in any negotiations that took place with Milosevic. See T. Youngs (*Kosovo: The Diplomatic and Military Options* (London: House of Commons Research Paper 98/93, 27 Oct. 1998), 11–12), who cites first *The Economist*, 8 Aug. 1998, and then Veton Surroi, editor of the Albanian-language newspaper *Koha Ditore*, who claims that 'nobody in the West was terribly unhappy about the offensive against the UCK' (*Guardian*, 19 Aug. 1998).

[64] Quoted in *Atlantic News*, 26 Sept. 1998.

[65] Quoted in Steele, 'Learning to Live', 20.

Britain and the USA wanted a stronger resolution than 1199, but it was clear from informal consultations that Russia and China would veto anything that legitimated the use of force against the Milosevic regime. Russia reluctantly supported the draft resolution but speaking before the vote, it stressed that this resolution did not authorize military action against the FRY. Ambassador Lavrov stated that 'no use of force and no sanctions are being imposed by the Council at the present stage . . . the use of unilateral measures of force in order to settle the conflict is fraught with the risk of destabilizing the Balkan region and of all of Europe and would have long-term adverse consequences'.[66] Also speaking before the vote, the Chinese Ambassador declared that his government could not support the draft resolution because it did not 'see the situation in Kosovo as a threat to international peace and security'. China argued that the draft resolution had 'invoked Chapter VII of the United Nations Charter all too indiscreetly in order to threaten the Federal Republic of Yugoslavia' and that this would adversely affect the possibilities for a peaceful settlement of the conflict.[67]

Resolution 1199 requested the Secretary General to provide an assessment of how far the parties were complying with it. On 5 October, Kofi Annan presented a report that concluded that he was 'outraged by reports of mass killings of civilians in Kosovo'.[68] The next day the Security Council met informally to discuss the Secretary General's report. Britain, which was President of the Security Council for October, took the lead in proposing a draft resolution specifically authorizing 'all necessary means' to end the killings in Kosovo. However, this met with a Russian declaration that it would veto any such resolution.[69] Two days later, Russian embassies around the world issued a statement 'that the use of force against a sovereign state without due sanction of the UN Security Council would be an outright violation of the UN Charter, undermining the existing system of international relations'.[70]

Given Russian and Chinese opposition to a new resolution specifically authorizing NATO to use force against the FRY, the Alliance was forced to justify its threat in terms of existing Security Council resolutions. This produced considerable misgivings on the part of some NATO members, especially Germany, which worried about the legitimacy of such a claim, given the Russian and Chinese statements in the Security Council during the vote on Resolution 1199.[71] The question of German participation in any NATO air

---

[66] S/PV.3930, 23 Sept. 1999, 3.   [67] Ibid. 2–4.

[68] Cited in Youngs, *Kosovo*, 13.

[69] 'Britain and US may Have to Go it Alone', *Electronic Telegraph*, 8 Oct. 1998. Russian Foreign Minister Igor Ivanov told Interfax news agency that 'Russia would definitely use its right of veto'. ('Russia Warns it will Use Veto to Halt Military Action', *Electronic Telegraph*, 7 Oct. 1998).

[70] 'Britain and US may Have to Go it Alone'.

[71] According to Catherine Guicherd, the then German Foreign Minister, Klaus Kinkel, was especially worried about relying on Resolution 1199 to justify NATO's action. For a discussion of the views of NATO members on this question, see C. Guicherd, 'International Law and the War in Kosovo', *Survival*, 41/2 (1999), 26–7.

strikes against the FRY was an extremely sensitive one, given that the action would be outside the NATO area and in a region where there are bitter wartime memories of German intervention. The legal basis of any future NATO action was the subject of a debate in the German Bundestag in mid-October, and the outcome of this was that the Bundestag gave its approval for Germany to join in any air strikes.[72] Despite his private reservations, Foreign Minister Kinkel argued that Resolution 1199 justified NATO's action. He stated: 'Under these unusual circumstances of the current crisis situation in Kosovo, as it is described in Resolution 1199 of the UN Security Council, the threat of and if need be the use of force by NATO is justified.'[73] However, he emphasized that Kosovo was a special case and that it should not be taken as a green light for future NATO actions outside the authority of the Security Council.[74] Kinkel stated that 'NATO has not created a new legal instrument which could be the basis for a general licence for NATO to do interventions . . . NATO's decision must not become a precedent'.[75] In arguing that the action should not set a precedent, Kinkel was emphatic that there should be no more deviations from the rule of Security Council authorization for the use of force. It is hard to resist the conclusion that Germany found itself in the difficult position of support-ing an action on ethical grounds, knowing that this at best had a dubious basis in international law, and at worst was illegal.

Whatever reservations Germany and other members of NATO had about the legality of relying on Resolutions 1160 and 1199 had been overcome by 13 October, when NATO issued an activation order for air strikes against Serbian targets and justified it in terms of existing Security Council resolu-tions. NATO's decision ratcheted up the pressure on Milosevic, and, in a last-minute effort to avoid the use of force, the Contact Group dispatched US Special Envoy Holbrooke to Belgrade. The talks ultimately proved successful, with Milosevic agreeing to a cessation of hostilities and a return of police and security forces to their barracks. In order to ensure compliance with the 'October Agreement', and to oversee the return of refugees to their homes, Milosevic accepted the presence of a verification mission of 1,700 inspectors from the Organization on Security and Cooperation in Europe (OSCE). The Yugoslav President also agreed to allow unarmed NATO aircraft to carry out inspection flights over Kosovo to monitor Serb compliance. The October Agreement was predicated on Kosovo remaining an integral part of Yugoslavia, but it represented significant concessions from Milosevic in that it provided for OSCE supervised elections in the province and the creation of an independent police force.

[72] B. Simma, 'NATO, the UN and the Use of Force: Legal Aspects', *www.ejil.org/Vol10/No1/abl-2html* (1999), 7.
[73] See Deutscher Bundestag: Plenarprotokoll 13/248 vom 16 October 1998, 21329.
[74] Simma, 'NATO', 7.
[75] See Deutscher Bundestag: Plenarprotokoll 13/248 vom 16 October 1998, 21329.

Although successful implementation of the October Agreement promised to heal the widening rift over the use of force among the Security Council's permanent members, it is clear from the statements of the USA, Russia, and China during the adoption of Resolution 1203 on 24 October that this issue remained highly divisive. The resolution repeated the Security Council's earlier positions on Kosovo and was passed by thirteen votes, with Russia and China abstaining. Despite growing Russian and Chinese sensitivities on the issue, the US Ambassador stated 'that a credible threat of force was key to achieving the OSCE and NATO agreements and remains key to ensuring their full implementation ... The NATO allies, in agreeing on 13 October to the use of force, made it clear that they had the authority, the will and the means to resolve the issue.'[76]

Opposing this argument was Russia which was determined to try and put the brakes on what it viewed as NATO's manipulation of Resolutions 1160 and 1199 to justify its threat to use force. The Russian Ambassador argued that the draft resolution did not take sufficiently into account the positive steps taken by Belgrade to resolve the conflict and that Russia could not, therefore, support what it viewed as the 'one-sided assertion in the preambular part of the text that the unresolved situation in Kosovo constitutes a continuing threat to peace and security in the region'. Moreover, Ambassador Lavrov once again emphasized that 'enforcement elements have been excluded from the draft resolution, and there are no provisions in it that would directly or indirectly sanction the automatic use of force which would be to the detriment of the prerogatives of the Security Council under the Charter'.[77] Russia stated that it expected NATO to rescind its activation order immediately now that Belgrade had consented to the OSCE verification mission. It was supported by China, which, speaking after the vote, indicated that NATO's activation order was a very worrying development, because the 'decision was made unilaterally, without consulting the Security Council or seeking its authorization [and this] created an extremely dangerous precedent in international relations'. The Chinese Ambassador pointed out that there had been attempts during the informal consultations to insert wording authorizing the threat or use of force but that this had been deleted from the final resolution. Consequently, China was explicit that the resolution 'just adopted does not entail any authorization to use force or to threaten to use force against the Federal Republic of Yugoslavia'. China abstained in the voting because of its reservations about those 'elements' in the resolution that it saw as interfering in the internal affairs of the FRY.[78]

The issue of NATO's authority to act against the FRY without explicit Security Council authorization touched a raw nerve among other members who in supporting the resolution expressed strong concerns about the legal

---

[76] S/PV 3937, 24 Oct. 1998, 15.   [77] Ibid. 12.   [78] Ibid. 11–15.

basis of any NATO military action. In an important statement, Costa Rica argued that, while the goals embodied in the resolution were 'ethically and morally unquestionable', they had to be achieved by means of law. 'The Security Council alone', Ambassador Niehaus argued, should 'determine whether there has been a violation of its resolutions, adopted in the exercise of its mandated powers'.[79] Expressing the same view even more pointedly, Brazil argued that regional organizations like NATO have no right to usurp the Security Council's authority to decide whether or not its resolutions were being complied with. The Brazilian Ambassador stated that 'non-universal organisms may resort to force only on the basis either of the right to legitimate self-defence . . . or through the procedures of Chapter VIII, in particular Article 53, which imposes on them the obligation of seeking Security Council authorization beforehand and abiding by the Council's decision . . . There is no third way.'[80]

Whatever hopes NATO had that the October Agreement would rescue it from the momentous decision to use force without express Security Council authority were dashed as the ceasefire failed to hold on the ground. The Kosovo Albanians had not been involved in the October Agreement and they resented a settlement that gave them less autonomy than they had had under the 1974 Yugoslav Constitution.[81] The UCK continued attacking Serb forces and they responded by destroying Albanian villages and killing civilians. On 15 January 1999, in retaliation for the deaths of two policemen, Serb forces massacred forty-five civilians in the village of Racak. This shocked world public opinion and spurred the Contact Group to seek a political settlement by inviting the Serbs and Kosovo Albanians to peace talks at the French château at Rambouillet.

The fundamental challenge that faced the negotiators at Rambouillet was how to reconcile respect for the territorial integrity of the Yugoslav state with the demand of the Kosovo Albanians for a referendum leading to eventual independence. After some tough negotiating, the Albanian delegation, which included Rugova and the UCK, eventually agreed to a transitional period of three years after which the future status of Kosovo would be determined. Under the agreement, the Albanians would have had a substantial measure of autonomy, including their own police forces, judiciary, and democratically elected assembly. Provisions were made for the disarmament of Serbian forces, although the FRY would retain a limited security presence in Kosovo. Finally, and what ultimately proved too much for Milosevic to swallow, in Appendix B of the 'Kosovo Interim Agreement for Peace and Self-Government in Kosovo', the Contact Group proposed that there should be a NATO led international force.

---

[79] Ibid. 6–7.   [80] Ibid. 6–7, 10–11.
[81] Bellamy, 'Lazar's Choice Deferred', 9

The negotiations broke down and the parties reconvened a week later in Paris, where the Serb delegation, led by Prime Minister Milutinovic, continued to reject the Contact Group's terms. At this point the Russians, who would have been part of any implementation force (the model being IFOR and SFOR in Bosnia), publicly claimed that they had not been consulted on the appendix detailing the rights of access of NATO forces and refused to sign the agreement. Marc Weller, who was an adviser to the Kosovar delegation at Rambouillet, characterizes the Russian position as 'startling'. He argues that the so-called military annex was presented to at least the Kosovar delegation and that it is inconceivable that the Russians did not know of its existence.[82] The fact that Russia did not raise complaints about it until Ambassador Mayorski's refusal to initial the Paris agreement suggests that their objections were somewhat contrived.[83]

After the breakdown of the Paris talks on 15 March, Serbian forces began a new campaign in Kosovo of ethnic cleansing. Holbrooke was sent on 22 March by the Contact Group to try and persuade Milosevic to accept Rambouillet and cease his new offensive. In the words of Weller, 'no progress was made' and the following day the Belgrade Parliament rejected the 'Interim Agreement'. In a last-ditch attempt to avert war, Holbrooke claims that he asked the Yugoslav President whether he realized what was going to happen if there was no agreement: Milosevic reportedly replied, 'Yes, you will bomb us.'[84] With negotiations going nowhere, the US Special Envoy left Belgrade for Brussels and the decision to launch air strikes against the FRY was taken by Alliance governments on the night of 23 March 1999.

Western governments invoked four key rationales to justify their intervention in Kosovo. They argued first that their action was aimed at averting an impending humanitarian catastrophe; secondly, that NATO's credibility was at stake; thirdly, that ethnic cleansing in Kosovo could not be allowed to stand in a civilized Europe and that it posed a long-term threat to European security; and finally, that NATO's use of force was in conformity with existing Security Council resolutions. Defending the action in the House of Commons on 25 March, the Foreign Secretary emphasized the first three of these rationales:

Since March last year, well over 400,000 people in Kosovo have at some point been driven from their homes

We have tried repeatedly, right up to the last minute, to find a way to halt the repression of Kosovar Albanians through negotiation. It was not possible, and the person who made it impossible was President Milosevic.

We were left with no other way of preventing the present humanitarian crisis from

---

[82] See M. Weller, 'The Rambouillet Conference on Kosovo', *International Affairs*, 75/2 (1999), 231, 237.

[83] I owe this argument to Alex Bellamy.

[84] Quoted in Tim Judah, *Kosovo: War and Revenge* (London: Yale University Press, 2000), 227.

becoming a catastrophe than by taking military action to limit the capacity of Milosevic's army to repress the Kosovar Albanians.

I defy any Honourable Member to meet the Kosovar Albanians, to whom I have talked repeatedly over the past three months, and tell them that we know what is being done to their families. That we see it every night on the television in our homes. That in the region we have a powerful fleet of Allied planes. And yet although we know what is happening and have the power to intervene we have chosen not to do so. Not to have acted, when we knew the atrocities that were being committed, would have been to make ourselves complicit in their repression. That is the first reason why Britain has a national interest in the success of this military action. And there are others.

Our confidence in our peace and security depends on the credibility of NATO. Last October it was NATO that guaranteed the cease-fire that President Milosevic signed . . . What possible credibility would NATO have the next time our security is challenged if we did not honour that guarantee? The consequences of NATO inaction would be far worse than the result of NATO action.

At some point [the conflict] would have spilled over into the neighbouring countries of the region, and then NATO would have been forced to act, but in circumstances more difficult and dangerous than now.

In the mid '90s, President (Milosevic) was the prime player in the war in Bosnia which gave our language the hideous phrase 'ethnic cleansing'. Only after three years of fighting in which a quarter of a million people were killed, did NATO find the resolve to use force.

Now we are seeing exactly the same pattern of ethnic violence being replayed again in Kosovo . . . We cannot allow the same tragedy to be repeated again in Kosovo.[85]

Although Britain, France, and Germany made a contribution to the air campaign against the FRY, the scale of the bombing was possible only because the USA committed over 650 planes to the region.[86] Clinton and his advisers argued, like the Blair Government, that the West had a moral responsibility to stop the terrible atrocities taking place in Kosovo. Moreover, the action was also justified to the American people on the grounds that a failure by the USA to act in defence of European security would jeopardize US national interests. Speaking on the day before Operation Allied Force was launched to the American Federation of State, County, and Municipal employees, the President argued that the world had stood aside as Milosevic had committed 'genocide in the heart of Europe' against the Bosnian Muslims and that this could not be allowed to happen in Kosovo, since 'it's about our values'. At the same time, he stressed that Europe's and America's security were indivisible and that, if the USA did not act now, it would have to act later when 'more people will die, and it will cost more money', since the USA had a long-term strategic interest in a stable and democratically ordered Europe.[87]

[85] Statement by the Foreign Secretary, Robin Cook, in the House of Commons, 25 Mar. 1999. See www.fco.gov.uk/news.

[86] This figure comes from the US Department of Defense. See www.defenselink.mil.

[87] President Clinton's remarks to the American Federation of State, County and Municipal Employees (AFSCME) Convention, 23 Mar. 1999. See www.usia.gov/regional/eur/balkans/kosovo/texts/99032304.htm.

The Russian Government was quick to challenge US humanitarian and security rationales as a cover for expanding its sphere of influence into the Balkans, and this raises the question as to how far the justifications of Britain and the USA equated with their motives for action. Boris Yeltsin commented, 'Bill Clinton wants to win . . . He hopes Milosevic will capitulate, give up the whole of Yugoslavia, make it America's protectorate.'[88] This perception was also widely shared by publics in Greece (traditionally sympathetic to the Serbs because of the shared Orthodox background), Italy, and Germany (there were considerable sensitivities among Germans about their government using force in a combat role for the first time since the end of the Second World War). However, neither Russia nor other critics have adduced any compelling evidence to support their contention that traditional motives of *realpolitik* explain Operation Allied Force. Instead, the evidence points to this being a case where a key determinant of the use of force was the Prime Minister's and the President's belief that this was a Just War. In his speech to the Economic Club of Chicago on 22 April 1999, Blair argued that the war against the FRY was 'based not on any territorial ambitions but on values', a point also stressed by Cook and Defence Secretary George Robertson.[89]

The argument is not that national interests were not involved, since both Cook and Clinton invoked the language of interests in justifying the use of force. Rather, the point is that, as Blair argued in his Chicago speech, there was no conflict between upholding humanitarian values and protecting national interests. The Prime Minister pressed the solidarist claim that there is a mutual compatibility between order and justice, declaring that 'our actions are guided by a . . . subtle blend of mutual self-interest and moral purpose in defending the values we cherish . . . values and interests merge'.[90] The facts of ethnic cleansing in Kosovo did not determine military intervention, since the British Government could have decided, like its Conservative predecessors, to interpret the violence in ways that legitimated non-intervention. National interests are not given but constructed, and the Blair Government reconstituted British interests to reflect its vision of Britain as a social-democratic state committed to defending, by force if necessary, internationally agreed human rights norms.

In his Chicago speech, Blair argued that one of the key criteria for a legitimate humanitarian intervention is, are there military operations 'we can sensibly and prudently undertake?'[91] As the Somali experience reminds us, military actions that begin with humanitarian claims can all too easily degen-

---

[88] Reuters, 'NATO: Flow of Kosovar Refugees Mysteriously Slows to a Trickle', 20 Apr. 1999, quoted by A. J. Bellamy and D. Kroslak, 'The Dawning of a Solidarist Era? The NATO Intervention in Kosovo', *Journal of International Relations and Development*, 3/1 (forthcoming).

[89] See speech by the British Prime Minister, Tony Blair, to the Economic Club of Chicago, Thursday, 22 Apr. 1999, 2, www.fco.gov.uk.

[90] Ibid. 8.

[91] Ibid. 9.

erate into policies that are the antithesis of humanitarianism. Controversy rages over how far the means of bombing employed by NATO to prosecute its first 'humanitarian war' undermined the very humanitarian rationales of Operation Allied Force. There are two key reasons that explain NATO's selection of air power as the chosen instrument of armed rescue.

The first is that the great attraction to Western policy-makers of air power is that it avoids the costs and risks of committing ground troops. Alliance governments publicly ruled out the use of ground troops from the outset of the air campaign, believing that soldiers returning in body bags would rapidly erode domestic support for the action against Milosevic. This concern with maintaining domestic legitimacy exerted a powerful constraint on NATO strategy and forced the Alliance to invest great faith in air power in achieving its humanitarian and security objectives.

This leads into the second reason for the reliance on bombing, which is that Alliance leaders were convinced that a serious show of force would compel Milosevic to back down after only a few days of bombing. Based on interviews in the USA, Britain, and the Netherlands, Adam Roberts argues that this illusion was widely shared in national capitals and at NATO headquarters.[92] This turned out to be a colossal miscalculation and it is yet another example of bad history making bad strategy, since the conviction that a few days of NATO air strikes would coerce Milosevic into surrendering was the lesson that British and US policy-makers drew from Operation Deliberate Force in Bosnia.[93] As I argued in the earlier part of this chapter, NATO air strikes were a significant but not decisive factor in bringing Milosevic to the negotiating table at Dayton.

The consequence of Alliance leaders learning the wrong lesson from Bosnia was that they underestimated how far the bombing would lead to an intensification of the barbarities against the Kosovars. There is evidence that Clinton and his senior advisers were aware of this possibility but had chosen to downplay its significance in their calculations over the efficacy of using force. For example, it was reported in the *Washington Post* on 1 April that CIA Director George J. Tenet had warned the administration weeks before the bombing that 'Serb led Yugoslav forces might respond by accelerating their

---

[92] Roberts, 'NATO's Humanitarian War', 111.

[93] Clinton, Secretary of State Madeleine Albright, and National Security Adviser, Sandy Berger all believed that the bombing campaign would compel Milosevic to accept the terms at Rambouillet within a matter of days. In the case of the Blair Government, when asked by Mr Woodward of the House of Commons Foreign Affairs Committee on 14 Apr. 1999 where 'historically would you find a precedent for achieving your humanitarian objectives with this particular military strategy which rules out the use of ground troops', Foreign Secretary Cook replied in a way that illustrated the depth of his conviction about the 'lessons' of NATO's use of force in the Bosnian War. Cook stated that the 'most immediate precedent and the most geographically relevant one is the Dayton peace process which involved the decision of NATO to commence military action from the air . . . Milosevic was brought to the Dayton negotiating table by the use of air power' (Minutes of Evidence on Kosovo, House of Commons Foreign Affairs Committee, 14 Apr.1999, 25).

campaign of ethnic cleansing'.[94] The American military made similar warnings. The *Sunday Times* reported on 28 March that a meeting had taken place between the President and his closest advisers with the Chairman of the Joint Chiefs of Staff, General Harry Shelton, at which it is reported that he said, 'bombing was likely to provoke a Serbian killing spree'.[95]

These words proved prescient ones as, within weeks of the start of the bombing, thousands of Kosovar Albanians were killed, over half a million were driven from their homes to become refugees in neighbouring countries, and hundreds of thousands more found themselves internally displaced within Kosovo itself.[96] The bombing almost certainly led the Serbs to intensify their campaign against the Kosovo Albanians, since, as Ken Booth argues, it created 'the cover of war for the ethnic cleansers . . . inflaming the latter's desire to extract revenge against the defenceless Albanians they despised'.[97] Indeed, as Deputy Secretary of State Strobe Talbott conceded in October 1999 at a conference on the future of NATO, the bombing campaign 'accelerated' the ethnic cleansing.[98] NATO leaders, then, stand accused of exacerbating the very humanitarian disaster that their actions were justified as averting.

The difficulty with this criticism is that it relies on the assumption that, in the absence of NATO bombing, the Serbs would have ended their killings and forced expulsion of ethnic Albanians. It is estimated that some 500 Kosovars had been killed and 400,000 displaced in the year leading up to NATO's action, but the justification for intervention was that without it many more Albanians would have been killed and forcibly driven from their homes.[99] Defending the Blair Government's actions before the House of Commons Foreign Affairs Committee on 14 April, the Foreign Secretary claimed that Milosevic had been planning a spring offensive, that it had commenced before the bombing began, and that Belgrade had developed a plan—Operation Horseshoe—to expel the Albanians from Kosovo.[100] In response to

---

[94] The report in the *Washington Post* is cited by Sir John Stanley MP in the House of Commons Foreign Affairs Committee Report on Kosovo, 14 Apr. 1999, 18.

[95] 'Stealth Fighter "Shot down" as Serbs Slaughter Hundreds', *Sunday Times*, 28 Mar. 1999.

[96] Roberts, 'NATO's Humanitarian War', 113.

[97] Booth, 'The Kosovo Tragedy: Epilogue to Another "Low and Dishonest Decade"?'

[98] Strobe Talbott was speaking at a conference organized by the Royal Institute of International Affairs and the Institute of World Economy and International Relations Russian Federation on 'NATO Development in Partnership: Engagement and Advancement after 2000' held at Chatham House, 7–8 Oct. 1999.

[99] The FCO's Memorandum on Kosovo stated: 'It was precisely because there was *good reason* to anticipate that Milosevic's forces would intensify represssion in Kosovo that NATO agreed unanimously that we had to act' (FCO Memorandum on Kosovo, 18; emphasis added).

[100] See Robin Cook, Minutes of Evidence on Kosovo, House of Commons Foreign Affairs Committee, 14 Apr. 1999, 26. It is believed that Operation Horseshoe began to be devised in early 1998 as a response to UCK violence. Because of the impossibility of separating UCK fighters from Kosovar Albanian civilians, the plan envisaged 'cleansing' regions where the UCK was active of all its Albanian inhabitants. These tactics were deployed in Drenica in 1998. The name 'Horseshoe' derives from the shape of the sweep that was envisaged in a more province-wide plan hatched in autumn 1998, and prepared throughout the winter of 1998–9. Alex Bellamy has argued to me that

Diane Abbott's question as to whether NATO's action had 'precipitated' the humanitarian emergency it was aimed at preventing, he replied that, had NATO not acted, 'I think the likelihood is that . . . I would now be giving evidence to you in circumstances in which much of what has happened had already happened, if not all of it, and you would very reasonably be asking me why I am doing nothing'.[101]

Even if it is accepted that Milosevic had a 'final solution' to depopulate Kosovo of its Albanian population, NATO's reliance on an air strategy could have prevented this only if two unlikely assumptions had proved to be correct: first, that the bombing compelled Belgrade within a short period of time to accept the deployment of a NATO-led force to protect the Kosovars; and, secondly, that NATO air attacks significantly degraded the Serbs' capacity to repress the Kosovo Albanians. The discovery of mass graves in Kosovo by the NATO-led international Kosovo Force (KFOR) in June 1999 and the stories of terrible atrocities tell their own grim tale of the limitations of trying to stop ethnic cleansing from the air.[102] As General Wesley Clarke, who commanded NATO forces during Operation Allied Force, put it in an unguarded moment at a press briefing, 'air power alone cannot stop paramilitary action'.[103] Averting the ethnic cleansing in Kosovo in March 1999 required not only air power but also a major commitment of ground troops.

Had the political will existed in the Alliance, a large expeditionary force could have been built up in Macedonia and Albania, signalling to Milosevic that NATO was serious about defending human rights. This might have been sufficient to persuade Milosevic to negotiate seriously over Kosovo, and it could have opened the door to other possibilities that might have avoided war, such as a UN- rather than NATO-led force. If, on the other hand, Belgrade's response had been to accelerate Operation Horseshoe, NATO could have launched a ground invasion to end the atrocities of Serb paramilitaries and regular forces. To reduce the risks, this would need to have been preceded by an intensive air campaign against air defence systems and Serb military targets in the FRY and Kosovo, remembering that every day NATO bombed was another day when Serb forces were able to kill or expel Kosovars. There is

it is possible to see a pattern of Serbian 'spring offensives' during the wars in Bosnia-Hercegovina and Croatia, and that it was always envisaged that Operation Horseshoe would be implemented in the spring of 1999. Bellamy contends that the international responses to Racak probably brought the plan forward somewhat, and that Milosevic initially hoped that he could maintain a dual front of prolonged international negotiation and armed aggression, as he had for long periods during the war in Bosnia-Hercegovina. For more on Operation Horseshoe, see 'Milosevic and Operation Horseshoe', *Observer*, 18 July 1999.

[101] For the exchange between Cook and Abbott, see House of Commons Foreign Affairs Committee Report on Kosovo, 14 Apr. 1999, 26.

[102] For example, see 'Captured on Paper, a Child's Vision of Death', *Guardian*, 20 May 1999, and 'British Team Verifies Atrocity Stories', *The Times*, 11 May 1999.

[103] 'Pentagon's Revenge as NATO Chief is Told to Go, *Guardian*, 29 July 1999.

no escaping the fact that this would have produced casualties, but this was the only realistic strategy for saving the Kosovars.[104]

Having failed to avert a humanitarian emergency by the use of air power, this instrument became the means of reversing the ensuing humanitarian catastrophe. Faced with the greatest exodus of refugees since the Second World War, Alliance leaders, led by Tony Blair, committed themselves to the war aim of returning all the refugees to their homes.[105] The problem was that the Kosovo Albanians would return to their homes only if they could be assured of long-term international protection. This required either convincing Milosevic that the Alliance could inflict unacceptable costs so that he 'consented' to a deployment of NATO forces; or blunting Serbian military capacity in Kosovo to such an extent that NATO ground forces could enter Kosovo in what came to be called by Alliance leaders a 'permissive environment'.[106]

NATO targeted Serb military forces in Kosovo throughout the campaign, but this met with limited success, owing to the fact that the Serbs hid their heavy weapons in the absence of any effective air defence against NATO forces.[107] The Alliance never deliberately targeted civilians, employing in the main the latest precision-guided weapons to avoid 'collateral damage'. But, as the pressure for a 'result' grew, NATO increasingly focused on infrastructural targets in the FRY, such as bridges, industries, oil refineries, fuel depots, and political buildings that were considered vital to the prosecution of the military effort in Kosovo. This led to an increasing number of Serb civilians being

[104] This position is rejected by both the British and French governments. When questioned on the lack of a ground-force option by Mr Woodward of the House of Commons Foreign Affairs Committee on 14 Apr., the Foreign Secretary claimed 'that ground forces are not a magic short cut. If we were to commit ground forces, it would take us two or three months to build them up in the theatre and it would require a force of a minimum of 100,000 and potentially double that . . . Ground forces are not a serious option and are most certainly not a short cut' (Robin Cook, Minutes of Evidence on Kosovo, House of Commons Foreign Affairs Committee, 14 Apr. 1999, 13–14). Similarly, French Defence Minister Alain Richard, who, releasing the French Government's report on the military lessons of the Kosovo campaign, stated on 10 Nov.: 'Sending in ground troops earlier would not have shortened the conflict and might have been a costly mistake . . . the air war was a crucial first phase' (quoted in 'Allies Emphasize Need to Prepare for Kosovo-Style Air Wars', *International Herald Tribune*, 12 Nov. 1999).

[105] Tony Blair became particularly animated on this issue after his visit to Stenkovec refugee camp in Macedonia at the beginning of May. See Tony Blair, 'Our Commitment is Total', statement made in Stenkovec refugee camp, Macedonia, 3 May 1999 (see www.fco.gov.uk), 'Blair: My Pledge to the Refugees', BBC World Service Bulletin, 14 May 1999. Blair had earlier included the return of refugees as a war aim: Tony Blair, 'There can be no Compromise on the Terms we Have Set out', House of Commons, 13 Apr. 1999 (www.fco.gov.uk). This view was also shared by Robin Cook. See e.g. Statement by the Foreign Secretary, Robin Cook, House of Commons, 10 May 1999 (www.fco.gov.uk).

[106] See Tony Blair, Prime Minister's Questions, House of Commons, 21 Apr. 1999. See also General Sir Charles Guthrie, 'Why Nato Cannot Simply March in and Crush Milosevic', *London Evening Standard*, 1 Apr. 1999.

[107] See 'Serb War Machine "surviving"', *Guardian*, 28 Apr. 1999. For more details on why the bombing was appearing to be less effective than hoped in diminishing the aggressive potential of the VJ and Serb paramilitaries, see P. Rogers, 'Ground Cover', *Guardian*, 29 Apr. 1999.

killed, and the moral character of the bombing campaign was further tarnished by stray bombs hitting civilian areas, and the diplomatic catastrophe of the bombing of the Chinese Embassy on 7 May.[108] Adam Roberts points out that NATO's selection of targets in the FRY was not only aimed at destroying the capacities supporting the Serb military machine in Kosovo; it was also to coerce the government in Belgrade into accepting a settlement by attacking key aspects of Serbian state power.[109]

Targeting civilian installations on the grounds that they were important to the regime's political control and could have military applications was highly controversial, as could be seen in the reaction to the attack against the Serb television station on 23 April.[110] The general dilemma that faced the Alliance was that bridges might be legitimate targets but not the buses and trains that happened to be crossing them the moment the bombs struck; similarly, should power stations have been attacked at night, when NATO knew that there would be civilian shift workers inside them? Since meeting the test of proportionality is a threshold criterion of a legitimate humanitarian intervention, did the level of force employed by the Alliance exceed the harm that it was designed to prevent and redress?

During the course of the war, this concern was raised by Mary Robinson, UN High Commissioner for Human Rights. She questioned whether NATO was being sufficiently careful in its targeting; there is a need, she said, 'not only to adhere to the principle of proportionality, but to err on the side of the principle'.[111] Failure to do this, she added, would undermine the humanitarian credentials of Operation Allied Force. The reluctance to deploy ground forces and the concomitant reliance on the air campaign reflected in her view a lack of moral courage on the part of NATO governments to place their service personnel in harm's way in defence of the values they claimed to be fighting for. She might have added that NATO could have reduced the risks of civilian casualties had it asked its pilots to fly at low level, since this would have have improved target discrimination. NATO's reluctance to bomb at low level reflected concerns not only about the safety of its air-crew, but also about losing aircraft and with them the sustainability of the air campaign.

---

108 ' "End the Bombing" Calls after Embassy Fiasco', *Observer*, 9 May 1999. On the immediate response to the bombing of the Chinese Embassy and the crisis of confidence within NATO, see 'Behind the Walls of the Besieged Embassy', *The Times*, 11 May 1999, and 'Besieged NATO Rejects Serb "Ploy" ', *Independent*, 11 May 1999. Reports in the *Observer* on 21 Oct. and 28 Nov. challenged the official version of events, which was that NATO had hit the wrong building, claiming that the Chinese Embassy was being used by Zeljko Raznatovic (the war criminal from the Bosnian war known as Arkan) to transmit radio signals to his death squads in Kosovo. The *Observer* claims that the 'Americans knew exactly what they were doing. The embassy was deliberately targeted by the most precise weapons in America's arsenal' ('Why America Bombed', *Observer*, 28 Nov. 1999).

109 Roberts, 'NATO's Humanitarian War', 115.

110 'Serb TV Station was Legitimate Target Says Blair', *Guardian*, 24 Apr. 1999.

111 P. Bishop, 'UN Rights Chief Warns NATO on Bombing', *Electronic Telegraph*, 5 May, www.telegraph.co.uk.

Roberts suggests that 'the disturbing lesson of the air campaign may be that its most effective aspect involved hurting Serbia proper (including its population and government) rather than directly attacking Serb forces in Kosovo and protecting the Kosovars'.[112] The bombing campaign certainly raises disturbing questions about whether NATO was employing means that sufficiently discriminated between combatants and non-combatants, but it has to be conceded that air power, as in the Bosnian war, played an important though not decisive role in persuading Belgrade on 3 June to accept an EU–Russian peace plan that provided for the withdrawal of all Serb forces from Kosovo and the deployment of a NATO-led multinational force that made possible the return of the refugees to their homes eleven weeks after the start of the bombing.[113]

In addition to the air campaign, three other key reasons prompted Milosevic to accept NATO's terms. The first was that NATO signalled in a series of developments in late May that it was increasingly serious about a ground intervention. Having promised the refugees that they would return home before winter, Blair was in the forefront of efforts to create a credible ground option, and, on 25 May, NATO approved a plan that increased the projected size of KFOR to 50,000 and, on 31 May, the Clinton Administration gave General Clark permission to strengthen the road in Albania that would carry NATO's heavy equipment from the port of Durres to the Kosovo border.[114] Nevertheless, no formal decision had been taken to intervene on the ground and there was considerable doubts in the Clinton Administration about the wisdom of such an action. It is possible that Britain and other European members of the Alliance might have acted without the support of US ground forces, but this would have been a risky undertaking that would have stretched British forces to the limit.

The second factor that critically influenced the Belgrade Government's calculations was its recognition that Russia would not actively support it against the West. Russia was eager to secure a settlement that gave it a political and military role in Kosovo and feared a NATO ground intervention because this would leave it isolated. It has been suggested by Zbigniew Brezinski that Milosevic capitulated only because a secret deal was hatched between Moscow and Belgrade to partition Kosovo, with a Russian military contingent controlling its own sector in north-east Kosovo. Brezinski argues that this plan explains why Russia landed paratroopers at Pristina airport,

---

[112] Roberts, 'NATO's Humanitarian War', 117–18.

[113] Even after the agreement on 3 June, there were several difficulties that plagued the negotiations between Serb military leaders and General Mike Jackson the NATO commander of KFOR. Finally, a military agreement was signed on 9 June that facilitated the withdrawal of Serb forces and this led to the adoption of Resolution 1244, which authorized the international presence in Kosovo, including Russian forces, the following day. See Roberts, 'NATO's Humanitarian War', 116–117.

[114] See ibid. 118, and 'NATO Secretly Planned an Invasion of Kosovo', *International Herald Tribune*, 20 Sept. 1999.

having given assurances to the contrary. It was only foiled, he claims, by the refusal of Hungary, Bulgaria, and Romania to allow Russian transports to over-fly their territory, and the determination of NATO to avoid giving Russia its own sector as part of KFOR. Whether this was the Machiavellian intent behind it, the fact is, that having been very hostile to NATO's position, Russia did come in late May and early June to accept NATO's demands for a full Serb withdrawal from Kosovo.[115] Finally, the changing balance of military forces in Kosovo influenced Milosevic. UCK operations in the last two weeks of the war forced Yugoslav forces into the open and this enabled NATO's B-52s to attack them with cluster bombs, causing substantial losses to Serbian forces.[116]

What judgement, then, should be made of the humanitarian success of Operation Allied Force? In terms of *rescue*, the means selected by NATO to stop Operation Horseshoe clearly accelerated it. This demonstrates, as in the Iraqi and Bosnian cases, the limits of air power as a means of humanitarian rescue. Having failed to avert the humanitarian catastrophe, bombing played, as in the Bosnian endgame, a significant though not decisive role in produc-ing a political settlement. This enabled the refugees to return home and provided them with a substantial measure of political autonomy that they would have been denied in the absence of NATO intervention. Jonathan Steele writing from Pristina in July 1999 declared: 'Those Western critics who condemn the bombing for turning a humanitarian crisis into a catastrophe get short shrift in Kosovo. Albanians were the primary victims and there is an almost universal feeling that although the price was far bloodier than expected, it was worth paying for the sake of liberation from Serb rule.'[117]

Yet if NATO's intervention in Kosovo was successful in restoring to the Albanians the civil and political rights that Milosevic's policy of repression had stripped away, it failed to stop a new round of ethnic cleansing, as thou-sands of Serbs fled in fear of Albanians seeking revenge. Far from creating the conditions for a new multiethnic polity in which Serbs and Albanians live under the protection of the rule of law, KFOR was unable in the early months to protect Serbs who now found themselves on the receiving end of a new order of ethnic apartheid.[118] This will only serve to store up the hatreds to fuel future violence between Serb and Albanian.

---

[115] See Z. Brezinski, 'Why Milosevic Capitulated in Kosovo', Balkan Action Council, 14 June 1999, and Roberts, 'NATO's Humanitarian War', 118.   [116] Ibid.

[117] 'Confused and Still in Denial, Serbs have a Long Way to Go', *Guardian*, 9 July 1999.

[118] It is estimated that 170,000 Serbs were forced to flee Kosovo. See F. del Mundo and R. Wilkinson, 'A Race against Time', *Refugees Magazine*, 116 (1999), and 'Kosovo's Wounded Women Find no Peace', *Guardian*, 19 Oct. 1999. Introducing an OSCE report in Dec. 1999 based on a year's investigations into human rights abuses in Kosovo, Daan Everts, head of the OSCE in Kosovo, stated that, since the arrival of KFOR, the 'capacity to investigate violations and enforce the law has been sorely lacking. Impunity has reigned instead of justice' (quoted in 'Scathing Kosovo Report Unveiled', *Guardian*, 6 Dec. 1999).

The jury is still out on the long-term humanitarian consequences of the Kosovo intervention: on the negative side, there are continuing concerns about the security of those Serbs who remain in Kosovo, uncertainties about whether KFOR troops will become the target for Albanian extremists if the Kosovars are frustrated in their bid for independence, and the danger that Albanian nationalism could lead to a 'Greater Albania', which could lead to a new round of instability and violence in the Balkans centred on Macedonia.

What is already evident is that NATO's intervention is not a good model of humanitarian intervention. As I discuss in the concluding part of the chapter, there are important questions to be asked over whether NATO's action meets the defining tests of necessity, proportionality, and a positive humanitarian outcome. Consequently, it is surprising to say the least that, with the exception of a small vocal minority of states, the international reaction to the bombing was so favorable. As we have seen several members of the Security Council were worried in late 1998 about the danger of NATO acting against the FRY without Security Council authorization, but when it came to responding to NATO's action, the majority of members legitimated or acquiesced in NATO's action. It is to these debates that we now turn.

NATO as Humanitarian Enforcer or Law breaker

At the request of the Russians, the Security Council met on 24 March to debate NATO's action and Ambassador Lavrov opened proceedings by accusing NATO of violating the UN Charter. In response to the justification of Alliance governments that military action was aimed at averting a humanitarian catastrophe, he argued that there was no basis in the accepted rules of international law to justify such a unilateral use of force. Russia did not defend violations of international humanitarian law, but it was only 'possible to combat violations of the law . . . with clean hands and only on the solid basis of the law'.[119] Russia was supported by Belarus, Namibia, and China, which pressed the point that it was only the Security Council that had the responsibility to authorize enforcement action in defence of its resolutions. India, which had asked to participate in the Security Council's deliberations, supported this position, arguing that 'No country, group of countries or regional arrangement, no matter how powerful, can arrogate to itself the right to take arbitrary and unilateral military action against others'.[120]

Set against this, NATO governments argued that the intervention was both legitimate and legal because it was aimed at averting a humanitarian catastrophe. Here, they invoked the language of Resolutions 1199 and 1203,

---

[119] S/PV.3988, 24 Mar. 1999, 3.   [120] Ibid.

which had been passed under Chapter VII of the Charter, and demanded that Serbian forces take actions to stop the impending humanitarian disaster. The Netherlands acknowledged that Security Council authorization was always to be sought when taking up arms to defend human rights. But if, owing to 'one or two permanent members' rigid interpretation of the concept of domestic jurisdiction, such a resolution is not attainable, we cannot sit back and simply let the humanitarian catastrophe occur'. Rather, Ambassador van Walsum argued that, in such cases, 'we will act on the legal basis we have available, and what we have available in this case is more than adequate'.[121]

Despite the Russian claim that there was no support in general international law for a doctrine of unilateral humanitarian intervention, Britain had taken the lead in late 1998 in arguing within the Alliance that there was a legal basis for NATO to use force in Kosovo even without explicit Security Council authorization. This reasoning was set out in an FCO paper circulated to NATO capitals in October 1998.

A UNSCR [US Security Council Resolution] would give a clear legal base for NATO action, as well as being politically desirable . . . But force can also be justified on the grounds of overwhelming humanitarian necessity without a UNSCR. The following criteria would need to be applied:

(a) that there is convincing evidence, generally accepted by the international community as a whole, of extreme humanitarian distress on a large scale, requiring immediate and urgent relief;

(b) that it is objectively clear that there is no practicable alternative to the use of force if lives are to be saved;

(c) that the proposed use of force is necessary and proportionate to the aim (the relief of humanitarian need) and is strictly limited in time and scope to this aim.[122]

This paper echoes the views expressed by Mr Anthony Aust when defending the legality of the safe havens to the Foreign Affairs Select Committee in late 1992. British ministers were quick to invoke the Iraqi case as a precedent supporting the legality of NATO's threat to use force against the FRY. In doing so the Blair Government emphasized that Security Council resolutions constituted 'convincing evidence' of the international community's judgement as to what counted as 'extreme humanitarian distress'. The government's evolving legal defence was set out by Baroness Symons, Minister of State at the Foreign Office, in a written answer to Lord Kennet on 16 November 1998:

There is no general doctrine of humanitarian necessity in international law. Cases have nevertheless arisen (as in northern Iraq in 1991) when, in the light of all the circum-

---

[121] S/PV.3988, 24 Mar. 1999, 3.
[122] Quoted in Roberts, 'NATO's Humanitarian War', 106.

stances, a limited use of force was justifiable in support of purposes laid down by the Security Council but without the Council's express authorization when that was the only means to avert an immediate and overwhelming humanitarian catastrophe.[123]

Two months before the air strikes began, Foreign Office Minister Tony Lloyd was questioned before the House of Commons Foreign Affairs Select Committee on this legal rationale. In response to questions from Ted Rowlands and Diane Abbott as to whether there was a legal right for NATO to take action given the divisions within the Security Council over how to respond to the humanitarian crisis in Kosovo, the minister replied: 'Within those terms, yes. International law certainly gives the legal base in the way that I have described . . . we believed at that time [October 1998] that the humanitarian crisis was such as to warrant that intervention.'[124]

Britain's argument that NATO did not need explicit Security Council authorization to act over Kosovo was supported by the new SPD–Green government under Chancellor Gerhard Schroeder. Although the new German Government was uncomfortable with participating in NATO air strikes without explicit UN authority, there was a greater willingness among ministers than in the previous government to advance new normative claims to justify NATO's position. The new Defence Minister, Rudolf Scharping, argued that international law should be developed so that massive human rights violations could be treated as a legitimate basis for the resort to force.[125] Moreover, the future Minister of State in the German Foreign Ministry, Günter Verheugen, addressed himself directly to the question of UN authorization when he declared that a veto in the Security Council should not block states from intervening in cases where the level of killing offends against basic standards of common humanity. He stated, 'one can imagine a situation in which the level of violence became so great that every decent person would say something had to be done to end the killing. If Russia . . . uses its Security Council veto one could say this was an abuse of the veto and argue the primacy of halting the slaughter is greater than formal respect of international law'.[126]

What is important about the German Government's position is that, in contrast to the stance taken by the British Government, ministers did not argue that there already existed a legal basis for unilateral humanitarian intervention. Instead, Günter Verheugen was explicit that the use of force without express Security Council authorization challenged the formal strictures of

---

[123] Baroness Symons of Vernham Dean, written answer to Lord Kennet, *Hansard*, 16 Nov. 1998, col. WA 140.

[124] Tony Lloyd, Minutes of Evidence on Kosovo, House of Commons Foreign Affairs Committee, 26 Jan. 1999, 12.

[125] Guicherd, 'International Law', 27.

[126] Quoted in 'Germany will Send Jets to Kosovo', *Electronic Telegraph*, 1 Oct. 1998.

international law. His argument was that the right of the veto in the Security Council brings with it a concomitant moral responsibility on the part of permanent members to uphold standards of common humanity. And where this is abused, unilateral humanitarian intervention is justified on moral grounds, even if this breaks the law.

Not surprisingly, the argument that NATO was morally justified in breaking international law did not figure in the defence given by the five NATO members on the Security Council. Rather, they emphasized that their action was supported by Security Council resolutions 1160, 1199, and 1203 adopted under Chapter VII of the Charter. This position was strongly supported by the EU, which Germany represented on the Security Council as holding the Presidency of the Union. The German Ambassador read out a statement endorsing NATO's action that had been adopted earlier in the day by the European Council at a meeting in Berlin.

Slovenia was less reticent than NATO governments in making the argument that Operation Allied Force was justified because Russia and China had abused the power of the veto. The Slovenian Ambassador expressed his regret 'that not all permanent members were willing to act in accordance with their special responsibility for the maintenance of international peace and security under the United Nations Charter'.[127] This was a veiled reference to the refusal of Russia and China to pass a resolution authorizing military action against the FRY in late 1998.

Less enthusiastically, Gambia acknowledged that the 'exigencies' of the situation justified NATO's action. Brazil did not challenge the action and neither did Bahrain, Malaysia, Gabon, or Argentina. Two days after the NATO bombing began, Russia tabled with Belarus and India a draft resolution condemning NATO's action as a breach of Articles 2 (4), 24, and 53 of the UN Charter and demanding a cessation of hostilities. States routinely invoke Article 2 (4) when they want to criticize the use of force by other states, but the claim that NATO was violating Articles 24 and 53 took the debate on the legitimate use of force into new territory. Article 24 refers to the primary responsibility of the Security Council for the maintenance of international peace and security, with UN member states agreeing that 'in carrying out its duties under this responsibility the Security Council acts on their behalf'.[128] Under Article 53 of the Charter, the Security Council is empowered to 'utilize Such ... regional arrangements or agencies for enforcement action', but the Charter is explicit that this can take place only with authorization by the Security Council. Consequently, NATO is charged with usurping the Security Council's primary responsibility, with the Russian Ambassador arguing that 'what is in the balance now is the question of law and lawlessness. It is a question of either reaffirming the

---

[127] S/PV.3988, 24 Mar. 1999, 6–7.   [128] Charter of the United Nations, Article 24.

commitment of one's country and people to the basic principles and values of the United Nations Charter, or tolerating a situation in which gross force dictates realpolitik.'[129]

In response to this charge, three of the NATO states on the Security Council and Slovenia robustly defended Operation Allied Force. The USA, the Netherlands, and Canada rejected the charge that they were acting outside the UN Charter, justifying their actions as being in conformity with existing resolutions and necessary to prevent a humanitarian catastrophe. The USA argued that NATO's action was not in violation of the Charter, because this did 'not sanction armed assaults upon ethnic groups, or imply that the international community should turn a blind eye to a growing humanitarian disaster'.[130] Canada stressed the international legitimacy behind NATO's actions arguing that supporting the draft resolution would place states 'outside the international consensus, which holds that the time has come to stop the continuing violence' by the FRY against the Kosovars.[131] Slovenia returned to the theme it had raised two days earlier, considering that, while it would have preferred direct Security Council authorization, 'the Security Council has the primary but not exclusive responsibility for the maintenance of international peace and security'. This argument represented an imaginative response to the Russian charge that NATO was acting contrary to Article 24 of the UN Charter, since the Slovenian Ambassador considered that 'all the Council members have to think hard about what needs to be done to ensure the Council's authority and to make its primary responsibility as real as the Charter requires'.[132] It was Russia and China who, by refusing to authorize military enforcement action, were in breach of Article 24, since it was only the threat of their vetoes that prevented the Security Council from exercising its 'primary responsibility for the maintenance of international peace and security'.

When the draft resolution was put to the vote, it was defeated by twelve votes to three (Russia, China, and Namibia). Speaking after the vote, the British Government argued that Resolutions 1199 and 1203 determined that Milosevic's policies had 'caused the threat to peace and security in the region', and that 'military intervention is justified as an exceptional measure to prevent an overwhelming humanitarian catastrophe'.[133] This position was endorsed by the French Government, which argued that the 'actions decided upon respond to Belgrade's violation of its international obligations under the resolutions which the Security Council has adopted under Chapter VII of the United Nations Charter'.[134]

The legal and moral position taken by NATO governments in the Security Council debate on 26 March is not surprising, but what has to be

---

[129] S/PV.3989, 26 Mar. 1999, 6.   [130] Ibid. 5.   [131] Ibid. 3.
[132] Ibid. 4.   [133] Ibid. 7.   [134] Ibid.

explained is why six non-Western states came to vote with Slovenia in comprehensively defeating a Russian draft resolution condemning NATO's bombing. Of the six, only three chose to justify their decision by making public statements. It is worth dwelling for a moment on the precise justi-fications given by these states. The Bahrain Government reiterated the standard NATO argument that the humanitarian catastrophe taking place inside Kosovo justified NATO's action, and that support for the draft reso-lution would encourage the Milosevic regime to continue its policy of ethnic cleansing.[135] The Malaysian Government regretted that, owing to irreconcilable differences within the Security Council, it had 'been neces-sary for measures to be taken outside of the Council'.[136] Although this was hardly a ringing endorsement of NATO's action, the Malaysian Government is a staunch defender of the non-intervention rule, and the fact that it was prepared publicly to excuse an action that bypassed the Security Council is highly significant. The position it took over Kosovo probably reflected the fact that NATO's intervention was in defence of Muslims. The Argentine Government was even stronger in its support for NATO's action, stating that rejection of the draft resolution was based on contributing to efforts to stop the massive violations of human rights in Kosovo. Indeed, the Argentinian Ambassador argued that the obligation to protect human rights and fulfil 'the legal norms of international humani-tarian law and human rights is a response to the universally recognized and accepted values and commitments'.[137] The implication was that, in exceptional circumstances such as those prevailing in Kosovo, states have a right to use force to put an end to human rights violations, even without express Security Council authorization. One important explanation for Argentina's public support of NATO's action is that its growing commit-ment to democratic values at home was being reflected in a commitment to defend human rights internationally. Gambia and Gabon did not partic-ipate in the debate, and Brazil, which had strongly opposed any use of force by NATO without Security Council authority in earlier debates, also remained silent.

The various justifications for Operation Allied Force proffered by the five NATO governments and the other members of the Security Council during the debate on 26 March were rejected by the sponsors of the draft resolution and their supporters. The FRY Ambassador deplored the 'flagrant aggression by NATO countries, led by the United States', which could not be justified under international law.[138] Ukraine and Belarus repeated the Russian line that NATO's actions were illegal, and this position was strongly supported by China, which opposed NATO's action as 'a blatant violation of the principles of the Charter . . . and of international law, as well as a challenge to the

---

[135] S/PV.3989, 26 Mar. 1999, 6.   [136] Ibid.   [137] Ibid. 7.   [138] Ibid. 11.

authority of the Security Council'.[139] The Indian representative stated that NATO 'believes itself to be above the law. We find this deeply uncomfortable.' Indeed, India challenged the international legitimacy of NATO's action by arguing that the 'international community can hardly be said to have endorsed their actions when already representatives of half of humanity have said that they do not agree with what they have done'.[140]

The vote in the Security Council was historic because, for the first time since the founding of the Charter, seven members either legitimated, excused or acquiesced in the use of force justified on humanitarian grounds in a context where there was no express Council authorization. The Russian draft resolution articulated the pluralist norms that had dominated earlier Security Council debates on intervention in the former Yugoslavia, and its rejection by the majority of the non-permanent members must have surprised the Russians. They would not, one suspects, have tabled such a motion had they known that it would be comprehensively defeated. Is the action, then, a transformative moment in the emergence of a new norm?

One explanation for the votes cast was supplied by the Cuban Ambassador, who described the vote as a 'shameful' one in which 'international legality is being violated', and he claimed that 'never before has the unipolar order imposed by the United States been so obvious and so disturbing'.[141] How far US power was responsible for the Security Council vote on 26 March, and how far it reflects a sea change in international norms on the legitimacy of unilateral humanitarian intervention, are questions that go to the heart of the theoretical issues raised in the book and I take them up in the concluding chapter.

Conclusion

The story of intervention in the Balkans in the 1990s confirms the old adage that prevention is always better than cure. The society of states missed so many opportunities to intervene decisively, with governments always finding reasons why they should pass by on the other side. It is probably too simple to imagine that sinking a few Yugoslav warships shelling Dubrovnik in late 1991 would have stopped Milosevic. But, since Western governments never tried this option, it cannot be known whether a limited use of force would have deterred the Serbs. Having failed to stop the killing in Croatia, the ghastly descent into violence that engulfed the civilians of Bosnia could surely have been prevented by the UN Security Council sending a multinational force and turning that country into a UN protectorate. The most

---

[139] Ibid. 9.   [140] Ibid. 16.   [141] Ibid. 13.

important lesson to draw from the experience of UN intervention in Bosnia in the 1990s is that the preventative deployment of forces could have averted the worst of the calamities that befell the peoples of the former Yugoslavia.

When intervention finally came, it did so in the form of armed escorts for humanitarian relief convoys. This was better than doing nothing, since to have left the civilians of Bosnia to their fate would have led to an even greater loss of life, the complete triumph of Serbian war aims, and the risk of the conflict escalating into a wider regional conflagration. Yet, while the policy of protecting aid convoys saved hundreds of thousands who would otherwise have perished during the harsh Balkan winters of 1992–4, helping the needy in this way is not the same as rescuing them from danger. The limits of the West's moral engagement with the human suffering in Bosnia was revealed most starkly in the débâcle over the safe-areas policy. The UN's promise to protect civilians was revealed to be a hollow one, as the UN Security Council failed to muster the 30,000 troops that UN military commanders in Bosnia considered necessary both to defend and to demilitarize them.

The failure of UN member-states to volunteer the troops to protect the safe areas led to a growing reliance on air power as the means to weaken the Serbs militarily. In a dry run of what was to happen four years later over Kosovo, NATO's air strikes degraded the capabilities of the Bosnian Serb army, but this did not prevent them from overrunning the UN protected areas. But, rather than learn the lesson that you cannot stop paramilitary murder and ethnic cleansing from the air, Alliance leaders wrongly concluded that the decisive factor in Milosevic's acceptance of a deal at Dayton was NATO air strikes against Bosnian Serb forces in September 1995.

The conviction that the threat and use of bombing could achieve quick results, and the belief shared by Clinton and Blair that NATO should have intervened more decisively in Bosnia, meant Alliance leaders were in no mood to compromise with Belgrade over ethnic cleansing in Kosovo. How far, then, did NATO's first war in defence of human rights meet the tests of a legitimate humanitarian intervention? Turning to the question of necessity or last resort, Blair claimed in his Chicago speech that, 'we should always give peace every chance, as we have in the case of Kosovo'.[142] Robert Skidelsky argues that, 'had NATO accepted from 1998 that force was ruled out . . . the diplomacy would have been different'.[143] The point overlooked by Skidelsky, and others who accuse NATO of giving up on negotiations too early, is that Milosevic made concessions in late 1998 only because NATO threatened air strikes.[144] NATO's objective of stopping Serb ethnic cleansing depended upon

---

[142] Blair, Economic Club of Chicago, 9.

[143] R. Skidelsky, 'Is Military Intervention over Kosovo Justified?', *Prospect Debate*, 5 June 1999.

[144] It has been suggested that NATO should have provided greater resources for the OSCE verification mission in late 1998, so that, instead of deploying only a few hundred inspectors, there were thousands of properly trained and equipped verifiers crawling over Kosovo with television

Milosevic accepting the deployment of a force that could protect Kosovars, and he was never going to permit this without a fight.

Equally problematic is the argument that NATO confronted the FRY with unacceptable terms at Rambouillet, the rejection of which legitimated NATO's use of force.[145] The argument that no sovereign state would have accepted the terms of an implementation agreement that gave NATO unprecedented rights of access in the FRY ignores the point that the whole purpose of Rambouillet was to limit severely the FRY's sovereignty over Kosovo. Milosevic was the source of the human rights violations against Kosovars, and the Interim Agreement was designed to end these. The argument that NATO should have persevered with the OSCE inspectors who were acting as a brake on Milosevic ignores the reality that the Serbs had begun their spring offensive under the cover of negotiations at Rambouillet and Paris. Had Milosevic been serious about entering into a dialogue with the Kosovars on autonomy for the province, his delegation would surely have come forward with constructive proposals at Rambouillet and Paris.[146] The fact that none was forthcoming made it easy for the Alliance to argue that it had exhausted all the available diplomatic options. The challenge to those who argue that NATO employed force without exhausting credible peaceful alternatives is to show that there was a non-violent strategy that could have established the conditions for the protection of human rights in Kosovo.

Ken Booth argues that outsiders 'could have looked after the refugees, built a hostile international consensus against Milosevic, imposed extremely rigor- ous sanctions on Serbia, helped in whatever ways possible the empowerment of Serbian civil[ized] society, and offered huge incentives in terms of regional economic and security building in return for a changed polity in Kosovo'.[147] Booth does not reject humanitarian intervention in Kosovo on pacifist grounds, but on the pragmatic ones that Operation Allied Force did not save lives and was counterproductive.

This is a damning indictment, but the problem with Booth's approach is that it would have taken years to work and in the meantime Milosevic could have carried on his ethnic cleansing and repopulated Kosovo with the Krajina Serbs. After all, Serbia was subject to mandatory economic sanctions through the 1990s and this did little to change the policies of the Milosevic regime. It might be countered that NATO's strategy of violent humanitarian intervention failed as a *rescue*, but there are two replies here: first, whilst the bombing accelerated Serb ethnic cleansing and led to thousands of Kosovars being killed, this has to be set against the fact that NATO's use of force made

---

cameras on hand to record any atrocities. The problem with this argument is that Milosevic permit- ted only 1,700 inspectors to be deployed.

[145] This is a view articulated by Ken Booth, John Pilger, and others.

[146] I owe this point to Alex Bellamy.

[147] Booth, 'The Kosovo Tragedy: Epilogue to Another "Low and Dishonest Decade?" ', 14.

possible KFOR and a measure of political autonomy that would have been unthinkable in any other context. Secondly, had NATO created a credible ground option, it would have had the option of intervening to halt Serb atrocities against the Kosovars in March 1999.

What has to be explained in the case of Kosovo is why the most powerful military alliance in history could not furnish a credible ground option. The answer is that no Alliance government argued for such a strategy, because they believed that casualties would undermine public support at home. The humanitarian motives behind NATO's action have to be located in the context of the overriding constraint that the operation be 'casualty free'. Without this assurance, there would have been no intervention in Kosovo. It was this requirement that dictated the selection of bombing as the means of humanitarian intervention, which, in turn, produced results that contradicted the humanitarian justifications of the operation. This judgement is softened by the fact that, without the bombing campaign, it is inconceivable that Milosevic would have agreed to KFOR. The question is whether the contradiction that opened up between the means of intervention and a positive humanitarian outcome is stark enough to disqualify Operation Allied Force as humanitarian. The moral judgement here is a complex one and it can in the nature of things be only an interim assessment. On the one hand, the intervention precipitated the very disaster it was aimed at averting, and KFOR failed to prevent the exodus of Serbs or guarantee the security of those who remained. On the other hand, through a combination of bombing, Russian diplomacy, and the threat of a ground invasion, Milosevic accepted a deal that returned the refugees to their homes, and created KFOR and a UN civil administration committed to helping the Kosovars build a multiethnic polity based on the rule of law.

The difficulty with balancing these conflicting moral considerations is that it can never be known how many more Kosovars would have been killed and driven from their homes had NATO not acted in March 1999. NATO acted preventatively and it was right to do so, but it employed the wrong means. The Alliance should have demonstrated its commitment to defending human rights by building up an invasion force so that, if diplomacy failed, it could have conducted a successful *rescue* mission. The reply to those who argue that bombing was the only strategy that could ensure Alliance cohesion is that, by ruling out the ground option, NATO governments demonstrated that their commitment to defending the human rights of Kosovars did not extend to accepting the risks to soldiers' lives of deploying ground forces.

Conclusion

This developing international norm in favour of intervention to protect civilians from wholesale slaughter will no doubt continue to pose profound challenges to the international community.

Any such evolution in our understanding of State sovereignty and individual sovereignty will, in some quarters, be met with distrust, scepticism, even hostility. But it is an evolution that we should welcome.

Why? Because, despite its limitations and imperfections, it is testimony to a humanity that cares more, not less, for the suffering in its midst, and a humanity that will do more, and not less, to end it.

It is a hopeful sign at the end of the twentieth century.[1]

Kofi Annan's statement supports the proposition that the practice of humanitarian intervention in the 1990s represented a new solidarism in the society of states. The purpose of this concluding chapter is to reflect on this claim in the light of the theoretical and empirical analysis in the previous chapters. How far is the new solidarity exhibited by the society of states with regard to the enforcement of human rights evidence that order and justice can be reconciled? The chapters in Part Three charted how international society became more open to solidarist themes in the 1990s. It also showed how pluralism and realism continue to limit the possibilities of international society recognizing humanitarian intervention as a legitimate normative practice. In this final chapter I examine how these constraints on developing the solidarist project might be overcome.

The Voice of Solidarism in the Diplomatic Dialogue

Kofi Annan's cautious welcome to the doctrine of humanitarian intervention stands in sharp contrast to the position taken by former UN Secretary Generals. It demonstrates how this question has moved to the forefront of policy concerns at the dawn of a new century. The 54th General Assembly in September 1999 witnessed a wide-ranging debate over the legitimacy and legality of humanitarian intervention, with many governments advancing

[1] Kofi A. Annan, 'Two Concepts of Sovereignty', Address to the 5th Session of the United Nations General Assembly, reprinted in *The Question of Intervention: Statements by the Secretary-General* (United Nations Department of Public Information: New York, 1999), 44.

the once inadmissible argument that human rights considerations could form a legitimate basis for the Security Council to authorize the use of force. Norms have clearly changed since the debates in the UN over India's and Vietnam's use of force in the 1970s, and Kofi Annan is right to believe that there is a 'developing international norm' in support of intervention. However, this normative change is subject to the very important caveat that the society of states shows little or no enthusiasm for legitimating acts of humanitarian intervention not authorized by the Security Council.

In his speech to the UN General Assembly introducing his Annual Report in September 1999, the Secretary General expressed his concern that unilateral interventions justified on humanitarian grounds might erode the foundations of international order. It is against this background that my study of the Bangladesh, Cambodian, and Ugandan cases assumes considerable significance. India, Vietnam, and Tanzania all resorted to force against a target state that was committing mass slaughter without Security Council authorization. In each case, humanitarian claims could have been invoked to justify the use of force, but, with the initial exception of India, governments preferred to rely on highly strained interpretations of pluralist rules that constituted the acceptable boundaries of permissible action. It is not that state leaders in the 1970s were unaware of the doctrine of humanitarian intervention, as the General Assembly debate over the Vietnamese intervention illustrated. Recall how Singapore's Ambassador refuted this justification on the grounds that humanitarian intervention will always be abused by the powerful. Other speakers emphasized the pluralist objection that the society of states was too divided on conceptions of justice to legitimate a right of humanitarian intervention. It was this combination of realist and pluralist arguments that legitimated the hostile international response to India, and especially Vietnam's use of force.

The argument in Part Two that humanitarian claims were not accepted as a legitimate basis for the use of force in the 1970s is open to the rejoinder that we should look beyond the words of states to their actual deeds. Here it is argued that the practical responses of states to India's, and especially Tanzania's actions, show that these were treated as humanitarian exceptions to the rules. I examined this argument in relation to Teson's analysis of the Bangladeshi and Ugandan cases. His view is that the conversation in the Security Council, General Assembly, and OAU, as disclosed through the justifications of the actors, is not as reliable a guide to the actual motivations of states as their deeds. It is the latter—rather than the *opinio juris* of states—that constitute the best description of the operative norms governing state practice.[2] I showed in

---

[2] Teson's specific argument with regard to humanitarian intervention finds general support in the following contention of the international lawyer D'Amato, who argues that scholars 'should be highly skeptical about . . . the briefs [governments] file in a court . . . the opinions of their attorneys general or their foreign offices . . . And skepticism is also a good antitdote to the all too easy tendency to view General Assembly resolutions, or Security Council condemnations of state actions,

Chapters 2 and 4 the limitations of Teson's account of the Bangladeshi and Ugandan cases, but it is the general claim that we should focus on 'deeds not words' that I have in my sights here.

It is a categorical error to posit a separation between words and deeds when thinking about how the social world hangs together; the former constitute the latter by establishing the boundaries of what is possible. This book has shown that, in the society of states, words *matter*. The legitimating reasons employed by governments are crucial because they enable and constrain actions. For example, the fact that the Nixon Administration named India's intervention in East Pakistan as a *violation* rather than a *rescue* (the alternative interpretation proffered by Senator Kennedy) is significant, because, once this meaning is fixed on an action, it immediately legitimates certain courses of action whilst rendering others as unacceptable.

Moreover, it is not the case that the Nixon Administration was free to create whatever discourse it liked: the cold-war mindset that drove US foreign policy at this time and the pluralist morality of the society of states were powerful constraints on the USA legitimating India's action as humanitarian. The fact that alternative solidarist interpretations were available to policy-makers reminds us that the meanings governments impose on actions are not natural nor inevitable. What is important, then, is to consider how the dominant discourse of legitimation worked to marginalize solidarism in US policy-making in the 1970s.

I have argued in this book that legitimacy is constitutive of state actions. But it might be objected that the pluralist rule structure of the society of states was not sufficiently constraining to prevent India, Tanzania, and Vietnam from using force. This appears to support the realist claim that states can always find a convenient rationale to justify actions that breach the rules. On the contrary, as Chapters 2 and 4 showed, whatever hidden motives India and Tanzania might have harboured, the creation of Bangladesh and the over-throw of Idi Amin would not have been possible without the legitimating reasons employed by both governments. Their justifications of 'refugee aggression' and Ugandan aggression were not *post hoc* rationalizations of deci-sions taken for other reasons; they were the essential enabling conditions of India's and Tanzania's decisions to use force. To reiterate one of the guiding themes of *Saving Strangers*, state actions *will be constrained if they cannot be justified in terms of a plausible legitimating reason*.

The logical corollary to this claim is that changing norms enable new state actions, and Part Three explored how Western states came to justify inter-vention in northern Iraq and Somalia on humanitarian grounds. How, then,

---

as expressive of international rules of law. Sometimes a Security Council condemnation that is not followed by any forcible action on the part of the Council is another way of saying to the ostens-ibly offending state, "We have to condemn you verbally, but don't worry we're not going to do anything about it" ' (quoted in Farer, 'An Enquiry', 188).

are we to explain Western states' invoking solidarist claims to justify their interventions in the 1990s when these governments took the lead in condemning India's and Vietnam's interventions that could and should have been legitimated on humanitarian grounds?

The realist answer is that the new practice of humanitarian intervention in the 1990s is a phenomenon of changing power relations. The end of the cold war dramatically changed the global balance of power, with Western states, led by the USA, occupying a hegemonic position in the global political order. As a result, there is no state or grouping of states capable of challenging Western political, economic, and military domination. This has allowed the USA, and its allies, to project military force into Iraq, Somalia, and the Balkans without worrying, as they did during the cold war, that intervention might generate superpowers, crises. Without this pre-eminent political position, Western states would have been much more cautious about acting without Russian support, as they did over northern Iraq, Bosnia, and especially Kosovo. Noam Chomsky argues that the new-found US enthusiasm for a doctrine of humanitarian intervention reflects the fact that this has become the legitimating ideology to justify the projection of US power necessary to maintain its economic hegemony now that the ideology of the cold war no longer serves this purpose.[3]

There are two problems with this realist explanation as I have argued in Part Three. First, it ignores the crucial point that, even if officials in the Bush and Clinton administrations invoked humanitarian justifications only for ulterior reasons, they found themselves constrained in their subsequent actions by the need to defend these as being in conformity with their humanitarian claims. Secondly, the view that US and Western policy-makers manipulated the legitimating ideology of humanitarianism to serve selfish interests ignores the extent to which the solidarist claims advanced by Western states are a result of normative change at the domestic level: the pressure for humanitarian intervention in the cases of northern Iraq and Somalia came from domestic publics, shocked by television pictures of slaughter and suffering, demanding that 'something be done'.

I will return to the possibilities of television and public opinion as transmission belts for solidarist values later in the chapter, but for the moment I want to consider how far the humanitarian claims advanced by Western states challenged the dominant pluralist legitimating principles of the society of states. As I showed in Chapter 5 and 6, the Security Council became progressively more open to solidarist values in 1991–2 as a result of Western governments seeking the flag of UN legitimacy for their interventions in northern Iraq and Somalia. This highlights how raising new humanitarian

---

[3] N. Chomsky, *The New Military Humanism: Lessons from Kosovo* (Monroe, Me.: Common Courage Press, 1999).

claims in the society of states depends upon material power resources, since, without the commitment of Western governments to act over northern Iraq and Somalia, the Security Council would not have adopted Resolutions 688 and 794. Both of these resolutions pushed against pluralist meanings of permissible Security Council action under Chapter VII: the former enabled intervention to create the 'safe havens' in northern Iraq and the latter mandated the USA to use force in defence of humanitarian values in a context where the Somali state had collapsed.

The key normative change in the 1990s was that the Security Council, under pressure from Western governments—who were themselves responding to the demands of public opinion at home—increasingly interpreted its responsibilities under Chapter VII as including the enforcement of global humanitarian norms. However, this norm of humanitarian intervention is crucially limited to cases where the Security Council authorizes action. The highly controversial issue concerns the legality and legitimacy of individual states, or groups of states, intervening to end human rights abuses when there is no Council authorization. This dilemma first arose over northern Iraq, when Western powers set up the safe havens without an explicit UN mandate, but it became a major issue of controversy during NATO's intervention in Kosovo.

The lack of international criticism of Western intervention in northern Iraq led Britain to invoke this case as a legal precedent when it came to justifying intervention in Kosovo. I showed in Chapter 8 how the legal advisers in the Foreign and Commonwealth Office tried to avoid NATO being projected into the role of a 'norm entrepreneur' by arguing that the case of northern Iraq provided a legal basis for the use of force in Kosovo. The argument is that the case of northern Iraq establishes a precedent for the use of force in support of humanitarian purposes laid down in existing Security Council resolutions, even in the absence of express Council authorization. The problem with this legal claim is twofold: first, it was not the justification invoked by the Western powers to defend the intervention in northern Iraq. Rather, the argument made in April 1991 by Western governments was that Resolution 688 provided sufficient authority by *itself* to justify the creation of the safe havens and a no-fly zone.

The second problem with the British Government's position is that there is an important difference between the two cases that goes a long way to explaining why they were treated so differently by the major powers of Russia, China, and India. The intervention in northern Iraq counts as humanitarian, whereas, as I argued in Chapter 8, the use of force to defend human rights in Kosovo has much weaker humanitarian qualifications, because, at best, it only barely satisfies the threshold tests of proportionality and a positive humanitarian outcome. The humanitarian justification for the safe havens and a no-fly zone in northern Iraq were clearly consistent with the means employed. As I argued in Chapter 5, the case of northern Iraq meets all the counter-restrictionist tests for a permissible use of force under Article 2 (4). Although there were attempts by Alliance governments after the intervention in Kosovo to legitimate NATO's use of force as not breaching Article 2 (4), this is a very difficult case to sustain. It is true that NATO intervention did not lead to a regime change or loss of territory by the FRY. But it is a very permissive interpretation of Article 2 (4) to argue that it permits states to conduct a sustained bombing campaign against military targets, factories, bridges, other lines of communication, and oil refineries of a state that is committing gross abuses of human rights on its territory. In a context where Serb civilians were being killed as a consequence of the aerial bombing of the FRY, and the initial result of rescue from the air was to accelerate the ethnic cleansing, Russia, China, and India were able to challenge the legitimacy of Operation Allied Force.

The reaction in the Security Council to NATO's bombing of the FRY was very different from the acquiescence that greeted Western intervention in northern and southern Iraq. As I argued in Chapter 5, members who privately opposed or were uncomfortable with the safe havens and no-fly zones acquiesced in them because they did not want to be seen criticizing actions that were saving lives. The shaming power of humanitarian norms did not operate to constrain Russia and China over Kosovo because the discrepancy between NATO's humanitarian justifications, on the one hand, and the failure of the means employed to achieve these purposes, on the other, exposed the Alliance to condemnation from these powers. Russia and China charged that NATO had not only flagrantly violated the UN Charter; it had also by its actions produced the very humanitarian catastrophe that it claimed to be preventing.

The opposition from Russia and China is not surprising, given their threat, prior to the bombing, to veto any resolution put before the Council authorizing NATO's use of force against the FRY. What has to be explained, however, is how on 26 March 1999 six non-Western states could support five NATO governments and Slovenia (no friend of the Milosevic regime) in comprehensively defeating a Russian draft resolution condemning the bombing. As I discussed in Chapter 8, the Cuban Ambassador was emphatic that the vote was a result of US hegemony, and this brings us back to the question whether power can always create a legitimacy convenient to itself.

The realist view is that the Security Council is an arena of power politics in which the strong manipulate the weak, and where all members engage in strategic bargaining to gain support for their positions. On this reading, the votes cast against the Russian resolution by the non-Western grouping are to be explained in terms of the pressure exerted by Western states. The problem with the realist view is that it does not sufficiently distinguish between power that is based on relations of domination and power that is legitimate because it is based on shared norms. A good example of this is the shaming power of humanitarian norms, which is a form of power not derived from the political and economic hegemony of Western states; rather, it stems from the fact that even repressive governments recognize the need to legitimate their actions as being in conformity with global human rights standards. It is important to differentiate theoretically and empirically between actions that are acquiesced in because of considerations of brute power, those grudgingly accepted because of the shaming power of humanitarian norms, and those validated because they are morally approved.[4]

A recent paper by an international lawyer draws attention to the problem of deriving legitimation from acquiescence. Nigel White argues that 'lack of condemnation by the Security Council cannot be seen as an authorisation to use force'.[5] While this is correct, the more pertinent question is whether the statements in the Council constitute *opinio juris* in support of *a right of unilateral humanitarian intervention*. With no explicit Security Council authorization owing to the threat of the Russian and Chinese veto, the five NATO states on the Security Council were forced to advance the following new claim: that in exceptional circumstances, states have a legal right to use force in support of existing resolutions adopted under Chapter VII, where this is necessary to prevent a humanitarian catastrophe.[6] The vote on 26 March lends some support to this proposition, but it is unwise to read too much into what was effectively a 7–3 vote, where only four of the seven spoke in support of NATO's action. As I argued in relation to the cases of Uganda and northern Iraq, acquiescence should certainly not be read as constituting the emergence of a new norm. Thus, it would be wrong to read into Gambia's, Brazil's, and Gabon's silence support for a new norm of humanitarian intervention outside express Council authorization. The realist explanation of their vote is a persuasive one, but it is not necessarily conclusive, since these states could have abstained. Consequently, two other explanations suggest themselves: first, that they felt constrained from doing anything other than tacitly supporting NATO's action by concern at being exposed as opposing an intervention to end atrocities; and, secondly, that, while they felt unable to argue the case publicly, they showed by their vote that they understood the political context within the Council that had forced NATO to act without authorization. There is no reason to choose between these three explanations, since all of them probably influenced the

---

[4] I owe this point to Andrew Hurrell.

[5] N. D. White, 'The Legality of Bombing in the Name of Humanity', paper presented to the British International Studies Association annual conference, University of Manchester, 20–22 Dec. 1999, 6.

[6] Speaking in South Africa three months before NATO launched Operation Allied Force, Prime Minister Blair considered that: 'people say you can't be self-appointed guardians of what is right and wrong. True, but when the international community agrees certain objectives and then fails to implement them, those who can act, must' (Tony Blair, 'Facing the Modern Challenge: The Third Way in Britain and South Africa', Cape Town, South Africa, 8 Jan. 1999).

reasoning that led Brazil, Gambia, and Gabon to acquiesce in NATO's action.

Only Argentina and Slovenia expressed moral approval for NATO's action. Realism would argue that Argentina's decision reflected considerations of interest, but this ignores how normative changes at the domestic level alter conception of national interests. Argentina's growing commitments to democratic values at home was being reflected in a new-found commitment to defend human rights internationally. Similarly, realists might explain Slovenia's condemnation of the Milosevic regime in power political terms, but there are no good reasons for doubting the sincerity of the claims it raised in the Council. (It might be significant in this regard that Slovenia's Permanent Representative at the UN was a former professor of international law.)

Now, even if it is conceded to the realists that Argentina and Slovenia were only using language strategically to further their interests, what is important is that they both sought to legitimate NATO's action by justifying it as being in conformity with the norms of human rights and Article 24 of the Charter, which constituted the givens of discourse in the Security Council over Kosovo. This reiterates the importance of Skinner's argument that, when actors want to justify actions that challenge existing norms, they seek to defend these as being in conformity with the dominant legitimating discourse. As I showed in Chapters 2 and 4, India tried to justify its use of force against Pakistan by appealing to a solidarist interpretation of the human rights norms in the UN Charter, and the new Ugandan Government sought to legitimate Tanzania's overthrow of Idi Amin by pointing to the contradictions between the normative principles enshrined in the OAU Charter and the practices of African states.

The other key point that emerges from this discussion of the Security Council debate on 26 March is that, having defended NATO's action as being in conformity with the legitimating discourse of the society of states, Argentina and Slovenia will be exposed as hypocrites if they adopt a different position in future cases where this argument is convincingly employed by other states to legitimate similar actions. Having defended an action in terms of a particular moral principle, actors that want to be legitimated find themselves constrained in their range of subsequent actions.

The justification advanced by the five NATO governments was roundly rejected by Russia, China, India, Belarus, and Cuba. Beyond the Security Council the action was greeted with approval by the EU (though there were significant bodies of opposition in states such as Germany, Greece and Italy) and the Organization of Islamic States (which, like Malaysia, welcomed an action that saved fellow Muslims), and, whilst the Organization of American States issued a statement regretting the action, it did not condemn it. Given that NATO's action drove a coach and horses through the pluralist understanding of the rules governing the use of force under the UN Charter, the international reaction was very favourable.

This raises the question as to how many states have to validate a new norm before it can be said to have acquired the status of a new rule of customary international law. And what if some of the objectors to a new rule are among the most powerful states in the world? Michael Byers makes the important point that, where there is only one case of past practice in support of a new rule, states can easily nullify it by acting against it in future instances.[7] Consequently, given the record of state practice against a rule of unilateral humanitarian intervention documented in this book, it will require additional cases to the Kosovo one where practice and *opinio juris* support this rule before a judgement can be made as to how far there is a new custom of unilateral humanitarian intervention in the society of states.

In this context, it is important to realize that Kosovo is limited as a legal precedent for unilateral humanitarian intervention. It could plausibly be invoked by other states in a future context only where the Security Council has already adopted Chapter VII resolutions identifying a government's human rights abuses as a threat to international peace and security, and where the threat or use of the veto prevented the Council authorizing the use of force. Restricting a legal right of unilateral humanitarian intervention to situations where the Council has already adopted Chapter VII resolutions reduces the dangers of states deciding for themselves when humanitarian intervention is permitted. As Vaughan Lowe put it in his Memorandum submitted to the Foreign Affairs Committee of the House of Commons, 'the right to act [claimed by NATO over Kosovo] is not a unilateral right, under which each and every State may decide for itself that intervention is warranted . . . The prior decision of the Security Council is asserted as a key element of the justification'.[8] This restriction on the right of humanitarian intervention suits Western members of the Council, since they have the power of veto to ensure that no resolutions are adopted in cases where their interests might be affected. But this cuts both ways. If a legal right of unilateral humanitarian intervention is to be restricted in this manner, then NATO could well find itself deprived of this legal argument in future cases where it wants to act. Having watched NATO governments defend their military action in Kosovo by appealing to three resolutions adopted under Chapter VII, it is likely that Russia and China will be considerably more cautious about passing such resolutions in the future.

Given the volatile domestic situation in Russia, and the heightened sensitivity of Russia and China to actions that erode the sovereignty rule, it is highly unlikely that the permanent members of the Security Council will

---

[7] Byers, *Custom, Power and the Power of Rules*, 159.

[8] V. Lowe, 'International Legal Issues Arising in the Kosovo Crisis', Memorandum submitted to the Foreign Affairs Committee of the House of Commons, Feb. 2000, 5.

become a humanitarian 'coalition of the willing' in future cases of gross human rights abuses. It could be argued that whether there is a new legal custom supporting unilateral humanitarian intervention is beside the point, since, when acts of brutality offend against the conscience of humanity, those with the power to end this have a moral responsibility to act. If the words 'We the Peoples', in the Preamble of the UN Charter, have meaning, then the threat or use of a veto in the Security Council cannot be allowed to stand in the way of humanitarian intervention. This sentiment was echoed by Kofi Annan in his opening speech to the 1999 General Assembly, when he asked in relation to the Rwandan genocide: 'If, in those dark days and hours leading up to the genocide, a coalition of States had been prepared to act in defence of the Tutsi population, but did not receive prompt Council authorization, should such a coalition have stood aside and allowed the horror to unfold?'.[9]

This voice in the dialogue over the legitimacy of humanitarian intervention echoes the view of Franck and Rodley. It may be recalled that they argued in the wake of the Bangladeshi case that, whilst humanitarian intervention breaks the law, this is morally justified in exceptional cases. The fundamental problem with this argument is that it plays into the hands of those states who maintain that humanitarian intervention is always a phenomenon of power, and that it issues a licence for the powerful to impose their values on the weak. This objection was expressed by Russia in the General Assembly in September 1999 when it warned that 'coercive measures . . . should not be allowed to turn into a repressive mechanism to influence States and peoples regarded by some as not being to their liking'.[10] The difficulty is that, if Western governments are perceived to be tearing up UN Charter principles when they want to intervene, other states might decide to treat these rules equally cavalierly in the future. Kofi Annan was well aware of this concern and cautioned those who welcomed NATO's action in Kosovo to remember that 'actions without Security Council authorization threaten the very core of the international security system founded on the Charter of the United Nations'.[11]

The challenge is to explore the possibilities of a solidarist third way that legitimates humanitarian intervention when the Security Council is prevented from authorizing the use of force, because of the threat or use of the veto, and that does not jeopardize existing restraints upon the use of force. Kofi Annan's response to the moral and legal dilemmas raised by the Kosovo crisis was to encourage the General Assembly to debate this question

[9] Annan, 'Two Concepts of Sovereignty', 39.
[10] Statement of Russian Foreign Minister before the General Assembly, Press Release GA.9599, http://srch 1.un.org:80/plweb-cgi/fastweb, 21 Sept. 1999.
[11] K. A. Annan, *Preventing War and Disaster: A Growing Global Challenge* (1999 Annual Report on the Work of the Organization; New York, 1999), 20.

at its 54th session. As I noted at the beginning of this chapter, several governments argued that the defence of human rights by force was legitimate if authorized by the Security Council, but no government expressly advocated a right of unilateral humanitarian intervention, and many states strongly opposed this.

The continuing reluctance of the society of states to concede a right of unilateral humanitarian intervention to states or regional organizations raises the question as to whether international society is right to treat the doctrine with such suspicion. Is the voice of pluralism correct to remind us that there is an irreconcilable conflict between order and justice, and that 'any principle of humanitarian intervention would issue a licence for all kinds of interference, claiming with more or less plausibility to be humanitarian, but driving huge wedges into international order'.[12] The solidarist reply that I have developed in this book is that the society of states is too timid in believing that a doctrine of unilateral humanitarian intervention will undermine the pillars of interstate order. States do disagree over the meaning and priority to be accorded civil, political, economic, and social rights, but these controversies should not obscure the fact that governments have signed up to legal instruments that commit them to upholding basic standards of humanity. Indeed, no government questions these normative standards, even when breaching them, and the dispute is over the means that can legitimately be employed to enforce these standards on governments that violate them.

The thesis advanced in *Saving Strangers* is that India's, Vietnam's and Tanzania's actions *were all justifiable because the use of force was the only means of ending atrocities on a massive scale, and the motives/means employed were consistent with a positive humanitarian outcome.* Vietnam and Tanzania should have justified their use of force on humanitarian grounds (India tried, of course), and this is the legitimating reason that should be invoked by states that can credibly make this case in the future. The response to the pluralist objection that unilateral humanitarian intervention will undermine order by opening the floodgates to intervention is that the society of states should recognize exceptions only where states can legitimately defend their actions as humanitarian. They would have to make a convincing case that a supreme humanitarian emergency exists and that the use of force satisfies the requirements of necessity and proportionality, and that the motives/means are not contradictory with the achievement of a positive humanitarian outcome. Establishing this criteria does not resolve the question of whether the conditions have been satisfied in hard cases like Kosovo, but it does create a framework within which actors can argue over the merits of the competing claims.

The need for legitimation is a powerful constraining force on state actions, and, if governments are unable to make a plausible defence of their interven-

---

[12] Vincent, *Human Rights and International Relations*, 114.

tion as humanitarian, they will be inhibited from trying to exploit a new norm permitting unilateral humanitarian intervention. But if states do try and abuse such a rule, the society of states should mobilize sanctions against these governments as a deterrent to others. At this point, realists and pluralists will retort that this ignores the fact that it is the powerful who decide what counts as humanitarian, and who control which states are sanctioned. Considerations of brute power cannot be ignored and they will clearly influence the level of sanctioning in particular cases, but what is crucial is that even the most powerful states know that they will be required to answer before the society of states and what Henry Shue calls 'the court of world public opinion'.[13] Even the powerful do not want to be exposed as hypocrites, and, once a state has legitimated an intervention as humanitarian, its subsequent actions will be constrained by the need to avoid acting in ways that undermine a positive humanitarian outcome.

The failure of the society of states to legitimate India's, Vietnam's and Tanzania's action as humanitarian demonstrates the moral bankruptcy of the pluralist discourse that constituted the limits of the diplomatic dialogue in the 1970s. However, there is evidence from the debate in the Security Council in the immediate aftermath of the Kosovo crisis that some governments are giving a new solidarist meaning to India's and Vietnam's interventions that is in conformity with the theory of humanitarian intervention I have developed in this book. The Slovenian Ambassador, speaking on 24 March 1999, offered a revisionist reading of state practice in the Bangladeshi case when he asserted that,

In 1971, in Asia, a State Member of the United Nations used force in a situation of extreme necessity. That was a case of the use of force without the authorization of the Security Council and without reference to legitimate self-defence. Nevertheless, the situation of necessity was very widely understood in the international community. I think that the historical lessons that can be drawn from that example should not be completely ignored today.[14]

Three months later, the Netherlands Ambassador, in defending NATO's action over Kosovo, offered a radically different interpretation of Vietnam's overthrow of the Pol Pot regime to that which prevailed in 1979. He acknowledged that his government had been wrong to name Vietnam's use of force as a violation of the rules, and asserted that traditional pluralist interpretation of the rules were under assault by a new solidarist doctrine that legitimated the use of force in defence of human rights.

Today, we regard it as a generally accepted rule of international law that no sovereign

---

[13] H. Shue, 'Let Whatever is Smouldering Erupt? Conditional Sovereignty, Reviewable Intervention and Rwanda 1994', in A. J. Padi, P. Jarvis, and C. Reus-Smit (eds.), *Between Sovereignty and Global Governance: The United Nations, the State and Civil Society* (London: Macmillan, 1998), 77.
[14] S/PV.3988, 24 Mar. 1999, 19.

State has the right to terrorize its own citizens. Only if that shift is a reality can we explain how on 26 March the Russian–Chinese draft resolution branding NATO air strikes a violation of the Charter could be so decisively rejected by 12 votes to 3 . . . Times have changed, and they will not change back. One simply cannot imagine a replay in the twenty-first century of the shameful episode of the 1980s, when the United Nations was apparently more indignant at a Vietnamese military intervention in Cambodia, which almost all Cambodians had experienced as a liberation, than at three years of Khmer Rouge genocide. As a result of that misconception, the large majority of delegations, including my own, allowed the Khmer Rouge to continue to occupy the Cambodian seat in the General Assembly for more than a decade.[15]

The implication of the above statements is that the international reaction to the Kosovo case marks a watershed in the society of states, and that we should expect to see it exhibiting a new solidarity in response to any future cases where states intervene to end atrocities without Council authorization. What is required is for international society to begin a genuine dialogue on the conditions that legitimate states using force for humanitarian purposes. A key solidarist claim to be raised in any such dialogue is that it is not acceptable for permanent members to exercise the veto in situations where states request Council authorization, and where there is significant international support for intervention to prevent or stop gross human rights abuses.[16]

This argument was invoked by Slovenia in justifying NATO's action in Kosovo, and it finds support in a speech by the Czech President, Václav Havel, who considered that it was time 'to reconsider whether it is still appropriate, even hypothetically, that in the Security Council one country can outvote the rest of the world'.[17]

There was another way that NATO could have substantiated its claim to be acting on behalf of the 'international community', and that would have been to place the issue before the General Assembly. Nigel White argues that the 1950 'Uniting for Peace' could have been invoked for this purpose. The background to Uniting for Peace was that the post-war expectations of cooperation between the permanent members in the Security Council had broken down with the onset of the cold war, and the West viewed the frequent use of the Soviet veto in the 1946–50 period as 'an abuse of the right [of the veto]'.[18] Consequently, it sought this resolution as a way of bypassing the Soviet veto in the Security Council. The procedure that NATO could have followed to secure greater international legitimacy was to place a draft resolution before the Security Council authorizing it to use force against the FRY

---

[15] S/PV.4011, 10 June, 1999, 12–13.

[16] Andrew Linklater suggests that 'one of the qualities of the good international citizen is the willingness to challenge the legitimacy of the veto by irresponsible powers which are prepared to block international action to prevent human rights violations' (Andrew Linklater, 'The Good International Citizen and the Crisis in Kosovo', unpublished paper in possession of author, 10).

[17] Quoted in ibid. 10.

[18] White, 'The Legality of Bombing', 10–11.

in the event that the Milosevic regime continued to fail to comply with Council resolutions. At this point, a Russian and Chinese veto would have exposed these states as the ones opposing intervention to end the atrocities. Even if Russia and China had cast their vetoes, NATO would then have been able to put a procedural resolution forward requesting that the matter be transferred to the General Assembly under the 'Uniting for Peace' resolution (the right of the veto does not exist in relation to procedural resolutions). This leads White to argue that, had NATO 'won both a procedural vote in the Security Council and a substantive vote in the General Assembly, NATO then would have had a sound legal basis upon which to launch its air strikes'.[19]

The reason why Alliance governments did not go down this road of securing collective legitimation from the General Assembly is that they could not guarantee securing the two-thirds majority to pass a resolution recommending military action. Western governments were not even prepared to risk putting a draft resolution before the Security Council authorizing the use of force, and this is a body that they can be much more confident about controlling than the General Assembly. Requiring a two-thirds majority in the General Assembly in cases where the Security Council has found a threat to 'international peace and security' but is unable to act constitutes a high standard of legitimacy, and it would minimize the risk that states would abuse a right of humanitarian intervention. However, making Assembly approval a precondition for intervention poses, by analogy, the same question that Kofi Annan raised in relation to Council authorization: should a group of states stand aside if they cannot secure the necessary votes in the General Assembly in cases where massive and systematic abuses of human rights are taking place? Had India and Vietnam relied on General Assembly resolutions recommending their proposed interventions, the victims of state terror in East Pakistan and Cambodia would have been left to their fate.

I have argued in this book that state practice is not the acid test of the legitimacy of humanitarian intervention. But a society of states that legitimates unilateral humanitarian intervention in situations where the Security Council is unable to authorize action because of the veto would exhibit a new collective capacity for global humanitarian law enforcement that was so tragically lacking in the 1970s. India's and Vietnam's interventions in the 1970s count as humanitarian because they satisfy the threshold requirements established in Part One, but interventions that progressively meet the requirements above the threshold have a greater claim to legitimacy. The Tanzanian case is instructive here because it has a greater claim to legitimacy than either India or Vietnam. Nyerere had spoken out against the Ugandan Government's human rights abuses after Amin's seizure of power and there is every reason to think that humanitarian motives played a significant role in Nyerere's determination

---

[19] White, 'The Legality of Bombing', 14.

to overthrow Amin. For this reason, Tanzania had much stronger humanitarian credentials than Vietnam, and the international response should have reflected this. My argument is that, while Vietnam should not have been condemned or sanctioned, it would have been equally wrong to praise or materially support a state that had intervened in the absence of any humanitarian motive. By contrast, the society of states should have praised Tanzania's action and provided Nyerere with the financial support he was desperately seeking from the West to pay for it. This solidarist framework is the one that should be employed by governments, NGOs, media, and domestic publics in judging the humanitarian attributions of particular interventions. Judgements will be contested but what is important is that the determination of whether an intervention is justified does not rest solely with governments. Instead, the challenge is to create a global public sphere in which the non-state actors listed above play an important role in the process of judging the humanitarian credentials of interventions. Here, I agree with Shue that, by building up a series of judgements that establish the norms of legitimate humanitarian intervention, states will have greater assurances that this practice will be approved by other governments and world public opinion.[20] And in future cases where governments are judged to have satisfied not only the minimum requirements but also criteria above the threshold, then collective legitimation should take the form of political, economic, and even military support for the intervening state, thereby encouraging other governments to incur the costs and risks of humanitarian intervention.

The weakness of this approach to humanitarian intervention in the society of states is that it makes it a *right* but not a *duty*. The development of a new solidarist norm enables practices of intervention that were previously unthinkable, but, as I argued in Part Three, they do not determine these. There is no guarantee that humanitarian intervention will take place in cases where it is desperately needed, as in Rwanda in 1994.[21] This highlights the real limits of the 'developing international norm' in support of civilians in danger. It also brings us back to the question of how far governments, especially those Western state leaders who intervened in the name of defending human rights in the 1990s, lived up to the solidarist responsibility of acting as guardians of 'human rights everywhere'.

How Much will We Sacrifice?

I argued in Chapter 7 that, had any state or group of states come forward in April or May 1994 requesting a UN mandate to end the atrocities in Rwanda, this would have been readily agreed to. The barrier to intervention was not

---

[20] Shue, 'Let Whatever is Smouldering Erupt?, 76.   [21] Ibid.

any doctrinal disagreement among members as to the legitimate purview of Security Council action. Instead, as Kofi Annan acknowledged in his 1999 Annual Report, 'the failure to intervene was driven more by the reluctance of Member States to pay the human and other costs of intervention, and by doubts that the use of force would be successful, than by concerns about sovereignty'.[22] A solidarist conception of ethical statecraft requires state leaders in exceptional cases of supreme humanitarian emergency to risk, and if necessary lose, soldiers' lives. As I argued in Part One, this must always be subject to considerations of necessity and proportionality. The appalling failure of Western states to end the killings in Rwanda demonstrates that, even in a case where there is good reason to think that the use of force would have been successful with only limited casualties, state leaders refused to risk their armed forces in order to save Rwandans in peril.

How to persuade state leaders that they have a moral responsibility to 'pay the human' costs of intervention in cases of genocide, mass murder, and ethnic cleansing is the challenge for a solidarist theory of international society. The fact is that no Western government has intervened to defend human rights in the 1990s unless it has been very confident that the risks of casualties were almost zero. This suggests that there are clear limits to the 'CNN effect', which is claimed to push hesitant governments into risky and costly interventions that they would prefer to avoid. Media coverage of the humanitarian emergencies in northern Iraq and Somalia was an important enabling condition (though not a determining one) in making intervention possible in these cases. But it was not sufficiently powerful to persuade Western governments to commit ground forces to Bosnia with an enforcement mandate to defend the safe areas. There was sustained media coverage of the war in the west, which generated increasing public pressures, especially in Britain and the USA, for more decisive intervention. Despite being faced with these growing humanitarian sensibilities among publics, Western governments chose to ride out the storm, considering that military intervention would not succeed and would rapidly lose public legitimacy once the casualties began arriving home. The Kosovo intervention does not alter this conclusion, because the ruling-out of a ground campaign reflected concern about the domestic political consequences of what Lawrence Freedman has called the 'bodybags effect'.[23]

Yet what the Kosovo case shows is that Western policy-makers do sometimes exercise foreign-policy leadership when it comes to saving the victims of atrocities. In the case of Operation Allied Force, media and domestic publics played catch-up with Alliance leaders, especially Clinton and Blair,

---

[22] Annan, *Preventing War and Disaster*, .21.

[23] L. Freedman, 'Victims and victors: reflections on the Kosovo War', *Review of International Studies*, 26/3 (2000), 337.

who took the lead in defining the repression of the Kosovars as a crisis that necessitated an urgent response on both humanitarian and security grounds. However, the reason why the Clinton Administration defended military intervention in Kosovo, when it had been ruled out in Rwanda, was that the bombing campaign carried little risk of casualties, there were important US security interests at stake in the Balkans, and the credibility of the Alliance was perceived to be on the line.

The implication of the above is that state leaders will accept anything other than minimal casualties only if they believe national interests are at stake. This is the conclusion to be drawn from India's, Vietnam's and Tanzania's interventions in the 1970s. As I argued in Part Two, these states did not act to stop the atrocities until their vital interests were threatened, and they were prepared to incur the costs of intervention—including the loss of soldiers—only because they had these interests at stake.

One response here is to argue that regional and subregional actors should take on the burden of humanitarian law enforcement, because neighbours will have a security interest in regional crises that produce an exodus of refugees and carry the risk that violence might spread to engulf the region.[24] A model here might be the Economic Community of West African States (ECOWAS) interventions in Liberia and Sierra Leone led by Nigerian troops. But, leaving aside the question of whether these interventions count as humanitarian, the larger problem remains that regional actors cannot be relied upon to act. The inaction of African states in response to genocide in Rwanda in those critical early weeks in April 1994 demonstrates this all too graphically.

Every effort should be made to build up a regional capacity for humanitarian intervention, but there is another response to the realist criticism that states will defend human rights only if they have an interest in doing so that is compatible with the regional approach. This is to press the solidarist claim that states have a long-term security interest in promoting and enforcing human rights because an unjust world will be a disorderly one. As I argued in Chapter 2, India and the UN Secretary General tried to interest the Security Council in Pakistan's human rights abuses on the grounds of the threat it posed to order. The result of the Council's failure to listen was war on the subcontinent. Similarly, I showed in Chapters 3 and 4 how Uganda and Cambodia were both gross violators of human rights at home and threats to regional security. There is no automatic relationship between domestic repression and aggression abroad, but this book provides strong support for that hypothesis in relation to the cases of Pakistan, Uganda, Cambodia, Iraq, and the SFRY. Consequently, there is good reason to endorse the solidarist claim that a foreign policy that places the defence of human rights at the centre of

---

[24] This idea is suggested by Morris, 'The Concept of Humanitarian Intervention',

its ethical code will make an important contribution both to protecting national interests and to strengthening the pillars of international order.

Kofi Annan reminded the General Assembly in September 1999 that the challenge was to protect human rights through building up a culture of non-violent preventative diplomacy, and, as I have shown in the case-study chapters, it is the small acorns of human rights abuses that grow into the oak trees of supreme humanitarian emergencies. Humanitarian intervention by force becomes the last resort, as in Kosovo, because opportunities are missed for preventative action. The society of states failed to address human rights abuses in Kosovo through the 1990s and the same story can be told in relation to Iraq, Somalia, and, of course, Rwanda. Western governments are to blame for failing to take preventative action seriously, but this responsibility is also shared by domestic publics, who have not done enough to challenge governments for placing political and economic concerns prior to the defence of human rights.

The solidarist argument that order and justice can be reconciled if states define their interests in enlightened ways is a very attractive one. However, there is a problem with this resolution of the order/justice conundrum, which is that it makes the pursuit of justice dependent upon considerations of order. The problem is that the extent to which order is dependent upon justice will vary from case to case. Thus, I argued in Chapter 8 that Western governments had both a moral obligation and a security interest in risking soldiers' lives to stop the supreme humanitarian emergencies in Bosnia and Kosovo, but what about a faraway African country like Rwanda in 1994? Can it really be argued that the genocide in Rwanda posed a threat to Western security interests and wider international order that justified the sacrifice of Western soldiers?

At this point, the solidarist claim that order and justice can be reconciled begins to unravel, and we are left with the argument that Western states should have rescued Rwandans in 1994 for reasons of humanity. This is the importance of Michael Ignatieff's observation that what connects the 'zone of safety' in the West to the 'zone of danger' in places like Africa is 'a narrative of compassion . . . that the problems of other people, no matter how far away, are of concern to all of us'.[25] He argues that this moral universalism was forged out of the horrors of the Holocaust and that it is predicated on humanity's shame at its 'abandonment of the Jews', which created 'a new kind of crime: the crime against humanity'.[26] Yet our collective 'abandonment' of the people of Rwanda demonstrates the limits of this moral universalism. Even when citizens in the West were exposed to television images and newspaper stories of appalling brutality in Rwanda at the end of April 1994, the genocide

---

[25] Ignatieff, *The Warrior's Honor*, 4–5.   [26] Ibid. 19.

was represented, especially in the USA, as the result of ethnic hatreds that were impervious to both reason and the military intervention of outsiders. There were demands for military intervention from NGOs, but this constituency was unable to mobilize wider domestic public opinion into joining it in pressurizing politicians to end the genocide. Citizens in the West were concerned about the plight of Rwandans, and there was a strong charitable response to the refugee crisis in the camps on the Rwanda–Zaïre border, but this was the limit of the West's solidarity with the victims of genocide.

What should have happened in April 1994 is that, in the absence of a timely and effective regional response, Western governments should have intervened with force and accepted the risk of casualties. Instead of being inhibited by the 'bodybags effect', state leaders—who had the power to save lives—had a responsibility to take the 'moral risks'.[27] It is arbitrary in the extreme to put a figure on how many British, American, Canadian soldiers should have been sacrificed to save hundreds of thousands of Rwandans, but what is clear is that the figure is well above the number lost by the USA in Somalia in 1993. No one can know in advance how humanitarian intervention will turn out, and, if it ends in disaster, then those who take the agonizing decision to sacrifice citizens to save strangers will have to answer before the bar of domestic public opinion and their own consciences. Assuming that there is no contradiction between the humanitarian claims justifying the use of force and the motives and conduct of the intervention, then even an intervention that fails can be judged legitimate. What is equally true is that we can judge a successful humanitarian intervention only in retrospect, just as we cannot know in advance the moral consequences of our failure to act, and this is why state leaders confront such appalling choices in deciding whether to intervene.

It is to be hoped that any loss of soldiers incurred whilst ending the genocide in Rwanda would have been accepted by Western societies. But to any sceptical voices in the media, opposition parties, or wider public opinion that asked why the lives of citizens were being sacrificed for Rwandan strangers, Western leaders should have employed the argument that Clinton invoked when he first set foot on Rwandan soil: putting out the inferno of genocide is in both the national and the global interest because failure to do so risks creating a contagion that will undermine the values of all civilized societies.

It is crucial that policy-makers in the West are not constrained in the future, as they were over Rwanda, from ending crimes against humanity because of the fear that domestic publics will not tolerate casualties. The loss of the US Rangers in Somalia is the only case that supports this hypothesis,

---

[27] Jackson cites Stanley Hoffmann, who quotes the following line from De Gaulle, who defined a statesman 'as somebody who takes risks, including moral risks' (Jackson, 'The Political Theory of International Society', 125).

and there are two reasons for thinking that it is unwise to generalize from this example: first, the Rangers died in a context where it was very unclear to US public opinion what their sacrifice had been for; secondly, the USA, as a consequence of Vietnam, is a ' "body-bag" culture'[28] in ways that is less obviously the case with other Western states. Consequently, are European governments significantly underestimating how far their publics will accept casualties if this sacrifice can be shown to be ending the appalling suffering that they have witnessed on their television screens?

One key policy prescription in neutralizing the pernicious consequences of the 'bodybags' in preventing humanitarian intervention is to make a reality of former Under-Secretary General Brian Urquhart's proposal of setting up a UN rapid reaction force of approximately 10,000 men with air support. This would be comprised of volunteer soldiers and could be sent to trouble spots at short notice. The great advantage of such a force is that the men and women who formed it would have chosen to serve as warriors for humanitarianism. Had such a force been dispatched to Kigali by the Security Council in the first two weeks of April 1994, it is very likely that hundreds of thousands would have been saved.

There are three drawbacks to such a force: first, as Gareth Evans pointed out in 1994, the UN fire brigade could not have been sent to save Rwandans, because it would already have been committed to fire-fighting in Somalia or Bosnia.[29] The response here is that we will have to create more than one fire brigade at the global level. Creating such forces will be costly and few governments have shown much enthusiasm for this project. The real problem is not cost but the lack of a solidarist commitment that could lead governments and citizens to view global firefighting in the same way as citizens view the provision of a fire service in domestic society. Moreover, the costs of providing such a force, as Brian Urquhart argues, have to be set against the long-term costs that attend the failure to prevent such conflicts.[30]

The second limitation of this approach is the vexed one of selectivity. By placing the control of such a force in the hands of the Security Council, the permanent members will always be able to veto the deployment of the force if it threatens their interests. This raises the question that I discussed earlier about the responsibilities that go with being a veto power on the Council. Yet, even if there is a consensus within the Security Council that force is morally and legally permitted, there will be occasions when humanitarian intervention will have to be ruled out on prudential grounds. I have argued that selectivity is not a threshold condition for an intervention to count as humanitarian,

---

[28] N. Ascherson, 'People Still Bleed in "Virtual War" ', *Observer*, 21 Nov. 1999.

[29] G. Evans, 'Cooperative Security and Intrastate Conflict', *Foreign Policy*, 96 (Fall 1994), 18–19.

[30] B. Urquhart and F. Heisbourg, 'Prospects for a Rapid Response Capability: A Dialogue', in O. A. Otunnu and M. W. Doyle, *Peacemaking and Peacekeeping in the New Century* (Oxford: Rowman & Littlefield, 1998), 192.

because the failure to act in one place to end human rights abuses does not disqualify other interventions that do end such abuses.

This view does not persuade public intellectuals like Noam Chomsky, who reminds us of the inconsistencies in Western responses to human suffering. For example, he points to the blatant selectivity of US action over Kosovo compared to its responses to Columbia's and Turkey's record of human rights abuses.[31] Nor does it cut much ice with China, Russia, and India among others who argue that humanitarian claims on the part of the West are always a cover for the pursuit of selfish interests. This argument when pressed by these states is designed to end the conversation on the legitimacy of human-itarian intervention. But this criticism needs to be addressed if humanitarian intervention is to gain a deeper legitimacy among those state leaders, public intellectuals, and citizens who complain about Western double standards.

I have argued that it is important to distinguish between interventions that are selective because of reasons of prudence and those that are selective because of selfish interests. This does not resolve the problem, because there will still be debate over whether governments are acting prudently or selfishly in particular cases. I argued in Chapter 3 that the West should not have put cold-war imperatives prior to the human rights of the Cambodian people, but others would contest this on the grounds that prudence required US decision-makers to act in this way, given the threat posed by the Soviet Union to US security interests at the end of the 1970s. And, as Russia's indiscriminate shelling of civilians in Chechyna showed several months after the Kosovo War, military intervention has to be ruled out on grounds of prudence in those cases where it risks war—including nuclear war—between the major powers.

The solidarist response to the charge of inconsistency in applying a rule of humanitarian intervention is to argue that a distinction be made between consistency and coherence. The latter depends upon a framework that starts from the premiss that like cases must be treated alike, but acknowledges that this does not mean that every case can be treated the same.[32] Deepening the level of solidarity in the society of states requires not only that human rights abuses be exposed to international scrutiny and censure, but that govern-ments that violate human rights *always* pay a heavy price in diplomatic, polit-ical, and economic terms. The challenge for politicians, NGOs, media, and concerned citizens committed to human rights is to ensure that governments do not evade this responsibility and are always held accountable for their actions in dealing with regimes that egregiously violate human rights. Clearly complex trade-offs are involved when dealing with nuclear armed states that

---

[31] N. Chomsky, *The New Military Humanism*.
[32] This general framework is suggested by Franck in *The Power of Legitimacy* and Tim Dunne and I have adopted it to the case of the selective response of governments to human rights abuses. See Wheeler and Dunne, 'Good International Citizenship', 868–70.

have the veto in the Security Council such as Russia and China. But, if these states are seen to be able to abuse human rights with impunity, the dangerous signal is sent that the way to avoid becoming a target for humanitarian intervention is to develop the military capabilities that make the costs of outside interference too prohibitive.

The last problem with the UN fire-brigade solution is that it is too limited to cope with the type of challenge posed by Bosnia, Kosovo, and Somalia, where what was required was the imposition of an international protectorate that could provide a security framework for years, if not decades, to come. The problem, as Walzer points out, is that the source of human rights abuses in the 1990s was very different from the cases of Bangladesh, Uganda, and Cambodia where what was required was forcibly to remove a tyrannical government. In the cases of Iraq, Somalia, Bosnia, and Kosovo, the causes of human suffering were deeply rooted in the political, economic, and social structures of societies.[33] Intervention that seeks to end the immediate symptoms of such suffering has to be coupled with a long-term commitment to address its causes through a commitment to conflict resolution and social reconstruction.

This is the significance of the Somali case, for the mandate given to UNOSOM II by the Security Council represented an attempt to address the underlying causes of the violence in Somalia. I argued in Chapter 6 that the manifest contradiction that opened up between the UN's humanitarian justifications, and the means it employed to bring Aidid to justice, led to appalling violence being inflicted on the Somali people. The Clinton Administration was developing a new political strategy to replace the discredited military one prior to the loss of the Rangers in October 1993. It can only be speculated whether this attempt at dialogue with Aidid and the other clan leaders would eventually have taken the gun out of Somali politics. But the troubling question raised by Somalia is whether a more culturally sensitive intervention could, ultimately, have avoided the escalation of violence that took place in the summer of 1993? At some point, the objective of building a law-governed polity required marginalizing the power of the warlords that rolled out of the barrel of a gun, and they were always going to resist this.

The reluctance of the USA to stay the course in Somalia after losing eighteen soldiers in October 1993 is symptomatic of a deeper failure on the part of liberal societies to address the problems of war-torn societies. This requires a long-term commitment to political, economic, and social reconstruction, and this type of intervention might prove costly in both lives and resources. This level of moral engagement was absent in Somalia, and the success of any future humanitarian interventions in sub-Saharan Africa will depend upon

---

[33] Walzer, 'The Politics of Rescue', *Dissent*, 42/1 (1995), 35–6.

making such a commitment to the long haul. At the end of the 1990s, the limited humanitarian energies and resources of the West were consumed with the Balkans, and the story in relation to the 'zone of danger' outside Europe was one of raising rather than lowering the moral drawbridge to the liberal castle of contentment.

Ignatieff's construction of the relations between the 'zone of danger' and the 'zone of safety' is superficially an attractive one, but the metaphor sets up a false dichotomy that overlooks how far global inequalities of wealth and power constitute the 'zone of danger' in the first place. This book has focused on the legitimacy of using force to end the 'loud emergencies' of genocide, mass murder, and ethnic cleansing, but this definition is open to the charge, mobilized by southern governments, that it ignores the plight of millions who are dying for want of the basic necessities of life. Many African governments emphasized this issue in their speeches before the General Assembly in September 1999, and it is a constant theme of China and other non-aligned states when they are attacked by the West for abuses of civil and political rights. This highlights the pluralist contention that states will define what counts as a supreme humanitarian emergency differently depending upon their ideological biases.

It is apparent, then, that developing a new West–South consensus on the legitimacy of humanitarian intervention in the society of states will depend upon a new dialogue between rich and poor. What is needed is a commitment by the West to the redistribution of wealth, and an acceptance by Southern governments that cases will arise where the slaughter of civilians by their governments is so appalling as to legitimate the use of force to uphold minimum standards of humanity. There is no guarantee that this dialogue would radically change the pluralist predispositions of many Southern states, but a genuine Western commitment to redistributive justice would begin to address the deeply held belief of many southern élites and their publics that Western states employ the legitimating ideology of what Chomsky calls 'the new military humanism' to mask their continuing political and economic hegemony, and the violence required to sustain it.

Critics of the society of states will argue that achieving a genuine West–South dialogue is utopian, because neither grouping wants to make the radical changes that would make it possible. On the one hand, it would force Western governments and societies to ask uncomfortable questions about their capitalist economies and consumption patterns, changes in which could do so much to end the 'Holocaust of neglect'[34] that excludes millions from basic subsistence rights. On the other, Southern élites that find themselves the target for criticism by human rights NGOs and Western governments do not want to legitimate intervention on human rights grounds for

---

[34] Shue, *Basic Rights*, 201.

fear that this could set precedents that might be employed against their own regimes.

The narrative of common humanity is sufficiently deeply rooted in Western societies for the victims of gross human rights abuses to be seen as deserving concern and charity. In this sense, globalization is bringing closer Kant's vision that rights violations 'in one place in the world [are] felt *everywhere*'. However, the West's conception of humanitarian intervention is so ideologically biased that the 'silent genocide' of death through poverty and malnutrition is rendered natural and inevitable. Bhikhu Parekh asks why 'suffering and death become a matter of humanitarian intervention only when they are caused by the breakdown of the state or by an outrageous abuse of its power'.[35] The answer is that humanitarian intervention to end starvation and poverty would require, in Mahatma Gandhi's telling words, 'that the rich . . . learn to live more simply so that the poor can simply live'. And, at the beginning of the new century, there is little evidence that the global rich in the West are ready to end their position of power and privilege.

The selective gaze of humanitarianism in the West relates not only to how human suffering is constructed, but also to the locations that become the site of attention. The media are notoriously partial in their coverage of atrocities, and, whilst governments devoted their limited humanitarian energies to Iraq, Somalia, Bosnia, and Kosovo, millions perished in Sudan, Angola, Liberia, Afghanistan, and countless other places where television was not present to record the outrages. Moreover, even in Somalia, Bosnia, and Rwanda, where there was considerable media coverage, solidarity did not run deep enough between Western publics, living in the secure sphere of global politics, and the victims of genocide, mass murder, and ethnic cleansing to persuade politicians that they should accept casualties to stop these crimes against humanity. This is the gap between the aspirations of solidarism and its attainments in practice.

The determination to conduct 'casualty-free' humanitarian interventions is laudable and there is a limit to the risks and costs that governments should accept in saving strangers. However, if the desire to protect soldiers' lives leads to unacceptable levels of violence being inflicted on civilians, as in the US–UN hunt for Aidid in Somalia in 1993, and to a lesser extent NATO's bombing of Serb civilians in March 1999, then the humanitarian qualifications of an intervention are called into question. At this point, domestic and international legitimation should be withdrawn from the intervention, since it is failing to satisfy the threshold tests of proportionality and a positive humanitarian outcome.

I have argued in the cases of Somalia and Kosovo that a positive humanitarian outcome was compromised by the refusal to accept greater risks to

---

[35] Parekh, 'Rethinking Humanitarian Intervention', 55.

soldiers' lives, and that Western governments were defining their moral responsibilities to suffering strangers too narrowly. But this prompts the reply, 'how many lives have to be sacrificed to satisfy this criticism?' This is a powerful counter but it perhaps misses the point, since what was required in both these cases was that governments were held accountable, both domestically and internationally, for the means they employed to achieve their humanitarian purposes. The Bush Administration should have been called to account for its decision not to disarm Somali warlords, and the Clinton Adminstration should have been required to justify the character of the means employed to hunt for Aidid. Similarly, NATO governments should have justified their decision not to create a ground option to save Kosovars. This would have exposed to public scrutiny how state leaders were resolving the appalling moral conflict between accepting a greater risk to soldiers' lives in order to save more civilians from slaughter.

Pluralist international society theory is deeply suspicious of a doctrine of humanitarian intervention because it argues that attempts to realize it in practice will be deeply subversive of interstate order. This legitimation of pluralist practices was endorsed by Bull, and it was even shared by Vincent, who cautioned at the end of his book that the society of states was not solidarist enough to issue a 'licence for intervention'.[36] I have argued in this book that there are two key grounds for rejecting this view: first, there is often a mutual compatibility between protecting the national interest, promoting international order, and enforcing human rights. In such situations, state leaders can escape making terrible choices between their duties to strangers and citizens, because risking soldiers' lives can be defended on grounds of both national interest and common humanity.

The second reason for rejecting the pluralist framing of the order/justice conundrum is that it exaggerates the threat posed to order by a practice of unilateral humanitarian intervention. Ideally, humanitarian intervention will always operate with Security Council authorization. If this is not possible, then interventions that satisfy the threshold tests should be legitimated as exceptions to the rules. Those that are judged to meet the more demanding criteria above the threshold should be praised and held out as examples for others to emulate. And, since the number of cases that could plausibly be defended in terms of these norms is limited, it is wrong to think that permitting a right of unilateral humanitarian intervention will open the floodgates to intervention as argued by realists and pluralists.

The conclusion, then, is not that solidarism is inevitably limited, because international society is characterized by a deep and abiding tension between its pluralist and solidarist conceptions. Rather, the solidarist project is 'premature', because state leaders have not taken the moral risks that would create

---

[36] Vincent, 'Human Rights and International Relations', 152.

in international law a doctrine that would give practical substance to Kofi Annan's claim that we are finally becoming 'a humanity that will do more' for fellow humans in danger. A key part of this moral transformation is an acceptance by governments in the West that humanitarian intervention is both morally permitted and morally required in cases of supreme humanitarian emergency.

In advancing this solidarist project in the next few decades, and widening it to embrace the humanitarian emergency of survival that confronts millions every day on this planet, we cannot rely on governments to act as guardian angels of humanity. It is no good being shocked by television images of atrocities or starvation, since what is required is that we all do something to end these and prevent them recurring. Liberal-democratic governments will seek to avoid taking risky decisions that could erode their support at home, and, as I have shown in this book, when it came to resolving the moral conflicts between realist and solidarist conceptions of moral responsibility in the Bosnian and Rwandan cases, Western state leaders believed that public opinion was not prepared to pay the price and bear the burden to end these atrocities. Had they judged that their policies of limited engagement in Bosnia, and non-intervention in Rwanda, were likely to lead to a moral outcry at home, and that public opinion was prepared to accept the human as well as the financial costs of intervention, politicians would have found it much more difficult to ignore the voice of solidarism in foreign-policy decision-making.

Governments are notoriously unreliable as rescuers, but where else can we turn to save those who cannot save themselves? At present, it is only states that have the capabilities to fly thousands of troops halfway round the world to prevent or stop genocide or mass murder. The challenge, then, for those working in human rights NGOs, universities, and the media is to mobilize public opinion into a new moral and practical commitment to the promotion and enforcement of human rights. This change in moral consciousness will not guarantee intervention when it is morally required. What it will do is heighten awareness on the part of state leaders that they will be held accountable if they decide not to save strangers.

BIBLIOGRAPHY

Abiew, F. K., *The Evolution of the Doctrine and Practice of Humanitarian Intervention* (The Hague: Kluwer Law International, 1999).

Adams, J., and Whitehead, P., *The Dynasty: The Nehru-Gandhi Story* (London: Penguin for the BBC, 1997).

Adelman, H., 'Humanitarian Intervention: The Case of the Kurds', *International Journal of Refugee Law*, 4 (1992).

—— 'Preventing Post-Cold War Conflicts: What Have We Learned? The Case of Rwanda', paper presented to the International Studies Association annual conference at San Diego, California, 17 Apr. 1996.

—— Suhrke A., and Klinghoffer, A. J., *The International Response to Conflict and Genocide: Lessons from the Rwanda Experience* (London: ODI, 1996).

Africa Watch and Physicians for Human Rights, *No Mercy in Mogadishu* (London: Africa Watch and Physicians for Human Rights, 1992).

Akehurst, M., 'Humanitarian Intervention', in H. Bull (ed.), *Intervention in World Politics* (Oxford: Oxford University Press, 1984).

Amnesty International, *Political Imprisonment and Torture* (London: Amnesty International, 1986).

Annan, K. A., *Preventing War and Disaster: A Growing Global Challenge* (1999 Annual Report on the Works of the Organization; New York, 1999).

Arend, A. C., and Beck, R. J., *International Law and the Use of Force: Beyond the UN Charter Paradigm* (London: Routledge, 1993).

Barnett, M. N., 'The UN and Global Security: The Norm is Mightier than the Sword', *Ethics and International Affairs*, 9 (1993).

—— 'The UN Security Council, Indifference, and Genocide in Rwanda', *Cultural Anthropology*, 12/4 (1997).

Bazyler, M., ''Reexamining the Doctrine of Humanitarian Intervention in the Light of the Atrocities in Kampuchea and Ethiopia', *Stanford Journal of International Law*, 23 (1987).

Becker, E., *When the War was Over: The Voices of Cambodia's Revolution and its People* (New York: Simon & Schuster, 1986).

Bellamy, A. J., 'If you Tolerate this . . . Two Decades of Human Wrongs in Kosovo', *International Journal of Human Rights*, 4/3–4 (2000).

—— 'Lessons Unlearnt: Why Coercive Diplomacy Failed at Rambouillet', *International Peacekeeping*, 7/3 (forthcoming).

—— 'Lazar's Choice Deferred: Serbs, Albanians and the Contact Group at Rambouillet', unpublished paper (University of Wales, Aberystwyth, 1999).

—— and Kroslak, D., 'The Dawning of a Solidarist Era? Nato Intervention in Kosovo', *Journal of International Relations and Development*, 3/1 (forthcoming).

Benjamin, B. M., 'Unilateral Humanitarian Intervention: Legalizing the Use of Force to Prevent Human Rights Atrocities', *Fordham International Law Journal*, 16 (1992–3).

Berdal, M., 'The Security Council, Peacekeeping and Internal Conflict after the Cold War', *Duke Journal of Comparative International Law*, 7/1 (1996).

Biberaj, E., 'Kosovo: The Balkan Powderkeg', *Conflict Studies*, 258 (1993).

Booth, K., 'Human Wrongs in International Relations', *International Affairs*, 71/1 (1995).

—— 'The Kosovo Tragedy: Epilogue to Another "Low and Dishonest Decade"?', unpublished lecture given at the South African Political Science Association Biennial Congress, held at the Military Academy, Saldanha, 29 June 1999.

Bourdieu, P., *In Other Worlds: Essays towards a Reflexive Sociology*, trans. M. Adamson (Stanford, Calif.: Stanford University Press, 1987).

Bowring, B., 'The "Droit et Devoir D'Ingérence": A Timely New Remedy for Africa', *African Journal of International and Comparative Law*, 7/3 (1995).

The British Yearbook of International Law 1992 (Oxford, Oxford University Press, 1993).

Brown, C., *International Relations Theory: New Normative Approaches* (Hemel Hempstead: Harvester Wheatsheaf, 1992).

Bull, H., 'The Grotian Conception of International Society', in H. Butterfield and M. Wight (eds.), *Diplomatic Investigations* (London: Allen & Unwin, 1966).

—— *The Anarchical Society: A Study of Order in World Politics* (London: Macmillan, 1977).

—— (ed.), *Intervention in World Politics* (Oxford: Oxford University Press, 1984).

Byers, M., *Custom, Power and the Power of Rules: International Relations and Customary International Law* (Cambridge: Cambridge University Press, 1999).

Carnegie Commission, *Preventing Deadly Conflict: Final Report with Executive Summary of the Carnegie Commission on Preventing Deadly Conflict* (New York: Carnegie Commission on Preventing Deadly Conflict, 1997).

Carr, E. H., *The Twenty Years Crisis 1919–1939*, (London: Macmillan, 1939).

Carruthers, S. L., *The Media at War* (London: Macmillan, 1999).

Chanda, N., 'Hanoi Ponders its Strategy', *Far Eastern Economic Review*, 7 (1979).

—— *Brother Enemy: The War after the War* (New York: Collier, 1986).

Chomsky, N., *The New Military Humanism: Lessons from Kosovo* (Monroe, Me.: Common Courage Press, 1999).

Clapham, C., 'Rwanda: The Perils of Peacemaking', *Journal of Peace Research*, 35/2 (1998).

Clark, J., 'Somalia', in L. F. Damrosch (ed.), *Enforcing Restraint: Collective Intervention in Internal Conflicts* (New York: Council on Foreign Relations, 1993).

Clarke, W,. and Herbst, J., 'Somalia and the Future of Humanitarian Intervention', *Foreign Affairs*, 75/2 (1996).

Claude, I., 'Collective Legitimization as a Political Function of the United Nations', *International Organization*, 20 (1966).

Cviic, C., *An Awful Warning: The War in Ex-Yugoslavia* (CPS Policy Study, 139; London: Centre for Policy Studies, 1994).

Davidson, J. S., *Grenada: A Study in Politics and the Limits of International Law* (Aldershot: Gower, 1987).

de Waal, A., 'African Encounters', *Index on Censorship*, 6 (1994).

—— 'Dangerous Precedents? Famine Relief in Somalia 1991–93', in J. Macrae and A. Zwi (eds.), *War and Hunger* (London: Zed Books, 1994).

Desch, M., 'Culture Clash: Assessing the Importance of Ideas in Security Studies', *International Security*, 23/1 (1998).

Destexhe, A., 'The "New" Humanitarianism', in A J. Paolini, A. P. Jarvis, and C. Reus-Smit (eds.), *Between Sovereignty and Global Governance: The United Nations, the State and Civil Society* (London: Macmillan, 1998).

Donnelly, J., 'The Social Construction of Human Rights', in T. Dunne and N. J. Wheeler (eds.), *Human Rights in Global Politics* (Cambridge: Cambridge University Press, 1999).

Doty, R. L., *Imperial Encounters: The Politics of Representation in North–South Relations* (Minneapolis: University of Minnesota Press, 1996).

Dunne, T., 'The Social Construction of International Society', *European Journal of International Relations*, 1/3 (1995).

—— *Inventing International Society: A History of the English School* (London: Macmillan, 1998).

Dunne, T., and Wheeler, N.J., 'Good International Citizenship: A Third Way for British Foreign Policy', *International Affairs*, 74/4 (1998).

—— —— (eds.), *Human Rights in Global Politics* (Cambridge: Cambridge University Press, 1999).

East Pakistan Staff Study by the Secretariat of the International Commission of Jurists, in *Review of the International Commission of Jurists*, 8 (1972).

Evans G., and Rowley, K., 'Kampuchea', *Age*, 29 Jan. 1985.

—— —— *Red Brotherhood at War: Vietnam, Cambodia and Laos since 1975*, 2nd edn. (London: Verso, 1990).

Falk, R., 'Hard Choices and Tragic Dilemmas', *Nation*, 20 Dec. 1993.

Farer, T. J., 'An Enquiry into the Legitimacy of Humanitarian intervention', in L. F. Damrosch and D. J. Scheffer (eds.), *Law and Force in the New International Order* (Oxford: Westview Press, 1991).

—— 'A Paradigm of Legitimate Intervention', in L. F. Damrosch, *Enforcing Restraint: Collective Intervention in Internal Conflicts* (New York: Council on Foreign Relations Book, 1993).

Feil, S. R., *Preventing Genocide: A Report to the Carnegie Commission on Preventing Deadly Conflict* (New York: Carnegie Corporation, 1998).

Fierke, K. M., *Changing Games, Changing Strategies: Critical Investigations in Security* (Manchester: Manchester University Press, 1998).

—— 'Dialogues of Manoeuvre and Entanglement: NATO, Russia and the CEEC's', *Millennium: Journal of International Studies*, 28 1 (1999).

Finnemore, M., 'Constructing Norms of Humanitarian Intervention', in P. Katzenstein (ed.), *The Culture of National Security* (Columbia: Columbia University Press, 1996).

—— and Sikkink, K., 'International Norm Dynamics and Political Change', *International Organization*, 2/4 (1998).

Fixdal, M., and Smith, D., 'Humanitarian Intervention and Just War', *Mershon International Studies Review*, 42/2 (1998).

Forde, S., 'Classical Realism', in T. Nardin, and D. R. Maples, (eds.), *Traditions of International Ethics* (Cambridge: Cambridge University Press, 1992).

Franck, T., *The Power of Legitimacy among Nations* (Oxford: Oxford University Press, 1990).

—— and Rodley, N., 'After Bangladesh: The Law of Humanitarian Intervention by Military Force', *American Journal of International Law*, 67 (1973).

Freedman, L., 'Victims and victors: reflections on the Kosovo War', *Review of International Studies*, 26/3 (2000).

Freedman, L., and Boren, D., ' "Safe Havens" for Kurds', in N. S. Rodley (ed.), *To Loose the Bands of Wickedness* (London: Brassey's, 1992).

Geras, N., *The Contract of Mutual Indifference: Political Philosophy after the Holocaust* (London: Verso, 1998).

Girling, J., 'Lessons of Cambodia', in J. Girling (ed.), *Human Rights in the Asia-Pacific Region* (Canberra: Australian National University, 1991).

Gourevitch, P., *We Wish to Inform you that Tomorrow we will be Killed with our Families: Stories from Rwanda* (London: Picador, 1998).

Gow, J., *Legitimacy and the Military: The Yugoslav Crisis* (London: Belhaven Press, 1992).

—— *Triumph of the Lack of Will: International Diplomacy and the Yugoslav War* (London: Hurst & Com., 1997)

—— 'Coercive Cadences: The Yugoslav War of Dissolution', in L. Freedman (ed.), *Strategic Coercion: Concepts and Cases* (Oxford: Oxford University Press, 1998).

Gowing, N., 'Real-Time Television Coverage of Armed Conflicts and Diplomatic Crises: Does it Pressure or Distort Foreign Policy Decisions?', occasional paper, Joan Shorenstein Centre, Kennedy School of Government, Harvard University, June 1994.

Greenwood, C., 'Is there a Right of Humanitarian Intervention', *The World Today*, 49/2 (1993).

Guicherd, C., 'International Law and the War in Kosovo', *Survival*, 41/2 (1999).

Habermas, J., *Theory of Communicative Action, i. Reason and the Rationalization of Society*, trans. T. McCarthy (London: Heinemann, 1984).

—— *Justification and Application: Remarks on Discourse Ethics*, trans. Ciaron Cronin (Cambridge: Polity Press, 1993).

—— (interviewed by M. Haller), *The Past as Future*, trans. M. Pensky (Cambridge: Polity Press, 1996).

Hariss, J. (ed.), *The Politics of Humanitarian Intervention* (London: Pinter, 1995).

Harper, M., 'Back to Somalia: A Report on his visit to Somalia', United Nations Association, UK, Mar. 1994.

Hasenclever, A., Mayer, P., and Rittberger, V., *Theories of International Regimes* (Cambridge: Cambridge University Press, 1997).

Hassan, F., 'Realpolitik in International Law: After Tanzanian–Ugandan Conflict "Humanitarian Intervention" Reexamined', *Willamette Law Review*, 17 (1981).

Heder, S. R., 'The Kampuchean–Vietnamese Conflict', in D. W. P. Elliot (ed.), *The Third Indochina Conflict* (Boulder, Colo.: Westview, 1981).

Heere, W. P., *International Law* (Leiden: A. W. Sijthoff, 1972).

Hendrickson, D. C., 'In Defense of Realism: A Commentary on Just and Unjust Wars', *Ethics and International Affairs*, 11 (1997).

Henkin, L., *How Nations Behave: Law and Foreign Policy* (New York: Columbia University Press, 1979).

Higgins, R., *Problems and Process: International Law and How We Use It* (Oxford: Oxford University Press, 1994).

Hirsch, J. L., and Oakley, R. B., *Somalia and Operation Restore Hope: Reflections on Peacemaking and Peacekeeping* (Washington: United States Institute of Peace, 1995).

Holbrooke, R., *To End a War* (New York: Random House, 1998).

Hollis, M., and Smith, S., *Explaining and Understanding International Relations* (Oxford: Oxford Univeristy Press, 1990).

Honig, J. W., and Both, N., *Srebrenica: Record of a War Crime* (London: Penguin, 1996).

Hurrell, A, 'Society and Anarchy in the 1990s', in B. A. Roberson (ed.), *The Structure of International Society* (London: Pinter, 1998).

—— 'International Society and Regimes', in V. Rittberger (ed.), *Regime Theory and International Relations* (Oxford: Oxford University Press, 1999).

Ignatieff, M., *The Warrior's Honor: Ethnic War and the Modern Conscience* (London: Chatto & Windus, 1998).

International Helsinki Federation for Human Rights, *From Autonomy to Colonization: Human Rights in Kosovo 1989–93* (Vienna: International Helsinki Committee, 1993).

Jackson, R. , *South Asian Crisis: India–Pakistan–Bangladesh* (London: Chatto & Windus for the International Institute of Strategic Studies, 1975)

Jackson, Robert H., *Quasi-States: Sovereignty, International Relations and the Third World* (Cambridge: Cambridge University Press, 1990).

—— 'Martin Wight, International Theory and the Good Life', *Millennium: Journal of International Studies*, 19/2 (1990).

—— 'Armed Humanitarianism', *International Journal*, 48 (Autumn 1993).

—— 'International Community Beyond the Cold War', in G. M. Lyons and M. Mastanduno (eds.), *Beyond Westphalia? State Sovereignty and International Intervention* (Baltimore: Johns Hopkins University Press, 1995).

—— 'The Political Theory of International Society', in K. Booth and S. Smith (eds.) *International Relations Theory Today* (Cambridge: Polity Press, 1995).

—— 'The Situational Ethics of Statecraft', unpublished paper in possession of the author.

Jakobsen, P. V., 'National Interest, Humanitarianism or CNN: What Triggers UN Peace Enforcement after the Cold War', *Journal of Peace Research*, 33/2 (1996).

Jennings, R. Y., 'The *Caroline* and *McLeod* Cases', *American Journal of International Law*, 32 (1938).

Jones, B. D., ' "Intervention without Borders": Humanitarian Intervention in Rwanda, 1990–94', *Millennium: Journal of International Studies*, 24/2 (1995).

Judah, T., *The Serbs: History, Myth and the Destruction of Yugoslavia* (London: Yale University Press, 1997).

—— *Kosovo: War and Revenge* (London: Yale University Press, 2000).

Kaldor, M., *New and Old Wars: Organized Violence in a Global Era* (Cambridge: Polity Press, 1999).

Keane, F., *Season of Blood: A Rwandan Journey* (London: Penguin, 1996).

Keesing's Contemporary Archives, Bristol.

Keen, D., 'Short-Term Interventions and Long-Term Problems', in J. Harriss (ed.), *The Politics of Humanitarian Intervention* (London: Pinter, 1995).

Klinghoffer, A. J., *The International Dimension of Genocide in Rwanda* (London: Macmillan, 1998).

Klintworth, G., *Vietnam's Intervention in International Law* (Canberra: Australian National University Press, 1984).

Koskenniemi, M., 'The Place of Law in Collective Security', in A. J. Paolini, A. P. Jarvis, and C. Reus-Smit (eds.), *Between Sovereignty and Global Governance: The United Nations, the State and Civil Society* (London: Macmillan, 1998).

Kratochwil, F., *Rules, Norms, and Decisions: On the Conditions of Practical and Legal*

Reasoning in International Relations and Domestic Affairs (Cambridge: Cambridge University Press, 1989).

Kratochwil, F., 'Neorealism and the Embarrassment of Changes', *Review of International Studies*, 19/1 (1993).

—— and Ruggie, J. G., 'International Organization: A State of the Art or an Art of the State', in F. Kratochwil and E. D. Mansfield (eds.), *International Organization: A Reader* (London: Harper Collins, 1994).

Kroslak, D., 'Evaluating the Moral Responsibility of France in the 1994 Genocide in Rwanda', paper presented to the British International Studies Association annual conference, University of Sussex, 14–16 Dec. 1998.

Kuper, L., *The Prevention of Genocide* (New Haven: Yale University Press, 1985).

Kuperman, A. J., 'The Other Lesson of Rwanda: Mediators Sometimes Do More Damage than Good', *SAIS Review*, 16/1 (1996).

Laberge, P., 'Humanitarian Intervention: Three Ethical Positions', *Ethics and International Affairs*, 9 (1995).

Leifer, M., 'Vietnam's Intervention in Kampuchea: The Rights of State v. the Rights of People', in I. Forbes and M. Hoffman (eds.), *Political Theory, International Relations and the Ethics of Intervention* (London: St Martin's Press for Macmillan, 1993).

Lemarchand, R., 'Rwanda: The Rationality of Genocide', *Issue: A Journal of Opinion*, 23/2 (1995).

Lewis, I., and Mayall, J., 'Somalia', in J. Mayall (ed.), *The New Interventionism 1991–1994: United Nations Experience in Cambodia, Former Yugoslavia and Somalia* (Cambridge: Cambridge University Press, 1996).

Lillich, R. B., 'The Development of Criteria for Humanitarian Intervention', unpublished paper in possession of the author.

Linklater, A., 'What is a Good International Citizen?', in P. Keal (ed.), *Ethics and Foreign Policy* (Canberra: Allen & Unwin, 1992).

—— *The Transformation of Political Community* (Cambridge: Polity Press, 1998).

—— 'The Good International Citizen and the Crisis in Kosovo', unpublished paper in possession of the author.

Lowe, V., 'International Legal Issues Arising in the Kosovo Crisis', Memorandum submitted to the Foreign Affairs Committee, House of Commons, Feb. 2000.

Lyons, T., and Samatar, A. I., *Somalia: State Collapse, Multilateral Intervention, and Strategies for Political Reconstruction* (Washington: Brookings Institute, 1995).

McNulty, M., 'France's Rwanda Débâcle: The First Failure of Military Intervention in France's African Domain', 6 Aug. 1998, http://www.kcl..ac.uk/kis/schools/hums/war/Wsjournal/rwanda.htm.

Mahbubani, K., 'The Kampuchean Problem: A Southeast Asian Perspective', *Foreign Affairs*, 62/2 (1983–4).

Makinda, S. M., *Seeking Peace from Chaos: Humanitarian Intervention in Somalia* (Boulder, Colo.: Lynne Rienner, 1993).

Manning, C., *The Nature of International Society*, 2nd edn. (London: Macmillan, 1975).

Mason, A., and Wheeler, N. J., 'Realist Objections to Humanitarian Intervention', in B. Holden (ed.), *The Ethical Dimensions of Global Change* (London: Macmillan, 1996).

Mayall, J., 'Non-Intervention, Self-Determination and the "New World Order"', *International Affairs*, 67/3 (1991).

Melvern, L., *The Ultimate Crime: Who Betrayed the UN and Why* (London: Allison & Busby, 1995).

—— 'Genocide behind the Thin Blue Line', *Security Dialogue*, 28/3 (1997).

—— *A People Betrayed: The Role of the West in Rwanda's Genocide* (London: Zed Books, forthcoming).

Minear, L., Scott, C., and Weiss, T. G., *The News Media, Civil War and Humanitarian Action* (Boulder, Colo.: Lynne Reinner, 1996).

Morris, J., 'The Concept of Humanitarian Intervention in International Relations', MA dissertationn (Hull, 1991).

Müller, H., 'The Internationalization of Principles, Norms and Rules by Governments: The Case of Security Regimes', in V. Rittberger (ed.), *Regime Theory and International Relations* (Oxford: Oxford University Press, 1999).

Murphy, S. D., *Human Intervention: The United Nations in an Evolving World Order* (Philadelphia: University of Pennsylvania Press, 1996).

Mysliwiec, E., *Punishing the Poor: The International Isolation of Kampuchea* (Oxford: Oxfam, 1988).

Natsios, A., 'Illusions of Influence: The CNN Effect in Complex Emergencies', in R. I. Roteberg and T. G. Weiss (eds.), *From Massacres to Genocide: The Media, Public Policy and Humanitarian Crises* (Washington: Brookings Institute, 1996).

O'Halloran, P. J., 'Humanitarian Intervention and the Genocide in Rwanda', *Conflict Studies*, 277 (1995).

Owen, D., *Balkan Odyssey* (London: Indigo, 1996).

Parekh, B., 'Rethinking Humanitarian Intervention', *International Political Science Review*, 18/1 (1997).

Pilger, J., 'The US Fraud in Africa', *New Statesman and Society*, 8 Jan. 1993.

Prunier, G.,*The Rwanda Crisis: History of a Genocide* (London: Hurst & Co., 1995).

Ramsbotham, O., and Woodhouse, T., *Humanitarian Intervention in Contemporary Conflict* (Cambridge: Polity Press, 1996).

Reisman, M., and McDougal, M. S., 'Humanitarian Intervention to Protect the Ibos', in R. Lillich (ed.), *Humanitarian Intervention and the United Nations* (Charlottesville, Va.: University of Charlottesville, 1973).

—— —— *Towards World Order and Human Dignity: Essays in Honor of Myers S. Mcdougal* (New York: Free Press, 1976).

Roberts, A., 'Humanitarian War: Military Intervention and Human Rights', *International Affairs*, 69/3 (1993).

—— 'NATO's Humanitarian War over Kosovo', *Survival*, 41/3 (1999).

Rodley, N. S., 'Collective Intervention to Protect Human Rights', in N. S. Rodley (ed.), *To Loose the Bands of Wickedness* (London: Brassey's, 1992).

Ronzitti, N., *Rescuing Nationals Abroad through Military Coercion and Intervention on Grounds of Humanity* (Dordrecht: Martinus Nijhoff, 1985).

Rubinstein, W., *The Myth of Rescue: Why the Democracies could not have Saved More Jews from the Nazis* (London: Routledge, 1997).

Sahnoun, M. M., 'Prevention in Conflict Resolution: The Case of Somalia', *Irish Studies in International Affairs*, 5 (1994).

Sarooshi, D., *The United Nations and the Development of Collective Security: The Delegation by the UN Security Council of its Chapter VII Powers* (Oxford: Oxford University Press, 1999).

Schachter, O., *A United Nations Legal Order* (Cambridge: Cambridge University Press, 1995).

Searle, J. R., *The Construction of Social Reality* (London: Penguin, 1995).

Shaw, M., *Civil Society and Media in Global Crises* (London: Pinter, 1996).

—— 'Global Voices', in T. Dunne and N. J. Wheeler (eds.), *Human Rights in Global Politics* (Cambridge: Cambridge University Press, 1999).

Shue, H., *Basic Rights: Subsistence, Affluence and US Foreign Policy* (Princeton: Princeton University Press, 1980).

—— 'Let Whatever is Smouldering Erupt? Conditional Sovereignty, Reviewable Intervention, and Rwanda 1994', in A. J. Paolini, P. Jarvis, and C. Reus-Smit, C., (eds.), *Between Sovereignty and Global Governance: The United Nations, the State and Civil Society* (London: Macmillan, 1998).

Silber, L., and Little, A., *The Death of Yugoslavia* (London: Penguin for the BBC, 1995).

Simma, B., 'NATO, the UN and the Use of Force: Legal Aspects', www.ejil.org/Vol10/No1/abl-2html (1999).

Sisson, R., and Rose, L. E., *War and Secession: Pakistan, India, and the Creation of Bangladesh* (Berkeley and Los Angeles: University of California Press, 1990).

Skinner, Q., 'Analysis of Political Thought and Action', in J. Tully (ed.), *Meaning and Context: Quentin Skinner and his Critics* (Cambridge: Polity Press, 1988).

—— 'Language and Social Change', in J. Tully (ed.), *Meaning and Context: Quentin Skinner and his Critics* (Cambridge: Polity Press, 1988).

Smith, M. J., 'Humanitarian Intervention: An Overview of the Ethical Issues', *Ethics and International Affairs*, 3 (1989).

Steele, J., 'Learning to Live with Milosevic', *Transitions*, 5 (1998).

Stevenson, J., 'Hope Restored in Somalia?', *Foreign Policy*, 91 (1993).

Stromseth, J. E., 'Iraq', in L. F. Damrosch (ed.), *Enforcing Restraint: Collective Intervention in Internal Conflicts* (New York: Council on Foreign Relations, 1993).

Tanner, M., *Croatia: A Nation Forged in War* (London: Yale University Press, 1997).

Teson, F., *Humanitarian Intervention: An Inquiry into Law and Morality* (Dobbs Ferry, NY Transnational Publishers, 1988).

Thant, U, *View from the UN* (London: David & Charles, 1978).

Thomas, C., *New States, Sovereignty and Intervention* (Aldershot: Gower, 1985).

Thompson, M., *A Paper House: The Ending of Yugoslavia* (London: Vintage, 1992).

United Nations, *The United Nations and Rwanda* (Washington: United Nations Department of Public Information, 1996).

Urquhart, B., and Heisbourg, F., 'Prospects for a Rapid Response Capability: A Dialogue', in O. A. Otunnu and M. W. Doyle (eds.), *Peacemaking and Peacekeeping in the New Century* (Oxford: Rowman & Littlefield, 1998).

Verwey, W., 'Humanitarian Intervention in the 1990s and Beyond: An International Law Perspective', in J. N. Pieterse (ed.), *World Orders in the Making: Humanitarian Intervention and Beyond* (London: Macmillan, 1998).

Vickers, M., *Between Serb and Albanian: A History of Kosovo* (London: Hurst & Com., 1998).

Vincent, R. J., *Human Rights and International Relations* (Cambridge: Cambridge University Press, 1986).

—— and Wilson, P., 'Beyond Non-Intervention', in I. Forbes and M. Hoffmann (eds.), *Political Theory, International Relations and the Ethics of Intervention* (London: Macmillan, 1993).

Walzer, M., *Just and Unjust Wars: A Moral Argument with Historical Illustrations* (London: Allen Lane, 1978).

—— 'The Politics of Rescue', *Dissent*, 42/1 (1995).

Weiss, T. G., *Military–Civilian Interactions: Intervening in Humanitarian Crises* (Oxford: Rowman & Littlefield, 1999).

Welch, C. E., 'The OAU and Human Rights: Towards a New Definition', *Journal of Modern African Studies*, 19/3 (1981).

Weller, M., 'Access to Victims: Reconceiving the Right to "Intervene" ' in W. P. Heere, *International Law and The Hauge's 750th Anniversary* (London: A. W. Sijthoff, 1972).

—— 'The International Response to the Dissolution of the Socialist Federal Republic of Yugoslavia', *American Journal of International Law*, 86/3 (1992).

—— 'The Rambouillet Conference on Kosovo', *International Affairs*, 75/2 (1999).

Wendt, A., 'Anarchy is what States Make of it: The Social Construction of Power Politics', *International Organization*, 46/2 (1992).

—— *Social Theory of International Politics* (Cambridge: Cambridge University Press, 1999).

Wheeler, N. J., 'Pluralist or Solidarist Conceptions of Humanitarian Intervention: Bull and Vincent on Humanitarian Intervention', *Millennium: Journal of International Studies*, 21/2 (1992).

—— and Dunne, T., 'Good International Citizenship: A Third Way for British Foreign Policy', *International Affairs*, 74/4 (Oct. 1998).

White, N. D., 'The Legality of Bombing in the Name of Humanity', paper presented to the British International Studies Association annual conference, University of Manchester, 20–22 Dec. 1999.

Wight, M., 'International Legitimacy', in H. Bull (ed.), *Systems of States* (Leicester: Leicester University Press and the LSE, 1977).

—— 'Western Values in International Relations', in M. Wight and H. Butterfield (eds.), *Diplomatic Investigations: Essays in the Theory of International Politics* (London: Allen & Unwin, 1966).

Woodward, S. L., *Balkan Tragedy: Chaos and Dissolution after the Cold War* (Washington: Brookings Institute, 1995).

Youngs, T., *Kosovo: The Diplomatic and Military Options* (London: House of Commons Research Paper 98/93, 27 Oct. 1998).

INDEX